PRISONER PARTICIPATION IN PRISON POWER

by

J.E. Baker

The Scarecrow Press, Inc.
Metuchen, N.J., and London
1985

The author gratefully acknowledges those who granted permission to reprint material from the following:

O. F. Lewis, The Development of American Prisons and Prison Customs, 1922, pp. 169-70, by permission of The Correctional Association of New York.

Howard B. Gill, "The Norfolk State Prison Colony at Massachusetts." Reprinted by special permission of the Journal of Criminal Law and Criminology, © by Northwestern University School of Law, Vol. 22, No. 1.

Harold M. Helfman, "Antecedents of Thomas Mott Osborne's Mutual Welfare League in Michigan." Reprinted by special permission of the Journal of Criminal Law and Criminology, © by Northwestern University School of Law, Vol. 40, No. 5.

J. E. Baker, "Inmate Self-government." Reprinted by special permission of the Journal of Criminal Law and Criminology, © by Northwestern University of Law, Vol. 55, No. 1.

Thomas Mott Osborne, Society and Prisons, New Haven, Yale University Press, 1916. Reprinted by permission of the publisher.

Fred E. Haynes, Criminology, New York, McGraw-Hill, 1935. Reproduced with permission of the publisher.

Nathan F. Leopold, Jr., Life Plus 99 Years. Copyright © 1957, 1958 by Nathan F. Leopold, Jr. Reprinted by permission of Doubleday & Co., Inc.

Kenyon Scudder, Prisoners Are People. Copyright © 1952 by Kenyon Scudder. Used by permission of Doubleday & Co., Inc.

Virginia V. Neto and LaNelle Marie Bainer, Offender Participation in Corrections: Methods for Involving Offenders and Ex-Offenders in the Correctional Process. Washington, D.C.: National Institute of Corrections, 1981. Used by permission of Virginia V. Neto.

Portions of this book are based on the author's The Right to Participate: Inmate Involvement in Prison Administration (Metuchen, N.J.: Scarecrow, 1974).

Library of Congress Cataloging in Publication Data

Baker, J. E., 1917-
Prisoner participation in prison power.

Includes bibliographies and index.
1. Prison administration--United States--History.
2. Prisoners--Legal status, laws, etc.--United States--History. 3. Prison reformers--United States--History.
I. Title.
HV9469.B17 1985 365'.068 85-8363
ISBN 0-8108-1820-5

Manufactured in the United States of America

for my sons

Joseph Edward and Steven Alan

CONTENTS

PREFACE

By 1870, with the holocaust of the Civil War a scant half-decade in memory, the present continental limits of the United States had been attained, and the attention of the nation was focused on the development of its tremendous natural resources. The demands of great national activities, while creating an unprecedented material wealth, left little time for consideration of those who for various reasons had offended the social order. In the backwash of that society languished more than thirty thousand human beings in a half-hundred prisons. Created as a substitute for brutal punishments, the prison had itself become in many respects a grim castle set apart from the populace in which the most unspeakable of indignities were practiced in the name of reformation and the public safety. The inhabitants of these monolithic monuments of inhumanity were deemed to have suffered a civil death, in which state, although they yet breathed as human beings, they had no rights other than what the law in its humanity saw fit to allow. And the humanity of the law as it pertained to the rights of the individual was at best in an embryonic state.

Social conscience, fortunately, is forever extant, although it has appeared at times to be comatose. Throughout the history of the nation, in fact, prior to the full development of the Colonies under other rule, some individuals and some groups had registered protest, first at the sanguinary nature of penalties imposed on offenders, and later at the degraded state of prisons. The fruition of this concern was the organization at Cincinnati, Ohio, in 1870, of the National Prison Association, now the American Correctional Association, in whose original declaration of Principles was one of particular significance:

> Principle V: The prisoner's destiny should be placed, measurably, in his own hands; he must be put into circumstances where he will be able, through his own exertions, to continually better his own condition. A regulated self-interest must be brought into play, and made constantly operative.

This principle gave, in effect, recognition to prior efforts and formed a foundation, at once philosophical and pragmatic, to further attempts to provide a place for the inmate to participate in both the program and the programming of the prison, i. e., inmate self-government and inmate advisory councils.

Since the birth of the American Correctional Association in 1870, there has been a phenomenal increase in the population of the nation, a sharp escalation in the number and variety of types of institutions, and the introduction of community corrections programs, all designed for the care and treatment of offenders. What has been described as the new penology is astir in many jurisdictions. New concepts, new directions, and new methods are creating a fresh atmosphere in which one can detect that most tantalizing quintessence of progress--hope. These facilities, these activities, and this promise came not as a sudden revelation, but resulted from the sustained effort of many correctional practitioners experimenting with many methods; a reawakening of the courts to the fact that citizens of the United States, even though sentenced to confinement, still retain rights guaranteed by the constitution, and are entitled to all due processes both inherent and specified constitutionally and statutorily; and a growing awareness by those subject to government directives and regulation that fair play demands that their suggestions and complaints be heard and responded to in a timely and rational manner. The arrogance of discretionary authority is under challenge. Those who would go beyond the mandate entrusted to them by virtue of holding an office of power, either elective or appointive, are being held accountable for both performance and consequence.

Alongside the judge and the prosecutor, the corrections administrator has, or has had, a vast discretionary authority. Although little has been accomplished regarding the judge and the prosecutor, the corrections administrator has been deluged with a veritable torrent of actions and demands designed to restrict that power of discretion. Additionally, efforts continue to identify and articulate a successor to the rehabilitative model of corrections that has dominated the field for a century or more. The major model, as yet amorphous and still in the process of formulation, is an emphasis of the importance of justice; thus the reference to the "justice model." Although the justice model calls for many things--determinate sentencing and the abolition of parole are two major items--a consequence of its emergence has been a realization that fairness must underlie any and all attempts to promote justice and to demonstrate the democratic process within an authoritarian setting. There must be rules known to all; those rules must be observed by all; there must be a process in which no threat or coercion is permitted against any person who expresses a complaint against the system, and which guarantees a reasoned reply within a reasonable period of time. The manifestation of that realization is the emergence of complaint mechanisms.

This volume is an account of the past and present of the various forms of complaint procedures, i. e., ombudsmen, grievance commissions, multi-level grievance procedures, and inmate councils, and the impact on correctional administration resulting from these processes, both individually and collectively.

Throughout, the confined offender is referred to variously as inmate, resident, student, ward, camper, or boy or girl. This is not an inconsistency. Insofar as it was possible to do so, the language of the source has been used here.

ACKNOWLEDGMENTS

The historical and current material for a prior book and for this one was obtained from a review of numerous books and periodicals in the field of corrections and through the cooperation of the men and women who direct and administer the adult, youth, and juvenile correctional residential facilities in the 50 States, the counties and cities contacted, the Federal Bureau of Prisons, the District of Columbia, the Department of Defense, and the Department of Health and Welfare. To these correctional colleagues, the author expresses his gratitude for the quantity and quality of responses to requests for information.

In 1960, the author became interested in inmate involvement in the administration of prisons, with a focus at that time on self-government programs and inmate advisory councils in penitentiaries. A research of the literature was augmented by a survey of 52 penitentiaries. Recipients were asked to give certain information if they "have or have had" such a group. The findings of both the literature research and the forty-four responses to the questionnaire were included in an article published in the Journal of Criminology, Criminal Law and Police Science, Vol. 55, No. 1, March 1964, under the title "Inmate Self-Government."

In 1966 and 1967, a survey was made of United States correctional institutions and agencies as listed in the 1966 edition of the Directory of Correctional Institutions and Agencies, published by the American Correctional Association. No contact was made with city and county correctional systems or institutions, other than the cities of Detroit, New York and Philadelphia, and Westchester County, New York. This was done because of literature references to or first-hand knowledge of past or current programs relevant to the survey. A literature reference indicating the possibility of a self-government program having existed several decades ago at the Essex County Penitentiary, Caldwell, New Jersey, was followed up, but no record of the organization was found.

Through the courtesy of the late E. Preston Sharp, Ph. D., then Executive Director, The American Correctional Association, and Norman A. Carlson, now Director, Federal Bureau of Prisons, copies of the indexes to the American Correctional Association Proceedings were provided to assist in the research of the literature of corrections. A selection was made of those citations believed to be references to self-government or advisory councils. Photocopies of those portions of the *Proceedings* referred to were then obtained from the American Correctional Association. Much information was gained which amplified accounts of self-government and advisory council programs found elsewhere, and leads found to others previously not known about. An example of the latter is the account of the Mutual Welfare League at the Kentucky State Reformatory in Frankfort, Kentucky. A reference to the League was made in an address at the General Session of the then American Prison Association on October 18, 1926, by Austin H. MacCormick, at that time Professor, Bowdoin College, Brunswick, Maine. An account of the origin, purpose, and functions of the League was found in the Kentucky State Archives.

Preparation of a book manuscript based on the literature research and the surveys made in 1960 and 1966-1967 was commenced in the spring of 1967. As the writing neared completion, the author opted for early retirement from the Federal Bureau of Prisons, to which he had devoted a 27-year span of his life. The occurrence which precipitated that decision was the proffer of the position of Warden, Penitentiary of New Mexico, at Santa Fe.

During the course of service in New Mexico as Warden and as Secretary of Corrections of the newly created Department of Corrections, and later as Deputy Commissioner, Kentucky Department of Corrections, interspersed with and followed by consulting contacts with state, county and city correctional agencies and facilities, principally for the Law Enforcement Assistance Administration technical assistance program administered by the American Correctional Association, and occasionally on personal contract, sufficient time to properly complete the manuscript never seemed to be available.

When the manuscript was finally completed, and tentatively accepted for publication, it was readily apparent that an updating of the survey data was necessary. The re-survey began in late 1972 and was completed in July, 1973. With each inquiry was sent an excerpt of the original manuscript as it pertained to the recipient, that account being based on information obtained in the 1960 and 1966-1967 surveys. The 1972 edition of the *Directory of Juvenile and Adult Correctional Institutions and Agencies*, published by the American Correctional Association, was used in the 1972-1973 survey.

The result of the foregoing was a book entitled *The Right to Participate: Inmate Involvement in Prison Administration*, published in 1974.

In addition to the previous surveys, a further survey was made of United States corrections departments, both adult and juvenile, as listed in the 1983 edition of the *Directory of Juvenile and Adult Correctional Departments, Institutions, Agencies and Paroling Authorities*. As before, the cities of Detroit, New York, Philadelphia, and Westchester County, New York, were contacted. Additionally, information from Cook County, Illinois, was obtained. The survey began in September, 1982 and was completed in September, 1983.

The author expresses his gratitude for the quantity and quality of the responses to requests for information received from his correctional colleagues throughout the nation.

With reference to the prior book, The Right to Participate: Inmate Involvement in Prison Administration, the following acknowledgments are reiterated:

To Daniel Glaser, Ph. D., Professor of Sociology, University of Southern California, the author is deeply indebted for two contributions. First, for the encouragement, counsel, and active assistance given in the original research efforts, and second, for the Foreword. Dr. Glaser is a luminary in the galaxy of activities comprising the science and art of corrections.

Special acknowledgment is made to the late Kenyon J. Scudder, career California correctional executive, who was the first Superintendent of the California Institutions for Men, at Chino; to Howard B. Gill, former Director, Institute of Correctional Administration, American University, eminent correctional practitioner and academician; and to the late Austin H. MacCormick, Executive Director, The Osborne Association, Inc., whose accomplishments in the correctional effort were legion.

Mr. Scudder amplified the published account of the origin and development of the Chino Advisory Council, and Mr. Gill did similarly with reference to the Norfolk Prison Colony. Mr. MacCormick made a critical review of draft portions of the manuscript dealing with the Mutual Welfare League at Auburn Prison, Sing Sing Prison, and the Naval Prison, providing new information and insights regarding the functioning of the League at each facility.

Although the author has already personally thanked him for the assistance rendered in researching the history of advisory councils in Federal prisons, that thanks is repeated here to J. C. Taylor, friend and correctional executive colleague. Rising through the ranks of the Federal Bureau of Prisons to Assistant Director, Ches Taylor later charted, by his three-year period of service, 1969 to 1972, as Commissioner, Kentucky Department of Corrections, the course which the Commonwealth of his birth is following to reach and maintain modern correctional practice.

In addition to former personnel of the Federal Bureau of Prisons Central Office--Mark S. Richmond, Assistant Director, retired; Louise L. MacKenzie, Librarian, retired; Jack H. Wise, retired--the author thanks the following for providing requested reference works: California State Library, Sacramento; University of California, Los Angeles; University of California, Berkeley; Claremont Graduate School, Claremont, California; Indiana State University, Terre Haute; University of Massachusetts, Amherst; University of Michigan, Ann Arbor; Cornell University, Ithaca, New York; the Library of Congress; and the Kentucky Department of Archives and Libraries, Frankfort. At the latter, Mrs. Lucy Chapman, Director of Information and Loan, was especially cooperative and helpful.

In the course of researching this subject and in the preparation of drafts of several portions of the manuscript, assistance was given by two men who were then residents of a correctional residential facility. To those men the author reiterates his thanks and best regards.

The permission of the Office of Chief of Naval Operations to use the material regarding the United States Naval Prison at Portsmouth, New Hampshire, is appreciated.

With reference to the present book, the author thanks the following persons and organizations for their assistance and encouragement in researching the literature and their attitude of helpfulness:

Linda Sherrow, Director of Information and Loan, Kentucky Department of Libraries and Archives, was of especial help in locating several reference works.

Joseph M. Callan, Executive Director of The Osborne Association, Inc., New York City, whose two predecessor organizations were The National Society of Penal Information and the Welfare League Association, Inc., provided copies of the *Handbook of American Institutions for Delinquent Juveniles*, Volumes I, II, and IV, and granted permission for use of the information gathered in site visits during the period 1937-1943.

The Center for Community Justice, Washington, D.C., graciously gave permission for use of the information contained in the several projects and surveys conducted by that organization concerning the establishment of complaint procedures in numerous correctional settings, the latest of which is *Complaint Procedures in Prisons and Jails: An Examination of Recent Experience*, published in 1980 by the National Institute of Corrections. Especial thanks is given to David D. Dillingham for his efforts in providing the reports. The projects were supported by grants in full or in part from one or more of the following: the Law Enforcement Assistance Administration, the National Institute of Law Enforcement and Criminal Justice, the American Bar Endowment, the Andrew W. Mellon Foundation, the Vincent Astor Foundation, the Herman Goldman Foundation, the Office of Economic Opportunity, and the National Institute of Corrections.

Contact, Inc., Lincoln, Nebraska, furnished a bibliography and several documents pertaining to inmate advisory councils which enhanced both the literature research and efforts to obtain current information about such groups.

Permission to use the information contained in a 1981 report entitled Offender Participation in Corrections: Methods for Involving Offenders and Ex-Offenders in the Correctional Process (and a Summary Report) was given by Virginia V. Neto, Criminal Justice Consultant. Ms. Neto was the Project Director for the Social Action Research Center, San Rafael, California, in a survey conducted to identify programs utilizing offenders as a correctional resource, including the participation of inmate advisory councils in prison management. The survey was supported by a grant from the National Institute of Corrections.

The Pennsylvania Prison Society, Philadelphia, granted permission to use the contents of its publication The Prison Journal, Volumes LV and LVII.

The National Prison Project, American Civil Liberties Union Foundation, furnished a copy of its Status Report--The Courts and Prisons, March 8, 1982, listing the states in which there are existing court decrees, consent decrees, or pending litigation involving the entire state prison system or the major institutions (no jails except for the District of Columbia), which deal with overcrowding and/or the total conditions of confinement.

Permission to use material from Corrections Magazine was given by The Edna McConnell Clark Foundation, New York City. The Clark Foundation assumed editorial rights when Corrections Magazine went out of business following publication of its June, 1983 issue.

As in the preparation of the previous book, the author especially recognizes and appreciates the assistance of his wife, Mary Elizabeth Baker, in researching, rewriting, and proofreading, and her continuing attitude of understanding throughout the preparation of this book.

J. E. Baker

Frankfort, Kentucky
December, 1983

INTRODUCTION

In a prior book a history of the participation by confined offenders in the administration of United States correctional residential facilities was recounted, covering the period from 1793 to 1973.

The focus of that history was on the involvement of inmates in prison administration via self-government programs and their modern counterpart, inmate advisory councils. In this volume the scope has been expanded to include other forms of participation by confined offenders in both the program and the programming of the prison.

Participatory management has always existed to some degree in American prisons, with inmates occupying roles having an impact on operations, procedures and, sometimes, policy. In some instances these roles were formal and officially sanctioned. In the main, most had no such recognition, but were tolerated because the services performed were needed by, or convenient to, the prison, the staff, or the inmates, individually or in combination. Sad to state, in many jurisdictions the significance of inmate participation was not within the awareness of staff. Untrained, underpaid, poorly motivated, and apathetic personnel too frequently abdicated their responsibilities to inmates, with no thought of or concern for the consequences.

Other than in upper-echelon administrative positions, inmates have been utilized throughout our national history in a variety of functions geared to the operation and management of the prison. It is obvious that prisons could not function without inmate participation in supportive and substitutive roles, and it does not stretch the imagination to conclude that these roles developed for reasons other than a philosophical belief in the value of inmate involvement. The most common reasons for substituting inmate manpower for that of employees are recruitment and retention difficulties and skeletal budgets. In some jurisdictions, however, the reason was naked exploitation. The labor of inmates represented profit to the states.

The functions referred to go beyond jobs involved with routine institution maintenance services, e. g. , food, laundry, and janitorial duties. Inmates have been used in a host of positions which normally would have been filled by civilian employees, e. g. , security (armed trusty), administrative-aide (Captain's clerk), admission (intake interviewer), and clerical duties providing access to records pertaining to other inmates and to staff (record clerks, casework typists, medical and psychiatric aides), and education (teachers, tutors, and librarians). Absent such inmate support, many prisons could not function.

Until fairly recent times inmate guards were used in three states: Arkansas, Louisiana and Mississippi. For years, in Texas, building tenders ran the day-to-day affairs of the institution. In 1973, the State Legislature passed a law: "An inmate in the Texas Department of Corrections or in any jail may not act in a supervisory capacity over other inmates [nor] administer disciplinary action." However, as late as 1978, critics alleged that the building tenders were as powerful as ever, still having disciplinary authority over other inmates.

A survey made in the summer of 1936 of the two penal farms in Arkansas, located at Tucker and Cummins, reported that inmate trustees served in a supervisory capacity as armed guards and "riders" or convict foremen bossing gangs of inmate field workers.

For many years in many jurisdictions, the inauguration of a new state administration, usually at four-year intervals and sometimes as often as two years, brought about wholesale changes in staff. With no permanence of either personnel or policy, not only were programs placed in jeopardy but also the operation of the prison itself, since the "new gang" seldom had even the remotest idea of how to proceed. Inmates filled that void of know-how, not always with an altruistic motive. But, motivation aside, inmate knowledge was the well-spring from which new employees drew in their transition to prison work.

In addition to providing the "what" as to operations and procedure, inmates provided the essential "how." Staff training and development was an idea observed principally in the breach until fairly recent times. Until the third decade of this century, new employees, particularly correctional officers, in most jurisdictions were on their own in developing the knowledge and skills, even those of the most rudimentary nature, to perform the tasks required of them. For instance, although uniformed officers were given assignments requiring the bearing of firearms, it was not unusual that training in their use was not, or was only minimally, provided. There was an almost total lack of instruction in the use of the nightstick, or baton, which was a standard issue item in many prisons.

In few instances did any written guidelines exist, and, in the main, those that did were simply statements of what the officer should do under given circumstances, or were rules of personal deportment. For example, officers were cautioned that "when in immediate charge of a gang of prisoners, guns must be kept in hand ready for instant use." Additionally, officers were "strictly forbidden to treat one another with disrespect or use any ungentlemanly epithets." Within the prison grounds they were required to "refrain from whistling, scuffling and immoderate laughter" or other acts "calculated to disturb the harmony and good order of the prison."

Prison officers were also instructed to conduct themselves "both in and out of the institution as to inspire sentiments of respect for their moral principles and character." They were advised to be circumspect in their way of life in society, careful as to the company they kept and the places they frequented. In many prisons it was the duty of the deputy warden to "make himself acquainted with the social habits and conduct of all subordinate officers and learn whether, when off duty, they frequent saloons or houses of ill repute, or associate with idle and loose characters, and report the facts to the warden."

All familiarity between employees and any inmate was prohibited, absolutely. No conversation with inmates was allowed, except as it pertained to the duty or labor of an inmate, without permission from a superior officer, ... "nor shall they listen to any convict's history of his crime and case on which he was convicted. Any employee who gets himself upon terms of intimacy or familiarity with a convict proves himself unfit for the position and shall be discharged therefor."

On the other hand, officers were enjoined to maintain "in their contacts with prisoners" a quiet demeanor under any provocation, and were prohibited from replying in like terms to impudent or insulting language. Usually officers "may not punish a prisoner or strike him except in self-defense or to quell an insurrection ... but shall uniformly treat them in a kind and humane manner. Jerking the prisoner around, punching him with a cane, or unnecessary rough treatment, will not be tolerated."

Other rules required an officer to watch a prisoner at least as closely as the prisoner watched him and to move around so as to exhibit awareness and alertness whenever an inmate came within sight of an officer's post. Sleeping on duty or entering the prison grounds while intoxicated were grounds for immediate discharge.

To these personal admonitions were added rules peculiar to the position of prison officer, such as controlling firearms within and outside the prison walls, especially when in the company of prisoners; restrictions on the transportation of articles in or out of the institution, either for inmates or otherwise, and procedures in instances of escape or attempted escape.

A few institutions (three of 88 surveyed in 1936) also set forth the specific duties of different positions. Almost all rules and regulations included some items of routine to be followed in the daily program; e.g., the issue of passes, taking counts, making inspections, supervising work crews and sick-call, and directing visitors. In most prisons, however, these were matters of such long standing that information about them was seldom published, although each was paramount to the administration of the institution. (To a large degree this is still true in 1983. Many correctional officers attribute a lack of clear guidelines for "job performance" as a major cause of job stress.)

In effect, the new employee was placed in a "sink or swim" predicament. If he did not perform his duties he could be readily fired since his job was secured only "at the pleasure" of the appointing authority. For the most part the only lifeline proffered was by inmates, at a price. The price was often special privilege, access to goods and services, and consequently power and control over other inmates. For even a conscientious employee, the price did not appear unreasonable, until he discovered, too late, that he had been co-opted. He found himself in a double bind: his tenure dependent on the whim of the administration and the performance of his role, keeping the lid on, possible only by cooperating with (pandering to) his inmate mentors.

Stories abound among veteran correctional employees of the authority given over to inmates; for example: the Captain's or Deputy Warden's clerk who determined the assignment roster, including not only the duty post, but shift-hours and days-off as well. As a rule, there was no appeal from the inmate clerk's action. The Captain, or Deputy Warden, had delegated (surrendered) his authority to the inmate clerk because he did not want to be bothered by such details; and in so doing it was made clear that any objection by an employee would be regarded as a bother. Woe be to the employee who became a "bother."

The potential for inmate impact on many aspects of prison operations and administration existed under the conditions heretofore mentioned. It would be naive to assume that no advantageous exploitation occurred.

The first attempts to formally enlist the participation of offenders in the administration of the prison were manifested by self-government programs, which evolved into an arrangement known as the advisory council. Chapter I is an account of both those entities prior to 1930.

During the past fifteen years, a new method of inmate participation has grown quite dramatically as both courts and correctional administrators have recognized the legitimacy of the right of inmates to complain. The method was originally conceived as a process by which an individual inmate could voice a personal concern--over an incident, problem, program, rule, regulation or policy--through established channels, with the guarantees of a reasoned reply within a specified time limit and no reprisals for such action. However, the process, a formal complaint mechanism, has become something far more significant than a means of airing legitimate complaints. It has become another method through which the inmate can have an impact upon the operations, programs, and administration of the prison. Formal complaint mechanisms have done much to resolve one of the paradoxes of the prison, the knowledge that the keeper and the kept share a common interest in the same problems and issues, surprisingly from similar perspectives, but have approached them, for the most part, in opposition because their respective systems for exercising power do not touch or encourage coexistence. A formal complaint procedure provides an interface between the two systems; a structure for the members of each to work in harmony. Complaint mechanisms have taken three forms: ombudsmen, grievance commissions, and multi-level grievance procedures in which inmates participate, in many jurisdictions, in both design and implementation as well as operation. These forms are discussed together with inmate advisory councils in Chapter II.

Chapters III, IV and V are accounts of formal complaint procedures and inmate councils in the states, the Federal Prison System and other jurisdictions from 1930 to the present.

Much has been written about the passing of the "hands-off" doctrine based on the theory that prisons were to be run by prison officials. During the past 15 years the judiciary, both state and federal, has made an adjustment of 180-degrees in its attitude, resulting in a veritable torrent of decisions designed to hold corrections officials accountable for the fair and reasonable exercise of the broad discretion inherent in the authority relegated to them by reason of default on the part of society as a whole. However, the courts did not of their own volition commence these actions; they did so only in response to initiatives by inmates alleging deplorable prison conditions and practices. This rediscovery of the Constitution by the courts has resulted in all prisons in eight states and one or more prisons in thirty others being under a court order or with challenges pending.[1] Examination of these court orders (some are consent decrees) is convincing proof that inmates have achieved a means of impacting upon practically every facet of prison management, including, in some instances, personnel administration.

Unlike previously mentioned forms of inmate participation initiated by the prison administration, the prisoner union movement began through the efforts of ex-offenders and confined offenders. True unions, based primarily on a labor union approach, were not successful and their existence was quashed by the U.S. Supreme Court ruling in June, 1977, that prisoners have no right to carry on union activities. Some organizations using the normative title of "prisoner union" still exist, but are actually only pressure groups which work outside the prison. The most active of such groups during the 1970s, the Prisoners Union, San Francisco, California, still exists as a private non-profit prisoners' rights advocacy group. It is an organization of volunteers with only one full-time paid employee. Its publication, The Outlaw, begun in November, 1971, continues as The California Prisoner.

Chapter VI is a review of the account herein of all forms of inmate participation in prison administration, an idea which, although in many ways already realized, continues in the main to be a controversial issue among those who labor in the correctional vineyard.

Note

1. "Status Report--The Courts and Prisons," The National Prison Project, American Civil Liberties Union, Washington, D.C., March 3, 1982.

CHAPTER I

NOTABLE EARLY EXPERIENCES

This chapter is an account of self-government and advisory council programs originating prior to 1930 in United States institutions for the confinement of adult and youthful offenders and juvenile delinquents. Until 1930, prison administration as either science or art was at best in an embryonic state. Humane treatment of offenders was the concern of only a dedicated few.

Life in the old prison was for the most part a deadly monotony under a stern and often brutal autocracy, excepting only the occasional administration whose chief characteristic was a condescending paternalism. There are few accounts of career administrators before 1930 and even fewer accounts of occupational mobility. Usually, a guard remained a guard. Supervisory personnel were generally hired at that level. Wardens and their deputies were appointed as part of a political patronage system, in which almost all personnel were as pawns.

Although the situation improved through the years, the 1966 and 1967 surveys made by the Joint Commission on Correctional Manpower and Training found widespread personnel recruitment and retention problems caused by low pay, heavy workloads, insufficient training and lack of merit system employment in the field of corrections. To some degree, these problems persist in many jurisdictions today.

Many of the early self-government and advisory council programs were both inadequately structured and improperly implemented. With few exceptions, all were superimposed on an untrained staff. The zeal of the originator of the program in most instances exceeded his correctional management ability. The programs were too heavily dependent upon the originator, since most expired rapidly when that person departed the scene.

However, it cannot go unsaid that almost all of the originators of those earlier programs were persons in advance of their time, innovators and experimenters, dynamic and creative, sometimes flamboyant, and always impatient with current conditions. None had a trained or professional staff recruited and developed under a merit system. There were no personnel development programs. Salaries were low, hours were long, tenure was insecure, and employee benefits were unheard of. All of these factors add up to extreme conditions, which was usually the state of affairs in most institutions (and is true today primarily because of overcrowding).

Involvement in the disciplinary process appears to have been a point of departure for the early programs of inmate participation. One need not ponder long the question as to why. If you examine only briefly the accounts of early prisons, the stark brutality of disciplinary practices assaults the senses. Revolting--yes, but they were the accepted methods of dealing with deviancy. The untrained personnel of the old prisons were ill-equipped to handle discipline problems. To several originators of the early programs this was apparently the area in most urgent need of change; also, this was an area offering the best prospects for effecting a positive change. There can be no denying that any provision for inmate participation in any part of the prison program was a dramatic if not downright audacious idea. Of all the features of self-government programs, inmate involvement in the handling of disciplinary matters was the most visible; this prominence created the still-lingering impression that participation in disciplinary matters was the whole of the self-government concept rather than merely a minor part.

Only at Gill's Norfolk State Prison Colony in Massachusetts, the Sleighton Farm School for Girls in Pennsylvania, the Clinton Farms in New Jersey, and the Long Lane School in Connecticut was staff support effectively enlisted. In the other institutions discussed in this chapter, those employees most affected, the line personnel, were often placed in situations subordinating them to their charges. Little comment is necessary regarding the administrative crassness of this arrangement. Modern management recognizes the need for interpretive communication in advance of putting a new procedure into effect. The presence of untrained and incompetent personnel intensifies that need. We can now only speculate as to the many positive changes which might have resulted had administrators of yesteryear focused their efforts on staff development.

At the same time these attempts to provide for inmate participation in the prison program were being sponsored by a few, and opposed by many, there was little realization on the part of all that inmates were already, in many ways, deeply involved in vital operational procedures which, in effect, gave them power over other inmates, over some of the staff, and over the allocation of goods and services, as described in the Introduction.

Walnut Street Jail

The earliest reference in correctional literature to inmate self-government in American institutions was made by the South Carolinian, Robert J. Turnbull. During his visit to the Walnut Street Jail in Philadelphia in 1793, Turnbull noted what he termed "a secondary and inferior government among the criminals for their own convenience and comfort." In his report he added: "One of their principal regulations relative to cleanliness was, that no one who found occasion should spit elsewhere but in the chimney (that is, in the night rooms). The punishment annexed to the person, who thought proper to infringe this general rule, was simply an exclusion from the society and conversation of his fellow convicts, and this is found to be sufficient."[1]

New York House of Refuge

In the winter of 1815-16 a small group of men held several meetings in New York City to discuss the treatment of poverty and crime. From these discussions in the home of Joseph Curtis and others came the Society for the Prevention of Pauperism, which became the Society for the Reformation of Juvenile Delinquents. The Society founded the New York House of Refuge which opened on January 1, 1825, with Curtis as the first superintendent.[2]

Curtis maintained that the House of Refuge could not be managed like a factory. Family life and the rule of a loving but determined paterfamilias were chief factors in his intensely personal administration. During the summer any boy finishing his work by Saturday noon was permitted to go for a swim in addition to an afternoon at liberty. Those who behaved very well were allowed to visit parents and friends in the city. Forgiveness was extended to any voluntarily returning runaway. He once stated: "Many things may be done that to a casual observer may seem inadmissable, but still, rightly managed, are productive of good."[3]

In a brief time Curtis found considerable distance between ideals and realities. To certain children, kindness and verbal reprimands meant nothing. An instance of this caused him to substitute punishment for kindness; four days later it was necessary to do so in an incident involving another boy. As time went on the security of the institution proved to be one of Curtis' greatest problems. Although he found it contrary to his convictions, he increasingly adopted severe modes of punishment. However, it appeared that nothing could prevent escapes. Almost in desperation, Curtis decided that the children might be more likely to accept a regime of punishment inflicted by themselves. Consequently he set up a jury system, which he described in his *Superintendent's Daily Journal* on March 30, 1825:

> We believe that many of the boys are disposed to do the things that are right, and would do so were they not provoked by those who are restrained by fear only. We therefore, to enable them to get rid of such company, have organized a court and trial by juror;--the jurors consist of 5 to be elected by themselves, before whom ... charges of misconduct are to be stated, and they are to pass sentence.[4]

A break occurred between Curtis and the board of managers because he refused to lash a boy who had voluntarily returned after running away. Though Curtis' position was deferred to, the resulting strained relations led to his resignation on May 5, 1826.[5]

Shortly after leaving the House of Refuge, Curtis became a partner in a jewel and pencil-case manufacturing concern. But his interest in the development of youth had not waned. He found fourteen apprentices, whose number was subsequently increased to thirty, and collected them into a residence adjoining his own. Characteristic of Curtis, the school placed equal emphasis on social as well as vocational education. Particular attention was given to social interaction and the acquisition of basic education. A sense of independence was to be achieved not only through savings--some accumulated as much as six hundred dollars--but also by each boy's contributing to the pay of the teachers employed. The school ended when the firm failed following disastrous financial investments in Virginia and North Carolina goldmining interests against which Curtis had counseled.[6]

Curtis' successor as superintendent of the New York House of Refuge was Nathaniel C. Hart, a former school teacher described as a tough-minded administrator and a thorough disciplinarian. He was superintendent for fourteen years. There is evidence that the jury system inaugurated by Curtis continued for some time. It is mentioned in an 1827 listing of rules and regulations. Additionally, the "guard," a detail of trusted inmates, kept watch along with the regular staff. However, the privilege of unsupervised visits to parents and friends in the city had been discontinued. An official report in January 1827 stated that those trusted for such visits had "disgraced the Institution by gross misconduct while absent." Records dated January 1844 refer to the selection of inmate monitors who safeguarded the discipline of the institution.[7]

Boston House of Reformation

Another reformatory for delinquent children, the Boston House of Reformation, established in 1826, was the setting for an early experiment which was broader in scope and lasted throughout the several years' tenure of its originator. A young Episcopal minister, the Reverend E. M. P. Wells, became superintendent of the institution in 1828, and promptly attracted considerable attention by his rather intensive education programming. Inmates were given a voting participation in the administration of the school. Corporal punishments were entirely excluded. Monitors were appointed from among the youngsters at the beginning of each month and the head monitor presided over the institution in the absence of the officers.[8]

Conceiving of his charges as citizens of a tiny republic, Wells made provisions for their participation in governing themselves. In contrast to Curtis at the New York House of Refuge who had resorted almost in desperation to self-government via a jury system of the children themselves, Wells instituted self-government because of its experience value. He viewed the institution as a laboratory to serve the child, with emphasis on positive behavior. The similarity of this approach and the current total environment or therapeutic community is startling, particularly since it occurred almost a century and a half ago.

Gustave de Beaumont and Alexis de Tocqueville, two young French prison commissioners on tour, commented on the positive aspects of Wells' system. They observed that nobody in the institution could be punished for a fault not provided for by divine law, or by those of the land, or of the House itself.[9]

A book of conduct was kept in which each youngster had his account of good and bad marks. At a daily evening assembly each was called upon to assign his own marks of merit or demerit. Such self-judgment was reportedly more severe than if it had been made by others. Violators of moral law and other offenses were tried before a disciplinary court consisting of twelve inmate jurors and the superintendent. A classification scheme provided three "bad" grades and three "good" grades. A schedule of promotions from one grade to another and a system of progressively increasing privileges are interesting to note as an early form of incentive program.

While his contemporaries had some reservations about his program there was a consensus as to the outstanding nature and ability of Wells himself. Disagreement with the Boston Common Council after an official inspection visit in 1832 led to his resignation soon afterwards.

Wells then became superintendent of a South Boston private school for the moral discipline of boys. This institution was regarded as without precedent or equal in America. With a capacity of forty and a tuition of $3.00 weekly, the school admitted unruly boys and those for whom a special kind of curriculum seemed fitting. Drawing on his experience at the House of Reformation, Wells instituted a daily schedule which can be regarded as insurgent in an era of dogmatic academic principles. Through a maximum of playtime, a broad academic curriculum, and an absence of compulsory and supervised industrial training Wells evidently sought to let each child find himself. Lewis observed that could Wells' scholastic and recreation methods be better known, in all probability it would be determined that he was a forerunner of Pestalozzi and Montessori.[10]

Massachusetts State Prison

The Massachusetts State Prison, Charlestown, opened in 1805 and served as a maximum security institution until it was officially closed in February 1956, when it was replaced by the Massachusetts Correctional Institution, South Walpole.

Frederic Robinson became warden of the Massachusetts State

Prison in 1843 and made many improvements in prison life. His views were remarkably modern even by current standards. He organized the Massachusetts State Prison Society for Moral Improvement and Mutual Aid, with himself as president and membership open to any inmate willing to give a formal promise to lead an orderly and virtuous life and to take a pledge of total abstinence from liquor. Meeting fortnightly in the chapel a discussion was held on some previously determined question. A committee to promote the objectives of the society was comprised of the warden, the chaplain, who was vice-president, the prison clerk as secretary, and six inmates chosen by a majority of the members and approved by the warden. Approximately 75 per cent of the inmates belonged to the society.[11]

Gideon Haynes, who was appointed warden of the Massachusetts State Prison in 1858, wrote in 1869:[12]

> Mr. Robinson, in conformity with his ideas of prison discipline started a society among the convicts called 'The Massachusetts State Prison Society for Moral Improvement and Mutual Aid.' The meetings were held in the chapel. The object as stated in the constitution, was, that 'every person, on becoming a member of this society, shall feel it to be his duty, and himself in honor pledged, to use all practicable means and helps for the improvement of his own mind and heart in knowledge and virtue, that by so doing it may be fitting himself for usefulness, respectability, and happiness, when he shall again enjoy the blessing of freedom and society; and furthermore, studiously to avoid everything which tends to corrupt, to debase, and to destroy; and thus to obtain the mastery over those passions and appetites, to whose influence and control so many owe their downfall and ruin.'
>
> The exercises at their meetings consisted of reading original or selected pieces, declamation, and discussion upon various subjects, in which officers and prisoners joined indiscriminately, sometimes ending in scenes of doubtful propriety.
>
> Each member in good standing was presented, on his discharge from prison, with quite an elaborate diploma, signed by the president, vice-president, and secretary of the society, 'recommending him to the confidence, patronage, and the kind aid of his friends and community at large.'

We have found no earlier references to any type of self-government or advisory council group in American adult institutions. The Society for Moral Improvement and Mutual Aid can be regarded as a noteworthy phenomenon in the progress of American prison administration, since it is the first recorded instance of an inmate being given a place, however slight, in a formal communication with the administration of an adult institution.

There is no record of any other form of inmate council at the Massachusetts State Prison, Charlestown, until 1952. Following the riot of that year an Inmate Council was organized under an agreement referred to as the Inmate Council Constitution. Each work-shop could, by two-thirds vote, elect one inmate to the Council. The entire population then elected six men from the Council to be councillors; the remainder were designated as representatives. The six councillors elected a chairman to be the overall representative of the institution and the entire Council. The only qualification for Council membership was six months residency in the institution. Term of office was six months. Together with the editor of the inmate newspaper, who was regarded as Council public relations officer, the councillors met with the warden to review and discuss matters referred by the full Council. The Council chairman appointed a secretary who could be a non-member if there was no qualified or voting member to fill the position. He also appointed one or more representatives to various committees approved by the warden --Finance (Commissary), Sports, Entertainment, Library, Kitchen, and Avocational. The duties of committeemen were to observe and report in writing to the full Council any complaints or suggestions inmates wished presented to the warden during the monthly meetings. The Council continued to function until the Charlestown institution was abandoned.[13]

In 1956 all inmates were transferred to the new maximum security facility, the Massachusetts Correctional Institution, South Walpole. The Inmate Advisory Council was continued at the new location.[14] Its intent and purpose according to the constitution was "to promote harmony and insure cooperation through greater knowledge and understanding of the policy of the Administration ... and to help provide for the general welfare of all." Provided he had six months left to serve and had been at the institution six months during which time he had not been confined to the punishment unit, an inmate was eligible for election to a six months term on the council of twenty-four members, comprised of three representatives from each medium security housing unit and two from each of the maximum security units. A plurality secret ballot vote by the Council determined which members would serve six months terms as chairman, vice-chairman, and secretary. These three together with four others formed an Executive Committee whose function was to recommend adoption or rejection of reports made by other committees on finance, sports, entertainment, commissary, and avocational activities. Required to meet twice a month and to conduct its deliberations according to Robert's Rules of Order, the Council prepared an agenda of items approved by a two-thirds majority vote for meetings with the superintendent.

In the March 1969 issue of Mentor, the inmate publication founded in 1898, there was a front page black-bordered box notice announcing that after considerable discussion at a special session held on January 8, 1969, the members of the Inmate Advisory Council voted to submit their resignations effective forthwith. The account stated: "Reasons for this action were multiple--most can be indexed under the heading of 'non-cooperation' and that the Councilmen's usefulness as representatives of the Inmate body had ceased to exist. Chairmanship, and all seats are now inactive, and vacant."

Detroit House of Correction

In his autobiography published in 1912, Zebulon R. Brockway, the first superintendent of the Detroit House of Correction which was established in 1861, reported an experiment in inmate self-government.[15] In discussing the case of a life-term prisoner he stated:

> Now to relieve his despondency and unrest, also to extend an experiment in prison administration then afoot to utilize intelligent prisoners for their mutual custodial and monitorial control, Brooks was assigned to some duties usually performed by civilian officers. He was entrusted with some inside prison keys and given our general confidence. He was entirely faithful and remarkably efficient. He seemed to recover his normal mental tone and cheerfulness and he was so engaged when I resigned my office and left the institution. Later he relapsed into melancholia, became a permanent hospital patient, and died.
>
> The experiment of engaging prisoners in monitorial and mechanical supervision and in educating their fellow prisoners, as it was conducted at the Detroit House of Correction during my Superintendency, was ennobling to the prisoners who were so assigned, and at one stage of the experiment it seemed feasible to establish in such a municipal prison (at least in the details of its administration) a system of almost complete self-government. So much confidence did this measure evoke that on an occasion when a majority of all the citizen officers conspired to force my compliance with an unreasonable demand by refusing further service, with the intent of closing the manufacturing activities of the establishment as the alternative, at the usual turn-out noon hour I ordered that the six hundred prisoners be sent from their cells to the factories in the enclosure, there to be guarded and directed by the fellow prisoner monitors selected and designated for such service. But this was not put to the test because the striking officers relented and returned to their duty.
>
> The promotion of prisoners to semi-official relations and duties, a practice that worked so well at Detroit and afterwards at the Elmira Reformatory, was very different from the use of "trusties" in common jails and prisons. The duties were less servile and the institutional social status of the prisoners thus engaged was much more elevated. It is an important and sound principle of reformatory prison science, as was attested by Maconochie at Norfolk Island, although it is disesteemed by many wardens. The inception of the practice in my prison experience is closely associated in memory with the service of Brooks,

> Stewart, McKay, and others of the longer sentenced United States prisoners who were confined with the common class of misdemeanants in the Detroit House of Correction, but who were more intelligent.[15]

Helfman has advanced the thought that no doubt Brockway felt that the civic opinion of the day would brand as sugar coating and coddling any deviation from the orthodox "watch dog" supervision of inmates and so made no public utterances at the time on the worthwhileness of his experiments.[16]

In 1926 Jesse O. Stutsman reported that about five years previously while superintendent of the Detroit House of Correction he conducted an experiment in self-government.[17] At that time the population was a mixture of city, county, state, and federal inmates, first offenders and recidivists of all ages serving both misdemeanor and felony sentences. The experiment originated as a plan to instill in the inmates responsibility for their own conduct during entertainments and movies which were held during evening hours when no more than five officers were present to supervise. Until then the number of entertainments was sharply limited since it had not been regarded as advisable to allow men out of their cells unless a large number of officers were present.

Eighteen men were elected by popular vote to be responsible for the deportment of the entire population. This Central Council was later enlarged to 36 when the population doubled. The system was in force for three years, working well with no serious violations despite an original dubious staff attitude.

Reportedly the good deportment of the men was engendered by knowing that added privileges had their genesis in this self-government arrangement in which the group sponsored its own conduct. The Central Council drew up a constitution, approved by the superintendent and adopted by unanimous vote of all inmates. Objectives were stated as:

1. To promote the general welfare of all inmates.
2. To maintain a harmonious feeling between inmates and officials.
3. To assist in the formation of constructive rules for the direction of the inmates.
4. To see that all accused inmates have a fair and impartial hearing and that every inmate has the opportunity for the highest possible physical, mental and moral development.
5. To cooperate with the officials to bring production of the shops to the highest quality of efficiency.

During the three years of the system, population turnover necessitated frequent reinterpretations of its purposes and conditions. Although Stutsman admitted the experiment was no acme of success, he cited several "features of excellence." For that institution and that particular time many constructive ends were attained whose accomplishment in any other manner might not have been possible. During the spring through fall months, a group of twenty men was selected each week for an outing at the prison farm located thirty miles outside of Detroit. With an inmate as driver, these men travelled in large open trucks. Return to the prison was usually after dark. No man attempted to escape and no depredations were committed along the way. However, it is reported that three of the most trusted members of the Central Council escaped (evidently from within the prison). This breach of trust was greatly disapproved by the rest of the men.

Although undertaking many additional duties, members of the Central Council were not excused from regular work assignments nor granted special privileges. The focus of Council members' activities was on better conditions for all. No destructive criticism was permitted, the objective of the system being to give the men opportunity to make suggestions and perform services for the benefit of the entire institution.

At their own suggestion, the men organized a Production Committee of inmate foremen whose weekly meetings resulted in closer inspection of finished products, better methods of repairing and replacing broken machinery, and a hundred percent increase in factory production. The Central Council also financed and directed the editing and publication of a periodical dedicated to informing the public on modern prison methods and to educating inmates.

Superintendent Stutsman retained the authority to censor all actions or to disband the entire organization. In all instances he fully interpreted his rulings. Discontinuance of the Central Council occurred when all long-term prisoners were transferred to the state prisons. The average length of sentence was about 30 days among the misdemeanant population remaining, being insufficient time to provide continuity of Council membership.

In 1928 the Detroit House of Correction was moved to farmland near the town of Plymouth, Michigan. Most of the records were lost or destroyed in the moving so that exploration for other experiments similar to those reported by Brockway and Stutsman seems not to be possible.

Assuming office in April 1972, the then superintendent of the Detroit House of Corrections initiated an informal inmate council in both the women's and men's facilities. The experience with both groups led to the adoption of a formal constitution and by-laws in the men's facility in November 1972, with similar work in progress at that time in the women's facility.

According to the constitution at that time, the purpose of the Resident Advisory Council "is the maintenance and promotion of a better understanding between residents, administration and society. The Council's powers are limited to recommendations concerning the welfare of the inmate body, with emphasis that members should not attempt to interfere in daily functions, particularly custodial matters. The Social Service Office supervises all nominations and elections. Any resident of thirty days or longer may be nominated by the residents of his dormitory as a representative or alternate representative. If screening by the Disciplinary Board reveals that he has had no major disciplinary reports in the month preceding the screening, the nominee is allowed one week to campaign in support of his election, at the end of which a secret ballot election is held. The Record Office clerk is secretary to the Council. Two members elected by the Council provide a liaison with the superintendent during the period between monthly meetings, which are held to discuss an agenda prepared a week earlier at a Council-member-only meeting. Tenure is limited to two consecutive four-month terms of office, with provision for removal for disciplinary reasons by the superintendent, or recall by a two-thirds vote of the Council and approval by the superintendent, for non-feasance or unexcused absence from meetings."[18] No current information has been received.

Elmira Reformatory

Zebulon R. Brockway was appointed as the first superintendent of the Elmira Reformatory, Elmira, New York, in 1876, and remained in that position until he resigned in 1900. In his autobiography published in 1912, Brockway described a system of martial control instituted in 1888:

> The reformatory became like a garrison of a thousand prisoner soldiers; more of the prisoners were utilized in the details of management, and prisoners to the number of nearly a hundred were given some military rank. They were assigned to participate in governing by service as monitors, instructors, inspectors, patrolmen, record clerks, etc. The military control was, at one time, so completely by the prisoners that on one occasion at the evening dress parade of the regiment, with a thousand men in line (no citizen but myself was present to observe it), the whole command from colonel to corporal was composed of prisoners.
>
> The court martial and the civil court procedure were both used for the trial of offenders against rules and regulations. The courts were a mixed composition of citizens, employees, and selected prisoners. Juries were impaneled, sometimes prisoner counsel was allowed, and always full stenographic reports of the trials were made and preserved and the right of appeal was conferred. The courts served well for a time, but they became too cumbersome, so that later the trials were held before a permanently assigned examining judge from whose decisions appeals were allowed to the general superintendent, thence to the board of managers. Appeals for clemency to the general superintendent, upon whom alone devolved the duty of imposing penalties, were frequently made, but rarely an appeal for

a new trial; and never except in one instance was an appeal for a new trial or review of judgment made beyond the general superintendent to the board of managers.[19]

Michigan State Prison

Hiram F. Hatch was warden of the Michigan State Prison from 1885 to 1891. His belief in the rehabilitation of amenable delinquents was in sharp contrast to the prevailing practices of the day. In 1888 he approved an organization for social betterment among the 457 inmates.[20] In an unsupervised meeting an inmate committee drew up a constitution, naming the organization The Mutual Aid League of the M.S.P. This constitution set forth the ideals of the group:

> The objects of this league shall be: by social intercourse to improve ourselves, and to aid in the moral, intellectual, physical and financial advancement of our fellowmen. To inculcate a higher appreciation of the value and sacred obligations of American citizenship, and the necessity of unconditional loyalty to the Federal and State government, as exemplified by a strict maintenance of the laws by them promulgated. To resist and oppose corruption and dishonesty in all forms and places and to promote honesty and efficiency in the discharge of all labor, tasks and duties assigned. To respect and aid by personal discipline, in the maintenance of all rules and regulations necessary to the discipline and good order of the prison.

Meetings were held monthly with the warden as presiding officer. Reports indicate he did this alone without guards. In line with the by-laws of the organization, Warden Hatch appointed nine members as an executive board who met with him weekly. The organization provided a means of communication between staff and inmates and was expected to assist in the orientation of new arrivals.

Warden Hatch received considerable criticism from contemporaries, which he answered by referring to a favorable record in the maintenance of prison discipline. The program was dropped with his resignation on February 3, 1891.

The George Junior Republic

The Junior Republic movement has particular importance in a study of self-government in institutions. Two of the later strong advocates for inmate self-government were associates of the founder. They were Thomas Mott Osborne, Member, Board of Directors, and Calvin Derrick, General Superintendent of the National Association of Junior Republics.

From his contacts with the people and institutions of an urban industrial setting (New York City), William Reuben George, a jewelry box manufacturer, developed an interest in improving the opportunities and lives of young people. He took a group of youths to West Dryden, New York, where he had spent the first 14 years of his life. The New York Tribune Fresh Air Fund provided the railroad fares, and food was supplied by farmers in the Dryden area for the two-week summer outing. In subsequent years, the motto "Nothing Without Labor" was adopted and put into practice, and offenders against group-determined rules were tried by a jury of their peers. In July 1895 George announced plans for a permanent Junior Republic. Subsequently, other Republics were formed and attracted national and international attention as experiments in self-government.[21]

Junior Republics known to be still in operation are located in Litchfield, Connecticut; Grove City, Pennsylvania; and Freeville, New York. The only connection between these Junior Republics is the name of the founder, as all were developed, financed, and governed autonomously.

The George Junior Republic, Freeville, New York, still operates under the self-government plan, essentially as designed when the facility was established in 1895, and codified in a constitution and by-laws.[22]

Auburn Prison--Women's Division

The records of the Women's Prison Association of New York for the year 1903 contain the comments of Alice L. Woodbridge, Prison Visitor, following a visit to the State Prison for Women at Auburn:

> The Superintendent, Mrs. Welshe, has organized a society among the prisoners. This is known as the 'Society of the Red Badge of Merit,' and women who break no rules for six months are eligible as members. When a rule is broken by a member, she is suspended for six months. This has had a wonderful effect upon the prisoners. The society meets once a month, and some kind of entertainment is provided. A badge made of common white cloth bound with red and bearing the letters 'S.R.B.M.' is worn by them but it is easily defaced and a more substantial one is needed. As this society has proved its efficiency as a means of discipline, the prison department should supply a proper badge for it. Twenty-five dollars would purchase a sufficient number of substantial badges to last for two years.
>
> For some unaccountable reason, the women employed as matrons in Auburn State Prison are not subjected to State Civil Service examination. In all other prisons and jails where women are employed, a Civil Service examination is required; and if efficient and intelligent supervision is needed anywhere, it is needed in a State Prison. Without it, the position is open to all sorts of abuses.[23]

In November 1913, Madeline Zabriskie Doty, a member of the New York State Commission on Prison Reform, together with Elizabeth C. Watson, voluntarily spent a week in confinement at Auburn Prison--Women's Division. Their identity was unknown to either staff or inmates. Both were committed on the evening of November 13, as Maggie Martin and Lizzie Watson. Supposedly each had been sentenced to serve 18 to 30 months for forgery. Their joint report revealed rather extreme conditions, and resulted in some improvements.[24]

Some months later, Miss Doty received letters from the inmates indicating that the matrons were not fully in accord with the changes. After she learned there was a new head matron, Miss Doty visited the prison and met with the inmates. Out of their discussions came the idea to organize a group to provide a channel for inmate communication to the head matron. The latter agreed to accord the group the same recognition given to employees. The new organization was called the Daily Endeavor League; its color emblem a blue bow.[25]

A charter of organization was drawn, providing for a president and representative of each housing unit to be chosen by the inmates. All inmates were to be members of the League and even though suspended for abuse, good behavior could make a new enrollment possible. Participation in the League turned the interest of the women toward the improvement of conditions from their prior sole concern with personal woes. A reign of good behavior resulted in the women's being allowed outside their cells on Sunday afternoons for a recreation hour. Correspondence and visiting rules were liberalized. The head matron proposed and held a Valentine Day party, lasting from four to nine p. m.

Soon, however, the matrons began reasoning that should the good behavior of the inmates continue, fewer matrons would be needed and this could result in a staff reduction of perhaps fifty percent. The situation deteriorated, and despite a work-training plan introduced by Miss Doty, staff antagonism to the League caused the head matron to reverse her original favorable stance. There then ensued an incident which marked the end of the League. A woman suspended by the group for poor conduct was befriended by the staff, putting the League in a position of ridicule and, in the opinion of Miss Doty, placing a premium on bad conduct. A few days later the head matron declared herself president of the League and directed the representatives to report misbehavior to her and the staff. Returning to the prison, Miss Doty called an assembly of all inmates, announcing that she believed self-government with the officials in command was a farce and that there could be no toleration of an organization whose representatives must become informers. A unanimous vote to disband the League was made.

The Women's Division of the Auburn Prison was merged with the Westfield State Farm at Bedford Hills, New York in 1933. The facility is now designated as the Bedford Hills Correctional Facility.

Sleighton School

The Sleighton School is a residential treatment center for juveniles of both sexes between the ages of 12 and 17 who have been adjudicated delinquent and committed by the courts. The school is located six miles southwest of Media, Pennsylvania. It is a private institution, owned and operated by a non-profit corporation and governed by a nineteen-member Board of Managers, of which four are court-appointed. The Commonwealth of Pennsylvania, by legislative act, gives an appropriation to the school, which is matched by the committing counties. This school may be the second oldest private institution accepting troubled youngsters in the United States. Originally called the Philadelphia House of Refuge, it began operation on December 8, 1828. In the early 1890s the boys' section was moved to Glen Mills and in 1910 the girls' section moved to its present location. The two schools were incorporated under the name of Glen Mills Schools, but on April 17, 1931, the girls' section was designated as the Sleighton Farm School for Girls. In July, 1975, the school became co-educational and its name was changed to Sleighton School.[26]

Superintendent Martha Platt Falconer took office in 1906 and established in 1910 a dynamic system of student government designed to place responsibility upon the girls for the maintenance of good morale and to make possible a large measure of freedom and self-expression.[27] The program was operating under the same concept and with basically the same procedures in 1967, and was referred to as Cottage Government.[28]

The purpose of student participation in government in the five Honor Cottages was to help each girl to develop inner controls so that she could become an acceptable citizen, first in her Honor Cottage, then in the school as a whole, and next in the community. Additionally, each girl was given the opportunity to develop leadership, gain ability to help others, and experience the satisfaction of cooperative work with adults.

After undergoing a period of orientation in the reception cottage, a girl moved into an honor cottage of her own choice, where she was accorded junior citizenship status. Upon completing a six-weeks' period of demonstrated mature behavior she could be voted citizenship privileges by other girls already in that status. If during the ensuing eight weeks she was regarded as making progress in her personal development and interpersonal relationships, she attained Leader standing. Following a like period, she was eligible for election to a Cottage Council. Council girls were largely responsible for morale in the cottage and the behavior of its residents. In weekly Council meetings they also assisted the housemothers and the student government director in making decisions regarding the discipline of other girls. The decision might be to talk with the girl involved and attempt to help her to improve, advise her that a recurrence of the unacceptable behavior could result in a restriction of movie attendance or participation in some other activity, or the actual imposition of a restriction. In extreme situations the offender could be removed from the Honor Cottage temporarily, or permanently, and placed in another type of living unit.

The following is based on information obtained in 1973.[29] During the 1960s there began a slow but obvious change in the characteristics of the population. A greater number of more disturbed and harder-to-reach youngsters, from all strata of society, rather than principally from the ranks of the underprivileged, were referred by the courts. These more sophisticated and educationally ambitious individuals, many the products of the drug culture, required a more intensive treatment program than had hitherto existed. Additional psychiatrists, social workers, and other professionally trained personnel were added to the staff. The original concept of student government was expanded to develop consultants among the girls in matters of clothing and other needs where adolescent taste is important. As they develop in insight and maturity the girls are assigned as junior staff and assist in group therapy. The fact that runaway attempts are minimal is attributed to this involvement in their own treatment process. The focus of school efforts is increasingly on helping the girls to gain greater independence and to assume greater responsibility as they move through the program. A Graduate Student Unit has been established for those who attend off-campus programs of vocational and business training and academic classes at the secondary and college levels. It is hoped that a half-way house can be developed within the year.

In addition to student government, which operates essentially as described in 1973, a Guided Group Interaction program has been added. Meetings are held daily and guided by staff. The program is a means of attempting to alter behavior through peer pressure.[30]

Preston School of Industry

Calvin Derrick utilized the pioneering work of William Reuben George who founded the George Junior Republic, when appointed superintendent of the Preston School of Industry, Ione, California, in October 1912. He outlined and formulated a program using inmate self-government as the keystone of its arch. It is significant to note that the Ione program represents the first acknowledgment and endorsement of inmate self-government by any state. At the inauguration of the second president of the self-government group, Governor Hiram Johnson of California went to the school and placed the stamp of his official approval upon the program.[31]

Prior to inaugurating the self-government program Derrick requested that the Department of Sociology of the University of California send out a questionnaire on the subject to various correctional institutions. His conclusions, based on the receipt of over one hundred replies, were:

1. Few people in correctional institutions thoroughly believed

in the principles of democracy and their application to populations in custody.

2. Almost all correctional institution personnel were ignorant of the manner in which these principles should or could be applied.

3. The rank and file of institution people were so prejudiced against the plan that they could not be induced to examine it with an open mind.

Perhaps Derrick's philosophy concerning self-government can best be expressed by his statement: "The principles of self-government are the principles of democracy. If democracy is right, then self-government is right. It is not, therefore, a question of principles; it is a question of the intelligent application of principles to a given set of conditions."

The Ione concept of the application of self-government was characterized by two ideas:

1. Self-government is not an end, but a means to a very definite purpose. While the prosecution of one inmate by another is not the main object of self-government, it does serve a definite purpose and affords splendid training in a variety of ways.

2. Since the home, school, church, and city have each in turn failed to make the boy fit into the established and approved pattern of civilization, we cannot place him in an institution which forces a much higher and more nearly perfect social order on him.

The sole purpose of this system of self-government was to furnish a medium in which the boys might develop a civilization of their own with as many degrees and gradations as necessary to meet their needs and interests, the ideal being to come as close as possible to standards of civilization.

As an introduction, boys were granted two hours a day of self-government under staff supervision. The institution was operated as a quasi-military organization, the population being divided into companies. Each company was given a brief and faulty constitution. Two experimented with a military government, but a civil form of government was developed by all after some 14 months of operation. Differences of opinion concerning interpretation of the constitution gave rise to political parties. Confusion resulting from the differing laws of the various companies brought about a House of Congress. Disagreement as to which laws should be retained or abolished caused the formation of a commission to codify civil and penal procedure and finally a body of uniform law. A prison was built to enforce the mandates of the courts. With prisoners to care for, it was necessary to provide work for them. A commissioner of labor was appointed to administer a work program of certain rough, unskilled labor. An orientation program was organized with the provision that its completion by newly admitted boys was a prerequisite to eligibility as a voter.

There were twenty-two marshals and deputy marshals responsible for an honor system operated among some 350 boys. These boy marshals had as much liberty and as much responsibility concerning the custody of the boys in their companies as did the staff within the grounds. Approximately ten per cent of the population were found unfit for participation in the self-government program and were controlled by employees.

It is understood that Derrick was granted a leave of absence effective July 1, 1916, to become assistant warden to Thomas Mott Osborne, then warden of Sing Sing Prison, Ossining, New York, and that the self-government program at the Preston School of Industry was discontinued the following year. No information has been obtained whether or not he took the Sing Sing Prison position (Warden Osborne resigned on October 16, 1916), but it has been verified that Derrick was superintendent of the Westchester County Penitentiary, Valhalla, New York, from 1917 to 1921, and established a self-government group known as the Effort League, which is later recounted.

A 1940 study found that while there was no truly representative system of student self-government at the facility, a variation existed in the form of a Cadet Council. The group was composed of cadet company captains appointed by the staff. At the time the council met only irregularly, but formerly had met each month at a luncheon in the superintendent's house to discuss athletics and other programs. To qualify for a cadet officer's commission, the student had to be over seventeen years of age, alert, capable, cooperative, and a demonstrated natural leader. In addition to their military duties (close order drill averaging about ten minutes a day and reviews), the cadet officers supervised the company locker rooms and maintained general order, but had no further disciplinary authority. They, and other students of especial trustworthiness, were designated on occasion to accompany staff members in efforts to apprehend runaways.[32]

Student monitors, known as cadet assistants, were placed with night supervisors in large dormitories. Occasionally, a cadet assistant nearing release was placed in charge of a cottage group for several hours at night because of a shortage of staff. The rationale for such assignments was that night supervision was "easy."

In January, 1973, each of the eight living units in the Preston School of Industry was designed to serve the specific needs of groupings such as drug users, recalcitrants, and parole violators. Ward participation was provided in a variety of opportunities, ranging from scheduled large group meetings attended by the superintendent and assistant superintendent to well organized student government in the drug program. Other formal communication was achieved in small groups. Wards assigned to the Food Service elected representatives who met weekly with the food manager and his staff to discuss assignee-related problems.[33]

New Jersey State Reformatory

The New Jersey State Reformatory at Rahway was opened in 1901. In 1948 it became an adult institution and is now known as the New Jersey State Prison.

Dr. Frank Moore became superintendent in 1909, bringing to the position many years of experience in school administration. He made many program changes based on a policy that life in the reformatory should approximate that outside to the end that a releasee might better be able to adjust himself to a normal existence. He conducted programs of public education by arranging for illustrated lectures to be given in all counties of the state upon the methods of reformation employed at Rahway.

In 1913 Dr. Moore established a tentative form of inmate self-government which he described in his annual report of 1914:

> One of the new features of the year has been the adoption of a plan of self-government. During the summer just passed there was organized a Council composed of thirty of the inmates elected by the inmates themselves. The duty of this Council is to assist in the discipline of the institution. They give particular attention to the keeping of order on the tiers, and to suppressing conversation with regard to crime and to preventing profanity. They have elected their own president and secretary, and meet twice a week. All new inmates after they have been addressed by the superintendent are taken into the Council meeting and given advice by the president of the Council as to how they may best conduct themselves while in the reformatory and as to what is the spirit of the inmates and the desire of the Council to lend them help whenever it can. The power has been given to the Council not to administer punishment in any way, but to deprive inmates whose influence is harmful from the privileges of the yard and from entertainments.[34]

In his annual report of 1915, Superintendent Moore reported:

> We gave the plan a trial for one year and then put the question to a vote of the inmates as to whether or not they desired to have the plan continued another year. A feeling had grown that there had been more or less unfairness by 'The Council.' Politics to some extent had entered from time to time in the selection of the councilmen, so that the two plans of being governed by council or officers of the institution were now put squarely before the young men for a decision as to which system of government they preferred. The result of their vote was overwhelmingly in favor of being governed by the officers rather than inmates. This vote shows that the young man who has been unable to control himself aright realizes that he is incapable

> of controlling others. He sees that it is best for him to be under proper control. When that control is fair and administered with a spirit of sincerity and kindness, he feels it is for his good and willingly yields to it. Especially will he do this, if he feels that he can look up to those who are governing him. But he will rebel, if those who assume to be his superiors are only his equals, who take advantage of their position to secure special privileges, violate rules or play favorites. Realizing these facts after giving the question sober consideration the inmates of the Reformatory felt that it was better for them that the institution should return to the original plan of being governed by the appointed authority of the institution and hence the council disbanded.[35]

Wines commented on Superintendent Moore's report:

> Lack of familiarity with governmental procedure would seem to be as strong a reason for continuing self-government as for abandoning it. Then, too, the inmate officers at Rahway who assumed to be 'superior' and took advantage of their position to secure special privileges might have been quickly dealt with by the other inmates, one would think, if these had been sufficiently induced to regard self-government as <u>their venture</u>--as something that they could make or mar as they chose.... One suspects that possibly the remedy ... was an arrangement for the 'recall' of arrogant and recalcitrant officials by the inmates themselves.
>
> Superintendent Moore's explanation did not appeal to the members of the New Jersey Prison Inquiry Commission [1917] as final. Referring to the fact that this experiment was said to have developed 'ward politics,' the commission pointed out in its report that 'that is an incident not unknown to self-government outside prison walls, and if it is a greater menace in correctional institutions than in the wards of a city, it is, on the other hand, more easily dealt with.' Of all correctional institutions, it went on, Rahways seems, 'both in the character of its population and in the strong and efficient government that it possesses, to be the one best adapted to work out such an experiment safely and successfully.' It finally suggested that 'another trial might wisely be made' before the method was wholly abandoned.[36]

Auburn Prison

Thomas Mott Osborne of Auburn, New York, had long been interested in the problems of prison management and in prisoner resocialization. As a member of the Board of Directors, George Junior Republic, he had learned first-hand of the self-government program initiated by William Reuben George. His belief that the principles of self-government could be utilized as a remedy for the evils of the prison system was expressed in his address to the National Prison Association in 1906:

> The prison system endeavors to make men industrious by driving them to work; to make them virtuous by removing temptation; to make them respect law by forcing them to obey edicts of an autocrat; to make them far-sighted by allowing them no chance to exercise foresight; to give them individual initiative by treating them in large groups; in short to prepare them again for society by placing them in conditions as unlike real society as they could well be made....
>
> Outside the walls a man must choose between work and idleness--between honesty and crime. Why not let him teach himself these lessons before he comes out? Such things are best learned by experience. Some can acquire their lesson in life by the experience of others; but most men are in prison for the very reason that they cannot do that. But everyone who is not an absolute fool can learn by experience, and the bulk of men in prison certainly are not fools....[37]

Late in 1913, Osborne spent a voluntary one-week term of confinement in Auburn Prison under the pseudonym of Tom Brown. Out of this grew the plan for establishing an inmate self-government program whose stated purpose and objective was to alter concepts of confinement then practiced routinely in the majority of penal institutions. A cardinal principle was that the prisoners must work out their own plan, rather than have an outside plan presented to them. Osborne noted: "This was real, vital democracy; this was solving the problem in the genuine American spirit."[38]

The first name proposed for the organization was Good Conduct League, followed by the Tom Brown League. The latter was rejected by Osborne as being too personal. Finally, Mutual Welfare League was agreed upon as the official designation. There then followed several meetings to implement the plan of self-government.[39]

On December 26, 1913 a free election was held in the institution to choose a committee of 49 to determine the exact nature and organization of the League. The first meeting of the elected Committee was held on December 28, and a chairman was selected. It was unanimously decided to make League membership available to all, with bad conduct as the sole reason for expulsion. In addition, a subcommittee of 12 members was selected to formulate by-laws. The League objective was stated as: "The promotion in every way of the true interests and welfare of the men confined in prison." The motto "Do Good--Make Good" was adopted. Emblematic of Hope and Truth, green and white were chosen as League Colors. It was agreed that there be a Board of Delegates of 49 members, elected for a six-month term, to serve as the governing body of the organization. Election of the Board of Delegates took place on January 15, 1914, and the members were installed in office on January 18.

On February 11, 1914, the Board of Delegates met in order that the inmate sergeant-at-arms could give instructions for conduct during the first general meeting of the League. The first general meeting of the Mutual Welfare League, featuring a piano and violin recital, was held on February 12, 1914.

It is significant to note that Warden Rattigan, of Auburn, with the approval of the New York State Superintendent of Prisons, proposed to hand over all infractions of discipline to the League except in five instances: assault on an officer, deadly assault upon another inmate, refusal to work, strike, and attempt to escape.

Prisoner cooperation was the foundation of the League. Its operations were based on the premise that the prison could be treated as a community. Tannenbaum espoused this by his comment: "Prisoners possessed among themselves a public opinion that if properly harnessed could be made effective in the enforcement of public policy and the development of public morale, which would make discipline both easier upon the Warden and more effective with the men."[40]

The Mutual Welfare League continued to function at the Auburn Prison until 1929, but its original purpose and procedures were deflected throughout the years. (See the report from the 1926 edition of the Handbook of American Prisons on page 30).

In 1966, the then warden at Sing Sing Prison, basing his comments on his service since 1926 with the New York State Department of Corrections, stated that the Mutual Welfare League was deeply involved in the riots of 1929 at the Auburn Prison and ceased operations thereafter. Leadership apparently had fallen into the hands of inmates who should not have been elected to represent others as they had actually strong-armed their way into leadership.[41]

Sing Sing Prison

In 1914, during his very brief administration, Warden McCormick succeeded in "opening up Sing Sing." He introduced a system of regulated leisure, allowing prisoners freedom of the yard on Saturday afternoon and all day Sunday. The dire predictions of chaos by others were not fulfilled. He also formed the first inmate self-government organization at Sing Sing known as the Golden Rule Brotherhood, whose design was similar to the Mutual Welfare League at Auburn Prison.[42]

Thomas Mott Osborne became warden of Sing Sing Prison, Ossining, New York, on December 1, 1914. He immediately organized a Mutual Welfare League which was described in Wines' book:

> At Sing Sing, the Secretary of the League was relieved of all other prison duties and gave his full time to this work. An office was fitted up for him next to that of the principal

> keeper, and here he kept his records, interviewed his callers and dictated his correspondence. He was one of the busiest men in prison.
>
> The real instruments of self-government at Sing Sing were the Committees. It was these that effectively expressed the wishes of the prisoners and took initiative in getting things done. The Warden's day was filled with appointments with Committee Chairmen who wanted assistance or advice. The Chairmen quickly came to realize that a great deal of power lay in their hands if they knew how to wield it. Not only were they the trustees of the wishes of their fellow-inmates, but the prison officials came to regard them as responsible makers of institution policy. Some of them became adept in the art of getting what they wanted without appearing to ask for much. Aside from the specific things they accomplished, their activity was beneficial in two ways: (1) It taught them some of the difficulties of administration, thus enabling them to pass that knowledge back to their constituents; and (2) It enabled the prison authorities, by means of the understanding the promoted, to rely upon cooperation where before they would have received only suspicion and distrust.[43]

Barnes commented on the program:

> A number of influences combined to bring Mr. Osborne's regime to a premature end at Sing Sing. Among these may be mentioned Mr. Osborne's failure to comprehend that his system was applicable only to non-defective convicts, and that it must be preceded by an adequate system of clinical observation, classification and promotion of convicts; his own unyielding and uncompromising attitude, so characteristic of the ardent reformer on the defensive; the opposition of the keepers and guards who had been trained wholly in the savage methods of the conventional repressive penology; the bitter enmity of grafting contractors who found Mr. Osborne as little susceptible to dishonesty as to conventionality; the opposition of political rivals among the most notorious 'rounders' of the machine politicians; and the jealousy of leading penologists of a more conventional and conservative cast.[44]

In his book, Twenty Thousand Years in Sing Sing, Lewis E. Lawes, who became warden there in 1920, described the Mutual Welfare League as then being part and parcel of the administration. League officers were permitted out of their cells long after midnight, and were assigned to the visiting room where they had unrestricted contact with outsiders. Also, they were in charge of all tours of the prison, an activity popular with out-of-town groups in 1920, and had full control of the store, making their own purchases, and banking and disbursing League funds with practically no supervision. The League's Executive Board appointed its sergeant-at-arms who selected his own deputies. In addition to functioning as monitors in the mess hall, they had charge of the recreation field, the chapel, and all athletic events and entertainment. It was their right and duty to report any prisoner for violation of rules or for delinquencies to the League Court. Before this group of seven judges the accuser and accused presented the facts. Sadly, not always being of the highest calibre, the judges often failed to examine facts impartially. Instances of double jeopardy were reported. Men disciplined by the Warden's Court were often held answerable for the same offense to the League Court.[45]

Lawes believed that the Mutual Welfare League was a worthwhile organization but that it had been badly administered. The membership was divided into two camps whose energies were concentrated on coralling votes. The better element remained aloof from the League, as a consequence of which it became a plaything of the less desirable men. On election day, apprehensively anticipated by the staff, the first-aid clinic was kept busy.

Within a brief time, Lawes abolished the League's Court, as well as party politics. He clearly defined the sphere of influence of the League in its relation to the prison administration. With the disappearance of partisanship, the type of men capable of exerting a good influence on others came to the fore. Lawes was of the opinion that the term self-government in prison was a much abused and greatly misconstrued term and that the true meaning of the term was the government of self.

Although Lawes cited Thomas Mott Osborne as being outstanding among prison administrators, he did not hesitate to point out what he believed to be mistakes made by Osborne in his dealings with the Mutual Welfare League. Lawes commented:

> I believe that prisoners should be allowed a measure of self-expression, a voice in the kind and character of their social and recreational activities. These, however, must at all times be subject to administrative supervision and censorship. The defect of Mr. Osborne's administration was in the overlapping of prisoner self-government with the Warden's responsibility as an administrator. His intense desire to raise the prisoner to a normal place led him to surrender his prerogatives. He became an advisor instead of a leader and ruler. The swing of the pendulum from severity to liberality was too wide. It resulted in chaos. Mr. Osborne was not given the opportunity to correct this fault. His term of office ended too soon.[46]

In the 1926 Handbook of American Prisons, editors Austin H. MacCormick and Paul W. Garrett stated that the following comments were equally true of the prisons at both Sing Sing and Auburn:

> While the League has, in all the different and varying conditions, never entirely ceased to be a factor in the administration of the prison, it has, unfortunately, ceased to be

> much more than an aid to prison management. The tendency is for the prison authorities to use the League as a convenient aid to secure easy prison administration: they do not guide and direct it so that it accomplishes its fundamental purpose of developing the right social viewpoint to replace the criminal viewpoint of individual selfishness. They use the League chiefly to serve the prison management rather than use both the League and the administration to serve society. To accomplish the fundamental and larger purpose requires a type of leadership, at once imaginative and constructive, which has not been given.[47]

The Mutual Welfare League is no longer in existence, having faded away in 1950.[48]

New Jersey Correctional Institution for Women

Opened in 1913, the Correctional Institution for Women, Clinton, was originally known as Clinton Farms and later as the New Jersey Reformatory for Women.

From 1914 until January 1973, student government, the core of programming, grew progressively less able to meet the needs of a changing population. In response to a request by inmates, a staff-inmate committee recently revised the system in the hope of providing a mutual relationship which will increase problem solving at the cottage level and open up channels of communication between inmates and administrative staff. The system is based upon the use of General Inmate Representatives (GIR's) elected by secret ballot for a term of six months. Since these women not only represent their cottages at meetings with administration but also are expected to assist staff in mediating and counselling with inmates, final approval of GIR's is given by the Classification Committee. Any staff member may meet at any time with their GIR's and a monthly meeting is held with the administrative staff and one GIR from each cottage to discuss problems affecting the entire population.[49]

Reports received in 1967 provided the following information regarding the Student Government Program from its inception in 1914.[50]

Student government was brought to the then Clinton Farms by Superintendent May Caughey from the Sleighton Farm School for Girls in Pennsylvania, where the theory had been introduced by Superintendent Martha P. Falconer in 1910. The insufficient physical accommodations of the institution and the small staff complement permitted no more than minimum security so that some form of student government honor system was necessitated.

The continued use of self-government meant a constant refining of its procedures and purposes. However, the basic philosophy that responsibility for one's own progress makes a most effective rehabilitative tool was not changed. Student officers were elected by each cottage. An Honor Group was made up of residents with a three months' clear conduct record who were recommended by their peers. An Honor Pledge was used as a symbol of acceptance of the effort that constitutes resocialization. The original requirement for "reporting anyone I believe to be planning to run away," was later deleted in consistency with a de-emphasis of implied authority of one inmate over another. The governing advisory group in 1914 consisted of an executive group called the Council of Commissioners and Improvement Committee, composed of representatives from each cottage. It was later renamed the Improvement Committee. Its functions were advisory and sanctions suggested required approval by the superintendent. In 1961 the duty of orienting the new girls to the rules of the institution was added as a function.

In 1948 overcrowding was regarded as the cause of numerous runaways. The staff consulted with the population on methods both to prevent and to discipline runaways, and to consider methods of rewarding cottages having no runaways. This is a good example of staff and student government integration. Group responsibility keynoted this cooperative effort which aided the institution during a crisis.

Several instances were advanced as to why student government had lasted at Clinton Farms:

1. It is functional.
2. It allows for open lines of communication.
3. The charisma of the superintendents.
4. The unity and cooperation of the staff.
5. Since it was an original part of the institution administration it has never posed a threat to the administration. The identification is now traditional.
6. Student government allows for flexibility in dealing with institutional and individual crises.
7. No outside political pressures to disband the form have been exerted.

Two instances of the spread of student government from Clinton Farms to other institutions are documented. Dr. Mary B. Harris, who was superintendent in 1918, became superintendent in 1927 of the Federal Reformatory for Women at Alderson, West Virginia; and Miss Grace Robson, who became superintendent on July 1, 1934, at the State Home and Industrial School for Girls, Eagle Springs, North Carolina, initiated student government in those institutions. The latter institution is now known as Samarcand Manor.

Connecticut State Reformatory

The October 1, 1914, report of the Board of Directors, Connecticut Reformatory, Cheshire, Connecticut, states:

> Recently a Welfare League has been established by the inmates, founded on a somewhat similar institution at Auburn, New York, and along the lines of the George Junior Republic, its object being to encourage the boys, not only to assist each other, but in certain minor matters to govern and police themselves, under the general supervision of the superintendent of the institution. The features of this League are of such recent establishment that little can be said at the present time of its success.... [51]

In September 1915, C. H. Johnson, who was assistant warden at Sing Sing Prison, New York, under Warden Osborne, became superintendent at the Connecticut Reformatory. The League was abandoned in May 1916, according to Superintendent Johnson's report:

> The reason for the dissatisfaction in the organization was that it lent itself readily to so much misrule and dishonesty that the inmates were tired of it. The young men in the reformatory were, to a large extent, foreigners from the industrial sections of the cities of the State. Many of them knew but little of the English language, some of them practically nothing. There were very few who knew anything about forms of government, and their ideas in such matters were extremely vague. When it came to the election of officials, the more clever inmates were able by threats, bribery and other similar means to secure their own election, and the more ignorant inmates had but a vague idea of what it was all about. In judicial matters it was extremely difficult to find in such a population inmates who had a mind which lent itself to judicial procedure and which could weigh evidence for or against the institutional offender. The result was that the judges were invariably those who had been selected by the inmate population because it was expected that they would be helpful to possible offenders in time of need. All kinds of adjustments were attempted to overcome these conditions, which were inherent in the nature of the population of the institution, but without success.... It was finally decided at a gathering of the inmates that the management of the institution should be placed with the superintendent and the officers appointed by law.
>
> There was then begun the development of a method of military instruction. It was found that the young men who came to the institution had done practically as they pleased most of their lives, had no respect for authority and had very little idea of obeying anybody when they were told to do so. Their physical carriage was just about as slouchy as their mental condition and social attitude. A military battalion was organized, inmate officers were selected on the grounds of merit and ability and not on the basis of purchased popularity, and beneficial results were quite noticeable in the physical appearance and attitudes of the inmates. It was quite evident that what the inmates needed

> was not more freedom, of which they had had an excess in their life, but direction and instruction in self-control and obedience to law and order.[52]

Westchester County Penitentiary

Calvin Derrick was superintendent of the Westchester County Penitentiary from 1917 to 1921. His philosophy of self-government as he had expressed it at the Preston School of Industry, Ione, California, was enunciated again when he approved an inmate meeting on September 17, 1917 to discuss forming an organization. Temporary officers were chosen and successive meetings resulted in the adoption of a constitution and by-laws on October 12. Known as the Effort League, the group had as officers a president, vice-president, judge, secretary, sergeant-at-arms, and a public defender. These officers formed a League Cabinet which met periodically with the administration.

As given in the constitution, the aims of the Effort League were:

> 1. To discipline ourselves.
> 2. To cooperate with the warden of this institution in the enforcement of all rules.
> 3. To educate ourselves by lectures, debates, and by whatever other means, making for uplift, we are capable of securing.
> 4. To promote our welfare by the improvement of conditions and by whatever material aid we can and are privileged to contribute.
> 5. To entertain ourselves by clean and healthy sports and amusements.

The warden was an honorary president and the associate wardens were honorary members. An officer was appointed by the warden to serve as League ambassador. The initiation ceremony was quite impressive according to a contemporary account:[53]

> It usually takes place during a Saturday evening social meeting. The new men, who have previously been instructed by a reception committee as to the League and its purposes, are called before the president, the judge and the other members of the cabinet. The president speaks a few words of welcome and the judge, after a short talk on the responsibilities and privileges of membership and the meaning and reality of the pledge, administers the latter. The new men in turn sign the constitution, the entire membership standing and singing 'America' meanwhile, after which the newly-made members file before the cabinet for a hearty hand-shake and personal greeting.

The Effort League sought to extend its influence and aid to

every member after his release. Those returning to the community were encouraged to contact the League for any readjustment assistance. The League sponsored cash donations and volunteer work for the Red Cross. It organized an evening school program whose principal purpose was social rather than academic education. Supervision was given to the cleaning of living and work areas by the appointment of a League inspector who made daily sanitation inspections.

An Inmate's Court for the Establishment of Good Relationship, regarded as the most important feature of the self-government work, was presided over by an inmate judge who, with two other members, heard all cases referred for trivial infractions of the rules, such as failure to have a clean cell or lack of attention to work. The Court had no punitive powers. Its effect lay in the ability of the members to motivate cooperation by counsel and advice. Failing this, the Court could expel the offender from the League.

In his annual report for the period January 1, 1917 through December 31, 1918, Superintendent Derrick stated:

> At the beginning of the year the matter of discipline was practically all in the hands of the institution officials. They were wholly responsible for the maintenance of good order and the proper behavior of the inmate population. In many cases the results were not all that were to be desired. How to handle some of the problems arising was a question not always easy of solution without resorting to older and harsher methods, which we would not under any circumstances consider. After many official conferences, and having in mind the growing influence of the Effort League and its possibilities for good, we determined to grant to the inmates the opportunity for governing themselves by assuming some of these disciplinary responsibilities. At first in a limited way, then, as our confidence increased, in larger measure. We found this method most successful. Minor cases were referred to the Inmates' Court, and as time went on, more important matters, until practically all complaints, both inmate and official, were handed over to this court, where they were handled in a most judicial and satisfactory manner, not only to the official force but also to the offending inmates. In this way our disciplinary problems were reduced to a minimum, and we had very few cases where it was necessary to in any way take matters into our own hands.
>
> On January 1, 1918, the Effort League of the Westchester County Penitentiary and Workhouse had been in existence just two and one-half months. It had demonstrated its right to continue, but while its ideals were worthy ones not much had been accomplished in a practical way. Nothing had been forced upon it, in fact nothing has ever been done at any time that savored of coercion, but the men, and particularly the members of the League Cabinet, realizing something of the possibilities of such an organization

> and its power for good to the inmate population, worked earnestly to advance the League's power and influence. The way was not always plain, either to the inmates or the officials, but one principle always prevailed, viz: every privilege must be earned by the men through their assumption of some work or responsibility connected therewith. The men, instead of avoiding these added burdens, voluntarily sought them, and when received made serious efforts to prove that they were worthy and could carry them out like men. A number of examples may be cited.
>
> In the beginning, the Inmates' Court had no punitive powers. All that could be done when an offender was brought before it was to endeavor by reasoning with him, by counsel and reprimand, to bring about a better understanding and to smooth out the difficulties. This plan was soon found to be wholly insufficient. Larger powers, powers involving fitting punishments and the power of enforcing its decrees, were needed, with the support of the administration behind it. To that end a penal code, prepared by the League judge and unanimously adopted by the members, was brought to the warden for his approval, which was readily given. It meant much more work for the Court, and consistent, loyal support from the membership. But from that time the Court became an increasingly important factor in the inmate life. More and more the confidence of the officials was won and held, until, as has been stated, practically every complaint was referred to this Court, and not a decision has ever been overruled by the warden.

In October, 1918, it was announced that a contract had been signed by officials of Westchester County and the federal government to use the penitentiary as a barracks in connection with General Hospital No. 38. The courts ceased committing offenders to the penitentiary on October 8, 1918. By mid-November, the population had rapidly reduced.

On September 19, 1919, the institution reverted to Westchester County jurisdiction. Twenty-two prisoners being boarded in other institutions were transferred to the penitentiary ten days later and the admission of newly sentenced offenders commenced. The Effort League was reinstated on October 1, 1919, by unanimous vote of the inmates.

The report of the Department of Corrections, Westchester County, for the period beginning January 1, 1921, through December 31, 1923, confirms the Effort League as still active and continuing to function in a highly satisfactory manner, handling matters of discipline through the Inmate Court, orienting new arrivals to their obligations to the League, explaining to them how good-time was earned and the significance of the Credit System. The League had been empowered to appoint inmates as foremen of inmate work groups, with the approval of the warden.[53]

In his 1926 book, Jesse O. Stutsman, who had been superintendent of the Detroit House of Correction in the early 1920s, referred to the initiation of an Effort League at the Westchester County Penitentiary by the then Superintendent Warren E. McClellan. He was no doubt referring to the League as it operated in the 1921-1923 period. The population was then comprised of males serving terms ranging from ten days to a maximum of one year. A system of four grades was established providing for the earning of a certain number of credits daily by cooperating in work and by perfect group or individual conduct. The higher the grade the greater the credit-earning potential. Payment for work was tied to the credits earned as was time served within certain limits.

Each work group was given credits based upon evaluations of its deportment, and to some extent the group was held responsible for the diligence and conduct of its members. The purpose of group credits was to instill a sense of value for cooperative effort. The rationale was that the average prisoner, being selfish and individualistic, needed to learn respect for the rights of others if he was ever to relate himself properly to the community.

A committee of the Effort League interpreted to each new arrival its purposes, regulations, and benefits of membership. After a ten-day trial period membership could be attained if the applicant proved himself worthy. About 90 per cent of the population so qualified. League officers were a president, vice-president, judge of the inner court, sergeant-at-arms, public defender, and secretary. Elected by popular vote to a four-months' term, the officers comprised a cabinet which acted as a link between the population and the administration.

In addition to being responsible for practically all conduct and order within the institution, the League had extensive powers of recommendation to the warden. These included recommendations for trusty assignments and gang foremen. Reportedly men in non-supervised situations were deterred from escape by loyalty to the League. The superintendent reported that many times the League had requested a more secure assignment for an individual it suspected of planning escape.

On the complaint of another inmate or of any prison official, a man could be brought before the prisoner's court. A description of the court, then still regarded as one of the most important parts of the League's machinery, reads:

> It has been found necessary to limit the severity of the court's sentences, and the maximum sentence has been placed at expulsion from the League, together with five days in a cell on limited diet. Expulsion from the League means that the offender is turned over to the warden for discipline ... separated from the other prisoners and loses all privileges.... The probation system, which was put into operation by the Effort League about three years ago,

> has proved very successful. First offenders are usually placed on probation for five or ten days and must report regularly to the probation officer assigned to their cases by the judge of the inmate court.[54]

Derrick left the Westchester County Penitentiary in 1921. The League continued to operate until the early 1930s when it reportedly deteriorated into "kangaroo courts" and died out. It was reestablished in May, 1938, under a new constitution which was revised in May, 1950. No disciplinary function was given to this new group. In 1966 it was reported that exploratory work was then in process with the Men's Council, started in 1955, under the guidance of a psychiatric team unit in a 135-bed living unit opened in January, 1965 as a therapeutic community. The by-laws of the group stated that its objective was "to set up an orderly and systematic method of communication with the staff, and other interested individuals and groups."[55]

In November, 1972, the League was still in existence but lacked both formal organization and recognition from the administration. In 1966 and early 1967, an Inmate Council, which in operation proved to be faulty by not providing a true representation of the population, was disbanded. Administration communication, in 1972, was through liaison committees.[56]

Currently, administrative staff met as needed with housing unit representatives to discuss matters of concern. The term "Effort League" still survives, even though it refers only to a checking account in which commissary profits are deposited, and by law may be applied only to the welfare of inmates. Although the inmates have some degree of input as to expenditure of funds, no formal mechanism for that purpose exists.

U.S. Naval Prison, Portsmouth, N.H.

In January 1917, Thomas Mott Osborne underwent twelve days' voluntary confinement at the U.S. Naval Prison in the Navy Yard at Portsmouth, New Hampshire, the first five days being spent on the *Southery*, the prison's receiving ship. His mission, undertaken at the request of Secretary of the Navy Daniels, was to study the operation of the prison and the treatment of the prisoners. In his report to Secretary Daniels, Osborne was severely critical. While the *Southery* was described as being well administered, clean, and conducive to instilling proper attitudes and creating good morale, the prison itself he indicated as having a degrading influence which was breeding criminals. He advocated abolishing the Naval Prison and establishing in its stead a detention school whose program would place emphasis on education, training, and work. Although this proposal was not adopted in its entirety, its underlying principles were accepted, as were Osborne's additional recommendations that restoration to duty or discharge from service be given at such time as was believed appropriate by a board of rehabilitation whose membership would consist of two officers, an educator, and a psychiatrist.[57]

During his period of voluntary confinement, Osborne had been accompanied by a former inmate of Sing Sing Prison and Austin MacCormick, then a young instructor at Bowdoin College and destined to become one of the world's leading figures in corrections. The three were listed as deserters, but their true identity and the fact that none of them had been in the Navy was an open-secret. Osborne used the alias of Tom Brown as he had in 1913 when serving a week of voluntary confinement at the Auburn Prison; MacCormick's assumed name was John Austin, and the former inmate used his true name.

During the summer of 1917, after the entry of the United States into World War I, Osborne and MacCormick were commissioned in the U.S. Naval Reserve Force and assigned to the Naval Prison. With the rank of Lieutenant Commander, Osborne was commandant of the Prison. Ensign MacCormick was the executive officer and second in command.

The Survey, a national magazine, in its issue dated August 18, 1917, reported:

> Mr. Osborne, it is understood, has been given a free hand by Secretary Daniels to apply his own theories of prison administration. Self-government will be introduced as soon as practicable. The inmates of a naval prison are in some respects better qualified to succeed with self-government than those in a large civil prison ... general level of intelligence of the prison is apt to be higher. The majority ... have not really committed criminal acts and the percentage of so-called habitual offenders is small.... In accepting his appointment as commandant, Mr. Osborne declared that young men sent to the naval prison should be returned to the navy as fit for the service as possible, and that he would endeavor to make this object the aim of his administration.[58]

The Naval Prison underwent a sudden and innovative change following Osborne's arrival. A Mutual Welfare League was organized, and adopted as its motto "Trust and be trusted," and as its colors, green and white signifying hope and truth. Its newspaper, The Mutual Welfare News, was published weekly. Following the established policies of the League the Marine sentries were relieved of all inside guard duties, but continued to guard the perimeter. They were replaced by League members. The League also had the responsibility of enforcing prison regulations through its police and court system. A Judiciary Committee of five prisoners was given the power to investigate and hear all charges of rules violations and to recommend punishments to the commandant. Prisoners could appeal their decisions to the commandant or his designated representatives. The practice of shaving heads and the use of yellow numbers and "red legs" on the inmates' clothing were discarded.[59]

Prisoners responded to the efforts to raise their morale. A Welfare League Dramatic Company presented plays and minstrels in the City of Portsmouth to raise money for the Red Cross, and on August 29, 1919, fifty men travelled in two trucks to York Harbor for that purpose.[60]

While education, recreation, trust, and an opportunity to exercise the duties and responsibilities of citizenship in the Mutual Welfare League were important factors in building morale and increasing the likelihood of success in civilian life after release, the Osborne administration's most significant contribution, at a time when the country was at war, was to develop the prisoners' desire to be restored to duty in the Navy and to prepare them for return. During the War and during the years immediately after its end, over 5000 prisoners convicted by general courts-martial, and usually sentenced to end their confinement with a dishonorable discharge, were restored to duty in the Navy, Marine Corps, and Coast Guard. While the exact figure is not known, the great majority of those restored had successful records. This success in restoring prisoners to duty furnished a precedent for the restoration program of the Army in World War II, under which 42,000 prisoners were restored to duty. More than ninety percent of those restored did not again become general courts-martial prisoners.[61]

The success of the restoration program at the Naval Prison under Commandant Osborne was not entirely due to the high morale developed in the prison body. Under Navy and Marine officers and non-commissioned officers, some of whom were former prisoners who had been restored and kept at the prison as instructors, an extensive and intensive training program was carried on, and restored men went back to duty with added technical knowledge and skills as well as a determination to "make good." Work of great value to the war effort was also performed. Prisoners volunteered to unload ships coming into the Navy Yard. Gangs worked in shifts around the clock, and the Portsmouth Navy Yard was credited with clearing cargo ships faster than any other Eastern port. Some of these volunteers were men who, because of the nature of their offenses, were not eligible for restoration to duty.[62]

It was inevitable, of course, that traditionalists would frown on Osborne's methods. Charges of lax discipline and immoral conditions among the prisoners were eventually made which resulted in the appointment by Secretary of the Navy Daniels of a special inquiry board. The distinguished membership of that board, Assistant Secretary of the Navy Franklin Delano Roosevelt, Rear Admiral H. O. Dunn, and Rear Admiral A. S. Halstead, found the charges untrue, stating:

> The board found the sanitary and physical conditions to be very good.
>
> The board found the general situation in regard to the guarding of prisoners and their well-being to be satisfactory. The question of dual control has been adjusted

> satisfactorily by the executive action of the commandant. The result of the guarding of prisoners by prisoners on the prison side of the deadline is proven to be justified by the result obtained, only eight prisoners out of a total of 6600 having succeeded in making good their escape over a period of more than two years....
>
> In particular no facts were developed to indicate conditions of lax discipline or immorality existing in the Naval Prison, or that the prisoners in any way constitute a menace to the safety of the Navy Yard, of the inhabitants or property in the communities of Kittery, Portsmouth, or surrounding territory.[63]

After the end of World War I, the number of prisoners decreased from more than two thousand to fewer than a thousand. Osborne resigned as commandant, returning to civilian life on March 17, 1920. He was succeeded at Portsmouth by Commodore A. V. Wadhams, USN; and MacCormick, then a lieutenant (senior grade) was recalled from sea duty to serve again as executive officer. Wadhams was impressed with the Mutual Welfare League. He became a firm advocate of its principles and continued the organization in its entirety until reassigned July 5, 1921. MacCormick had returned to civilian life in May 1921. Commodore Wadhams' pamphlet describing the League states:

> Among the recreational activities of the prisoners may be counted the Farragut Club, which is just like any Y.M.C.A. hut having a gymnasium replete with all kinds of athletic gear, and containing a large recreational room where men may, during their leisure hours come and enjoy themselves. We have also a library, which contains some four thousand volumes, fiction and non-fiction, which is one of the most important factors in the educational activities of this institution. There are also two other activities or branches of the Mutual Welfare League, which deserve mention. One is the Tom Brown Club, a literary club, named after its founder Thomas Mott Osborne (Tom Brown being the name adopted by him when he first went into prison work) which holds its meeting every Sunday night. Before it are presented talks by prominent men of affairs as well as debates and literary discussion by the prisoners themselves. There is also a Bible Study Club, which is presided over by the Chaplain, who every Saturday night delivers a heart-to-heart talk on Christian life and endeavor, sometimes illustrating it by lantern slides.
>
> A campaign of education is carried on continually through the machinery of the League. The Commanding Officer is constantly in touch with the League's activities, for he reviews for approval or disapproval the minutes of all the meetings of the Board of Delegates and the Executive Committee. The League Chief-Sergeant-at-Arms makes report from time to time to the Commanding Officer of all offenders for violations of orders and rules and also of the general

> state of discipline; and the Commanding Officer transmits these reports to the Judiciary Committee for investigation.
>
> The systematic supervision and administration stated above and the wise guardianship of the League by the Commanding Officer and his aides, without undue interference in the essentials of self-government, is in essence the modus operandi of the Commanding Officer in his relation to the prisoners.
>
> ... [T]he greatest factor is the growth of self-respect, pride in the institution and a sense of loyalty to those over them which has developed under the League. The men do their work conscientiously, not from fear of punishment, but because they take pride in seeing it well done. They maintain excellent discipline, not because offenses will bring punishment upon themselves, but because bad conduct will destroy what they feel is their own personal project, the League.[64]

Under Osborne and Wadhams the Naval Prison had been a Naval command. After Wadhams left, it again became a Marine command. Commodore Wadhams' successor did not share his views of the Mutual Welfare League. He felt that under the system shrewd inmates managed to gain control of the League and manipulated it to their own advantage. He also believed that inmates did not have the scientific attitude or technique necessary for dealing with violations of regulations and were likely to be more cruel and less judicious in their treatment of difficult prisoners than were the prison officials themselves. Under the Welfare League system the prison populace had enjoyed considerable freedom. Living quarters had lacked the traditional bars and dull drabness of most prisons. The cell block, with a capacity of 320 men, was practically empty. To house the increased number of prisoners, 2600 at its peak, during World War I, open barracks housing about 2000 prisoners were constructed inside the wire fence. The cell block had been used for new prisoners and those under punishment. After dissolving the League, the new Commandant filled the cell block and divided the remaining men into two battalions of ten companies each. The suddenness of this drastic change in policy naturally had a depressing effect upon morale and this was sharply reflected in a decided rise in the incidence of rules violations.[65]

Until 1974 the Naval Prison was commanded by a series of Marine officers who, while not operating under the Mutual Welfare League plan, accepted and followed the basic philosophy and policies of modern corrections.[66] The Prison was closed in July, 1974, because a dwindling prisoner population made further operation economically unfeasible.[67]

The Long Lane School

The Long Lane School at Middletown, Connecticut, opened in 1869 as a training school for delinquent girls. Information was received in 1966 that the facility had a self-government program dating back to 1917 which had changed from time to time in concert with turnover in students and staff. Each cottage had its own council which could suggest action to be taken upon staff-reported incidents of misconduct. Staff made the final decision as to the kind and extent of penalties, usually some degree of privilege loss.[68]

After three months at the school, a new girl could be admitted to the responsibilities of citizenship in student government by vote of her peers, if they believed she had learned and practiced the seven ideals of the school: self-control, self-respect, loyalty, honor, obedience, appreciation, and courtesy. On becoming a citizen the girl pledged: "I pledge my loyalty to the United States of America and to Long Lane School. On my honor I will assume responsibility as a citizen to promote an interest in the welfare of others and do everything in my power to uphold the ideals for which self-government at Long Lane School stands." The school motto was "Not Self--But All"; colors were yellow and white; the school flower was the daisy; and the 121st Psalm had been chosen as reflecting the purpose and hope of the group.

For current information regarding the Long Lane School, see the section on Connecticut in Chapter III.

U.S. Disciplinary Barracks, Governors Island, N.Y.

In his annual report for the fiscal year beginning July 1, 1918, and ending June 30, 1919, Colonel John E. Hunt, commandant of the Atlantic Branch, U.S. Disciplinary Barracks, Governors Island, New York, gave credit to the cooperation of the inmate Honor Association for the maintenance of proper discipline.[69] Formed in November 1918, at Colonel Hunt's suggestion, the Association proved its value when the population increased considerably and it was necessary to occupy additional quarters. Proper discipline was maintained with no increase in the staff complement due to the assistance of the members of the Honor Association.

Disciplinary infractions decreased as a result of the Honor Association's influence. A disciplinary board of inmates conducted a trial under staff supervision and meted out punishment to any man reported by Association members. Those men reported by staff were tried by the staff disciplinary board.

Colonel Hunt's remarks on the philosophy underlying the utilization of inmate organizations show keen insight for the time:

> It seems to me that such an experiment, although it has proved successful here, cannot be inaugurated at any time and under all conditions. It requires for its successful operation, a group of earnest prisoners and a sympathetic advance by the administration. Its operation needs careful watching lest the group of earnest workers be replaced by

> a less trustworthy element. It is purely a measure for local administration and its continuance or dissolution must be solely in the hands of the local authorities. When such an association works with the end in view that in whatever way it benefits the institution it benefits its own individual members, it will prove successful, but if members use the association for purely selfish ends it is doomed to failure and may become a positive menace.
>
> It appears to me that the value of a properly conducted association aside from the immediate local benefits mentioned above has a wider application. It teaches members in a very concrete way, the necessity for and benefits derived from a social order, and I believe it cannot but have its educational effect on some when they again assume their places in organized society.

Kentucky State Reformatory

The Kentucky State Reformatory at Frankfort was in existence from 1797 until 1937, when heavy floods forced evacuation to nearby temporary quarters with subsequent transfer of all prisoners to the not then completed new State Reformatory at LaGrange, some 50 miles northwest.

A Mutual Welfare League, organized at the Frankfort institution in 1920, had as its objective "the promotion in every way of the true interests and welfare of the men confined in prison." At one time reportedly 90 per cent of the institution population were members. Reports as late as 1931 mention the League as still active.[70]

Activities of the League were entirely of a charitable nature, and were not connected with the management or operation of the institution. The organization received no financial or other support from the State except occasional investigations by parole agents in the course of other duties.

Membership, open to any prisoner, was divided into three classes:

1. Active members--those paying monthly dues, the amount paid being determined by the amount of compensation received by the member. For instance: members receiving as much as ten cents a day were assessed twenty-five cents a month, while those receiving less than ten cents paid twelve cents a month.
2. Inactive members--described as those who through unfortunate conditions for which they were not to blame were not able to pay dues.
3. Honorary members--those who merited membership by reason of charitable deeds.

The League derived income from the profits of several enterprises--a mercantile store, a printing shop, and various recreational activities. Charitable work included aid to dependent families which was initiated in 1921, burial of deceased members, if no other funds were available; and the furnishing of such extras as fruit or milk for hospitalized members.

The aid to dependent families program was known as the Department of Dependent Welfare. Any member of the Mutual Welfare League could apply for aid to his dependents, including wife, children, parents, and siblings, by completing an application form which called for certain identifying data, the amount of money remitted in the past by the member to the dependent, and the listing of four references acquainted with the dependent. Investigation was then made, often by a parole agent. Occasional contributions were made to the Salvation Army, the Eastern Kentucky Flood Relief, and similar causes.

Management of the Mutual Welfare League was exercised by a Board of Directors composed of nine prisoners selected for a one-year term. The prison chief clerk was the custodian of all funds. Activities proposed for League undertaking were subject to the approval of the superintendent.

On January 11, 1929, a conference was held at the invitation of Governor Sampson between members of the State Board of Charities and Corrections and a group of educators and social and religious leaders of the Commonwealth to discuss the establishment of schools of citizenship and moral training in Kentucky penal institutions. Five of the community group members were appointed as a Committee of Laymen which filed its report and recommendations on April 24, 1929, a portion of which concerned the Mutual Welfare League:[71]

> We believe that the Mutual Welfare League offers large opportunities for moral training. Among the present avenues for citizenship training through the activities of the League there are: (1) The Mutual Welfare League Courier. This paper gives an opportunity for self-expression and for the prisoners to correlate the problems of the institution with those of the outside world. (2) Commissary. This affords the satisfaction of certain individual wants and might also serve as a practical problem in economic relationship. (3) Social Service. This consists in raising money, contributing to needy families and paying the expenses of prisoner and guard on visits to sick relatives. (4) Education. This consists in the payment of fifteen cents a day to teachers of night school and the contribution of one-half fee for any correspondence course taken by any inmate.
>
> An analysis of the Mutual Welfare League shows that it is well planned for the field of work allotted to it. There is much conflicting opinion as to whether or not greater responsibility can be given the prisoners, the weight of opinion seeming to indicate that an honor system in a modified form such as exists at the Reformatory, coupled with an organization like the League, works for the most good.

There is a question as to whether the League might not be consulted with regard to changes in school curriculum since it virtually pays for instruction. Furthermore, the recommendation of the United States Children's Bureau might be restated, for in it seems to lie the possibility of valuable training in social relations and the problems arising out of these relations. The recommendation is as follows: 'Employment by the State Board of Charities and Corrections of a sufficient number of trained family case workers to investigate all families of newly committed prisoners in order to assist them in the readjustments made necessary by the imprisonment of the father, and give such friendly supervision as may be necessary. This work should be coordinated with the parole work, for which it will be an excellent foundation, preparing the family and the community for the prisoner's return. The case workers should also render assistance to the Mutual Welfare League in the investigation and supervision of cases.' It also seems to the committee that the privileges of the league should be extended to women prisoners.

New Castle Correctional Institution

An Honor Court was in operation at the New Castle Correctional Institution, Wilmington, Delaware, from 1921 to 1931, under the administrations of two wardens. Factors cited as contributing to its demise were the release of inmates competent to carry out the purposes of the organization, declining administrative interest, and the nonavailability of suitable staff supervision.[72] The institution was replaced in April 1971 by the Delaware Correctional Center at Smyrna.

Haynes described the Wilmington Honor Court as composed of eight members and dealing with all matters of discipline, recreation, entertainment, and welfare of the inmates. The Court made rules and selected the three judges before whom offenders were given a hearing. The approval of the warden was required on all penalties. There was no regular term for the members of the Court. Whenever a vacancy occurred, an election was held, but members were subject to recall at any time. Inmates replaced guards to the extent that only two guards during the day and one at night were required for the custody of 400 men. Conceding that the reduction of guards may have been carried too far, Haynes nonetheless felt it was a striking demonstration that a prison can be conducted practically without guards, without serious internal disturbances and without an unusual number of escapees, raising the question whether a very considerable part of the cost of the employment of guards is necessary.[73]

New Jersey State Prison

In a 1919 article, Winthrop D. Lane stated that a moderate

degree of inmate control had been suggested as a remedy for publicly exposed administrative difficulties in the New Jersey State Prison, Trenton. A site visit report of November 12, 1923 is the only indication that any action was taken on the recommendation. A committee of three representatives named by petition of the other inmates, and approved by the principal keeper, acted as spokesmen to the administration.[74] It is not known when the committee plan was established or how long it lasted.

Massachusetts State Prison Colony

The State Prison Colony, Norfolk, was opened in 1931. Currently, it is designated as Massachusetts Correctional Institution. During the period 1927-1934, Howard B. Gill, the first superintendent of the State Prison Colony, Norfolk, inaugurated a program of individual and group treatment of inmates called the Norfolk Plan. Mr. Gill described the Plan in an article published in 1931 and in a letter to the author in 1966.[75]

The Norfolk Plan utilized balanced programs in the following five broad areas:

1. Normalcy--affecting the inter-personal relationship between officials and inmates, the nature of structures in the institution, all institutional activities, rules and regulations, and the general overall climate of the institution.
2. Small Group Principle--applied to living quarters, dining, bathing, industries, leisure time activities including hobbies, athletics, entertainment, visiting, religious services, education, medical care.
3. Inmate-Staff Organization--based on joint participation of officials and inmates through joint action and joint responsibility for all institution activities except discipline, parole, finances, and similar official administrative matters.
4. Community Contacts--bringing the community into the prison and taking the prisoners, as much as possible, into the community.
5. Individual and Group Treatment--through individual problem-solving in five main areas, namely situational, medical, psychological, anti-social (ethical), and custodial, and through group discussions in meetings of the Inmate Council, 15 standing joint committees, and weekly House Meetings.

It soon became evident that under the Norfolk Plan only a select population of the more tractable, adult, "normal" prisoners who would cooperate on a basis of mutual trust could make up the prison population. At first this precluded escape risks while the inmates were housed in an open camp. Later, however, upon completion of the walled enclosure, such inmates could be included provided other criteria for normalcy, cooperation, and ultimate adjustment were met. Inmates and officials regarded each other with courtesy and respect. Except in the Receiving Building, housing was in normal rooms, not cells. There were only two prison rules --no escapes and no contraband. All regulations affecting routine operations were regarded merely as procedural matters. There were no limitations on correspondence or visiting. The typical prison uniform was replaced with ordinary clothing. Only watch officers (tower guards, gate keepers, patrol) wore uniforms. Inmates had freedom of movement within the walled enclosure. There were no marching formations. The test of any suggestion was, "Is it normal?"

The small group principle applied not only to housing inmates in groups of 50 men under the direction of two house officers acting as resident caseworkers, but also to all other activities. For example, there were 14 play spaces including four large athletic fields. The auditorium was purposely designed to hold no more than half the population. The chapel provided only approximately 100 seats. Four-man tables were used in each of the dining rooms, each of which in turn was limited to 50 inmates. Each dining room had its own small service kitchen where all except main dishes (meats, vegetables, desserts) could be cooked for small order service. The central bathhouse, typical of prisons at that time, was replaced by ordinary toilets and baths on each of the three floors of each house of 50 men. Access to these toilets and baths could be had at any time.

The third phase of the plan, an inmate-staff organization, was built around an Inmate Council, which developed as a direct outgrowth of the group system of housing and supervision, and the need to foster inmate responsibility because of limitations in numbers of staff. Together the staff and this council, through a system of joint committees, were responsible for the conduct of all institutional activities except as noted above. This was neither an honor system nor an inmate self-government program, and this was a basic essential in the success of the Norfolk Plan.

The Norfolk Plan of joint participation and joint responsibility of many inmates and many staff members was in sharp contrast to the advisory councils in many prisons where a small inmate committee worked with a single staff member, for instance the warden or associate warden. One of the outstanding features of the Norfolk Plan in its most successful phase was the involvement of some 30 or more staff members and some 60 or more inmates who made up the joint committees.

In an address before the Conference on the Treatment of Criminal Delinquency at Cambridge, Massachusetts, December 4, 1930, Gill reported:

> This is not to be confused with the strictly penal administration of the Colony which is in the hands of the Superintendent and his assistants. Also in contrast to inmate organizations in some institutions which are founded on the principle of self-government in the hands of inmates only,

> this community operates on the principle of joint responsibility in which both officers and inmates take part.
>
> The Council consists of fifteen inmates, three nominated and elected by the inmates from each of the five houses (referring to inmate living quarters) for a term of three months. The three councilmen from each house and the house officers act as a house committee which meets weekly, and a weekly meeting is also held in each house with all members and the house officer present. Questions affecting the welfare of the house or the institution are discussed at these meetings. Such questions are then carried by the council-men to the weekly staff meeting. The Council elects its own chairman and secretary and appoints its own committees on construction, education and library, entertainment, athletics, food, maintenance, store, etc. The Staff also has its chairman and committees on construction, education and library, entertainment, athletics, food, maintenance, store, etc.
>
> Questions relating to any of these fields of activity are taken up in weekly joint meetings of the respective committees and by them referred also to the weekly meetings of the Council and the Staff. The Staff and the Council meet weekly with the Superintendent who refers any action taken in the meeting to the other for confirmation. The Council has advisory powers only and final action always rests with the Staff; suggestions may originate in either body, however, and are referred to both before final action. However, in the thirty months in which the plan has been in operation, the two have failed to agree finally on only one decision. The plan does not always give the 'best men' the leadership--frequently otherwise, and it has been interesting to note what responsibility does for these others. That the plan has not run into difficulties frequently encountered by inmate self-government organizations where control has soon passed into the hands of the bold and unscrupulous, is due to the very important and sincere part played in it by the officers, who (contrary to the usual circumstances) are wholeheartedly a part of it and who act as a proper balance wheel....
>
> In general the plan has worked, although it is neither an 'honor system' nor 'self-government,' because it is founded frankly on a basis of results for both Staff and men.... Neither officers nor men give up their independence or their responsibilities, and each continually checks the other to insure square dealing; but both agree that cooperation works better than opposition where men must work and eat and live together, whatever the circumstances.

Mr. Gill has summarized some of the more obvious advantages of the inmate-staff organization under the Norfolk Plan as originally operated.

> The joint committees, for example, furnished the most

effective means of communication between staff and prisoners. A valuable fringe benefit of these committees also was the release of tensions which are inevitable in any institution. In both committee and house meetings grievances were aired and resolved before minor problems became major crises. There has never been a riot at Norfolk in its entire forty years' history. It was once the proud boast that there had been only three fights among inmates in one three year period--a remarkable record for any institution. Due to the cooperation between inmates and official personnel all activities within the institution were enhanced. At one time construction work doubled its production as a result, winning a special commendation from the Commissioner of Correction, Sanford Bates.

Naturally, the sense of responsibility engendered by inmate participation tempered by Staff cooperation developed a kind of civic pride and interest among many prisoners who may never before have experienced any such feelings. Cooperation with responsible officials sometimes gave criminals for the first time the notion that they too could belong to the side of law and order. To other prisoners it gave opportunity to express much that was sound in their personalities. Instead of developing leaders among the worst prisoners, the Plan brought out the better element in the prison population because such prisoners through cooperation with the Staff could secure the most benefits for all prisoners.

While group treatment had not then become the vogue in prisons, at Norfolk individualized treatment was paralleled by something called 'Socialized Treatment.' Such socialized treatment was naturally developed in the joint committees of the Norfolk Plan. There the influence of law-abiding officers on prisoners, and vice-versa, had its therapeutic effect. While present day 'group discussions' had not been introduced in correctional work, the informal discussions in council or committee meetings at Norfolk often had the same effect.

The May 1, 1964 issue of the inmate newspaper, The Colony, contains the remarks made by Mr. Gill earlier that year at a meeting of the Norfolk Protestant Fellowship and mentions the recent placement in the administration building of a plaque inscribed:

In Recognition of the Establishment
at Norfolk, Massachusetts, of the first
COMMUNITY PRISON FOR MEN
in the United States under the leadership of:
HOWARD B. GILL
Superintendent, 1927-1934

An Inmate Council was organized in February 1937 under a constitution, revised periodically thereafter, which provided for the secret ballot election of two representatives from each housing unit to serve a six-month term.[76] The superintendent and the community service director were designated as ex-officio members. Several standing committees were established. A Financial and Store Committee of five, with the community service director as an ex-officio member, was charged with responsibility for the conduct of the Inmate Store and the making of recommendations regarding any appropriations involving the expenditure of store profits.

The constitution also established the Cooperative Aid Society of Norfolk whose purpose was stated as being to provide financial aid to any inmate, or his family, when the need was imperative and could not be obtained from the usual sources, or when such aid was necessary to forestall a definite approaching need; to finance transportation for family members, or surrogates, to visit inmates who had not had a visit for a lengthy period because of the visitor's indigency. A five-member Board of Directors composed of three inmates elected by the Inmate Council and two staff members, the institution treasurer and the family welfare director, guided the Society. The staff members were designated, respectively, as treasurer and secretary. Fifteen per cent of the net profits of the Store was committed to finance this assistance.

Article V of the constitution, entitled Inmate Joint Responsibility for Escapes, stated that in return for community privileges granted to the inmates, the inmate body at large assumed a joint responsibility with the staff for orderly and efficient institution operations, especially in regard to escapes. In the event of escape by an inmate entitled to Council privileges, it was stipulated that the inmate body would forfeit Council privileges for a period not to exceed one week.

Information was received in 1966 that the Inmate Council still functioned, with its actions subject to staff veto. Three factors were cited as contributing to the decline in some of the actual practices of joint participation attained by Superintendent Gill: the larger number of inmates, a dilution of the criteria for selection of those to be sent to the institution, and changing leadership. At that time the opinion was expressed that inmates were not as likely to accept much responsibility. for escapes. It was reported that at times they had defaulted on other obligations to maintain orderly and efficient operation of the institution, notably kitchen work.[77] In 1983, the only active inmate advisory council in any Massachusetts facility was at the Norfolk Correctional Institution.

Illinois State Penitentiary

In the summer of 1929, Major Henry C. Hill was appointed warden of the Illinois State Penitentiary at Joliet, and of its branch at Statesville. The following autumn he introduced into both prisons the idea of electing a grievance committee composed of two representatives from each cell house. The committee was to meet with him periodically to present requests or complaints referred to it by other inmates. However, after two or three meetings the plan was disbanded. Disagreement among the committee members and a lack of sound suggestions contributed to the warden's decision that the idea was not productive.[78]

Notes

1. Turnbull, Robert J. As quoted in: The Cradle of the Penitentiary, by Negley K. Teeters. The Pennsylvania Prison Society, 1955, p. 46.
2. Sedgwick, C. M. Memoir of Joseph Curtis. New York: Harper & Bros., 1858, p. 66.
3. Lewis, O. F. "Inmate Self-Government a Century Ago," The Delinquent, vol. 8, no. 1 (January 1918), p. 9-15.
4. Pickett, Robert Stanley. "The New York House of Refuge: A Case Study of Nineteenth Century Humanitarian Reform, 1825-27." Unpublished doctoral dissertation, Syracuse University, 1963, p. 112.
5. Lewis, O. F., op. cit.
6. Sedgwick, C. M., op. cit., pp. 107-135.
7. Pickett, Robert Stanley, op. cit., pp. 135, 170-71, 259.
8. Lewis, O. F., op. cit.
9. Pierson, George Wilson. Tocqueville and Beaumont in America. New York: Oxford University Press, 1938, pp. 435-36.
10. Lewis, O. F., op. cit.
11. Lewis, O. F. The Development of American Prisons and Prison Customs, 1776-1845. Prison Association of New York, 1922, pp. 169-70.
12. Haynes, Gideon. Pictures from Prison Life. Boston: Lee and Shepard, 1869, pp. 62-63.
13. Letter from then Supt. Palmer C. Scafati, Massachusetts Correctional Institution, South Walpole, Mass., February 9, 1967.
14. Letter from then Supt. Palmer C. Scafati, September 30, 1966.
15. Brockway, Zebulon R. Fifty Years of Prison Service: An Autobiography. New York: Charities Publication Committee, 1912, pp. 96-97
16. Helfman, Harold M. "Antecedents of Thomas Mott Osborne's 'Mutual Welfare League' in Michigan," Journal of Criminal Law and Criminology, vol. 40 (May-April 1949-50), pp. 597-600.
17. Stutsman, Jesse O. Curing the Criminal. New York: Macmillan, 1926, pp. 215-219.
18. Constitution and By-Laws, Resident Advisory Council, Men's Division, Detroit House of Correction, Plymouth, November 1972.
19. Brockway, Zebulon R., op. cit., pp. 302-303.
20. Helfman, Harold M., op. cit.
21. Bakken, Douglas A., ed. The William R. George and George Junior Republic Papers, 1807-1967. Ithaca, New York: Cornell University Press, 1970, pp. 9-11.
22. Letter and enclosures from Gabriel Viada, Associate Executive

Director, George Junior Republic, Freeville, New York, July 14, 1983.

23. Letter from Executive Director Carolyn M. Thompson, The Women's Prison Association of New York, New York City, May 9, 1967.
24. Doty, Madeline Zabriskie. "Maggie Martin, 933," Century Magazine, October 1914, pp. 843-857.
25. Doty, Madeline Zabriskie. "Maggie Martin's Friends." Century Magazine, April 1915, pp. 875-883.
26. Letter from Gloria M. Levister, ACSW, Executive Director, Sleighton School, Lima, Pennsylvania, August 5, 1983.
27. Letter from then Supt. Myrtle E. Gray, Sleighton Farm School for Girls, Darling, Pennsylvania, March 22, 1967.
28. Memorandum re Honor Cottage Standings, Sleighton Farm School for Girls, March 1966; and Brochure, 1966, p. 5.
29. Letter from Supt. Adeline F. Tabourin, Sleighton Farm School for Girls, January 8, 1973.
30. Letter from Gloria M. Levister, ACSW, op. cit.
31. Derrick, Calvin. "Self-Government." The Survey, September 1, 1917, pp. 473-478.
32. Cox, William B., and Shelley, Joseph A., eds. Handbook of American Institutions for Delinquent Juveniles: Pacific Coast States. Prepared by the Osborne Association, New York: Vol. III, First Edition, pp. 83-84. (At that time, 1940, California law regarding the Preston School of Industry provided that the facility be subject to military discipline.)
33. Letter and Reports from Director Allen F. Breed, Dept. of the Youth Authority, Sacramento, California, January 25, 1973.
34. Barnes, Harry Elmer. A History of the Penal, Reformatory and Correctional Institution of the State of New Jersey. Trenton, N.J.: MacCrellish and Quigley Co., 1918, p. 293.
35. Wines, Frederick Howard. Punishment and Reformation: A Study of the Penitentiary System. Revised by Winthrop D. Lane. New York: Thomas Y. Crowell, 1923, pp. 408-409.
36. Ibid., pp. 409-410.
37. Osborne, Thomas Mott. Society and Prisons. New Haven, Conn.: Yale University Press, 1916, p. 164.
38. Ibid.
39. Ibid.
40. Tannenbaum, Frank. Crime and the Community. Boston: The Athenian Press, Ginn & Company, 1938, p. 416.
41. Letter from then Warden W. L. Denno, Sing Sing Prison, Ossining, New York, September 20, 1966.
42. Lawes, Lewis E. Twenty Thousand Years in Sing Sing. New York: Ray Long & Richard E. Smith, 1932, pp. 104-105.
43. Wines, Frederick Howard, op. cit., pp. 397-398.
44. Barnes, Harry Elmer. The Evolution of Penology in Pennsylvania. Indianapolis: Bobbs-Merrill Co., 1927, p. 426.
45. Lawes, Lewis E., op. cit., pp. 112-120.

46. *Ibid.*, pp. 105 and 107.
47. MacCormick, Austin H., and Garrett, Paul W., eds. *Handbook of American Prisons*. Prepared by National Society of Penal Information, Inc. New York: G. P. Putnam, 1926, pp. 450-451.
48. Denno, W. L., *op. cit.*
49. Letter and Reports from Director Albert C. Wagner, Division of Correction and Parole, Trenton, New Jersey, March 5, 1973.
50. Quarles, Mary Ann. "A Comparative Study of the Relation of the Treatment Program at the New Jersey Reformatory for Women for the Fifty Year Period, 1910 to 1960, to Concepts of Penology." Unpublished doctoral Dissertation, pp. 187-222; Brochure, "The Functioning of the New Jersey Reformatory for Women," July 1, 1966, pp. 10-13.
51. Letter from then Supt. Robert T. Grey, Connecticut Reformatory, Cheshire, Connecticut, September 19, 1966.
52. Wines, Frederick Howard, *op. cit.*, pp. 407-408.
53. Letter from Commissioner Louis P. Kurtis, Dept. of Public Welfare, County of Westchester, White Plains, New York, December 13, 1966; First Annual Report, Commissioner of Charities and Corrections, Westchester County, January 1 to December 31, 1917; Second Annual Report, Westchester County Penitentiary and Workhouse, January 1 to December 31, 1918; Reports of Dept. of Corrections, Westchester County, September 1 to December 31, 1919, and January 1, 1921 to December 31, 1923.
54. Stutsman, Jesse O., *op. cit.*, pp. 219-222.
55. Letter from then Warden William J. O'Brien, Westchester County Penitentiary, Valhalla, New York, November 29, 1966; Constitution and By-Laws, Effort League, Rev. May 1, 1950; By-Laws, The Men's Council, September 1965 and July 1966.
56. Letter from Commissioner Roberts J. Wright, Dept. of Correction, Westchester County, Valhalla, New York, November 29, 1972.
57. Verge, Robert J. *A History of the U.S. Naval Prison at Portsmouth, New Hampshire*. Portsmouth, N.H.: U.S. Naval Print Shop, 1946, pp. 16-18.
58. *The Survey*, August 18, 1917.
59. *Op. cit.*
60. *The Mutual Welfare News*, Naval Prison, Portsmouth, New Hampshire, September 14, 1919.
61. Correspondence from Austin H. MacCormick, Executive Director, The Osborne Association, Inc., New York City, January 24, 1973.
62. *Ibid.*
63. *The Survey*, March 27, 1920.
64. Verge, Robert J., *op. cit.*, pp. 20-21.
65. *Ibid.*, pp. 22-23.
66. Correspondence from Austin H. MacCormick, *op. cit.*
67. Letter from A. A. Davis, Commander, U.S. Navy, Director, Law Enforcement and Corrections Division, Dept. of the Navy, Washington, D.C., September 30, 1982.

68. Letter from then Supt. Ethel D. Mecum, Long Lane School, Middletown, Connecticut, October 7, 1966.
69. Annual Report, Atlantic Branch, U.S. Disciplinary Barracks, Governors Island, New York, June 30, 1919, pp. 16-17.
70. Report of Board of Prison Commissioners, Kentucky Public Documents, 1927-1929, pp. 48-49; Report for Biennial Period ending June 30, 1931, pp. 96-98.
71. *Ibid.*, pp. 51-55.
72. Letter from then Commissioner William Nardini, Ph.D., Dept. of Correction, Smyrna, Delaware, October 13, 1966.
73. Haynes, Fred E. *Criminology*. 2d ed. New York: McGraw-Hill, 1935, Chapter XII.
74. Lane, Winthrop D. "Democracy for Law Breakers," *The New Republic*, March 8, 1919, pp. 172-174; *Handbook of American Prisons*, prepared by National Society of Penal Information. New York: G. P. Putnam's Sons, 1925, p. 168.
75. Gill, Howard B. "The Norfolk State Prison Colony at Massachusetts," *Journal of Criminal Law and Criminology*, Vol. 22 (1931), pp. 107-112; Correspondence from Howard B. Gill, Director, Institute of Correctional Administration, American University, Washington, D.C., October 4, 1966.
76. Constitution and By-Laws, Inmate Council, Massachusetts Correctional Institution, Norfolk, Mass., as amended and compiled January 1962.
77. Letter from Director of Treatment Raymond W. Brennan, Massachusetts Correctional Institution, Norfolk, August 12, 1966.
78. From Nathan F. Leopold, Jr. *Life Plus 99 Years*. New York: Doubleday, 1958, pp. 232-233.

CHAPTER II

COMPLAINT PROCEDURES

A complaint procedure is an administrative, as opposed to legislative or judicial, means through which inmates may express and resolve their grievances. It is formal in the sense that it establishes explicit channels to be followed in attempting to resolve problems.

The premise of a complaint procedure is that by providing inmates with a formal avenue for challenging departmental and institutional policies and creating a forum in which individual actions of staff and other inmates can be reviewed, institutional violence and litigation will decrease. The procedures apply the techniques of mediation and reconciliation and are designed to achieve the resolution of problems through the cooperative efforts of staff and inmates.[1]

Historically, inmates have relied on a number of informal methods of making known their complaints. Riots, work stoppages and other illegal acts have received the greatest publicity. Other methods have included "open-door" policies, and informal requests or arrangements with sympathetic personnel. Despite their usefulness in providing some relief, these informal methods guaranteed neither action nor response. Often the recipient of the complaint lacked either the authority to make a needed change or the access to those who did. Even when directed to a person who could act, the response was all too frequently, "I'll look into it." When a response did occur, it was not subject to review, the absence of which mitigated against the fullest consideration of alternatives and the strongest possible effort at resolution of each complaint.

Since 1970, correctional administrators have made heavy investments of time, effort and money to develop formal methods of responding to inmates' complaints. A 1979 survey of 115 jurisdictions (the 50 states, the Federal Prison System, District of Columbia, the Canal Zone, Puerto Rico, American Samoa, and 60 jails located in major metropolitan centers or identified by the National Institute of Corrections Jail Center as having a tradition of innovative programming) revealed that nearly every correctional system currently has some formal means of responding to inmates' complaints. Of the states, only Rhode Island reported no formalized method, written or unwritten, for handling complaints at that time.[2] However, a multi-level grievance procedure was established by the Rhode Island Department of Corrections on January 7, 1980.

What events brought about the post-1970 interest in establishing meaningful procedures for dealing with warranted grievances of inmates? Deeper still, what caused correctional administrators to recognize as legitimate the right of prisoners to complain?

Though there may have been others, the cumulative impact of the following events undoubtedly was the catalyst which caused correctional administrators to recognize what elementary psychology and fundamental justice dictate: whenever large numbers of human beings are confined involuntarily in close quarters, there must be effective, credible machinery to provide an outlet for their complaints and dissatisfaction.[3] Those events were increasing prison violence, inmate militancy, the intervention of the courts, and the growing recognition by professional correctional organizations of grievance mechanisms for inmates as a fundamental requirement in correctional institutions.

During the past several years, there has been an increasing level of violence in prisons. Subsequent investigations have often revealed widespread and traditional disregard of inmate grievances irrespective of their legitimacy. This is not to imply that the absence of grievance mechanisms caused riots or other forms of disturbance. However, considering the mounting demands for change, inherent in other events as will be delineated, that absence probably made them inevitable. Absent or restricted communication patterns which seriously impaired the airing of legitimate inmate grievances and the detection of impending unrest was cited in 1973 by Flynn as one of the major contributing factors in a then recent wave of prison violence.[4]

The development throughout the criminal justice system of alternatives to confinement has altered considerably the nature of the typical prison. The acquiescent "good inmate" of yesterday seems to have disappeared. Among the confined population today there is an increasing militancy which is reflective of the aroused political activism of minorities in general society. A growing awareness by inmates of their rights has been matched by a readiness to challenge any authority perceived as being blind or insensitive to their needs or requests.

Beginning in the late 1960s as court after court was confronted with what were alleged to be, and in many cases proven as, deplorable and inhumane prison conditions and practices, judges began to abandon their "hands-off" doctrine which essentially had been based on the theory that prisons were to be run by prison personnel and the role of the courts was to judge only the legality of verdicts and sentences. The courts recognized as legitimate the right of an inmate to complain, thus subjecting to court review a broad range of official decisions formerly made in complete autonomy by prison personnel. This 180-degree change in attitude by the courts had an interesting outcome, favorable to the development of formal grievance mechanisms, which is discussed later.

Advocacy for the creation of a mechanism for registering and responding to inmate complaints began almost thirty years ago. The Fourth United Nations Congress on Prevention of Crime and Treatment of Offenders adopted, on August 30, 1955, the Standard Minimum Rules for the Treatment of Prisoners. Section 35, pertaining to complaints by prisoners, states

> Every prisoner shall be allowed to make a request or complaint ... to the central prison administration, the judicial authority or other approved channels.... Unless it is evidently frivolous or groundless, every request or complaint will be dealt with and replied to without delay.

Despite the U.N. principle, impetus for the establishment by correctional agencies of just and effective procedures for dealing with inmate grievances did not occur until the 1967 Task Force Report on Corrections of the President's Commission on Law Enforcement and Administration of Justice so urged. Subsequently, virtually every major study group and commission on corrections has reiterated the principle.

In its October, 1970 publication on a series of riots and major disturbances in correctional institutions in 1968, the American Correctional Association reported:

> Prompt and positive handling of inmates' complaints and grievances is essential in maintaining good morale. A firm 'no' can be as effective as granting his request in reducing an individual inmate's tensions, particularly if he feels his problem has been given genuine consideration by appropriate officials and if given a reason for the denial. Equivocation and vague answers create false hopes and thus increase the man's anger when nothing is done. A most dangerous situation arises however when inmates have grievances they feel can be corrected only if the proper officials are made aware of their problems. Inmates know that disturbances are certain to give their complaints wide publicity when less drastic measures fail.

Additionally, in 1979 the Commission on Accreditation for Corrections, in affiliation with the American Correctional Association, specified as an essential standard for correctional agencies the existence of written policies and procedures for filing of grievances, including an appeals procedure.

The National Council on Crime and Delinquency, in 1972, identified as fundamental the right of an inmate to have access to a grievance procedure by stating: "The Director of the State Department of Correction (or the equivalent official) shall establish a grievance procedure to which all prisoners within the system shall have access. Prisoners shall be entitled to report any grievance...."

In 1972, the Annual Chief Justice Earl Warren Conference sponsored by the Roscoe Pound-American Trial Lawyers Foundation recommended that "... prisoners should be permitted to organize, without fear of reprisal, for the purpose of effective expression and negotiation of grievances. Even in the absence of grievances, and as a method of avoiding abuses leading to grievances, there should be regular meetings between duly elected prisoners' representatives and prison authorities."

In January, 1973, the National Advisory Commission on Criminal Justice Standards and Goals observed that all correctional agencies have not only a responsibility but an institutional interest in maintaining procedures that are, and appear to offenders to be, designed to resolve their complaints fairly.

The significance of these events was not lost on correctional administrators, although some were slow in getting the message. However, a growing number have followed the lead of the courts and are increasingly willing to recognize the right of inmates to complain. Additionally, there is a perception of the validity of inmate complaints about such conditions as overcrowding, outmoded facilities, and inadequate programs, all conditions against which administrators also are struggling. Even more significant, administrators recognize the legitimacy of the process of complaining, apart from the validity of particular complaints. Furthermore, perceptive administrators are realizing that the establishment of just and effective procedures for dealing with inmate grievances pays several dividends. Formal procedures can provide reliable information about the implementation of policies and permit ongoing review and modification of outmoded policies. Most important, formal procedures can enlist the cooperation of inmates and staff in implementing change when it is needed.[5]

In a 1973 survey of adult institutions, responding administrators identified some of their objectives in establishing a complaint procedure as follows (ranked in descending order of priority):[6]

1. To provide opportunities for all inmates to voice grievances and receive official responses.
2. To assist management by identifying institutional problems.
3. To reduce inmate frustration.
4. To aid in inmate rehabilitation.
5. To reduce the level of violence.
6. To reduce the amount of litigation.

Ironically, judicial vexation with both the subject matter and volume of inmate petitions caused courts to endorse the establishment of credible complaint procedures in order to <u>reduce</u> judicial intervention in corrections. This endorsement was consistent with a view, long prevalent among administrators, that judges have no special expertise qualifying them to dictate changes in corrections, that such intervention in the day-to-day operations of institutions constituted an overextension of both the authority and the capacity of courts, and that responding in court to inmates' complaints is both time-consuming and expensive.

Chief Justice Warren E. Burger, U.S. Supreme Court, in a speech to the American Bar Association on August 6, 1973, related with dismay the case of an inmate who engaged the primary attention of "one district judge twice, three circuit judges on appeal, and six others in a secondary sense--to say nothing of lawyers, court clerks, bailiffs, court reporters, and all the rest" in an attempt to recover seven packs of cigarettes allegedly taken improperly by a guard.

Nine months earlier the Chief Justice had suggested that grievance procedures common in industrial plants might be applicable to correctional institutions, and in November, 1974, Judge Donald P. Lay, U.S. Court of Appeals for the Eighth Circuit, similarly identified the establishment of credible administrative mechanisms as one important means of reducing judicial intervention in corrections:

> The second and perhaps more immediate solution to many of our problems is to create within the prison system an administrative grievance adjustment policy which will be attractive to the prison population. As prisoners come to realize that their complaints will be processed on an administrative level in a fair, expeditious and impartial manner, and that relief will be afforded where justified, inmates will begin to elect their administrative remedy rather than the delayed process of the courts.

Other examples considered inappropriate for the exercise of judicial intervention, cited by the U.S. Court of Appeals for the First Circuit, included the claimed right to keep a pet in a correctional institution, the right to receive personal clothing from the state, and the duty of the institution to repair broken toilets.

Courts in some jurisdictions have been quick to grant approval and encouragement when administrative complaint procedures have been introduced. For example, the U.S. Court of Appeals for the Fifth Circuit suggested strong approval for the requirement imposed by a subordinate Federal District Court that Federal prisoners exhaust administrative channels for remedy of grievances offered by the newly implemented and then experimental Federal Bureau of Prisons Grievance Procedure before submitting their petitions to the lower court.

Although courts have supported the concept of administrative complaint procedures, the shape of their design and details of operation have been determined by individual administrations or, occasionally, by state legislatures. As a result of differing approaches, a variety of models exists.[7] These models fall into three broad categories: Ombudsmen, Grievance Commissions, and Multi-Level Grievance Procedures. All are hereinafter discussed, together with inmate councils.

A. OMBUDSMEN

The office of ombudsman originated in Sweden. It was established by the Swedish Parliament to keep a watchful eye on royal officials who wielded executive power. The ombudsman was expected to insure, through his independent powers of investigation and censure, that authority was not abused.

Although the position was first created by the Swedish Constitution Act of 1809, the word ombudsman originated in the primitive legal order of Germanic tribes who had devised two punishments for lawbreakers. One was banishment as an outlaw, leaving the offender a free mark for slaying. The other, an alternative to outlawry, was a fine payable to the family of the aggrieved by the family of the culprit. To avoid the violence which a face-to-face payment meeting might create, an impartial person was designated to collect the fine (om--about; buds--messenger collecting "fine").[8]

Each of the Scandinavian countries followed Sweden's lead in creating governmental ombudsmen offices. All are appointed by the legislature, entirely independent of the executive, are empowered to make information public, and must report annually to the legislature.[9]

Since the early 1970s, the ombudsman concept has become increasingly popular in United States prisons and jails. The survey made by the author in 1982-83 identified 15 states with an ombudsman program. Seven are independent of the state corrections department; six were established by the State Legislature, and the seventh, Connecticut, was created by a written agreement between the State Department of Correction and the Hartford Institute of Criminal and Social Justice.

From its inception in 1974 to 1981, the Indiana ombudsman position was funded by the legislature and was thus independent of the Department of Corrections, but since then has functioned as a department employee. An ombudsman for Alabama adult corrections, established in 1978, was discontinued in late 1982 or early 1983. A survey published in 1980 reported that an ombudsman for Mississippi adult corrections was established in 1978.[10] However, no mention is made of the position in the 1981 revised edition of the Inmate Handbook of the Mississippi Department of Corrections.

Ombudsmen established in Oregon in 1971, and Ohio in 1972, were discontinued in 1981 and 1975, respectively.

Eight ombudsmen accept complaints from both adult and juvenile offenders. Five are concerned only with problems of adults.

The ombudsman position in New York was established to deal only with youth under the jurisdiction of the Division for Youth of the State Executive Department. The same is true for the ombudsman in the Alabama Department of Youth Services.

The ombudsmen in Alaska, Hawaii and Nebraska cover the entire scope of governmental activities, with prison problems only a part of their work load.

A grievance procedure is also available to the inmates in one or more of the institutions in each of the fifteen states having an ombudsman.

In some jurisdictions, a crisis in prison conditions sparked the establishment of an ombudsman program. Following the uprising in 1971 at the New Jersey State Prison, Rahway, both an ombudsman and an inmate council were authorized. A short-lived ombudsman program, begun in late 1971 at the Holmesburg Prison, City of Philadelphia, was commenced in part because of the riot there in 1970.

Inmates have access to ombudsmen by mail or through direct contact with them when they visit the institution. Inmates in segregation are not excluded from petitioning the ombudsman.

The function of an ombudsman differs from that of a multi-level, or inmate/staff, participation procedure. The primary function of an ombudsman appears to be deciding the merits of a complaint alleging that an act or decision is unfair or improper, or that the corrections department, or the institution, failed to act. In contrast, the primary function of the multi-level procedure is to stimulate change through mediation of individual grievances.[11]

Ombudsmen handle a wide range of problems with few restrictions on the issues that can be raised. One exception is parole decisions, which generally are made by autonomous boards and thus are outside the jurisdiction of ombudsmen or other types of complaint mechanisms.

In the 1982-83 survey by the author, no information was specifically sought regarding the frequency with which inmates complain to ombudsmen. However, Alaska reported 192 complaints for 1982, with 738 projected for 1983. Connecticut reported 3,099 complaints from inception of the program in September, 1973 through 1978.

Much energy and argument have been expended in attempts to establish the qualifications for the person who will serve as ombudsman. In 1974, the Ombudsman Committee of the American Bar Association's Section of Administrative Law published a model statute for state governments interested in creating an ombudsman. The model includes the following provisions, which closely reflect the essential features of the Scandinavian model:

1. Appointment: The ombudsman is to be elected by a two-thirds vote of the members of both houses of the legislature or, alternatively, appointed by the governor, subject to confirmation by a two-thirds vote of both houses.

2. Qualifications: ... an individual of "recognized judgment, objectivity and integrity ... well equipped to analyze problems of law, administration, and public policy." Compensation is set deliberately high to attract highly qualified people (the same salary and benefits as the chief judge of the highest state court).

3. Removal: ... can be removed only by a two-thirds vote of both houses of the legislature and only for mental and physical incapacity or other grounds suitable for removal of state court judge.

4. Powers: Included in the ombudsman's powers is the authority to use the courts to enforce compliance with his investigation.

5. Reports: ... may publish through the media recommendations in separate special reports or in general periodic reports of his activities, provided that replies for criticized agencies also are published.

The Center for Community Justice has pointed out that it may be preferable not to spell out the qualifications for an ombudsman in great detail, citing that persons of varying background, education and experience are working effectively as correctional ombudsmen, including a former social worker, a businessman, a correctional officer, legal aid attorneys, and an ex-offender. Determination of ombudsman qualifications in a specific jurisdiction should include input from correctional administrators, line staff and inmates. Involving those persons can enhance the possibility of successfully initiating an ombudsman program.[12]

The Center for Community Justice reported the following in 1980 on the number of complaints to ombudsmen for the periods indicated:

Indiana	Approximately 5,000, 1974-1978
Iowa	Approximately 2,300, 1973-1978
Kansas	1,204, September 1975-July 1978
Kentucky	518, January-October, 1978
Michigan	3,400, 1978
Minnesota	6,854, 1972-1978
New Jersey	1,827, 1978
Oregon	6,000, 1971-1978
South Carolina	512, 1978
Virginia	Approximately 4,000, 1977-1978

Current ombudsmen programs are listed in Section E of this chapter. Detailed accounts of past and present programs are presented in Chapters III, IV and V.

B. GRIEVANCE COMMISSIONS

Grievance commissions have features of both the ombudsmen and the multi-level grievance procedures (discussed in the following section), and exist only in the Maryland, New York and North Carolina adult systems. In those jurisdictions, a commission of outsiders, generally with an investigative staff, is empowered to receive and investigate complaints and make recommendations to correctional administrators.

In Maryland, a complaint arising as a result of disciplinary action within the institution must be processed through the institution adjustment procedure prior to submission to the Grievance Commission.

In some systems, an ombudsman or grievance commission is combined with multi-level appeal procedures in piggy-back fashion; that is, the ombudsman or commission constitutes the level of appeal from the internal departmental grievance procedure. This is the case in the adult systems of North Carolina and New York (grievance commissions) and in Michigan (ombudsman).

In New York, the Commission of Correction, a state agency responsible for inspecting and monitoring the level of care provided prisoners in all New York correctional facilities, municipal lockups and county jails, acts as the grievance commission in the adult system.

In North Carolina, an inmate seeking procedural review of a disciplinary action may appeal directly to the Inmate Grievance Commission. With respect to other grievances, the internal institution grievance procedure must be used before an appeal may be made to the Commission.

C. MULTI-LEVEL GRIEVANCE PROCEDURES

Multi-level grievance procedures involve the submission of complaints to a designated individual within an institution, with provision for appeals to successively higher levels within the organization and, in some instances, to a person or group outside the corrections agency. Outside reviews are advisory in all cases.

The 1982-83 survey identified 38 states having a multi-level grievance procedure for both adult and juvenile offenders; nine states with procedures for adults only; and one, Maryland, with a procedure for juveniles only (adults present their grievances to a Grievance Commission). In five states there is no grievance procedure for juveniles. However, some of those states have ombudsmen who respond to complaints by juveniles. In Oklahoma institutions for juveniles, the superintendent, staff and students attempt to resolve grievances within ten days and periodic reviews are made of those not resolved.

All institutions of the Federal Prison System may submit complaints under the Administrative Review System, which is a multi-level procedure. Grievance procedures are available to all inmates in District of Columbia institutions, as they are at the two county systems, Cook County, Illinois, and Westchester County, New York, and the city systems of New York City and Philadelphia, Pennsylvania.

In some procedures, inmates are not involved at any level. In others, inmates may be involved at the initial, and occasionally, at the second level. The rationale for both staff and inmate participation is two-fold: to place the greatest amount of decision-making authority on the persons who must live with the results of the decisions, and to provide a forum for accommodation between opposing points of view.[13]

The 1982-83 survey also found that inmates participate in decision-making levels in both adult and juvenile procedures in seven states; in only adult procedures in ten states; in only juvenile procedures in five states; in the cities of New York and Philadelphia; and not at all in the Federal Prison System or the counties of Cook, Illinois, and Westchester, New York.

Multi-level grievance procedures have been developed primarily by a Washington, D.C.-based organization, the Center for Community Justice. The Center was founded in 1971 by a group of lawyers, correctional officials and ex-offenders to develop non-violent, administrative mechanisms for correctional institutions. The Center first designed and operated a pilot program for delivering legal services to prisoners and parolees in the District of Columbia. In the course of providing legal services to individuals, the Center also came to serve as an ad hoc ombudsman, mediating disputes between inmates and correctional staff.

The Center's early experiences led to the development of formal procedures for handling problems within correctional agencies. Variations of the procedures were implemented in the Massachusetts Department of Correction and the California Youth Authority. Because of that direct participation, the Center became a source of technical assistance for other states, institutions, planning agencies and inmate groups interested in developing grievance mechanisms of their own.

Based on its analysis of grievance mechanisms, the Center for Community Justice identified the following principles as essential for establishing a procedure which will effectively handle inmate grievances. The principles also present a framework within which successful procedures may be introduced in correctional institutions.[14]

1. The procedure must include some form of independent review, i.e., review by people outside the correctional structure. The more totally independent of official governmental control such review is, the more likely it will be to promote inmates' belief in the mechanism's fairness and their willingness to use it.

2. Line staff and inmates must participate in the design and operation of a grievance mechanism. Only participation can give these critically important constituencies a vested interest in the success of the mechanism. In addition, participation seems to be the only possible way to overcome initial apprehension on the part of line staff and distrust on the part of inmates.

3. The mechanism must have relatively short, enforceable time limits. These limits must apply to both the making and implementation of decisions. Every mechanism also should provide for the handling of emergency grievances.

4. There must be guaranteed written responses for every complaint submitted to the mechanism. Written answers must give reasons for adverse decisions.

5. The implementation of a successful grievance mechanism requires effective administrative planning and leadership. Correctional administrators must take the lead in assessing needs, determining resource requirements and allocating sufficient resources in order to create successful mechanisms. In addition, they must participate actively in an effort to win the commitment of subordinate administrators to establishing effective mechanisms.

6. Administrative, line staff and inmate personnel, key to the operations of a mechanism, must be trained thoroughly in the skills and techniques requisite for the effective investigation hearing and disposition of inmates' grievances.

7. Every institution with a grievance mechanism must develop an effective, persuasive, continuing program for the orientation of staff and inmates to the nature, purpose and functions of the grievance mechanism.

8. There must be a continuing system to monitor and evaluate the effectiveness of each operating grievance mechanism. At a minimum, the monitoring and evaluation system should operate at the institutional and departmental levels; it is preferable that some outside monitoring take place at least periodically.

9. Once a department has tested and evaluated its mechanism thoroughly, it should move to make it a permanent part of its program by having it statutorily enacted in appropriate legislation.

It is important, however, to remember that, while there is no prescribed formula that can guarantee success, no procedure can hope to succeed without the total commitment of top administration to the concepts of fairness and justice inherent in grievance procedures.

Both the American Bar Association[15] and the Commission on Accreditation in Corrections[16] have issued standards based on the principles developed by the Center. In addition, the principles served as guideposts to measure the progress of state and local correctional facilities in a report by the Comptroller General of the United States to the Subcommittee on Courts, Civil Liberties, and the Administration of Justice of the House of Representatives Committee on the Judiciary. That report and a later one[17] by the Comptroller General were of assistance to the same House Subcommittee in its deliberation on H.R. 9400, which (with a companion bill in the Senate, S. 1393) eventually resulted in Public Law 96-247, the Civil Rights of Institutionalized Persons Act. Under the Act, the Attorney General of the United States developed procedures by which states, and their political subdivisions, voluntarily may submit for certification prisoner grievance mechanism plans for adult correctional and detention facilities. Upon certification by the Attorney General that a proposed plan is in substantial compliance with the standards, actions sought by inmates of that facility, pursuant to 42 U.S.C. 1983, may be continued by a court for a period of up to ninety days in order to require the exhaustion of administrative remedies available under the grievance procedure, if the issues raised can reasonably be expected to be resolved by the grievance procedure.

As defined in the standards developed by the Attorney General, a grievance is a written complaint filed by an inmate on his or her own behalf regarding a policy applicable within an institution, a condition in an institution, an action involving an inmate of an institution, or an incident occurring within an institution. Complaints relating to a parole decision are specifically excluded; nor may a grievance procedure be used as a disciplinary procedure.

Substantial compliance means that there is no omission of any essential part from compliance, that any omission consists only of an unimportant defect or omission, and that there has been a firm effort to comply fully with the standards.

The text of the Civil Rights of Institutionalized Persons Act, together with the standards for inmate grievance procedures developed by the U.S. Attorney General, and a summary of the actions taken by both Houses of Congress on the bills, H.R. 9400 and S.B. 1393, which culminated in the Act, is given in Appendix A.

Information on the use of multi-level procedures was not sought in the 1982-83 survey. However, the California Department of the Youth Authority reported that, in 1980, a total of 9,968 grievances were filed and resolved. Of that total, there were 3,657 individuals filing grievances; 37% or one of every three wards filed a grievance. From the inception of the procedure in 1973 through 1980, a total of 41,294 grievances were filed. It is interesting to note that the number of grievances started to increase in March, 1979, as the population of the institutions continued to rise. Usage peaked in August, 1980, when grievances rose to an all-time high of 1,058 for that month.

The majority, 56%, of the 1980 grievances dealt with individual problems. Approximately half, 53.5%, were resolved in favor of the grievant, usually at the living unit level. In only sixty-two instances (.57%) was use made of the option of referral to an outside arbitrator for resolution.

The Federal Prison System reported that 13,187 complaints were filed in 1982 under the Administrative Remedy Procedure. Of that number, fifteen per cent were granted; eighty-five per cent were denied. Approximately one-third were appealed to the Regional Office and a slightly higher number were appealed to the Central Office.

The 1980 publication of the Center for Community Justice, Complaint Procedures in Prisons and Jails: An Examination of Recent Experience, reported the following usage totals:

California (Adult Authority)	1973-1978	25,194
Delaware	1978	Approx. 300
Florida	1975-1978	7,720
(6,183 at institution level; 1,537 appealed to Central Office)		
Georgia	1974-1978	288 (to final level of review)
Hawaii	1969-1978	356
Illinois	for 1978 only	3,745
Iowa	1973-1978	300
Kentucky	1977-1978	160
Michigan	1976-1977	2,657 (final level of review)
Mississippi	1976-1978	680
Montana	1974-1978	626
Nevada	7/1977-7/1978	280
New Jersey	1978	111
New York	1976-1978	18,000
North Carolina	1975-1978	20,261
North Dakota	for 1978	208
Ohio	FY 1978	2,183
Pennsylvania	1976-3/1978	5,935
South Carolina	1976-1978	307 (at one institution)
South Dakota	1977-1978	62
Virginia	1974-1978	Approx. 11,000
Washington	1976-1978	Approx. 50 (one institution)
Wisconsin	11/1972-10/1977	25,125
Federal Prison System	1973-1978	Approx. 80,000
District of Columbia	1978	200

A listing of multi-level grievance procedures will be found in a Summary of Complaint Mechanisms in Section E of the present chapter.

In addition to the foregoing, Wisconsin reported 5,687 complaints filed, of which 39% (2,195) were filed by inmates of the Waupun Correctional Institution (the largest institution), in 1981.

Most jurisdictions provide for orientation of newly admitted inmates to the grievance procedure. Several have prepared a booklet which includes not only department and institution rules and regulations, but also the rights of inmates and information about available legal services.

Staff orientation to the grievance procedure is ordered by some jurisdictions. Staff responsibility for insuring the integrity of the procedure is often emphasized.

As a rule, inmates are encouraged to seek informal resolution of complaints by discussing the issue with staff members. In some jurisdictions the complaint is not written at this level.

While the number of procedure levels varies, the final level in all multi-level procedures is the person or group in charge of the correctional system, and advisory opinions of outside groups or individuals are sometimes allowed.

Confidentiality is a basic premise of the procedure. In many jurisdictions no adverse information concerning use of or participation in the procedure by either inmates or staff may be placed in the individual's personnel files.

Written responses, including reasons for decisions, within specified time limits are mandatory in most procedures. The length of time permitted for review of and an answer to a complaint is rather generous in all procedures. Almost all include a proviso for an extension of response time limits, some only with the grievant's concurrence and some by unilateral action of the administration. In those instances, the grievant is notified when a reply will be made. Some procedures specify that an extension of the response time may not exceed the original specified time period.

Several jurisdictions have established a continuing management information system to measure the operations and impact of their grievance procedure. Many of these systems incorporate recommendations made in the October 17, 1977 Report of the Comptroller General of the United States, Managers Need Comprehensive Systems for Assessing Effectiveness and Operation of Inmate Grievance Mechanisms:

- Compile data on the operations of the mechanism to determine (1) whether grievances are handled within prescribed time limits, (2) that decisions under the mechanism are carried out, (3) that no reprisals occur as a result of submitting grievances to the mechanism, and (4) that procedures are adhered to.
- Maintain records for determining the impact of the mechanism, such as reduction of legal actions and clarification and change in policies.

- Interview institutional and departmental administrators to ascertain the extent of their knowledge of the responsiveness to the mechanism.
- Interview or administer questionnaires to line staff, e.g., correctional officers, to ascertain data on familiarity with and belief in the mechanism.
- Interview or administer questionnaires to inmates to obtain their views and general knowledge of the mechanism and their willingness to use it.

A standard form for registering a complaint is provided in most jurisdictions. Accessibility to the forms is usually via a specified staff member--either the inmate's housing unit officer or caseworker. Provision is made for replies at all levels of the procedure on some forms, providing at any time a cumulative record of consideration given to the complaint. In some procedures, a new form is required for appeal to successive levels, to which must be attached a copy of any previous form used.

Citing reasons for an appeal to the next higher level is a requirement in some procedures, in a few of which the appellate level may decline consideration, but must advise the grievant in writing of the reasons for denial.

Assistance in preparing a grievance, in some procedures, may be given either by staff or inmates to a grievant who is illiterate, unable to properly express him/herself in writing, or has a language difficulty.

Parolees are included under the grievance procedure in some jurisdictions. However, no information of any special processing for parolee complaints is given in the accounts of past and current procedures in chapters III, IV and V.

D. INMATE COUNCILS

Contrary to some reports made during the past several years, the inmate council is not a concept that administrators of correctional systems and facilities are increasingly turning away from. This is made readily apparent by a reading of the many active councils in Chapters III, IV, and V.

Inmate councils have been included in this chapter on complaint mechanisms, not because the author believes they are such, but only for purposes of content organization and in recognition of the fact that, in some instances, a council does present for resolution matters of institution-wide concern.

The Center for Community Justice found that the advisory nature of the inmate council is antithetical to its use as a grievance mechanism. By its very nature, an inmate council deals with institutional problems. Wisely, most inmate councils do not permit consideration of individual complaints during meetings; the view is that to do so would be obstructive of a principal goal, the advocacy of new or changed institution policy. This approach excludes a substantial portion of grievances from the jurisdiction of the mechanism.[18]

Our 1982-83 survey determined that inmate councils exist in 45 states in one or more adult and/or juvenile institutions. No information was received regarding either adult or juvenile institutions in Illinois. Likewise, no information was obtained about juvenile institutions in three other states, nor about adult institutions in two states. Neither Pennsylvania nor Vermont has institutions for juvenile offenders. Four institutions in the Federal Prison System have inmate councils, two established in 1977, one in 1979, and one in 1981. Two youth institutions in the District of Columbia system have councils, but there are none in the juvenile institutions. Neither Cook County, Illinois, nor Westchester County, New York, has councils. All institutions in the Cities of New York and Philadelphia systems have councils. No current information was received regarding Department of the Army or the U.S. Marine Corps confinement facilities. There is a council at the single institution of the Department of the Air Force. Establishment of a council is discretionary with the officer-in-charge at each Department of the Navy brig.

Until the early 1970s, the primary channel for communicating inmates' points of view to administrators was the inmate council. Massachusetts was the setting for the first actual experimentation with formal inmate participation in administration, involving both youth and adult populations. Although the experience at the New York House of Refuge antedated that of the Boston House of Reformation by approximately three years, it was only at the latter that inmate participation was purposefully used for its experience value to the individual. At the Massachusetts State Prison, the Society for Moral Improvement and Mutual Aid represented the first instance of adult inmates being placed in a formal communication with administration.

As we review the scene from 1793 to 1983, it appears that the concept of offender participation in prison management as embodied in the advisory council has seldom been utilized in many jurisdictions in more than a superficial manner. Many administrators regard the advisory council as simply a device for the communication of inmate complaints to the administration. This narrow view has produced the term "gimme" groups.

The various rationales for the existence of advisory councils range from the pragmatism of providing an administrative peephole through which inmate plots may be discovered to the altruism of learning democracy by experiencing it. Some practitioners accept the view that the inmate must be a part of the service process rather than simply an object of service, but few have done little to translate the view into action.

The Manual of Correctional Standards, 1959 issue, of the American Correctional Association, states that inmate participation in planning and operation of institutional programs is slowly passing out of the controversial stage, and that many prison administrators recognize the approach and method as being sound in educational theory and practical as a means of prison administration. Additionally, with the appointment of more imaginative and socially-minded wardens and officials, its use in institutions will come to be taken for granted.

The 1966 issue of the Manual of Correctional Standards further stated:

> One of the most significant privileges which can be extended to persons confined is opportunity to take some limited responsibility for the planning and operation of the institution program. Opportunity for participation in constructive social action while under custody, usually in the form of an inmate advisory council, can be one of the most successful and effective means for developing high institutional morale and good discipline.

In its 1972 publication, The Emerging Rights of the Confined, the South Carolina Department of Corrections endorsed the American Correctional Association Manual of Correctional Standards, and suggested a concept of "maximum feasible participation":

> This term means little more than the notion that those who are allowed a voice in the rule-making process are more likely to obey such rules. It does not mean that the prisons would be run by a town meeting of the cell blocks or even that there would be any real power given to inmates to control the prisons. All that is implied by the notion is that at some point along the line the inmate, either individually or through a representative, is allowed to make a meaningful input into the decision-making process that surrounds him with rules. One means of accomplishing this goal would be the establishment of an inmate council with elected representatives. Such a council should be able to present questions to the administration concerning various rules and practices of the institution and receive a straightforward answer. If such an answer cannot be given, then there should be serious doubt concerning the utility of the rule. The inmate council would then be able to accept the explanation or suggest alternatives for the consideration of the administrators.

While there has been some discussion about and limited experimentation with assigning management responsibilities to inmate councils, as pointed out in 1975 by the Center for Community Justice, most jurisdictions have followed the 1966 Manual of Correctional Standards of the American Correctional Association guidelines:

> The inmate advisory council's functions always remain advisory. No actual administrative powers are ever delegated to it. The council encourages, develops, and supports projects for the general welfare of inmates, but all responsibility for management remains in the hands of regularly employed personnel.

As will be noted in the accounts of past and present inmate councils, inmate council members assume a varied range of responsibilities and interact with the administration as representatives of all inmates, not as individuals. Although councils are in the main advisory in nature, which is a criticism leveled by those who dispute the idea that a council can have any effect, it must be remembered that most study groups, commissions, and task forces in the outside world are also only advisory in nature, yet their importance for citizen input and their contribution to decision-making are significant.

Views and pronouncements on the use and value of advisory councils appear to vary in accordance with the group, or the purpose of the group, doing the talking. For instance, in May 1953, the Committee on Riots under the auspices of the American Correctional Association, reported on the unprecedented number of riots in American prisons during the period 1951-1953. Effective communication between management and inmates was mentioned in a report, entitled "Prison Riots and Disturbances," as one measure that might prevent such outbursts of mass violence and mutinous behavior. A representative inmate council was cited as one method of effecting this two-way communication.

In 1960, reportedly the Wardens Association of America went on record as being opposed to the idea of inmate self-government (advisory councils). The number of persons present and voting is not known, but it is understood that prior to the meeting there had been a canvassing of wardens on the issue. Subsequently, the American Correctional Association was prompted to revise the 1953 report, "Prison Riots and Disturbances," by the beginning of a series of riots and major disturbances in correctional institutions in 1968. The report of the revision committee was made in an October 1970 publication entitled "Causes, Preventive Measures, and Methods of Controlling Riots and Disturbances in Correctional Institutions."

According to the report, some administrators believe that it is necessary to develop a formal structure for communications between inmates and administrative personnel. The formation of ad hoc advisory groups was cited as appearing to be the most feasible way of dealing with particular problems or issues. In the opinion of the revision committee this practice would ensure inmate involvement and at the same time prevent selected inmates from capitalizing on their tenure on an advisory panel to exploit other inmates, since the ad hoc committees would be dissolved upon resolution of the particular problem or issue. The issue of advisory councils occasioned a rather heated discussion at the 1972 meeting of the American Association of Wardens and Superintendents. The consensus appears to be that the ranks for and against were about even.

The history of advisory councils, since 1930 in particular, reveals that often the first step taken to create a positive relationship between inmates and staff has been the organization of an advisory council. Additionally, advisory councils have been organized following a crisis situation, such as a riot, as an agency to bring order out of chaos. In many respects, an advisory council formed under such conditions may be likened to a peace tribunal to which each side may send its most enlightened and capable representatives to determine upon what terms and by what means future difficulties might be averted.

Then, on the other hand, there are institutions where an advisory council has never been organized for any reason or under any circumstance. There is no evidence that the presence or the absence of an advisory council has had any marked influence on the destiny of an institution. The best evidence which can be adduced from the past and the present is that open communications between inmates and staff does seem to facilitate the adjustment of both groups.

Why do some correctional administrators look with disfavor upon inmate advisory councils while others turn to the concept for succor in periods of program malaise and in the aftermath of disaster? Further, why, during the course of our surveys, did many administrators qualify their admissions of no councils with statements reflecting a belief that councils offer many advantages to an institution program, that serious thought was being given to establishing a council, or that the organization and operation of a council had not been ruled out for the future. Certainly these reflect more than a suggestion of uncertainty about not having a council.

This ambivalence is believed to be the product of an erroneous equation of inmate advisory councils with self-government systems of the past in which inmates functioned as disciplinarians. This belief is buttressed by the results of a survey published in 1964 in the _Journal of Criminology, Criminal Law and Police Science_. The principal objection to advisory councils was that they permitted one inmate to have authority over another. Yet a properly drawn advisory council plan can easily and effectively rule out any possibility of this occurring.

The author is of the opinion that discipline is a part of the treatment process which must be retained in toto by prison personnel. The proper administration of discipline requires a degree of objectivity which is not to be found in the object itself. This does not imply an exclusion of inmate opinions and suggestions in determining the disciplinary process. However, it does imply that those who administer the process must be qualified to do so.

Many administrators are obviously concerned that some inmates will use membership on an advisory council to their personal advantage and at the expense of sound administration. It has been postulated that since many inmates have grievances they may tend to regard the advisory council as a forum for the expression of those grievances. All of this may well be true. Also true is the fact that some staff members may have views similar to those of the inmates and in that light define their own role as one of advocacy and align themselves with the inmates. So, both inmates and staff can use an advisory council to their personal advantage and at the expense of sound administration.

The foregoing should be regarded by the administrator as a challenge to his correctional management skill rather than as a reason not to have an advisory council if he believes that such a group will be of value. The administration simply needs to recognize that this attitude may underlie the approach by some inmates and some staff members to the advisory council concept. A necessary part of the development of both groups is to recognize the defined role of an advisory council. And only management can make that definition.

Opponents of the advisory council point out that some inmates will use their advisory council membership to create centers of personal power which can subvert the authority of the administration. There is no doubt that politics can be involved, since prisoners are people and people do engage in politics of one fashion or another. Properly designed and monitored procedures can do much to reduce the creation of power centers--for instance, frequent elections and rotation of positions in which power may be implied or inherent, such as committee chairmanships.

If the decision is to have an advisory council, the purpose and scope of the group's function must be fully communicated to and understood by both staff and inmates. This should be accomplished before a group is organized. The method most frequently employed for this communication is the drawing up of a constitution and a set of by-laws. Another approach is the issuance of a directive by the central authority setting forth the official policy regarding advisory councils--or staff-inmate communications, or inmate organizations--and providing organizational and procedural guidelines. These approaches are adequate, but each lacks any means or method of insuring that the intent of the decision maker is effected.

Despite the best structuring, the most careful planning, or the most meticulous implementation, there is no absolutely certain method by which the intended purpose of an advisory council, or any program for that matter, can be assured. But we do know that people respond when their personal interest is involved. A staff response of acceptance and support for an advisory council can be facilitated if management makes it explicit that such acceptance and support are factors in personnel performance expectations.

If an advisory council is organized, it is assumed that the

administrator is serious about it, that he is accepting the group as an element in the organizational structure, and perhaps even recognizing the inmates as members of the staff, even though in a subordinate status. Granted all of this, it is his intention then that the advisory council function as an integral agency of the institution. He recognizes that in order for this intent to be translated into reality, the involvement of staff at all levels is necessary. A fatal defect of most of the early experiences with advisory councils, and with many of those that came after 1930, was the dependence of the organizations on a lone individual. When that person departed the scene, the council ceased to exist. To avoid this, the base of personnel involved with council activities should be broadened. A warden and his associate wardens should be actively interested in council functions, of course, but can best demonstrate that interest by insuring budgetary support, for instance, leaving operational contacts to other staff. Whatever staff works directly with the council should be empowered to make decisions and take actions, at least within limits in certain areas.

The question is often raised as to what are the proper functions of an advisory council. The answer lies in the purpose for which the organization is formed. Almost without exception, the expressed purpose of a council is to effect or to improve inmate-staff relationships, and consequently insure the proper functioning of the institution, by providing a free-flow channel of communication. With this as a basis, there is really no function of the institution from which the input of council views should be excluded; even in those involving personnel recruitment, selection, and retention, management should be alert to the possibilities for staff development inherent in effective communication. Staff can learn much about itself by being attentive to the nuances of that communication.

All functions of the advisory council should be continuously monitored and frequently evaluated. Top management should be actively involved in this evaluation, according it the same serious consideration given to other program evaluations. This brings us to what the author regards as the most powerful of all rationales for the inclusion of inmates in both the program and the programming of corrections: the use of council membership as a treatment method. To do so offers an opportunity for effecting attitudinal changes through which more satisfactory modes of coping with social-role demands can be realized. A properly organized and functioning advisory council can be an excellent vehicle for the abundant energies and unusually high abilities of many offenders that are not amenable to conventional treatment forms. Some men need an experience of working for the welfare of others. Others require ego-satisfying assignments in which they can escape the feeling of being engulfed in the crowd.

As the accounts in chapters III, IV and V reveal, council membership often changes recalcitrants to rather agreeable persons; often, too, the inward viewpoint of the self-centered personality is redirected outward to a genuine interest in others. The use of membership in an advisory council as a part of the development plan for a particular inmate certainly will call for a different method by which council members are selected. One method would be to appoint members to the council. There are reasons against this so obvious as to make discussion of them unnecessary. However, in that connection the best accepted and most dynamic advisory council the author has ever known of had 75 per cent of its members appointed by the staff sponsor. The reason for this was a series of vacancies created by transfers of elected representatives to other housing units or to other institutions, and the brevity of the unexpired portion of their terms made special elections not feasible. Such appointments were provided for in the council constitution.

Probably the best method is to use the individual's council membership as a part of his treatment development plan, after he has attained membership through the regular ballot process. Those persons for whom it is believed that advisory council membership would be beneficial can be encouraged to seek election. In this regard, classes in the principles of legislative duties, responsibilities, and techniques can be included in the educational program.

It has been the experience of the author, and the experience of many others as related in the accounts herein, that placement in a formalized situation, such as an advisory council, can have a salutary effect on dominating or aggressive individuals--those who demonstrate a big-shot complex. In such a situation, where discipline and ability rather than toughness or muscle are the factors important to personal stature, a distinct toning-down process can occur. Conversely, those who are shy and withdrawn in the confinement situation, where a high value is placed on physical prowess, and who have lost confidence in themselves because of this, can attain some degree of stature and regain a large measure of self-esteem in a formalized structure where calmness and logic are superior to the strident voice and the balled fist.

An advisory council, properly utilized, has a two-way function. It is an agency for communicating to inmates the responsibilities which the administration expects of them and to present a picture of administrative problems in the areas with which inmates are concerned. For instance, by showing them the budget and soliciting their suggestions as to how a better job might be done with available resources, a structure is created which provides for and encourages thoughtful, constructive feedback. This approach involves the same psychological principles basic to management efforts to provide employee job satisfaction--call it morale.

E. SUMMARY OF COMPLAINT MECHANISMS

Jurisdiction	Type of System	Date Begun	No. of Levels	Responses: In Writing	Responses: Within Time Limits	Formal Hearing	Final Level of Review
ALABAMA							
Adult	GP	1977	Unk.	Yes	No	No	Warden
	Ombudsman	1978		Yes	No	Unk.	
Juvenile	GP	Unk.	5	Yes	Yes	Yes	Dir. Dept. Youth Svs.
	Ombudsman	Unk.		Yes	Yes	Yes	
ALASKA							
Adult	GP	1977[1]	3	Yes	Yes	No	Dir. Div. of Corrs.
	Ombudsman	1975[2]		Yes	Yes		
Juvenile	Ombudsman	1975 (Ombudsman serves both adults and juveniles)					
ARIZONA							
Adult	GP	1975[3]	6	Yes	Yes	Yes[4]	Outside Review Board
Juvenile (Same as Adult)							
ARKANSAS							
Adult	GP	1974[5]	3	Yes	Yes	No	Dir. Dept. Corr.
Juvenile	GP	1978[6]	4	Yes	Yes	Yes[6]	Dep. Comm. Div. Yth. Svs

1. Rev. 7/83 to conform to Commission on Accreditation of Corrections Standards.
2. Eff. 7/1/78, Correctional Ombudsman position established to serve both adult and juvenile offenders.
3. Procedure last modified 1/15/81.
4. Three-person Review Committee has one inmate member.
5. In 1974 only at Tucker and Cummins Units; in 1981, all adult institutions.
6. Four-person Grievance Committee has one student member.

Jurisdiction	Type of System	Date Begun	No. of Levels	Responses: In Writing	Responses: Within Time Limits	Formal Hearing	Final Level of Review
CALIFORNIA							
Adult	GP	1973	3	Yes	Yes	Yes	Dir., Dept. Corrs.[7]
Juvenile	GP	1973[8]	3	Yes	Yes	Yes[9]	Outside Review Board
COLORADO							
Adult	GP	1976-78[10]	3	Yes	Yes	Yes	Outside Review
	GP	1981[11]	3	Yes	Yes	No	Exec. Dir., Dept. Corrs.
Juvenile	GP	1978(c) Each facility has its own operational procedures.					
CONNECTICUT							
Adult	GP	1983[12]	4[13]	Yes	Yes	Yes	Comm'r. Dept. Corr.
	Ombudsman	1973[14]		Yes	No		
Juvenile	GP[15]		1	Yes	Yes	Yes	Grievance Board[16]

7. Inmates assigned to corrections industries may appeal to State Labor Commissioner in certain situations.
8. Established in Sept. 1973 as pilot program, Karl Holton School, Stockton, Calif. By mid-1975 procedure operative in all youth authority institutions.
9. Equal number wards and staff on grievance committee.
10. Only at Colorado Territorial Correctional Facility, Canon City; 3 inmates and 3 staff on grievance committee.
11. Established in all adult institutions.
12. Only at the Community Correctional Center, New Haven.
13. Inmates involved in decision making at first two levels.
14. Originally served only two institutions. Now serves all adult institutions.
15. Letter of 10/18/82 indicated GP (Grievance Board) would be established in near future. (Only one juvenile institution in Connecticut.)
16. Two students will be members of the Grievance Board, together with four staff members.

Jurisdiction	Type of System	Date Begun	No. of Levels	Responses: In Writing	Responses: Within Time Limits	Formal Hearing	Final Level of Review
DELAWARE							
Adult	GP	1978	2	Yes	No	Yes[17]	Chief, Bur. Adult Corr. or Comm., Dept. Corr.
Juvenile (same as adult)							
FLORIDA							
Adult	GP	1975	2	Yes	Yes	No	Regional Dir. or Secy., Dept. Corrs.
Juvenile	GP[18]	1982	4	Yes	Yes	Yes	Supt.
GEORGIA							
Adult	GP	1974	4	Yes	Yes	No	Commr., Dept. Offender Rehab.
Juvenile	GP	1982	3[19]	Yes	Yes	Yes	Dir., Div. Youth Svs.
HAWAII							
Adult	Adm. Review	1970	4	Yes	Yes	Yes	Admin'or. Corrs. Div.
Juvenile (same as adult)							
IDAHO							
Adult	GP[20]	1974	4	Yes	Yes		Dir., Dept. Corrs.
Juvenile	Grievances sent to Superintendent						Superintendent.

17. Two inmates and two staff members comprise the Resident Grievance Resolution Committee.
18. An advisory panel of persons outside the facility may be formed at any level of the procedure under certain circumstances.
19. At the second level of review a committee of one or two staff or residents may be appointed by the facility director to make or share in the decision.
20. For adjustment process only.

Jurisdiction	Type of System	Date Begun	No. of Levels	Responses: In Writing	Responses: Within Time Limits	Formal Hearing	Final Level of Review
ILLINOIS							
Adult	GP	1972	3	Yes	Yes	Yes[21]	Dir., Dept. Corrs.
Juvenile	GP	1975	3	Yes	Yes	Yes[22]	Dir., Dept. Corrs.
INDIANA							
Adult	GP	1979	3	Yes	Yes	Yes[23]	Comm'r., Dept. Corr.
	Ombudsman	1974		Yes	No		
Juvenile (same as adult)							
IOWA							
Adult	GP	1973	3	Yes	Yes	Yes	Comm'r., Dept. Soc. Servs.
	Ombudsman	1972		Yes	Yes		
Juvenile (same as adult)							

21. Administrative Review Board conducts hearing at institution; makes disposition recommendation to Director.
22. Same as #21.
23. Regulations provide for inmates and staff to serve as members of first level grievance committee, but this occurs only at Indiana State Prison and Indiana Girls' School.

Jurisdiction	Type of System	Date Begun	No. of Levels	Responses: In Writing	Responses: Within Time Limits	Formal Hearing	Final Level of Review
KANSAS							
Adult	GP	1972[24]	2	Yes	Yes	No	Secy., Dept. Corrs.
	GP	1975[25]	3	Yes	Yes	Yes	Secy., Dept. Corrs.[26]
	Ombudsman	1975		Yes	Yes	Yes	
Juvenile	GP[27]	1981 (Atchison)	2	Yes	Yes	Yes	Superintendent
	GP[28]	1982 (Beloit)	2	Yes	Yes	Yes	Superintendent
KENTUCKY							
Adult	GP	1977	4	Yes	Yes	Yes[29]	Outside Review/Comm'r. Corrs. Cabinet
	Ombudsman	1974		Yes	No	No	
Juvenile	GP	1982	2	Yes	Yes	Yes	Comm'r., Dept. for Soc. Services
LOUISIANA							
Adult	GP	1973	Unk.	Yes	Yes	Yes[30]	Secy., Dept. Corrs.
Juvenile (same as adult)							

24. In operation only at Kansas State Penitentiary.
25. Established at all institutions. At first level institution Supt. may designate 2 or more employees and a like number of inmates to participate in advisory capacity in decision making.
26. Secy. may refer complaint to ombudsman or some independent agency outside Dept. Corr's. for an advisory recommendation.
27. Youth Svs. directives require each facility to establish grievance procedure based on Comm. on Accreditation in Corrections standards. Information received from only two institutions.
28. A student is member of 3-person grievance committee at first level of review.
29. Inmates participate in decision-making roles in hearing.
30. Inmates participate in decision-making roles in hearing.

Jurisdiction	Type of System	Date Begun	No. of Levels	Responses: In Writing	Responses: Within Time Limits	Formal Hearing	Final Level of Review
MAINE							
Adult	GP[31]	1974	2	Yes	Yes	No	Comm. Dept. Corrs.
Juvenile (same as adult)							
MARYLAND							
Adult	Grievance Comm.	1971	2	Yes	Yes	Yes	Secy. Dept. Public Safety & Correctional Svs.
Juvenile	GP	1983	5	Yes	Yes	Yes	Dir. Juv. Svs. Admin.
MASSACHUSETTS							
Adult	GP	1973 (at MCI, Concord 3/73 to 6/73)					
	GP	1979 (at MCI, Walpole; never implemented system-wide)					
	GP	1982	2	Yes	Yes	No	Dept. Corr. Grievance Coordinator
Juvenile--All institutions closed in 1972-1973.							
MICHIGAN							
Adult	GP	1973	3	Yes	Yes	No	Warden[32]
	Ombudsman	1975		Yes	No		
Juvenile--No grievance procedure.							

31. This is description of proposed client grievance procedure as reported September, 1982. Original GP established in 1974 had no provisions for written responses, time limits, or formal hearings; number of levels unknown.
32. Grievant may appeal to ombudsman.

Jurisdiction	Type of System	Date Begun	No. of Levels	Responses: In Writing	Responses: Within Time Limits	Formal Hearing	Final Level of Review
MINNESOTA							
Adult	Ombudsman	1972		Yes	No		
Juvenile (same ombudsman as adults)							
	GP	1983	No other information.[33]				
MISSISSIPPI							
Adult	GP	1976	2	Yes	Yes	No	Warden.
	Ombudsman	1978		Yes			
Juvenile--No grievance procedure.							
MISSOURI							
Adult	GP	1974	Unk.	Yes	Yes	Yes	Dir., Dept. Corrs.
Juvenile--No grievance procedure.							
MONTANA							
Adult	GP[34]	1974	Unk.	Yes	Yes	Yes	Outside review board
	GP	1982	3	Yes	Yes	No	Dir., Dept. Insts.
Juvenile	GP[35]						

33. Procedure only at Minnesota Correctional Facility, Red Wing (juveniles).
34. This probably applied only to Montana State Prison, Deer Lodge.
35. Only at Mountain View School, Helena, Montana; concerns only disciplinary actions.

Jurisdiction	Type of System	Date Begun	No. of Levels	Responses: In Writing	Responses: Within Time Limits	Formal Hearing	Final Level of Review
NEBRASKA							
Adult	GP	1971	Unk.	Yes	Yes	No	Dir., Dept. Corr'l Svs.
	State Ombudsman	1973(c)		Yes	No		
Juvenile	GP (same as adult)						
	Ombudsman (same as adult)						
NEVADA							
Adult	GP	1977(c)	3	Yes	Yes	Yes[36]	Dir., Dept. Prisons
	Mediator	1976		Yes	Yes		
Juvenile--No information received.							
NEW HAMPSHIRE							
Adult	GP[37]	1977	Unk.	Yes	No	No	Warden
Juvenile	GP	1978	3	Yes	Yes	No[38]	Board of Trustees
NEW JERSEY							
Adult	GP	1978	Unk.	Yes	Yes	Yes[39]	Comm'r., Dept. Corrs.
	Ombudsman	1973		No	No		
Juvenile--Same ombudsman as adult.							

36. Inmates participate in decision-making roles in hearing.
37. Information of 3/31/83 states: "Presently, inmate complaints are handled individually through the use of request/complaint forms which are forwarded to appropriate agency within the prison."
38. A student grievance committee screens complaints at first level.
39. Inmates participate in decision-making roles in hearing.

Jurisdiction	Type of System	Date Begun	No. of Levels	Responses: In Writing	Responses: Within Time Limits	Formal Hearing	Final Level of Review
NEW MEXICO							
Adult	GP	1974[40]	Unk.	Yes	Yes	Yes	Secy., Dept. Corrs.
	GP	1982	4	Yes	Yes	Yes	Secy., Dept. Corrs.
Juvenile	GP	1970[41]	5	Yes	Yes	No	Secy., Dept. Corrs.
	GP	1975[42]	5	Yes	Yes	Yes	Dir., Juv. Insts. Div.
NEW YORK							
Adult	GP[43]	1976	4	Yes	Yes	Yes[44]	Comm'r.,[45] Dept. Corr'l. Services
Juvenile	Ombudsman	1972		Yes	Yes	Yes	
	GP[46]	1983	4	Yes	Yes	Yes	Dir.,[47] Div. for Youth

40. Reported in 1979.
41. At New Mexico Youth Diagnostic Center, Albuquerque.
42. At New Mexico Boys' School, Springer.
43. In 1972 an Inspector General Service was established to investigate inmate complaints; its fate is unknown.
44. First level committee: 2 inmates and 2 staff; non-voting chairperson may be an inmate.
45. State Commission on Corrections, the fourth level of review, may delegate its function to independent arbitrator. The Commissioner, Dept. of Corrections Services, may accept or reject recommendation of the Commission and/or independent arbitrator.
46. Inmates serve in equal number as staff at second level of review.
47. Grievant may request advisory opinion of an independent review board.

Jurisdiction	Type of System	Date Begun	No. of Levels	Responses: In Writing	Responses: Within Time Limits	Formal Hearing	Final Level of Review
NORTH CAROLINA							
Adult and Youth Services Complex	GP and Grievance Commission	1975	4	Yes	Yes	Yes	Secy., Dept. Corr.
Juvenile	GP	1979	4	Yes	Yes	Yes	Treatment Team[48]
NORTH DAKOTA							
Adult	GP	1972	4	Yes	Yes	Yes	Dir. of Institutions
Juvenile--Disciplinary actions, release dates, and treatment decisions are appealable under three different processes.							
OHIO							
Adult	Ombudsman[49]	1972-75		Unk.	Unk.	Unk.	
	GP	1972	3	Yes	Yes	No	Chief Inspector, Dept. Rehab. & Corrs.
Juvenile--No grievance procedure.							
OKLAHOMA							
Adult	GP	1978	3	Yes	Yes	No	Dir., Dept. Corrs.
Juvenile--Superintendent, staff and students attempt resolution of grievances within ten days. Unresolved grievances are reviewed periodically.							

48. The third and fourth levels of review are not available for complaints regarding the grievant's level status.
49. Origin, procedure and reason for demise of ombudsman program given in Chapter III.

Jurisdiction	Type of System	Date Begun	No. of Levels	Responses: In Writing	Responses: Within Time Limits	Formal Hearing	Final Level of Review
OREGON							
Adult	Ombudsman[50]	1971-81					
	GP	1977	3	Yes	Yes	Yes	Admin. Corr's. Div.
Juvenile	GP	1982	5	Yes	Yes	Yes	Supt. /Court of Appeals[51]
PENNSYLVANIA							
Adult	GP	1976-83	2	Yes	Yes	No	Comm'r., Bur. Corr.
	GP	1983	3	Yes	Yes	Yes	Warden/Comm'r. Bureau Corr.[52]
Juvenile--Each institution has an internal grievance procedure.							
RHODE ISLAND							
Adult	GP	1980	4	Yes	Yes	Yes	Dir., Dept. Corrs.
Juvenile	GP	1979	3	Yes	Yes	Yes	Outside Reviewer/Asst. Dir. Inst'l. Svs.
SOUTH CAROLINA							
Adult	Ombudsman	1972		No	Yes		
	GP[53]	1977	4	Yes	Yes	Yes[54]	Outside Review/Comm'r. Dept. Corrs.
Juvenile	Ombudsman (same as for adults)						

50. Reason for demise of ombudsman program given in Chapter III.
51. If issue concerns disciplinary action it may be appealed to Court of Appeals; otherwise, superintendent is final level of review.
52. Warden is final level of review on issues covered by bureau directives or policies.
53. GP functions in some but not all institutions.
54. Inmates participate in decision-making roles in hearing.

Jurisdiction	Type of System	Date Begun	No. of Levels	Responses: In Writing	Responses: Within Time Limits	Formal Hearing	Final Level of Review
SOUTH DAKOTA							
Adult	GP	1977	4	Yes	Yes	Yes	Exec. Dir., Bd. of Charities and Corrs.
Juvenile--Same as adult.							
TENNESSEE							
Adult	GP	1976	4	Yes	Yes	Yes[55]	Comm'r., Dept. Corr.
Youth and Juveniles	GP[56]	1979	4	Yes	Yes	Yes	Comm'r., Dept. Corr.
TEXAS							
Adult	GP	1975	2	Yes	Yes	No	Dir., Dept. Corrs.
Juvenile	GP	1976	3[57]	Yes	Soon as Possible	Yes[58]	Exec. Dir., Texas Youth Council
UTAH							
Adult	GP	1972	3	Yes	Yes	No	Dir., Div. Corrs.
Juvenile	GP	Unk.	2	Unk.	Unk.	Unk.	Superintendent
VERMONT							
Adult	GP	1978	2	Yes	Yes	Yes[59]	Comm'r., Dept. Corrs.
Juvenile--No state facilities for juveniles							

55. Inmates participate in decision-making roles in hearing.
56. As of May, 1983, GP in only one institution; being developed in remaining four.
57. Grievance subject matter determines whether all levels are used.
58. Inmates participate in decision-making roles in hearing.
59. Inmates participate in decision-making roles in hearing.

Jurisdiction	Type of System	Date Begun	No. of Levels	Responses: In Writing	Responses: Within Time Limits	Formal Hearing	Final Level of Review
VIRGINIA							
Adult	GP	1974	4	Yes	Yes	Yes	Dir., Dept. Corrs.
Juvenile--As of March, 1983, GP being initiated in all facilities.							
WASHINGTON							
Adult	GP	1976[60]	Unk.	No	No	Yes	Warden
	GP	1981	4	Yes	Yes	No	Secy., Dept. Corrs.
Juvenile	GP	1982	3	Yes	Yes	Yes	Outside Review/Dir. Div. Juvenile Rehabil.
WEST VIRGINIA							
Adult	GP	1977	2	Yes	Yes	Yes	Comm'r., Dept. Corrs.
Juvenile--Same as adult.							
WISCONSIN							
Adult	GP	1972	3	Yes	Yes	Yes[61]	Secy., Dept. Health and Social Services
Juvenile--Same as adult.							

60. This may have been operative only at Washington State Penitentiary, Walla Walla. Inmates participated in decision-making roles in hearing.

61. At first level, institution superintendent, the issue may be referred for advisory opinion to a Complaint Advisory Board composed of two inmates and two staff.

Jurisdiction	Type of System	Date Begun	No. of Levels	Responses: In Writing	Responses: Within Time Limits	Formal Hearing	Final Level of Review
WYOMING							
Adult	GP[62]	1977	Unk.	Yes	Yes	Yes	St. Bd., Charities and Reform
	GP[63]	1983	2	Yes	Yes	Yes[64]	St. Bd., Charities and Reform
	GP[65]	Unk.[66]	3	Yes	Yes	Yes	Warden/Outside Review
Juvenile	GP[67]	Unk.	2	Unk.	Unk.	Unk.	Superintendent

62. Applied only to Wyoming State Penitentiary, Rawlins.
63. Applies to Wyoming State Penitentiary, and Wyoming Honor Farm, Riverton.
64. Inmates participate in decision-making roles if issue challenges general policy or practice.
65. Applies only to Wyoming Women's Center, Evanston.
66. Outside review is made by three persons: chairperson is someone not on institution staff; one member appointed by warden; one member, chosen by grievant, may be a staff member, inmate, or an approved volunteer.
67. Applies to Wyoming Girls' School, Sheridan, and Wyoming Industrial Institute, Worland.

Jurisdiction	Type of System	Date Begun	No. of Levels	Responses: In Writing	Responses: Within Time Limits	Formal Hearing	Final Level of Review
FEDERAL PRISON SYSTEM	GP	1973[68]	3	Yes	Yes	No	Gen. Counsel, F. P. S.
COUNTY OF COOK, ILLINOIS	GP	1983	3	Yes	Yes	No	Exec. Dir., Dept. Corrs.
DISTRICT OF COLUMBIA	GP	1978	3	Yes	Yes	No	Dir., Dept. Corrs.
CITY OF NEW YORK	GP	1982	4	Yes	Yes	Yes[69]	Comm'r., Dept. Corrs.
CITY OF PHILADELPHIA	GP	1981	4	Yes	Yes	Yes[70]	Grievance Appeals Committee/Warden
WESTCHESTER COUNTY, NEW YORK	GP	1981	5	Yes	Yes	Yes	Comm'r., Dept. Corr. / State Comm. of Corr.

68. Beginning in September, 1973, procedure test-piloted at four institutions. On October 18, 1974, procedure became effective at all institutions.

69. Two inmates, elected by peers, serve as voting members, as do two staff members, on Inmate Grievance Resolution Committee. A fifth member, who is non-voting chairperson, may be a staff member, volunteer associated with the institution, or a civilian grievance coordinator.

70. Three-member internal grievance committee includes one inmate. Four-member grievance appeals committee which considers appeals from warden's decisions includes one inmate.

Notes

1. *Prevention and Control of Conflict in Corrections*, Final Report, Center for Community Justice, Washington, D.C., April 15, 1979 (LEAA Grant ED-99-0009, October, 1975-December 31, 1978), pp. 1-2.
2. Dillingham, David D., and Singer, Linda R. *Complaint Procedures in Prisons and Jails: An Examination of Recent Experience.* Washington, D.C.: National Institute of Corrections, U.S. Dept. of Justice, 1980.
3. Keating, McArthur, Lewis, Sebelius, Singer. *Grievance Mechanisms in Correctional Institutions.* Washington, D.C.: National Institute of Law Enforcement and Criminal Justice, U.S. Dept. of Justice, 1975, p. 6.
4. Flynn, Edith E., Ph.D. "Sources of Collective Violence in Correctional Institutions," National Institute of Law Enforcement and Criminal Justice, *Criminal Justice Monograph: Prevention of Violence in Correctional Institutions*, 1973, p. 28.
5. Dillingham, David D., and Singer, Linda R., *op. cit.*, pp. 3-4.
6. McArthur, Virginia A. "Inmate Grievance Mechanisms: A Survey of 209 American Prisons," *Federal Probation*, December 1974, p. 44.
7. *Op. cit.*, p. 1.
8. Keating, et al., *op. cit.*, pp. 15-16.
9. *Ibid.*
10. Dillingham, David D., and Singer, Linda R., *op. cit.*, p. 52.
11. Bookwalter, James R. "A Response to: Complaint Procedures in Prisons and Jails; An Examination of Recent Experience," Office of the Connecticut Correctional Ombudsman, The Hartford Institute of Criminal and Social Justice, Hartford, Connecticut, December 1981.
12. Keating, et al., *op. cit.*, p. 18.
13. Dillingham, David D., and Singer, Linda R., *op. cit.* p. 5.
14. Keating, et al., *op. cit.*, p. 33.
15. *A Model Act for the Protection of Rights of Prisoners.* National Council on Crime and Delinquency, 1972, p. 10.
16. *Manual of Standards for the Administration of Correctional Agencies.* Commission on Accreditation for Corrections, 1979, p. 8.
17. Reports of the Comptroller General of the United States: *Grievance Mechanisms in State Correctional Institutions and Large City Jails.* Washington, D.C.: U.S. General Accounting Office, June 17, 1977.
    Managers Need Comprehensive Systems for Assessing Effectiveness and Operation of Inmate Grievance Mechanisms. Washington, D.C.: U.S. General Accounting Office, October 17, 1977.
18. Keating, et al., *op. cit.*, p. 23.

CHAPTER III

THE STATES

Although there is no common correctional administration model in the United States, all correctional residential facilities are under a central administration. New Hampshire was the last state to centralize when it established a Department of Corrections on August 1, 1983. In some states, both adult and juvenile facilities are under a single department or division of a department. As a rule, facilities for juvenile offenders are administered by an agency independent of adult corrections. That agency is often an element of a larger organization.

With increasing frequency, state officials have restructured their adult and juvenile corrections agencies during the past two decades. The reorganizations have, in almost every instance, involved consolidating corrections administration into fewer agencies.

Despite the variety of organizational structures in all the states, most share a past history of and/or a current experience with all or some of the programs designed to include the offender in the operational dynamics of correctional residential facilities, i.e., ombudsmen, grievance commissions, multi-level grievance procedures and inmate advisory councils. However, all too frequently a practioner may be totally unaware of either the past or the present in this regard in his own state or, in some instances, in his own institution. For example, during the course of surveys made in 1966-67 and 1972-73, occasionally the first response received from a state or an institution administration was that no self-government or advisory council program had ever existed. With leads provided to them, these same respondents were often able to find the details of prior programs.

The foregoing gives rise to the question of just how much valuable information about other programs lies buried in forgotten files. How much and what kinds of experiences have been relegated to oblivion as corrections has coped with its problems on a crisis-oriented basis? It has been said that of all American enterprises, corrections apparently has been the least dependent on organized facts, either past or present. The validity of this observation is the result of several factors, of which two seem to be major.

First, corrections has always been and largely remains a mix of facilities and programs whose operations are administratively fragmented among many governmental levels. This mix has been in a continual state of flux, as society has struggled to define its attitude toward the ever-growing problem of what to do about those who offend the social order.

Second, the turnover of personnel in corrections has been of such magnitude that continuity of programs and the establishment of a rational data system on which to base planning, monitoring, and evaluation have been nigh impossible in many jurisdictions. For instance, a 1981[1] study of the 50 states, the District of Columbia, and the New York City corrections organizations revealed changes of chief administrators as follows:

18 in 1980
19 in 1979
18 in 1978
14 in 1977
13 in 1976

In 1981, only eight state corrections departments had the same chief as in 1970 and only 18 had the same chief as in 1978. In the period 1976-1980, eight states changed leadership three times; two changed four times.

The foregoing changes represent only the tip of the iceberg. Each exodus of a director/commissioner/secretary/administrator activates a chain reaction in which wardens, deputy wardens, and numerous others, usually administrative aides and central office personnel, are replaced. In most jurisdictions the positions mentioned are not covered by a merit system, and are subject to summary dismissal with each change of administration.

The tempo of change in correctional administration continues unabated. As an example: the American Correctional Association publishes informational directories each year, usually in November or December, containing comprehensive data on the nation's prisons, jails and detention centers, and probation, parole and after-care services based on information supplied by the institutions and agencies as of July 1 each year. However, it is impossible for the information to be completely accurate when published because of the volatility of corrections and the political influences that have major effects on personnel.[2]

The 1967 report of the President's Commission on Law Enforcement and Administration of Justice, and the subsequent creation in 1968 of the Law Enforcement Assistance Administration under the provisions of the Omnibus Crime Control and Safe Streets Act, did much toward mobilizing public and legislative support for improvement and innovation in correctional services. Only an informed public can be an interested public. And only an interested public can resolve the paradox in the handling of offenders, establish realistic objectives for corrections, and provide the means to insure the realization of these objectives. Although the Law Enforcement Assistance Administration was discontinued in 1982, correctional training and research is being continued by the National Institute of Corrections, the American Correctional Association, and the Federal Prison System.

Considerable progress has been made in the past decade-and-a-half to alleviate, if not resolve, the problems of recruitment and retention which have plagued corrections, especially prisons. For some years, federal funds were available through the Law Enforcement Education Program (LEEP) to assist not only students interested in preparing for a career in corrections, but also correctional personnel wishing to augment their education. The same period saw a tremendous rise in the number of colleges and universities offering curricula concerned with corrections. Despite a diminishment of federal funding, corrections curricula offerings yet survive. Such programs, together with the somewhat phenomenal growth of in-service training programs in all jurisdictions, sustain the hope that correctional institutions will be increasingly staffed by persons with a professional education or a professional attitude (or both, since one usually nurtures the other).

As previously noted, intervention by the courts as a result of inmate initiatives has brought about a reexamination of attitudes and procedures within every corrections jurisdiction. Additionally, the growing ranks of professional corrections workers have had a significant impact on correctional philosophy and practice, not the least of which is the importance of establishing a viable system of communication between inmates and all levels of staff. The past and present of those efforts are related in this chapter.

Notes

1. Terrell, Don Hutto, "Legislative-Legal Issues and Liability-Regaining the Policy Initiative." 1981 Proceedings, 111th Annual Congress of Correction, American Correctional Association, pp. 161-164.
2. 1983 Directory, Juvenile and Adult Correctional Departments, Institutions, Agencies and Paroling Authorities, American Correctional Association, p. v. (The other two directories published annually by the American Correctional Association are the National Jail and Adult Detention Directory and the Probation and Parole Directory.)

ALABAMA

Department of Corrections

The Department of Corrections administers ten institutions for adult felony offenders, and 14 community-based facilities.

An Ombudsman makes regular visits to the institutions to process inmate grievances. No specifics of the program were provided. A 1980 report indicated that an Ombudsman program was established February 15, 1978; also, a grievance procedure was established in 1977, in which written responses were required. However, no formal hearings were provided for. The Warden was the final level of appeal.[1]

According to recent information, the Ombudsman position was abolished in late 1982 or early 1983. The grievance procedure was revised in May, 1983, and a new procedure was established on July 7, 1983. Other than it being a multilevel procedure, no other details were given.[2]

Currently, inmate councils recommend the disbursement of available welfare funds.[3] In 1973 it was reported that half the profits from a canteen at each institution, and commissions from inmates' purchases of craft materials, were credited to an inmate welfare fund controlled by a welfare committee comprised of inmates appointed by the Warden.[4]

Although in 1966 it was reported that there was no current program involving inmates in institution administration,[5] by 1973 each major institution had an inmate council. Councils had been established to afford a better means of inmate-staff communication. Council members were reportedly elected on a representative basis. However, some inmates stated that usually only a tiny percentage of the inmate population participated in the elections, and only a few inmates were aware of the actual functions of the councils.[6]

Department of Youth Services

In 1973, the Department of Youth Services was created by an act of the State Legislature, replacing the Board of Trustees at each of the three institutions. All commitments to the Department are processed at the co-educational Diagnostic and Evaluation Center, Mount Meigs, Alabama, from where placement is made, in accordance with individual needs identified in a treatment plan, to one of three institutions, four group homes, or the work release center.[7]

An Ombudsman of the Department Advocacy Unit is responsible for investigating any alleged abuse and mistreatment, by either staff or another student, reported by a student on a complaint form. The Ombudsman is described as a fact finder, not a decision maker, who may act as a spokesman at any level of the procedure if so requested by the student. The Ombudsman visits each of the three institutions on an assigned day, and as needed at the group homes and the work release center. Each student is advised at the Diagnostic and Evaluation Center of the right to fair and equitable treatment and in an Acknowledgment of Rights Form (signed by the student and countersigned by a staff member) agrees to the understanding "... that I must be reasonable and responsible when filing a complaint and should not file a grievance just to get even with someone ... if I deliberately lie or slander someone, disciplinary action will be taken against me." An Operational Manual contains a proviso guarding the student against any reprisal, punishment, or negative happening for using the grievance procedure, and states that such an occurrence is grounds for a grievance.

Grievances concerning programmatic and discipline procedures are first considered by the facility staff, whose decision may be appealed to the Ombudsman, who attempts to resolve the issue at its point of origin within ten working days. Successive appeals may be made to the following, who must reply within the number of working days indicated:

Facility Head	- 7
Student Review Committee	- 10
Department Director	- 10

As a final step, a student may appeal to one of the State Circuit Courts.[8]

In 1973, it was reported that while there was no student council at the Alabama Youth Services-Vacca Campus (until 1975, the Alabama Boys' Industrial School), Birmingham, in each cottage "Lieutenants" assisted in the supervision of other boys, and all boys were encouraged to make suggestions regarding procedure and program.[9]

In 1971 and through early 1972, a pre-release program was developed under a Law Enforcement Assistance Administration grant at the Alabama Youth Services-Mt. Meigs Campus (until 1975 the Alabama Industrial School). A feature of the program was the development of a self-governing unit. The group process was the methodology of choice of the trained staff who implemented the program. The dynamics of resident turnover soon resulted in the orientation of new arrivals in the unit by those already there. Rules of self-governing behavior emerged as the groups acquired expertise. Additional efforts were underway to involve students in self-governing behavior in 1973.[10]

At the Alabama Youth Services-Chalkville Campus (until 1975 the State Training School for Girls), Birmingham, planning was commenced in the latter part of 1971 to initiate treatment through modern programs. This required much study, considerable planning, and intensive staff training. The latter included extensive leadership training in behavior modification and sensitivity training to impress staff with the need for change and ways to cope with it. The students became involved in policy changes, program planning and campus government. In November 1972, announcement was made of a plan to elect in each of the four cottages a Cottage Council to be composed of a president, vice-president, secretary, cottage recreation leader, and a representative to a Campus Council Committee. The latter group was to include the president and representative of each Cottage Council as interim members until an election was held.[11]

Notes

1. Letter from Associate Commissioner Merle R. Friesen, Ed.D., Dept. of Corrections, Montgomery, September 28, 1982; Dillingham, David D., and Singer, Linda R. Complaint Procedures in Prisons and Jails: An Examination of Recent Experience. Washington, D.C.: National Institute of Corrections, U.S. Dept. of Justice, 1980, p. 50.
2. Telephone conversation with Sarah Sellers, Dept. Grievance Officer, Dept. of Corrections, Montgomery, September 6, 1983.
3. Letter from Associate Commissioner Merle R. Friesen, op. cit.
4. Alabama Prisons, report of the Alabama Advisory Committee to the U.S. Commission on Civil Rights, November 1974, p. 26.
5. Baker, J.E. The Right to Participate: Inmate Involvement in Prison Administration. Metuchen, N J.: The Scarecrow Press, 1974, p. 87.
6. Alabama Prisons, op. cit., pp. 26-27.
7. Letters from John E. Moore, Program Specialist for Advocacy, Dept. of Youth Services, Mt. Meigs, September 29, 1982; October 15, 1982.
8. Operational Manual, Advocacy Unit (amended), Alabama Dept. of Youth Services.
9. Baker, J.E., op. cit., p. 87.
10. Ibid., pp. 87-88.
11. Ibid., p. 88.

ALASKA

Division of Adult Corrections

The Division of Adult Corrections, Department of Health and Social Services, administers all institutions for adult and youthful felony and misdemeanor offenders. Until 1982 the Division also administered the facilities for juvenile offenders.

An Inmate Grievance Procedure, established in 1977, provided for written responses within specified time limits. No formal hearing was held on any grievance. The final level of appeal was the Director, Division of Corrections.[1]

In July 1983 a new policy was written requiring grievances of prisoners in adult institutions to conform to Commission on Accreditation for Corrections standards. Under the tri-level procedure, an inmate may file a written complaint via a prescribed form if attempts to resolve the problem through discussion with concerned staff have failed. The shift supervisor assigns an employee to conduct an investigation and, within five working days, ensure that the requested relief is granted, or give a written report to the institution superintendent indicating findings and recommending whether or not the complaint is frivolous and requires no further action or merits additional investigation. The superintendent must reply in writing within five working days. An appeal may be made to the final level of review, the Director, Division of Adult Corrections. A written response must be given in the subsequent fifteen working days.[2]

Exceptions to the grievance procedures are disciplinary actions, decisions of the Parole Board or any agency outside the Division of Adult Corrections, and classification matters such as institution placement and security designation. The policy ensures the right of every prisoner to use the grievance procedure without fear of reprisal.

A state Ombudsman was authorized by the legislature, effective April 15, 1975, to investigate complaints from aggrieved persons and to investigate the administrative acts of agencies on his or her own motion. The office began operations July 1, 1975. Findings of the Ombudsman may be reported to state agencies or to the public. On July 1, 1978, a special position to work only with corrections issues was established. That process remained in effect until 1981 when it was decided that better service could be provided by having each of the three regional offices of Ombudsman respond to complaints from the correctional institutions within its own area.[3]

Inmates of any institution, either adult or juvenile, may register a complaint by telephone, in writing, or during the Ombudsman's visits to the institution. Complaints are investigated, and attempts at resolution made, at the institution. When recommendations will affect overall corrections policy, remedies are sought at the division or department level. A written reply is given to the grievant within ten days. Correctional complaints rose from 192 in 1982 to a projected 738 for 1983.

At the present time (1983) there are no Division of Adult Corrections directives regarding inmate advisory councils.

From circa 1980 to late 1982 there was an inmate council at the Juneau Correctional Center, Juneau, operating under a constitution and by-laws. Its demise was attributed to inmates' lack of interest.[4]

In 1973 it was reported that the situation regarding inmate advisory councils had changed several times during the past few years. At that time, inmate councils were permitted in all institutions, but were not required. The most active group was the Council at the Adult Conservation Camp, Palmer, a minimum security facility (now Palmer Correctional Center). A member of the Council could sit in on a disciplinary committee hearing if requested to do so by the inmate charged with a rule violation. This Council was organized in 1964. The five democratically selected representatives-at-large met monthly with staff members to discuss matters of mutual concern. It was regarded as a well functioning organization whose existence provided a meaningful experience for both inmates and staff.[5]

In a 1966-67 survey it was found that Alaska was then the only state requiring by administrative order the establishment of an inmate council in each of its jails. A representative from each major living area of the jail was selected by the inmates under officer supervision to serve for one month. Men in segregation and those who had received a misconduct report in the preceding two weeks could not be selected. Total representation could not be more than three nor less than two. The group met weekly with a staff committee composed of the superintendent or his designee, an officer selected at large by the jail staff through balloting, and a member of the local probation staff selected by the jail commander with the approval of the chief probation officer. It was required that replies to all questions and problems presented by the Council be made no later than one week after the meeting. Several features of the "Policy Memorandum" on council procedure are interesting and worthy of note, since each was an affirmation of the administration's interest and sincerity:

> (1) One Councilman is permitted to confer with each segregation inmate for a period not to exceed five minutes unless a time extension is granted by the Jail Superintendent, subject only to visual supervision.
> (2) Preferably Council meetings are to be held between nine and eleven a.m. in a suitable room or office, at which coffee is to be available to contribute to an informal, relaxed atmosphere.
> (3) Meetings are to be held despite no items of business to be presented by the Council. The staff is charged with utilizing the time to promote a better understanding of matters in general.
> (4) If he believes the meetings are not being held properly, any representative, either staff or inmate, may send a letter explaining the problem to the Director, Youth and Adult Authority.

Exceptions to the policy were permitted at the Ketchikan and Nome State Jails, at the extreme ends of the state. At these facilities the superintendent contacted the inmates several times a month regarding any complaints they might have. A complex population of sixty-five per cent unsentenced prisoners, disciplinary transfers from the Adult Conservation Camp, and a high turnover at the Anchorage State Jail reportedly made for considerable difficulty in maintaining a balanced council there.[6]

Youth Services

The Youth Services, Department of Health and Social Services, administers the facilities for juvenile delinquents. No information has been received regarding grievance procedures. However, as previously noted, confined juveniles have access to the state Ombudsman's services for the redress of complaints.

A student government program at the McLaughlin Youth Center,

Anchorage, provides a formal structure through which residents can provide suggestions and have input to the decision-making process about their group living situation. Each cottage elects a president, vice-president, secretary, and sergeant-at-arms to serve for a one-month term, to which there is no succession limitation. A staff member is appointed by the cottage director to serve as advisor and to meet weekly with the elected officers. Minutes of each meeting are distributed the following day. Ad hoc committees may be appointed by the president. All suggestions and requests made at a meeting are subsequently responded to by the administration. Reasons are given for decisions made.[7]

Notes

1. Dillingham, David D., and Singer, Linda R., op cit., p. 50; telephone conversation with Allen J. Cooper, Policy and Procedures Coordinator, Division of Adult Corrections, Juneau, June 17, 1983.
2. Administrative Policies and Procedures, "Prisoner Grievances," Division of Adult Corrections, Juneau.
3. Letter from Duncan C. Fowler, Regional Representative, Office of Ombudsman, Juneau, July 5, 1983.
4. Telephone conversation with Allen J. Cooper, op. cit.
5. Baker, J. E., op. cit., p. 88.
6. Ibid., p. 89.
7. Letter from David E. Arnold, Youth Services Administrator, Youth Services, Anchorage, June 7, 1983; memorandum by Dean Dixon, Program Director, McLaughlin Youth Center, Anchorage, May 18, 1983; statement re Student Government, McLaughlin Youth Center.

ARIZONA

Department of Corrections

The Department of Corrections administers seven adult institutions, two juvenile correctional institutions, and eight community correctional centers (three adult and five juvenile).[1]

Under an Administrative Grievance Procedure,[2] any inmate having a complaint is expected to attempt informal resolution through direct personal contact with the appropriate staff member within ten working days of the date on which the basis for the complaint occurred. Failing this, the inmate may file a written complaint which will then be processed through the multi-level procedure, as follows:

1. A staff member appointed by the institution head as Grievance Coordinator will attempt resolution within a period of five working days, documenting such efforts and providing a written reply to the inmate. The Coordinator is responsible for any further processing of the complaint.

2. Rejecting the proposed resolution, the inmate may appeal to the Grievance Review Committee, composed of two staff members and one inmate appointed by the institution head. The latter must have served not less than six months, with no record of disciplinary isolation time for a like period, be literate, and shall have displayed a maturity commensurate with the responsibilities of the position. The committee is required to provide a written response to the inmate, following a hearing, documenting reasons for its decision, within five working days.

3. A decision of the Grievance Review Committee may, within five working days, be appealed to the institution head for review and written response within five working days. Should an extensive investigation be required, an additional five working days may be granted if the inmate agrees in writing. If the complaint concerns a health matter, the inmate may appeal to the Administrator of the Department Health Services. Should the written response from that service not be acceptable to the inmate, appeal may be made to the next level.

4. An appeal within five working days may then be made to the Director (or designee) of the Department of Corrections for review and written response within ten working days.

5. Should the inmate reject the response of the director, an appeal may be made to an Outside Review Committee composed of persons appointed by the Governor from other than Department of Corrections personnel, for review and written response within 15 working days.

6. Suit may be filed by the inmate in the appropriate court if the decision rendered by the Outside Review Committee is not accepted.

A 24-hour response will be made to complaints when the institution head "... determines that normal processing might result in serious physical or psychological harm to an inmate or a threat to the safety or security of the institution."

To ensure that no reprisal will result as a consequence of utilizing the procedure, the Department has specifically forbidden any harassment, punishment, or disciplinary action for so doing, or the filing of written grievances in the inmate's institutional file. A Master File of Grievances is kept in the Director's office.

To discourage the filing of frivolous or repetitive complaints, the Grievance Review Committee is authorized to advise an offender, in writing, that time required for the consideration of such complaints is at the expense of legitimate complaints and that a continuation will result in the return of the complaint unprocessed.

In those instances in which a complaint involves alleged loss or damage of property as a result of staff negligence, and the inmate is seeking reimbursement, the Grievance Coordinator is authorized to conduct an investigation and settle a claim of not more than 25 dollars when staff negligence or Department of Corrections responsibility is determined. The head of the institution, upon recommendation of the Grievance Review Committee, may settle a claim not in excess of 100 dollars. Any recommendation for reimbursement in excess of 100 dollars requires approval by the Assistant Director of Administration. All payments are made from a Department Grievance Reimbursement Fund financed by a one per cent of gross sales levied on each institution canteen.[3]

The Department is exploring the certification process for the Administrative Grievance Procedures under the provisions of Public Law 96-247, the Civil Rights of Institutionalized Persons Act, and is planning to require soon the training and certification of all Grievance Coordinators.[4]

In 1978 the establishment of inmate advisory councils was authorized by a newly appointed Department Director. Currently, all but one of the adult institutions have a council or are developing one. In the juvenile institutions, students participate in student councils and food services meetings. Other inmate organizations and clubs provide inmates the opportunity to voice their opinions on food services and recreational leisure-time activities.[5]

In 1972 it was reported that in the three Community Correctional Centers then in operation, each populated by 12 offenders in their early teens, a family-style participation in the development of behavior standards and the planning of outside activities was regarded as having been successful. However, the administration at that time looked with disfavor upon the establishment of inmate councils in extremely large institutional settings.[6]

Notes

1. Letter from Deborah Lou Roepke, Research Assistant to the Director, Department of Corrections, Phoenix, November 3, 1982.
2. Policy and Procedure No. 430, "Administrative Grievance Procedure for Inmates," Arizona Department of Corrections, January 15, 1981. (A survey made in February, 1977, by CONTACT, INC., Lincoln, Nebraska, of all state Department of Corrections, indicates Arizona reporting a Grievance Procedure. A 1980 publication, Complaint Procedures in Prisons and Jails: An Examination of Recent Experience, by David D. Dillingham and Linda R. Singer, Center for Community Justice, Washington, D.C., listed Arizona as reporting the establishment of a Grievance Procedure in 1975.)
3. Policy and Procedure No. 448, "Grievance--Inmate Reimbursement Procedure, Adult Services," Arizona Department of Corrections, June 17, 1982.

4. Letter from Deborah Lou Roepke, *op. cit.*
5. *Ibid.*
6. J. E. Baker, *op. cit.*, p. 90.

ARKANSAS

Department of Correction

The Department of Correction administers nine adult institutions, including a Diagnostic Unit, Pine Bluff, which opened in 1979, to receive, diagnose, orient and classify each person committed to the custody of the Department.

A multi-level Inmate Grievance Procedure was established in 1974 at the Cummins Unit, Grady (formerly the Arkansas State Penitentiary) and the Tucker Unit, Tucker (first known as the Tucker Intermediate Reformatory, later as the Arkansas Intermediate Reformatory).[1] Other than the Women's Reformatory, Grady (closed in 1975 when the present Women's Unit, Pine Bluff was opened), those were the only institutions in the state system at that time. Currently, all institutions have a Grievance Procedure, established in 1981.[2]

Inmates are encouraged to attempt resolution of a grievance by contacting the immediate supervisor. A grievance is defined as a complaint by an inmate on his/her own behalf regarding an institution policy, a condition within the institution, an action involving another inmate, or an incident having an impact on the grievant. Probation and/or parole matters are excluded, as are appeals of disciplinary action. A separate procedure is available for the latter.

If the immediate supervisor cannot resolve the grievance, an inmate may submit a written grievance to the Administrative Review Officer. Assistance in completing the grievance form may be sought from the supervisor or a member of the Inmate Council. Within ten working days, or less if an emergency situation exists, the Warden will make a written response setting forth the reason for the decision in clear, well-reasoned terms, with advice that an appeal is possible and showing how it may be obtained. A grievant may declare a situation as an emergency if it is believed that a substantial risk of personal injury or other serious and irreparable harm would result in the time required for ordinary processing.

Appeals may be made to the following levels, from which responses must be made during the time limits cited: Assistant Director--20 working days; Director--30 working days.

The Director, within the time limit allowed, may appoint an Administrative Review Board consisting of an Assistant Director, other than the one who had reviewed the grievance previously, and two other staff members to review the matter and make recommendation for resolution.

Reprisals against an inmate for making use of the procedure are forbidden. Any charge of a reprisal is investigated by the Department Internal Affairs Division, and employees determined to be guilty may be disciplined, the minimum sanction being a written reprimand.

Employees are protected from reprisals for carrying out their responsibilities to execute the procedure.

No record of an inmate's participation in the procedure may be placed in the inmate's file. Access to procedure files is limited to those persons directly involved in the process.

Administrators at each level of the procedure submit an annual report to the Director on inmate use of the procedure, whether such use has resulted in meaningful consideration of complaints and where appropriate and adequate remedies were made. This review and evaluation is sent to the U.S. Attorney General in compliance with the certification requirements of the Civil Rights of Institutionalized Persons Act (Public Law 96-247).

It is assumed that an Inmate Council exists in the institutions because of the statement in the Inmate Handbook that an inmate may seek assistance from a member of that group in completing a grievance form.

In 1972 it was reported that each of the three institutions then in operation had an inmate council whose members were elected to represent their living quarters. The councils made recommendations for expenditures from the Inmate Welfare Fund, sponsored projects promoting the welfare of inmates, and presented to the staff problems of general concern together with suggested solutions.[3]

The constitution and by-laws of the Inmate Council at the then Arkansas State Penitentiary provided for the election of two representatives and one alternate from each living unit to serve a six-month term of office, with tenure limited to two terms. Candidates must have been at the institution for at least two months and have a minimum of six months' time remaining prior to expected release. Additionally, candidates must not have been subjected to major disciplinary action during the three months preceding election, and be in not less than Class II status. The meritorious good-time statute of 1971 provided for a system of grading for the purpose of determining the number of days' sentence-credit to be allowed monthly to each inmate. All newly classified inmates were placed in Class II.[4] A chairman, vice-chairman, and treasurer, elected within the membership, constituted an Executive Committee. Two meetings of the Council were held each month. One meeting was a closed session. At the other, the superintendent or the commissioner of correction was in attendance. Special meetings could be called by the Executive Committee with administration approval. Additional members could be appointed by the chairman subject to approval by the Executive Committee. A permanent Finance Committee composed of two appointed members and the treasurer, the latter serving as chairman, made monthly and semi-annual financial reports. Special committees, each chaired by a Council member, were appointed to carry out specific projects and tasks.[5]

Division of Youth Services

The Division of Youth Services, Department of Human Services, administers two facilities to house adjudicated juvenile delinquents, the Pine Bluff Youth Services Center, Pine Bluff, and the Alexander Youth Services Center, Alexander. An Intake and Evaluation Unit, located within the latter facility, receives all commitments to the Division for diagnostic classification and evaluation services, to determine which of the two facilities, or whether an alternate community-based program, best suits the individual's needs. An Intensive Treatment Unit opened in 1981 within the same facility.[6]

In September, 1978, a grievance procedure was established as a means of resolving student claims of unfair treatment or dissatisfaction with some aspect of confinement subject to control by the Division of Youth Services. A four-member Grievance Committee was appointed by the institution superintendent to represent the administration, treatment services, cottage life, and the student body.[7]

Within 30 days of an alleged incident, a student, with assistance from his/her counselor, may complete a Student Grievance form. The counselor shall attempt resolution through counseling, clarification and/or negotiation. Should the attempt fail, the grievance is forwarded to the Grievance Committee. Within five working days, that group shall review the grievance and conduct a hearing with the student for the purpose of obtaining evidence on which to base a decision, which must be made within two working days following the hearing.[8]

The student may, within three working days after the committee decision, appeal to the superintendent, who must respond within a like period after reviewing the grievance and the efforts already made toward its resolution. At the discretion of the superintendent, a meeting may be held with the grievant.[9]

An appeal from the superintendent's decision may be made within two working days to the final level of review, the Deputy Commissioner, who has a like period to respond, during which meeting with the grievant is discretionary.[10]

No information was received concerning advisory councils. In June 1967 it was reported that no council had ever been established at the four facilities then in operation: The Arkansas Training School for Boys, Pine Bluff (now the Pine Bluff Youth Services Center); the Arkansas Training School for Boys, Wrightsville (now closed); the Arkansas Training School for Girls, Alexander (now the

Alexander Youth Services Center, a co-ed facility); and the Arkansas Training School for Girls, Fargo (now closed).[11]

Notes

1. Corrections Compendium, CONTACT, INC., Lincoln, Nebraska, August, 1977; Dillingham, David D. and Singer, Linda R., Complaint Procedures in Prisons and Jails: an Examination of Recent Experience, Center for Community Justice, 1980, p. 50.
2. "Inmate Handbook," Department of Correction, May, 1981, pp. 19-20(i).
3. Baker, J.E., op. cit., p. 90.
4. This practice is still in effect. "Inmate Handbook," op. cit., pp. 22-23.
5. Baker, J.E., op. cit., pp. 90-91.
6. Letter from Commissioner Scott R. Gordon, Division of Youth Services, Little Rock, September 29, 1982.
7. Ibid.
8. DYS Policy No. 5009, "Student Rights, Dignity, Privileges, and Responsibilities: Student Grievance," September 21, 1978.
9. Ibid.
10. Ibid.
11. Baker, J.E., op. cit., p. 91.

CALIFORNIA

Youth and Adult Correctional Agency

The Youth and Adult Correctional Agency provides institutions for adult and youthful felony offenders and for adjudicated delinquents.

Department of Corrections

The Department of Corrections administers 12 institutions for adult and youthful felony offenders.

A tri-level Inmate Appeal Policy (now the Inmate/Parolee Appeal Procedure) was introduced in 1973 and fully implemented in all adult institutions by mid-1974.[1] Although the procedure applies to any inmate, resident, parolee or outpatient under the jurisdiction of the Department of Corrections, references will be only to confined offenders.

The purpose of the procedure is three-fold:

1. To provide a vehicle for review of staff decisions which may adversely affect an inmate's welfare, status, or program.

2. To provide for the resolution of grievances at the lowest possible level with a timely response to the appellant.

3. To audit the internal processes and operation of the department, to identify, modify, or eliminate practices which may not be necessary or may impede the accomplishment of correctional goals. [2]

All inmates have the right to appeal any decision, action, policy or regulation of the department which is perceived as severely affecting his/her welfare. Appeals (complaints) may include, but are not limited to, matters of classification, transfer, housing, mail, visiting, and lost property. A court decision, in re Muszalski, 52 Cal. App. 3rd 500, held that normally before a writ of habeas corpus is filed by an inmate over a grievance with the department, he or she must first use the departmental appeal procedure. Board of Prison Terms decisions to schedule a hearing may not be appealed. [3]

Within 15 days of the action or decision on which a complaint is based, an inmate must make every effort toward resolution with the appropriate staff member(s). At staff discretion, this time period may be extended. There is no time limit, however, within which to file a complaint on lost or damaged personal property. The warden may delay the implementation of a decision being appealed when the delay will pose no threat to institution security, the safety of persons, or other serious operational problems. Group complaints on the same issue may be made, with one inmate signing as the principal grievant and the others as co-signers. [4]

Should attempts at informal resolution fail, the inmate may then file, on his/her behalf only, a prescribed form with the institution appeals officer, who must be of not less than correctional administrator rank. Assistance in preparing the form by another inmate, a staff member, a family member or other interested person, or the grievant's attorney is permissible at this and subsequent levels of the procedure. [5]

Under certain conditions the appeals officer may refuse to accept a complaint. If the complaint is accepted, the appeals officer will assign it to the appropriate staff member for review and investigation, which must include an interview with the grievant, unless the reviewer decides to grant the request on the basis of the written information given by the inmate. A written response must be made within 15 working days. The response must speak to the complaint issue and set forth the specific decision being rendered. This requirement applies to responses at all levels. [6]

The second level of the procedure is the Warden. The requirement for a personal interview with the grievant, or its waiver, is the same as that for the first level. A written response within ten working days is specified.

The third and final level is the Director, Department of Corrections, who must reply within 20 working days, with the exception of the following conditions:

1. Issues concerning major departmental policy may be submitted to the next scheduled administrators' meeting. A reply must then be made within twenty working days following the meeting.

2. When the institution is under a state of emergency, the time constraints may be suspended by the Warden.

At any level of the procedure, when exceptional delays prevent closure within the specified time limits, the grievant must be given a written reason for the delay and an estimated completion date.[7]

At the Minimum Security Unit, California Institution for Men, Chino, an inmate clerk attempts to resolve potential complaints before they enter the formal procedure. When a complaint is filed, the first level of review is a committee composed of both staff and inmates.[8]

Special procedures are specified in complaints involving property loss or damage. Inmates employed by correctional industries are instructed to submit any complaints concerning perceived health or safety hazards to the Correctional Industries Safety Committee. If after so doing the inmate believes a retaliatory action against him/her has taken place as a result, a complaint may then be filed under the Inmate Appeal Procedure. After exhausting that process, and still of the belief that a retaliatory action occurred, the inmate may then file an appeal directly to the Labor Commissioner in the manner prescribed by the Division of Industrial Safety.[9]

The appeals officer may take certain actions when it has been determined that the procedure is being subjected to abuse which includes a disciplinary charge for knowingly making false or slanderous statements, or the written complaint contains gross derogatory or obscene statements. An excessive number of complaints may result in all but the first one submitted being deferred. Lack of clarity may be reason to return the complaint for revision. Refusal to cooperate in the investigation of a complaint by declining to be interviewed can result in cancellation of the complaint.[10]

No reprisals may be taken against an inmate for use of the procedure. A copy of each complaint, noting the actions taken at all levels, is placed in the inmate's file at the institution and in the department central office.[11]

Inmate councils have been utilized in the adult institutions as a means of direct communication between inmates and staff. Currently, as in the past, the Department of Corrections emphasizes that the councils do not have administrative or executive authority.[12] Department regulations require that the title of a council must adequately convey the advisory role.[13]

Each adult institution warden, under present regulations, is directed to establish an inmate advisory council and a plan for its operation, for two purposes, each held to be of equal importance:

> 1. To provide inmates with representation and a voice in administrative deliberations and decisions affecting the welfare and best interest of all inmates.
> 2. To provide the warden and staff with a means whereby administrative actions, and the reasons for same, may be communicated to and understood by inmates.[14]

Representation must be provided for housing, program, and activity units, and all ethnic segments of the institution population. The staff-supervised election process must be by secret ballot, or by any other democratic means that insures against irregularities, coercion, duress, or reprisal in or resulting from an individual's choice, and guarantees participation by all who so wish. Eligibility for nomination, selection, and retention as a council member may be limited only by the inmate's ability to function effectively in that capacity. Disciplinary violations not reflective of behavior patterns which, if continued, would be detrimental to the council or the individual's effectiveness, will not bar nomination, election, or retention.[15]

Except as specifically authorized by the warden, the council may not function as a grievance committee. However, should the basis for an individual's grievance affect, or be of concern to the institution population, the issue may be called to official attention. The grievance procedure may be used by a council when use of council procedure fails to effect a satisfactory resolution. Any grievance relating to an employee may not be discussed with any employee below the rank of lieutenant or higher-level program supervisor. Members are not permitted to confront employees or threaten recourse to higher authority because of a questioned decision or action. By the same token, employees may not do likewise simply because the inmate is a council member.[16]

Minutes of all formal meetings of a council are required, with intra-institutional and inter-institution distribution as approved by the warden. The council may correspond with legislative and appointed officials, and with news media representatives. At the warden's discretion, such correspondence may be confidential.[17]

All inmates must be kept aware of council topics and discussion results, with conspicuously located bulletin boards mentioned as one means of so doing. In order for all inmates to know who the council candidates and members are, wardens are encouraged to provide them high visibility by publishing photographs and names and by issuing shirts and jackets of such design as to readily identify the wearers. Timely written responses must be made to all issues referred by a council, specifying the action taken, the reasons for it, and a statement of the manner and approximate time of implementation.[18]

Council input on proposed departmental rules, or changes, is obtained by providing copies to which a response may be made by the council or an individual member, either via the warden or directly to the Department Policy Documentation Unit.[19]

All staff members are directed to support the council process. At each institution the warden appoints a coordinator who must be of a relatively high rank. A central office staff member is designated as the departmental liaison with all councils. Wardens are urged to meet with the council no less than once a month.[20]

At a warden's discretion and in keeping with resources available, certain privileges may be granted to council members for services rendered, e.g., establishing council membership as a part or full-time assignment so as to provide the same participation credit available through other work and program assignments, and granting pay status.[21]

Upon good cause, a warden may suspend the membership of an individual or all council activities if there is reason to believe a threat exists to institution security, safety of persons, or the best interests and general welfare of the institution population. The department must be notified of such action and its basis, as must the inmates. Commensurate with security and safety, every effort must be made to reactivate the council as quickly as possible.[22]

The foregoing regulations spell out in much more detail the purposes, policies, and procedures regarding inmates advisory councils than did a 1963 Inmate Activities Manual reported in a previous book.[23]

The California State Prison at San Quentin, established in 1852, is the oldest correctional institution in the state. In the summer of 1941, less than a year after Clinton T. Duffy became Warden, an Inmates' Departmental Representative Committee of thirty-five members was organized to succeed an Inmate Athletic Committee organized in 1940. In a letter dated November 18, 1941, Warden Duffy described the group and said it had paid dividends because the men were permitted to share with officials the problems which face them:

> ... Weekly meetings are held, and suggestions received from the entire inmate body are culled and studied and passed on to the warden with recommendations for approval or disapproval.
>
> The Committee is a sort of clearing house for ideas and 'beefs.' Many of the recent improvements in San Quentin have been brought about through the group. Many matters that would not ordinarily reach the warden's desk are handled by the Inmates' Departmental Representative Committee, and conditions that have prevailed as a matter of course for decades have been remedied by means of the close cooperation which exists between the officials and the Committee.

> The Inmates' Departmental Representative Committee assisted in establishing the canteen; a plan was worked out by committee members for the installation of motion picture and sound equipment; radio programs are worked out by a sub-group of the Committee.
>
> No officials or guards are present during the meetings of the group, unless especially invited. The members have been told, explicitly, by the warden that they are free to discuss any and all matters that pertain to the betterment of conditions in the prison, and that even if their recommendations do not meet with his approval at first, they are at liberty to re-submit them. In other words, Warden Duffy believes the inmates should have the privilege of making themselves heard on any subjects that affect their welfare....[24]

In 1966 it was reported that an Inmate Advisory Council then in operation had been organized in 1944. The administration at that time expressed the opinion that a council system works well in certain areas, such as the serving of equivalent kinds of food at particular meals, but did not believe the real inmate leaders become involved, the example being cited that Council members sometimes were not even aware of portending major disturbances. Conversely, however, it was admitted that Council efforts in resolving many minor grievances no doubt reduce the potential for serious discontent resulting from an accumulation of petty gripes.

The current Men's Advisory Council (no doubt a continuation of the council reported in 1966) operates under a procedure established on February 10, 1967 to promote cooperation among inmates and act as a staff-inmate liaison group. The council is comprised of representatives of the work and housing areas elected by majority vote. There are 16 working committees to consider problems presented to the council. Membership ranges from a minimum of five but is usually 65.[25]

The California State Prison at Folsom, Represa received its first group of prisoners by transfer from San Quentin in July 1880. A maximum security institution, Folsom is programmed for recidivists, management problems, and severe escape risks. An Inmate Advisory Council became active in 1956 under a constitution and bylaws developed in September 1955 and later revised on several occasions, according to information received in 1972. The group, known as the Men's Advisory Council, was composed of 20 members elected to represent their housing units. A chairman, vice-chairman, and secretary were elected within the membership. Meetings were held bi-weekly without staff representation present, and with the warden and other staff members as the need arose. Minutes of all meetings were widely disseminated within the institution. The Council sponsored charity drives and assisted with the selection of movies and radio programs.[26] Currently, there is no inmate council. The last group, Folsom Auxiliary Committee, was suspended in August 1979 by order of the Warden.[27]

The California Correctional Institution at Tehachapi was reopened on January 3, 1955. (Constructed originally as an institution for female prisoners, the facility was so operated until serious earthquake damage forced evacuation in August, 1952.) The initial program was designed to care for parole violators and recidivists who could be managed in a minimum security setting. Late in 1957, a shortage of minimum custody men gave rise to plans for additional security features necessary for conversion to a medium security institution. However, required group counseling for medium security men was substituted for the proposed additional physical security features. This approach was in line with the underlying philosophy at Tehachapi and in 1973 was reported as quite successful.[28]

The community living program, patterned somewhat after Dr. Maxwell Jones' therapeutic community concept, had an Inmate Advisory Council as one of its features. The council was organized soon after the institution opened in 1955, and functioned in accordance with a Department of Corrections Inmate Activities Manual issued in 1963. In August, 1967, a 640-bed Medium Security Unit was opened to house all medium security inmates. By 1973, that Unit had an Inmate Advisory Council, as did the Minimum Security Unit.[29]

At the present time both the Medium Unit and the Minimum Unit have Men's Advisory Councils. The chief function of each is to act as a staff-inmate liaison group. Each is organized under Department of Corrections regulations. In the Medium Unit each dormitory annually elects three councilmen who must be representative of each major ethnic group. At-large members, one for each of the other ethnic groups, are chosen by the council. An Executive Council of five, who may serve only two consecutive terms, is selected by the membership; it includes a chairman, vice-chairman, secretary, sergeant-at-arms, and parliamentarian. The chairman and secretary positions are regarded as full-time assignments and are paid from the Inmate Welfare Fund. Executive Council members are required to become knowledgeable of institution policies and procedures in order to relate more effectively to both inmates and staff. The Minimum Unit Council is similar in organization and procedure.[30]

Business meetings, held weekly with program staff, are conducted in accordance with Roberts' Rules of Order. While this does not eliminate an occasional emotional delivery, the procedure sets the tone of the meeting, which is described as primarily that of relating to the hard facts of prison economics. Not an easy task. The administration within each unit believes that, while inmates must be reasonable and prudent in approaching institution problems, it is equally critical that a sometimes reluctant staff be made to realize that inmates can be a source of assistance in the solution of inmate problems. It is noted that personnel of both units have, as a rule, asked for and received helpful input by inmates regarding critical altercations and disturbances present in the prison environment.[31]

The California Institution for Men, Chino, was opened in 1941. Approximately six months later, when the population numbered 170, problems affecting general morale began to arise and Superintendent Kenyon J. Scudder believed it would be helpful to discuss the matters with representatives of the men. An Advisory Council of ten members representing the housing units was elected by secret ballot. A constitution and by-laws provided weekly meetings with the Superintendent during which no discussion of staff or other inmates was permitted. Various committees assisted in planning and organizing special holiday events, and regular athletic and recreational programs. Term of office was six months. Council officers were a president, secretary, and executive committee of three or four. The Superintendent met alone with the Council believing that this was conducive to freer discussion. Further, it was a means of his "feeling the pulse of the institution." During Superintendent Scudder's 15 years at Chino it was necessary on only two occasions to remove administratively a member who tried to use the council for personal advancement.[32]

Superintendent Scudder consistently emphasized his belief that councils should be of an advisory nature only, and that this can be assured by a carefully drawn constitution, and that a principal purpose of a council is to bring attention to those problems whose impact on the men is unknown to the administration and thus potentially harmful. As an example of the latter, he related an incident which occurred at Chino some years ago:

> Periodically the subject of coffee came up at a meeting. Any correctional administrator knows the value of good coffee. The men wanted to know why the taste of the coffee varied so from week to week. We asked the Chief Steward to discuss this with the Council. He told the Council that we had the best equipment for making coffee and the coffee was the same as that for personnel. It was a case of the man on the coffee assignment simply not doing his job. The Chief Steward thanked the Council for calling the matter to attention, then took the opportunity to discuss ration procedures. The reaction of the Council was good, especially the next morning when the coffee was pronounced excellent.[33]

Early in 1966 the Chino Advisory Council was discontinued, having reportedly lost the confidence of the responsible inmates. This was attributed to the nomination of poorly qualified persons, for instance, the "clown," and the seeking of membership by militant individuals. The Council was replaced with a procedure under which a representative from each housing unit met with the Superintendent once a month. Reportedly, these meetings seemed to accomplish the same objectives as did the Council.[34]

In 1973 it was reported that the Chino institution was a complex of four facilities encompassing the Southern Reception Guidance Center; a Medium Security Unit which functioned as a reception center for the complex; a Minimum Security Unit which was an academic and vocational education center; and a new 400-man unit to be probably designated as Reception Guidance Center-East. A short time prior to the 1973 report, a Men's Advisory Council was organized. An inmate committee, with a staff advisor, was preparing a constitution and by-laws, the format of which was expected to follow along previous lines to allow for maximum inmate representation to the administrative staff.[35]

The four facilities at Chino are now designated: CIM-Minimum Reception Center-Central; Reception Center-West; CIM-East. Each has a Men's Advisory Council whose purpose is two-fold: to provide inmates a representative voice in administrative deliberations affecting their welfare and best interest, and to establish a vehicle by which administrative actions and their basis may be communicated to inmates. The councils have been very active and of use to the administration in calling attention to problem areas and in relaying policy changes to the inmates.[36]

The CIM-Minimum council has 27 members and one clerk. Three representatives are elected by majority vote from each housing unit: one white, one black, and one hispanic. The Reception Center-Central council represents the permanent work crew inmates of the facility (the remainder being new commitments for processing). The council has a membership of three, elected by majority vote: one white, one black, and one hispanic. The Reception Center-West council also represents only the inmates permanently assigned to work crews. Membership consists of two persons from each of the previously mentioned ethnic groups. Election is by majority vote. The CIM-East facility is presently in a period of transition from a protective custody unit to one of medium security. When the conversion is completed, a racially balanced council will be elected by majority vote.[37]

The Correctional Training Facility, Soledad, originally consisted of three distinct facilities. An Inmate Advisory Council was established as each facility was opened: South Facility in January, 1948; Central Facility in July, 1952; and North Facility on December 1, 1958. South Facility was closed on January 3, 1970. In 1973, the councils in North and Central Facilities were still in operation. Any inmate who had been nominated by three others could become a nominee for a 12-month term of office as a representative of his housing unit, providing he had been at the facility a minimum of six months, had at least ten months to serve, and his record of adjustment warranted approval by the administration. Elections were by secret ballot. There were ten permanent committees, including an executive committee composed of a chairman, vice-chairman, secretary, and sergeant-at-arms, which met with the administration at the call of the latter.[38] No current information has been received regarding the council.

The Deuel Vocational Institution, Tracy, was moved to its present location in July, 1953, following use of a temporary site on the desert near Lancaster since 1946. An Inmate Advisory Council was established in March, 1958. The name was later changed to Men's Advisory Council. A constitution provided for secret ballot election of three representatives from each housing unit to serve terms of six months. The chairman, vice-chairman, secretary and sergeant-at-arms composed an Executive Committee which met monthly with the administration to discuss topics referred from meetings of the full council membership.[39] The council was disbanded in 1977 due to its loss of trust and credibility among the inmates and because of its unreasonable demands on the administration. In 1979 an informal committee was selected by a Program Administrator to re-establish the avenue of administration-inmate communication lost by disbandment of the previous council. Initially, a considerable degree of suspicion and skepticism was manifested by the population toward those selected as committee members. However, as time passed, trust in the committee grew and communication was enhanced. Eventually the committee came to be referred to as the Convict Communication Committee. The group has no formalized constitution. Each of the seven general population housing units is represented by three committee members who are selected by the Program Administrator on the basis of each individual's popularity with his peers, maturity, interest in carrying out committee member duties, and personal credibility. At any time the Program Administrator can remove an inmate from committee membership. The twenty-one members present issues of constituent concern to a nine-member Central Committee. If necessary, the latter group can contact the Program Administrator daily on such issues. The administration reports the committee as being helpful in maintaining a daily reading of population climate.[40]

The mission of the California Medical Facility, Vacaville, is to provide medical and psychiatric services to disturbed inmates in the population of the Department of Corrections. In 1972, the institution also served as a reception and guidance center for all newly committed felons for the 47 northern counties. It was reported that a Men's Advisory Council was established under a constitution and by-laws adopted on September 9, 1963, and revised periodically afterward. Council objectives included encouragement to inmates to be interested and participate actively in the advancement of the institution by contributing advice and suggestions for the improvement of the conditions under which they live. An Executive Committee met monthly with the Superintendent and his executive staff.[41]

A Men's Advisory Council is currently active in the facility, operating under a constitution and by-laws originally adopted in March, 1981. The Correctional Administrator, Custody/Operations is the staff advisor to the group, which consists of 30 voting members, each elected to a one-year term of office to represent the various housing units and racial and ethnic groups. From its members the council elects an executive body, consisting of a chairman, vice-chairman, executive secretary, executive treasurer, and executive public information officer, which meets weekly with the staff advisor, and monthly with the advisor, the associate superintendent for Business

Services and the superintendent. Volunteers from the institution population may be, by two-thirds vote of the council, appointed as ad hoc members to provide abilities and knowledge vital to council functions. The full council meets twice a month. Special meetings may be called at any time by the executive body. There are eight standing committees, any of which may meet at the call of its chairman and two members. Meetings of the council and all committees are governed generally by Roberts' Rules of Order. The constitution provides for the recall and/or impeachment of any council member who has a poor work record, does not properly represent the inmates, or conducts himself in such manner as to be discreditable and detrimental to the council.[42]

The California Men's Colony, San Luis Obispo, is composed of four quads, each with two 600-man buildings arranged in 50-man living units. In 1972 the following information, obtained in 1966, was reviewed by the institution administration, which made no changes.

An Inmate Advisory Council was active in each of the two existing facilities within the institution (West, opened in 1954, and East, opened in 1961). An institution general order provided guidelines for the formation of groups and stressed the development of those habits and skills of membership most likely to be transferrable to community organizations, such as Alcoholics Anonymous. A constitution and by-laws set forth the procedures of each council.

A Resident Advisory Council, organized shortly after the opening of the West Facility in 1954, had reportedly operated successfully. Meetings were held on the housing unit level and all decisions requiring administrative action were forwarded by an officer who monitored the meeting.

An Inmate Advisory Council was organized in the East Facility soon after its opening in 1961. The Facility was divided into four quads and council meetings were held on that level. The council was abandoned for approximately a year when it was determined to have been a factor behind a food demonstration. It was reestablished, however, and was reported as operating satisfactorily.[43]

Currently, a Men's Advisory Council is operating in each of the four quads under a constitution and by-laws dated December, 1981. Each of the 50-man units elects by secret ballot one representative to serve a one-year term of office. Representation must encompass all ethnic groups in the population. From its members, the council elects a chairman, vice-chairman, secretary, and sergeant-at-arms to serve as an Executive Committee. The chairman appoints council members to six standing committees and other subcommittees as needed. The council meets twice monthly, one of the meetings being with the Program Administrator who acts as staff liaison. Meetings with the superintendent as scheduled by him are attended by the chairman and secretary of each quad council. All meetings are conducted under Roberts' Rules of Order and minutes are subsequently distributed to the Program Administrator and other administrative staff. A process for recall of councilmen and/or executive committee members is provided in the constitution.[44]

The California Conservation Center, Susanville, opened in February 1963. An Inmate Advisory Council was organized soon afterwards. Emphasis was placed on the advisory nature of its functions. According to a 1966 report, no serious incidents or problems had been encountered and the administration had had no occasion to consider discontinuing the group. Non-involvement in disciplinary action for a 90-day period was the membership eligibility requirement given in the constitution and by-laws, with representation by housing units, four members for each.[45]

Presently, a Men's Advisory Council is composed of 34 members elected to serve a six-month term of office by their peers in each of the two program units. The electees of each unit must include five white, five black, five Mexican-American, one Asian, and one American Indian inmate. Each unit also elects a four-man Executive Committee from the council members. The council meets weekly; the executive committee meets once a month during which an agenda is prepared for a subsequent meeting with the superintendent. With approval of two-thirds of the members, the chairman appoints councilmen to serve on five standing committees. Two paying positions have been established for equal distribution between each council. Any member may be removed from office for cause upon petition of no less than two-thirds of the ethnic group he represents, for example, three or more unwarranted or two consecutive absences from council meetings.[46]

An Inmate Advisory Council at the Southern Conservation Center, Chino, was organized in 1963 when the facility was the Chino Branch of the California Rehabilitation Center. Officially established on August 1, 1964, to assist the superintendent in determining inmate reaction and the welfare of the inmate body as a whole, the council reportedly served these purposes very well. Guidelines for operation were set forth in an institution administrative order. A constitution provided for the secret ballot election, every 90 days, of one representative. Eligibility for membership was limited to those free from disciplinary action during the month prior to election. By 1973, the camp had been redesignated as Unit D., the Medium Security facility of the California Institution for Men Complex, Chino.[47]

According to information received in 1966, the Sierra Conservation Center, Jamestown, opened on July 15, 1965, and organized an Inmate Advisory Council in its minimum custody unit and its medium custody unit on April 1, 1966. The constitution and bylaws of the minimum custody unit (Calaveras) provided for the secret ballot election of one representative from each housing unit to a six-month term. No qualifications of conduct or length of time served were noted. Six standing committees were authorized, including an Executive Committee composed of the council officers, the chairman, vice-chairman, executive secretary, vice-secretary and sergeant-at-arms.

Today the Sierra Conservation Center provides housing for approximately 1600 inmates in two housing units, one medium custody, the other minimum. Additionally, the Center administers a Conservation Camp program for about 1200 men in 14 satellite camps. (Because of rapid turnover and the small population of each camp, which makes close staff-inmate working relationships possible, no formal procedures for discussion of matters of concern, such as an advisory council, have been organized.)[49]

Each of the units elects ten representatives to the Men's Advisory Council General Council, ethnically balanced to insure representation for all. One member is elected to represent the inmates housed in the Fire House, making a total of 21 councilmen. Term of office is six months, limited to two terms. Any inmate may stand for nomination and election unless he is in administrative segregation pending transfer or further prosecution, or has been involved in a disciplinary incident related to abuse of council activities. Five officers, a chairman, two vice-chairmen, secretary and parliamentarian, are elected by the council members as an Executive Committee. To insure proper representation, the chairman and vice-chairman must be of different ethnic backgrounds. A Program Administrator is the staff sponsor of the council and provides such assistance as is needed to meet periodically with supervisory and administrative personnel via several subcommittees, e.g., recreation, food service and canteen. The council sponsors a variety of special events, some of which are designed to raise funds for the council account. Disbursement of account funds is authorized by the executive committee subject to approval by the staff sponsor, for events of benefit to the institution population.[50]

The California Rehabilitation Center, Norco, is the program/rehabilitation center for civilly committed narcotic addicts. Additionally, it has been designated as a medium security institution for adult felony offenders. There are four separate units within the facility, three for males, one for females.[51]

Information was received in 1966 and 1972 that a male Resident Central Committee had been organized in May, 1964. It operated under a constitution which provided for the secret ballot election of two representatives from each living unit to terms of four months. An executive committee, consisting of the chairman, secretary, sergeant-at-arms and two other central committee members, met periodically with the administration to accomplish the principal objective of the organization, which was stated as: "to improve relations and foster better communications and understanding between residents and staff at all levels; to keep staff and residents advised of their respective problems so these problems may be dealt with in an appropriate manner." In the women's section at the Patton State Hospital, San Bernardino, one representative and an alternate were elected from each living unit to serve a six-month term of office. The total council membership was ten. Meetings were held every other week with the Program Administrator.[52]

At the present time, the Inmate Advisory Council in each of the units for males is composed of three representatives, one for each major ethnic group, elected by staff-supervised secret ballot to a one-year term of office. An executive committee, consisting of a chairman, vice-chairman, secretary, and sergeant-at-arms, is elected by the membership. The first three mentioned officers may not be of the same ethnic group. Each council meets weekly with the unit administrators and counseling staff. Twice a month the executive committee meets with the Associate Superintendent for programs. Periodically, all executive committees meet with the superintendent, deputy superintendent and the associate superintendent to express the concerns, issues and grievances of the general population. Removal of members may be made by administrative order or by a two-thirds vote of the council membership.[53]

The California Institution for Women, Frontera, was established when legislation in 1929 provided for the removal of women from the State Prison at San Quentin. A site was selected at Tehachapi and four buildings to house 150 persons were completed and dedicated in May, 1932. Legal difficulties delayed occupancy until September, 1933, when the institution formally opened as a unit of San Quentin. In December, 1936, it was designated as a separate institution. The remoteness of the Tehachapi location caused eventual relocation in 1952, hastened by a severe earthquake, to the present site. The institution provides care for all types of felony commitments and may admit referrals from the Youth Authority. The unusually active program, designed to purposefully engage the inmate at all times, prompted one of the women to utter a remark which became a catch phrase: "I haven't got time to do my time."[54]

In 1940 each cottage had an inmate committee, appointed by the inmates for the purpose of planning and discussing Monday night cottage entertainments with the superintendent. The superintendent also met with the inmate population to discuss and interpret proposed changes in institution rules and regulations.[55]

In 1973, it was reported that a Resident Council, possibly organized when the institution was located at Tehachapi (probably the cottage committees described in the foregoing paragraph), continued active until the summer of 1964, when numerous housing reassignments made impossible the continuation of a representative elective group. In lieu of the council a Liaison Committee was formed whose members were recommended by cottage supervisors and confirmed by the superintendent. While each cottage had active representation, there was feeling among the women that members did not actually represent the inmate body, but had attained membership by winning recognition of the cottage supervisors. The administration could discern no difference in the operation of this group and the Resident Advisory Council, and in January 1966 the latter was reactivated.

Projects carried out by the Resident Advisory Council were cited as possibly being the greatest value of its existence. Enumerated as disadvantages in council operations were: the length of time required for the group to acquire cohesiveness--estimated to be six months, which is the term of office--and the likelihood of disproportionate representation of the more vocal and demanding inmates. The latter was not considered to be totally disadvantageous since it did provide an opportunity for the superintendent to deal first-hand with the demands. It had been found that quite often members of a pressure group became fairly good representatives in the course of their six-month term of office.[56]

After being disbanded for a considerable period of time, the Resident Advisory Council was reestablished in May, 1976, and subsequently renamed the Women's Advisory Council. This council provides a direct channel of staff-inmate communication. Advisory only, the group relays inmate concerns and keeps the inmates aware of administrative decisions affecting policies and procedures. The living units elect a total of six members by secret ballot to a six-month term of office, with one successive term allowed. The Psychiatric Treatment Unit also elects two members. The top vote getter in each unit is designated as the chairperson, who may serve a one-year nonrenewable term. An executive body, elected within the membership, acts as the liaison with the administration. Each member is assigned to two of the various sub-committees concerned with clothing, canteen, medical service, mail and visit privileges, food service, hobby craft, and education. The council meets with the appropriate department head to deal with specific concerns.[57]

Department of the Youth Authority

The Department of the Youth Authority administers 14 facilities for young adult felony offenders, misdemeanants, and commitments from juvenile courts.

In the fall of 1972, the director of the Youth Authority determined that all the program units, both institutional and community-based, should develop formal grievance procedures which could be used by those committed to its jurisdiction to settle complaints in a fair and equitable manner. Twelve principles were established jointly by line staff and wards, and issued April 4, 1973 as Principles for Ward Grievance Procedures. Included in the principles were requirements that complaints be responded to in writing within specific time limits, and levels of appeal, with the final level being to someone outside the Youth Authority for advisory arbitration. (See Appendix B for a recounting of the twelve principles).[58]

Experimentation with the principles began in July, 1973, in one of the four 100-bed living units of the Karl Holton School, Stockton. A committee representing staff and wards met with the superintendent and staff of the Center for Community Justice[59] to design a procedure based on the principles, but tailored to the needs of the unit. In the resulting procedure, the first level consisted of a committee of four voting members (two staff and two wards) with a non-voting chairman acting as mediator. At the second level, the committee decision (in living unit matters) or recommendations (on institutional questions) could be appealed to the superintendent by the complainant or the staff members involved in the grievance. The final level involved review of appeals from the superintendent's or, where appropriate, the department director's decision by an independent review panel, composed of one ward representative, one staff representative, and a local professional arbitrator from the American Arbitration Association.[60]

Administrators of the school, together with wards and staff members chosen to serve on the first level grievance committee, participated in a three-day program in mediation and other conflict resolution skills conducted by the Institute for Mediation and Conflict Resolution, a New York-based organization with broad experience in teaching those skills. The unit's procedure went into operation in early September, 1973. Thereafter, implementation throughout the Karl Holton School continued on a unit basis, and, by mid-1974, all units had functioning grievance procedures.[61]

Based on a favorable evaluation of procedure operations at the Karl Holton School by the Youth Authority Research Division, the director decided to extend the program to each institution and program unit, and chose a unit of the Youth Training School, Ontario, the largest facility, as the next development site. This was accomplished by the summer of 1974.[62]

By mid-1975, the ward grievance procedure was operational in all youth authority facilities, and in 1976 was made operational in parole units throughout the state. In September, 1976, the procedure was given mandated legal status when Section 1766. 5, added to the Welfare and Institution Code, required the Youth Authority Director to establish and maintain a grievance procedure meeting specific conditions. Those conditions largely parallel the aforementioned twelve principles which are contained in Appendix B. Additionally, an on-going monitoring system and an annual report regarding the operation of the program is required, to include data on usage, types of issues resolved, dispositions made of complaints, and information concerning levels of compliance with procedural requirements to promote the fairness and efficacy of the program.[63]

A ward with a complaint normally goes first to a Ward Grievance Clerk who has been elected by wards housed on his/her living unit. With this clerk's help, he/she completes a grievance form which basically asks the nature of the problem and what the ward thinks needs to be done to solve it. By policy, almost anything can be grieved. The only exceptions are issues over which the Youth Authority has no control or decisions of the Youthful Offender Parole Board and disciplinary matters where already existing appeal procedures are available. An example of the latter would be a disciplinary matter resulting from a rule infraction. Any disagreement about the fairness or outcome of a disciplinary hearing is dealt with through a separate disciplinary appeal process.

Once the grievant writes down a complaint, an attempt must be made to resolve the issue within a specific period of time--normally five to seven days. During this time, the ward has a right to a hearing before a grievance committee, usually composed of equal numbers of wards and staff and with a neutral chairperson, which will attempt to mediate or mutually work out an acceptable solution.

However, it is also possible for the matter to be resolved informally. That is to say, a solution agreeable to all parties is worked out before the formal committee hearing is held and the matter is considered resolved. Such informal resolutions are encouraged, but are not required in order to gain access to the formalized procedure. In either situation, a written response is given to the grievant setting forth exactly what has been decided. If dissatisfied with the response, any party to the grievance can make an appeal to a higher level of review. This higher level is normally the institution's superintendent, except in cases where a departmental policy is questioned. In the case of departmental issues, the matter goes directly to the Youth Authority's director. Again, a written answer must be given within specific time limits stating the reasons for the action. At a few locations, an additional level of review is used involving a middle manager (Treatment Team Supervisor or Program Administrator) who attempts resolution prior to the appeal's going to the superintendent.

If still not satisfactorily resolved, the grievance can be appealed to an independent arbitrator from the American Arbitration Association or Barrister Association of the Los Angeles County Bar, who will conduct a hearing and render an advisory recommendation. While advisory, this decision must be followed unless it is in violation of the law, would result in physical danger to anyone, would require expenditure of funds not available, or, in the director's judgment, would be detrimental to the public or the proper operation of the department. Two exceptions to the general process exist. First, if the matter is of an emergency nature and requires more immediate handling than would be given in normal processing, the ward can request that the matter be handled as an emergency grievance. The ward then has a right to a timely review by the institution's superintendent, or designee, before the issue becomes moot (usually within twenty-four hours or less). The superintendent decides if the matter is truly an emergency and, if so, what action is to be taken. The superintendent can also deny the grievance as an emergency. If dissatisfied with the superintendent's response, the grievant's recourse is to use the regular system to seek further redress. A second exception occurs when a grievance is filed with allegations which, if found true, could result in some form of formal punitive action being taken against an employee. Under these circumstances, the grievance is sent directly to the institution's superintendent or parole administrator for an investigation, by-passing the regular grievance committee. The sufficiency of the superintendent's investigation is appealable to an arbitrator by either the ward or the employee involved. However, the actual disposition in terms of disciplinary action, if any, taken against the employee is not.[64]

Freedom from reprisal is supported by department policy. Only when there is a clear-cut case of slander with intent and potential for harm of an employee can disciplinary action be initiated against a ward filing a grievance. On only two occasions in 1980 was it thought that misuse had occurred and disciplinary charges brought against wards.[65]

Student Advisory Councils within Department of the Youth Authority facilities have taken on a different appearance and role since 1973 when the Ward Grievance Procedure was first implemented. Under the procedure each living unit (50 wards) is required to have a representative, selected by peers, to serve as the unit grievance clerk. Shortly after the procedure inception, many facilities identified their grievance clerks as the Student Advisory Council. The councils continue to meet with the superintendent regularly, but as a rule do not address the broad issues of institutional and departmental policies and procedures as was once done.[66]

As a result of the success and general acceptance of the grievance procedure by wards and staff, the Student Advisory Councils have taken on a secondary role. In most facilities, the council, whether composed of grievance clerks or other elected wards, deals with the institution food service, e.g., the kinds of foods served; the canteen; the expenditure of ward benefit funds which are derived from vending machine profits; special religious, holiday or entertainment programs; community involvement, and any other issues of general interest to the wards. It is believed that a much greater impact on institution and department procedures and policies is available to the wards through use of the grievance procedure in which the ward's voice becomes more than advisory and the administration must respond specifically to each grievance filed.[67]

In January 1973, the Youth Authority director provided information concerning the status of student councils which, together with the results of earlier surveys as specifically noted, is the basis for the following accounts.

Due to the short time spent by wards at the Northern California Reception Center-Clinic, Sacramento, it was impractical to attempt to organize an ongoing advisory council. However, eight to ten wards met periodically with a Citizens Advisory Council to discuss ward recreation and program needs, and to develop volunteer services.

There was no formal student council at the Southern Reception Center-Clinic, Norwalk, because wards were there usually less than thirty days. As an alternative, weekly meetings were held in each living unit to discuss and resolve problems pertaining to unit operation. Any individual dissatisfied with answers received at these meetings could request to see the superintendent. A grievance procedure was being developed in order to establish a permanent channel of communication between wards and policy-makers.

In 1966 it was reported that each student was assigned to

one of eight small groups. A representative of each group and the resident newspaper editor made up the membership of a Cottage Council which had been in operation for more than a year. The Council examined various problems of community living, solicited suggestions from the groups, made recommendations on means to effect constructive changes, supervised a bi-monthly rating system in which groups rated each of the members as to how they were doing in program basic areas, and counseled boys who presented serious behavioral or attitudinal problems. Committees on entertainment, activities, crafts, and the newspaper were active and could seek Council assistance.[68]

The Ventura School, Camarillo, was originally opened on July 1, 1891 as the California School for Girls, located on the grounds of the Whittier State School (originally the State Reform School for Juvenile Offenders, now the Fred C. Nelles School for Boys). In 1916 a separate institution was opened at Ventura and designated as the Ventura School for Girls. The school moved to its present location in 1962, and has been a co-educational facility since October, 1970. A Reception Center-Clinic, for girls only, was added in 1964.

A 1940 survey reported that some years earlier an experiment in student cooperation was undertaken in one of the cottages but had to be disbanded very soon because the girls "dished out" punishments to offenders that were too harsh. In further explanation of the plan, it was said that the cottage mother was an interested listener who, upon report of a suggested disciplinary measure which seemed too harsh, would remark, "Don't you think that is a little severe?"[69] The same survey found that girl monitors, appointed in each cottage by the supervisor, were assigned to care for the locker room (each girl was assigned a clothing locker) and to assist in supervision of the other girls, substituting for the supervisor in the latter's temporary absence. The monitors had no disciplinary authority other than that of advising newly-arrived girls when their beds were made improperly and "for similar causes." Honor cottage girls who assisted supervisors in the successful apprehension of runaways were rewarded by an earlier release.[70]

In 1973 a Student Advisory Committee was reported as being active. Although no details were given as to how members were chosen, it was indicated that the group held a one-hour meeting each week with the superintendent, assistant superintendent, and the supervisors of the Treatment Teams to talk informally about anything regarding the institution which had impact on the wards. Additionally, a group of officers and student body members held monthly discussions with the supervisor of education regarding educational facilities and curriculum. A Recreation Committee of two representatives from each living unit met with two social workers to develop ongoing as well as holiday recreation projects and events. The Protestant chaplain met monthly with an advisory committee of students.

A 1966 report told of a Student Advisory Committee then in

operation, whose members were chosen by a Progress Evaluation Committee. A minimum of two months' residence in the institution was an eligibility requirement. The six-month average length of stay obviated the necessity for a time limit on membership. Removal could occur if a girl's attitude or behavior deteriorated. If she did not participate in the meetings, the superintendent might ask that she be replaced, although this had been done only twice in four years. The Committee met weekly with the superintendent, at which time other staff members might attend in relation to the problems presented. Topics discussed might include food, recreation projects, clothing, personal care items, policies on progress evaluation, and parole referrals.[71]

The Fred C. Nelles School for Boys, Whittier, was originally opened on July 1, 1891 as the State Reform School for Juvenile Delinquents for the care of both boys and girls. In 1893, the name was changed to Whittier State School. In 1916 a separate institution for girls was opened at Ventura (in 1962 moved to its present location at Camarillo). Since then the facility has housed only boys, ages eight to sixteen.

Shortly after his appointment in 1933, Superintendent E. J. Milne called together a group of boys, one from each cottage, and expressed his wish to organize an honor club in each cottage to give the boys an opportunity to develop self-government and an opportunity to use initiative in problems of discipline for violation of rules and regulations. The name, Paramount Honor Club, was selected by the boys. By-laws were adopted providing for the secret ballot election of seven officers in each cottage to serve a term of 90 days. The president, vice-president, secretary and four directors met monthly to consider affairs of the cottage. A special meeting could be called to take up a particular case of discipline. Any boy who had at least 30 days of satisfactory grade could apply for club membership. Upon a two-thirds favorable vote of the membership, conditional acceptance for 30 days was granted, following which he became a member upon again receiving a like vote. Each member signed his intention to abide by the following three articles of the by-laws:

> Article I ... shall not escape or attempt to escape; ... do ... utmost to prevent and persuade others from escaping. Article II ... when out on absence leave ... so conduct myself as to reflect credit upon myself and the institution. Article III ... hereby pledge to put forth an honest and honorable effort to stamp out the use of tobacco among the boys....[72]

The Honor Club of Placement Cottage (boys about to be paroled were placed there two months prior to release), was regarded as the grand body of all honor clubs, handling the major initiatory work and the induction of new officers. Club officers were on call for emergencies and were expected to assist supervisors in maintaining order among the boys to prevent unnecessarily loud noise or destruction of property. Reportedly, within two years the Paramount

Honor Clubs had brought about a marked improvement in boy morale and the clubs were said to be of major importance as a function of the facility, not only in the cottages but also in the vocational and academic programs. When there was no runaway from a cottage for 60 days, each club member was entitled to: attend a movie in Whittier, and a credit of 50 merits (a system originally intended as a means of estimating a boy's progress). [73]

In 1940 it was planned to establish a student body organization within the academic school to provide boys a reasonable degree of self-government. Principally affected would be the more mature boys of high school caliber. The organization was to be patterned after those in public schools. [74]

The same 1940 study of the institution was critical of the honor clubs, expressing the opinion that they were simply an instrument for the enforcement of rules and regulations and so used the boys. Additionally, it was charged that the officers chosen were not truly representative of the student body; that a sampling of cottage meeting minutes indicated a somewhat artificial functioning, with enthusiasm whipped up sporadically by cottage supervisors. The hope was expressed that the academic school plan to organize a student body would supplant the honor clubs. [75] The administration did not agree, pointing out that many boys had testified to the honor club as having been very helpful in their lives at the school. Finally, the administration stated, it also hoped the projected student body plan might bring improvements in the system of self-government, but if it were adopted it would not be because the honor clubs had failed. [76]

Information obtained in 1966 on the Nelles School reflected considerable autonomy in the activities of each cottage. At that time each cottage had a five-boy Recreation Committee responsible for suggesting program and activities modifications. Members were chosen from those who had been residing in the cottage for at least 60 days and whose conduct and attitude were regarded as being among the best. The purchase of a tug-of-war rope was mentioned as an example of an accepted suggestion. [77]

In 1973, community meetings were being held as required by each living unit, and attended by all wards and cottage Treatment Team members available. The Treatment Teams were given a large degree of autonomy by the School administration, which was reflected in the differential of structure and purpose of the community meetings in the various living units.

The Los Guilucos School, Santa Rosa, was opened in 1943 as a school for girls, became co-educational during 1970-71, and was closed in June, 1973. During the co-educational period, a Student Advisory Committee met once a month with the superintendent. The purpose of the group was to provide an opportunity for articulate, participating students to review their experiences at the school and to suggest changes which would in their opinion ensure more effective programs.

Weekly community meetings, also held at the Santa Rosa facility, were described as having been the primary vehicle for the conveyance of student opinion and suggestions for program changes. The meetings were attended by the Treatment Team supervisor who subsequently held discussions with his staff on student suggestions, and presented proposed program changes at weekly meetings of the administrative staff.

In 1966 there was a Girls' Advisory Committee, composed of two representatives of each cottage, that met weekly with the superintendent and assistant superintendent to discuss topics referred by the various cottages. Length of time in the program and general leadership ability were the criteria for the selection of representatives.[78]

In 1973, the Youth Training School, Ontario, opened in 1960, had had a formal Student Council since 1970. The 12 to 15 members, elected by students and staff, represented their cottages at twice-a-month meetings with the superintendent and six of his administrative staff, seeking clarification of policies and procedures, registering group grievances, and recommending program and policy changes. The superintendent maintained a positive posture relative to the group and often sought reactions to pending decisions that would affect housing unit social activities. The council also participated in housing unit meetings. Additionally, there was a 12-member Food Advisory Council which met with the food administrator each month.

The Mt. Bullion Youth Conservation Camp, Mariposa, in 1973 had a Student Council which met each week with a senior youth counselor. Selection of a representative was made by each work crew. Work crews frequently discussed camp program problems during "tail-gate" counseling sessions. Community counseling sessions were held on alternate weeks.

A Camp Council of six representatives selected at large by the population was, in 1973, scheduled to be reactivated in the near future at the Pine Grove Youth Conservation Camp, Pine Grove, to meet with the superintendent each week to discuss anything of concern to the membership.

At the Ben Lomond Youth Conservation Camp, Santa Cruz, in 1973, the senior youth counselor supervised the Advisory Council, whose members were chosen on the basis of demonstrated positive leadership ability and interest in the program. The principal function of the council was to provide a means of communication between wards and staff. An open-door policy permitted wards to talk to administrative staff members at any time they believed their assigned counselor could not help them. This program was reported as being in operation in 1966, then being designated as the Ward Council.[79]

As of 1973, a four-member Ward Council met regularly with

the superintendent to discuss suggestions for program improvement and to maintain open lines of communication between wards and administration at the Washington Ridge Youth Conservation Camp, Nevada City.

The Northern California Youth Center, Stockton, is a complex of three facilities, each with an approximate capacity of 400:

O. H. Close School for Boys. There was no formal student council in 1973. Ad hoc committees from each living unit met as needs indicated. Community meetings, five days each week, were held in the living units. Those meetings were attended by seven Treatment Team members--team supervisor, a social worker, three teachers, and two youth counselors. Discussions dealing with any operational problem of each unit and any inter-personal problems between wards and staff and between the wards themselves were conducted in a democratic atmosphere. This facility opened in 1966 and the program described herein was reported as being in operation the same year.[80]

Karl Holton School for Boys. In 1973 the school had no formal student council. However, community meetings held in all 50-bed living units, daily attended by the Treatment Team supervisor, social worker, teachers, and youth counselors, dealt with unit operational problems, program planning, and inter-personal relationship problems between the wards and staff. In addition to the community meetings, the Ethnic Studies Program had a Ward Advisory Committee comprised of the various minority groups who advised staff on curriculum content in that area. Each 50-bed unit also had a Student Recreation Committee which worked with a staff member to plan and develop recreation for the unit. All units had an Orientation Committee of wards and one staff member to develop and conduct ongoing orientation programs for all new wards.

DeWitt Nelson Training Center. As of 1973, a trainee Advisory Council met twice a month with the superintendent for two or three hours. The five dormitories each elected three members to the council whose duties included:

1. Orienting new arrivals and assisting staff in acquainting them with rules, regulations, and programs.
2. Acting in an advisory capacity to the superintendent in disseminating ward benefit funds.
3. Acting as spokesmen for their ethnic groups.
4. Advising what items of value should be placed on the canteen list.
5. Assisting as leaders in preparation of school-wide activities.
6. Acting as a sounding board directly to the superintendent, giving him feedback on the overall morale of the ward population.

The Paso Robles School for Boys, Pasa Robles, was opened

in 1947 and closed effective October 1972. Information received in 1966 indicated that while there was no centrally organized ward-staff advisory council, the program of the school was designed to encourage operation of the nine living units as semi-autonomous therapeutic communities. There were student government activities of varying degree in each unit. Four of the cottages had popularly elected committees working closely with staff in ongoing programs.[81]

The past and the 1973 scene regarding student councils at the Preston School of Industry, Ione, were reviewed in chapter I on Early Experiences.

Notes

1. Keating, McArthur, Lewis, Sebelius, Singer. Grievance Mechanisms in Correctional Institutions. Washington, D.C.: National Institute of Law Enforcement and Criminal Justice, U.S. Department of Justice, 1975, pp. 36-37.
2. "Inmate/Parolee Appeal Procedure," Administrative Manual, Department of Corrections, Sacramento, Chapter 7300.
3. Ibid. (In re Muszalski holds that the Department of Corrections inmate appeal procedure provides "... viable, efficacious administrative remedies which must be exhausted by an inmate before resorting to a petition for habeas corpus in the courts." The opinion does not, however, apply to court actions challenging the criminal proceedings leading to sentencing to the department.)
4. Ibid.
5. Ibid.
6. Ibid.
7. Ibid.
8. Ibid.
9. Ibid.
10. Ibid.
11. Ibid.
12. Baker, J. E., op. cit., p. 91.
13. "Inmate Activity Groups: Inmate Advisory Council," Administrative Manual, Chapter 7100, Article 1, Department of Corrections, August 1, 1977.
14. Ibid.
15. Ibid.
16. Ibid.
17. Ibid.
18. Ibid.
19. Ibid.
20. Ibid.
21. Ibid.
22. Ibid.
23. Baker, J. E., op. cit., pp. 91-92.
24. MacCormick, Austin H., ed. Handbook of American Prisons and Reformatories, Vol. II, First Edition. New York: The Osborne Association, Inc., 1942, p. 245.

25. Letter from J. A. McCullough, Administrative Assistant, California State Prison, San Quentin, November 3, 1982, and "Inmate Advisory Council and Committee," Institution Procedure No. 303, California State Prison, San Quentin, February 10, 1967; Revised December 10, 1980.
26. Baker, J. E., _op. cit._, p. 92.
27. Letter from Gil Miller, Administrative Assistant, California State Prison at Folsom, Represa, November 5, 1982.
28. Baker, J. E., _op. cit._, p. 93.
29. _Ibid._
30. Program Procedure No. 208A, "Men's Advisory Council," Medium Unit (Revised December 15, 1981); Program Procedure No. 208B, "Men's Advisory Council," Minimum Unit (Revised December 15, 1981); California Correctional Unit, Tehachapi.
31. Letter from John G. Henderson, Program Administrator, Minimum Unit, California Correctional Institution at Tehachapi, November 18, 1982.
32. Baker, J. E., _op. cit._, p. 93.
33. Baker, J. E., _op. cit._, p. 94.
34. _Ibid._
35. _Ibid._
36. Letter from Superintendent M. Carroll, California Correctional Institution, Chino, November 12, 1982.
37. _Ibid._
38. Baker, J. E., _op. cit._, p. 95.
39. _Ibid._
40. Letter from K. W. Prunty, Administrative Assistant, Duell Vocational Institution, Tracy, November 8, 1982.
41. Baker, J. E., _op. cit._, pp. 95-96; letter from D. R. Custard, Public Information Officer, California Medical Facility, Vacaville, November 3, 1982.
42. "Inmate Advisory Council," Operations Plan No. 26, September 20, 1982 (supersedes plan dated March 4, 1981); "Constitution and By-Laws, Men's Advisory Council," California Medical Facility, Vacaville.
43. Baker, J. E., _op. cit._, p. 96.
44. Letter from Superintendent D. J. McCarthy, California Men's Colony, San Luis Obispo, November 4, 1982; "Constitution and By-Laws, Men's Advisory Council," December, 1981.
45. Baker, J. E., _op. cit._, p. 96.
46. Letter from Carol V. Roddy, Community Resources Manager, California Correctional Center, Susanville, November 18, 1982; "Inmate Advisory Group," Operational Procedure No. 59.00, Revised January 7, 1982.
47. Baker, J. E., _op. cit._, pp. 96-97.
48. Baker, J. E., _op. cit._, p. 97.
49. Letter from Superintendent K. D. Britt and T. E. Williams, Program Administrator, Sierra Conservation Center, Jamestown, November 17, 1982.
50. _Ibid._
51. Letter from Superintendent C. J. Villalobos, California Rehabilitation Center, Norco, October 17, 1982.

52. Baker, J. E., *op. cit.*, p. 97.
53. "Constitution and By-Laws, Inmate Advisory Council," California Rehabilitation Center, Norco.
54. Baker, J. E., *op. cit.*, p. 98.
55. MacCormick, Austin H., ed., *op. cit.*, p. 343.
56. Baker, J. E., *op. cit.*, p. 98.
57. Letter from D. M. Martel, Associate Superintendent for Operations, California Institution for Women, Frontera, December 1, 1982.
58. Keating, J. Michael, Jr., Gilligan, Kathleen M., McArthur, Virginia A., Lewis, Michael K., and Singer, Linda R. *Seen But Not Heard: A Survey of Grievance Mechanisms in Juvenile Correctional Institutions.* Washington, D.C.: Center for Community Justice, 1974.
59. The Center for Community Justice (originally named the Center for Correctional Justice) is directly involved in the development of correctional grievance mechanisms. In 1971, a group of lawyers, correctional officials, and ex-offenders founded the Center to develop alternatives to prison violence and litigation. The Center first designed and operated a pilot program for delivering legal services to District of Columbia prisoners and parolees, which led to the development of formal procedures for handling problems within correctional agencies. Because of its direct participation in the design and implementation of the procedures, the Center has become a source of technical assistance for other states, institutions, planning agencies, and inmate groups interested in developing grievance mechanisms of their own.
60. Keating, J. Michael, Jr., et al., *op. cit.*, p. 71.
61. *Ibid.*, pp. 71-72.
62. *Ibid.*, p. 72.
63. *Ward Grievance Procedure, Annual Departmental Report*, Department of the Youth Authority, 1980, p. 1.
64. *Ibid.*, pp. 3-5.
65. *Ibid.*, p. 21.
66. Letter from Walter H. Friesen, Ward Rights Specialist, Department of the Youth Authority, Sacramento, October 6, 1982.
67. *Ibid.*
68. Baker, J. E., *op. cit.*, p. 99.
69. Cox, William B., and Bixby, F. Lovell, Ph.D. *Handbook of American Institutions for Delinquent Juveniles, Pacific Coast States*, Vol. III, First Edition. New York: The Osborne Association, Inc., 1940, pp. 122-123.
70. *Ibid.*, pp. 129-130.
71. Baker, J. E., *op. cit.*, p. 100.
72. "The Paramount Honor Club," *The Sentinel*, Whittier State School, Vol. XXXII, No. 3, July-August 1935, pp. 25-26.
73. *Ibid.*
74. Cox, William B., and Bixby F. Lovell, Ph.D., *op. cit.*, p. 169.
75. *Ibid.*, pp. 205-206.
76. *Ibid.*, pp. 211-212.

77. Baker, J. E., _op. cit._, p. 100.
78. _Ibid._, p. 101.
79. _Ibid._, p. 102.
80. _Ibid._, p. 102.
81. _Ibid._, p. 102.

COLORADO

Department of Corrections

The Department of Corrections, established in 1977 to replace the Department of Institutions, administers all institutions for adult and youthful felony offenders.

A grievance system was established at the Colorado Territorial Correctional Facility, Canon City (then the Colorado State Penitentiary), in February 1976. A grievance committee of three staff and three inmates, the warden, and an outside review panel comprised the three levels of consideration available. The procedure was discontinued in December, 1978 because it was complicated and failed to achieve established goals.[1]

The current inmate grievance procedure was established in all adult institutions on November 26, 1979.[2] The tri-level process provides for consideration of inmate grievances concerning an incident or condition within a facility by a staff member designated by the superintendent, the superintendent, and the executive director, Department of Corrections. However, the first level of review for complaints relating to conditions or operations within correctional industries is given by an employee of that activity designated by the director, Division of Correctional Industries, and complaints about medical or mental health are first reviewed by a representative of those services.

Complaints regarding classification, administrative segregation and disciplinary board actions are not grievable under the procedure since there is a separate review process for each. Parole board actions are also precluded because the Department of Corrections has no jurisdiction. Also, regulations and procedures governing the general operation of the department and its employees which do not personally affect an inmate are not grievable.

All grievances must be made on an official form. Assistance by other inmates or by staff is authorized for illiterates or those who cannot write legibly. A grievance must be filed within 14 days from the date the inmate knew or should have known of the facts giving rise to the complaint, or within 14 days after a final action which might result in a complaint. An extension of this time may be granted by the superintendent if the inmate can clearly demonstrate that filing within the initial period was not feasible.

Inmates are provided a written response within 30 days following receipt of the grievance. An appeal to the executive director may be made within the following 30 days. The inmate must provide substantial reason for the appeal. The executive director may reject an appeal if it is determined that the reasons given lack support. Written replies are given to accepted appeals within 30 days.

An extension of the time limits may be extended for a period not to exceed 30 days when circumstances require additional time for decision making. The grievant is notified in writing of any such extension.

When there are indications of potential and substantial risk to the life or safety of the grievant or when irreparable harm to the grievant's health is imminent, the superintendent shall declare an emergency and the grievance be forwarded to the level where corrective action can be taken; a response shall be made within 48 hours. Appeals shall be handled initially by phone to the executive director level when conditions warrant.

Employees and inmates are encouraged to make comments on the operation of the grievance procedure by addressing the issue in a grievance or by writing directly to the executive director or the Department Inspector General. Such comments will be reviewed at least twice annually at a meeting with appropriate administrative personnel. To the extent practical and consistent with rules, regulations, and procedures, the executive director will attempt to implement the suggested changes and recommendations.

Currently there are no inmate councils in the adult institutions, all having been phased out within the past few years.[3]

In November, 1972, it was reported that an Inmate Advisory Council that met regularly and had quite an influential voice in the administration, making a number of contributions, was in operation at one of the institutions. (At that time the Colorado State Penitentiary, Canon City, and the Colorado State Reformatory, Buena Vista, were listed as the adult institutions, each with subsidiary units). The process of electing members to a similar group in the other institution was underway. Information as to which institution the references pertained was not obtained. However, information obtained in November, 1966, as given in the following paragraph, was confirmed as being essentially valid in 1972.[4]

At the State Penitentiary, Canon City, in 1966, a number of groups were reported as having fairly complete control of their activities under the supervision of sponsors. Cited as examples were Alcoholics Anonymous and the Dale Carnegie Alumni Group. The latter had developed a crime prevention program working with schools, churches, and various community groups. Its main function was to evangelize the "crime does not pay" message to teenagers and to impress parents with the importance of taking an active interest in the affairs of their children.

Division of Youth Services

The institutional Treatment Services, Division of Youth Services, administers five facilities for juvenile delinquents and children in need of supervision.

Although the central office has issued no directives on the activity, a student grievance procedure was established circa 1978 in all facilities. Each facility has developed its own operational process. The grievance procedure is an integral part of the unit management system.[5]

No directives have been issued by the central office regarding student councils.[6]

In January, 1973, it was reported there were no student councils at any of the facilities. However, residents participated in discussions on cottage administration and in decision-making during daily housing unit meetings at the Mount View School, Denver (then the Mount View Girls' School), and Lookout Mountain School for Boys, Golden. Regular boy/staff meetings and occasional marathon meetings were held at the Lathrop Park Youth Camp, Walsenburg, and the Golden Gate Youth Camp, Golden.[7]

A February 1967 report stated that an attempt several years prior to form a student council at the then Mount View Girls' School was cancelled after various girls ganged up on others to coerce votes during the election campaign.[8]

Notes

1. Letter from Robert W. Thurlow, Public Information Officer (Acting), Department of Corrections, Colorado Springs, May 11, 1983. Another source, however, indicates that the procedure was implemented following a June, 1976 training seminar. An early monitoring visit found that although the staff and inmate grievance committee members were proving adept at reaching reasonable solutions to problems, administration responses to a number of grievances were so unspecific that it was unclear that members of the prison administration were to take follow-up action. By September two problems had reached critical proportions--responses from the administration so vague as to be meaningless, and even in those instances in which the response specified an action to be taken, no one was directed to perform it, nor was a time specified for completion. Before an agreement could be reached on steps to correct these operational deficiencies, a series of events took place which effectively suspended the procedure. In mid-August, 1976, a series of inmate-versus-inmate assaults occurred in the institution, resulting in a complete lock-up of all inmates and the suspension

of all institutional programs. In April, 1977, with all inmates still in lock-up, the grievance procedure project was discontinued. (See: Singer, Linda R., "Prevention and Control of Conflict in Corrections," Final Report, LEAA Grant No. 77-ED-99-0009, Center for Community Justice, Washington, D.C., April 15, 1979.) Colorado was one of four states involved in the 1975 LEAA Grant to aid in the development of model methods of resolving disputes in correctional institutions.

2. DOC Regulation 305-4, "Inmate/Parolee Grievance System," Dept. of Corrections, Colorado Springs, February 11, 1982.
3. Letter from Robert W. Thurlow, Public Information Officer (Acting), Dept. of Corrections, Colorado Springs, March 11, 1983.
4. Baker, J. E., op. cit., p. 104.
5. Telephone conversation with Loren G. Adlfinger, Director, Institutional Treatment, Division of Youth Services, Denver, June 21, 1983.
6. Ibid.
7. Baker, J. E., op. cit., p. 104.
8. Ibid.

CONNECTICUT

Department of Correction

The Department of Correction administers five institutions for adult and youthful felony offenders and eight community correctional centers for felony offenders whose sentences are less than a year, misdemeanants, and civil cases.[1]

An Ombudsman program was established by written agreement between the Department of Corrections and the Hartford Institute of Criminal and Social Justice on September 12, 1973, which is applicable to all department institutions.[2] An inmate with a grievance of any kind, including complaints about policies and procedures of the institution or department, is interviewed by the Ombudsman, who may reject the complaint or agree to investigate it. There is no appeal from the Ombudsman's rejection of a complaint. The Ombudsman has full and immediate access to all locations and persons in the institution. Findings and recommendations are reported to the warden, who is free to accept or reject them. Should the warden reject the report, the Ombudsman may forward it to the Department Commissioner.[3]

A grievance procedure was established on January 1, 1983, at the Community Correctional Center, New Haven, a 480-capacity facility opened in 1975. Complaints dealing with an inmate's treatment under institutional and/or department policies and procedures are accepted, except: matters outside department jurisdiction;

personal conflicts not related to policies or procedures; disciplinary or classification committee decisions; medical diagnostic or treatment decisions; and situations in which there is a clear potential for disciplinary action and/or criminal prosecution against any person.

Within five days following an event, an inmate may complete a prescribed grievance form which will be considered by a warden-appointed Grievance Procedure Coordinator and one inmate member of a grievance committee pool who will investigate and attempt resolution within seven working days. Should resolution not be possible, the grievance will be referred to the Grievance Committee, which will consist of a non-voting chairperson (a staff member), two inmates, and two line personnel, one of whom must be a correctional officer. The committee conducts a hearing at which the grievant, the coordinator, and relevant witnesses may be present. A written recommendation will be made to the warden within five working days, who has a like time in which to respond. If still dissatisfied, the grievant may file within two days for a review by the Department Commissioner. An Advisory Committee appointed by the commissioner meets monthly to consider appeals and make recommendations. Within 15 days following the advisory committee meeting, the commissioner will make a written response to the grievant and the warden. [4]

The Grievance Committee pool is made up of eight volunteer inmates who have a projected minimum of three months time remaining to serve; eight staff non-supervisory personnel, each with a minimum of one year experience at the facility, and two chairpersons selected from the supervisory staff. The latter are appointed for a one-year period. [5]

Exceptions to the time limitations at each level are possible if the grievant agrees. The procedure provides for emergency processing should an inmate's claim of such be sustained by the shift supervisor or the grievance coordinator. Multiple grievances concerning the same issue may be combined, with the final resolution being applicable to all. Decisions of the commissioner are regarded as precedents. [6]

The Department of Correction has not issued any directives on inmate councils and there was an indication in information received that no councils exist in any of the institutions with the exception of the Honor Cottage at the Connecticut Correctional Institution, Niantic, which is later described.

Information obtained in 1966 and 1967 was reviewed by the Department of Correction administration prior to inclusion in a previous book. The same material was again reviewed by the current administration and no changes made except information regarding the number of facilities, and an affirmative response to the query whether the Honor Cottage at the Niantic Institution was still in operation.

The first prison in the Colony of Connecticut was an abandoned copper mine, opened at Granby in 1773 and named Newgate Prison. Its use was discontinued on September 28, 1827, when the Connecticut State Prison at Wethersfield opened. In 1963, the latter was replaced by the Connecticut Correctional Institution, near Somers.

The warden at the Connecticut State prison until 1969 stated in 1966 that from information available it would appear that an inmate committee was functioning in the late 1950s, but was not apparently officially sponsored or recognized. The warden from September 1956 until December 1961 took office following an inmate uprising which necessitated calling out the National Guard. He found a self-appointed inmate committee which, if not the focal point of inmate unrest, had succeeded in gaining a great deal of public and official recognition through its ability to verbalize feelings of discontent and unrest. The group gradually dissolved when recognition was denied it. Selected inmate committees were used thereafter for a variety of special purposes but no central council was organized.

The Connecticut State Farm and Prison for Women at Niantic, now designated as Connecticut Correctional Institution, was first opened in 1917 as a farm. Although no records are available, it is known that a type of self-government was used in the early twenties. The reason for its discontinuance has been conjectured as a change in staff. Currently the Honor Cottage is self-governing and its 15 to 22 residents are carefully screened by the administration. The latter also determines policy and guidelines on behavior and operational procedures. A staff member is on duty at all times but it is seldom necessary for her to become involved in discipline or management. The residents elect, for three-month terms, officers who may request additional privileges on behalf of the others. Residents may also voice disapproval of the administration's choice of girls for the Honor Cottage. Some time ago the request of another cottage group of 28 girls for some self-management was approved. This plan appeared to hold promise but it expired after about three months when the leaders were released.

An account of the Welfare League at the Connecticut State Reformatory from 1914 to 1916 was given in chapter I on Early Experiences. The institution was opened in 1913, and later designated as the Connecticut Correctional Institution, Cheshire. No institution of that name is currently listed among Connecticut institutions, but there is a Connecticut Youth Institution, Cheshire, indicated as having been opened in 1982.

Department of Children and Youth Services

The Department of Children and Youth Services has jurisdiction over the co-ed Long Lane School, Middletown, which opened in 1869 as the Long Lane School for Girls. In 1973 the facility was merged with the Connecticut School for Boys, Meriden, which had opened in 1851.

A Grievance Board procedure has been proposed and will be instituted soon.[7] The Board will be chaired by an impartial, permanent chairperson, designated by the superintendent, who will appoint three staff or community volunteers as members. Two students, selected by students, also will be included. A student may initiate a grievance, either written or oral, to the chairperson, who will schedule it for board consideration. Board meetings will be held on an as-needed basis, but must be held once each month. The grievant must personally present the complaint to the board, may call other students as witnesses, and may introduce any relevant written material. A written decision must be given within 30 days following receipt of the complaint. Emergency grievances involving situations of potential or actual harm to students must be immediately referred to the superintendent or the ranking person on duty. Students will not be subject to any reprisals or disciplinary sanctions for use of the grievance procedure.[8]

The stated purpose for the establishment of a formal grievance procedure is to provide an appropriate means for students to influence their environment through constructive challenge and criticism as well as the opportunity to develop abilities in problem solving, negotiating, and working cooperatively with others. Should there be no grievances for the board to consider, the membership will be expanded to include representatives from each cottage group for a general discussion of program suggestions and, as well, any recommendations for changes in the design or function of the grievance board procedure.[9]

Currently, a grievance process is provided in Incident Meetings. Such meetings may be called by a student, with a staff member's approval, when an incident occurs which is notable either for the behavioral management difficulties it presents, or for its potential positive or negative impact on the group members' interactions and behaviors. In dealing with a negative incident, the meeting serves to defuse the incident, to involve the group in the problem situation, and to give the members an opportunity to make a plan to minimize the possibility of the incident leading to further trouble. A meeting relative to a positive incident serves to direct attention to the fact that one or more members are helping themselves or others, thus furnishing an illustration to the group as to how it can help each member. Incident Meetings are of five to ten minutes duration.[10]

A 1966 account of a self-government program dating to 1917 was given in chapter I on Early Experiences.

A July 1973 Constitution for the Long Lane School, adopted shortly after the merger with the Connecticut School for Boys, contained the School Statement of Purpose, established a preference for the use of positive reinforcement, and provided a structure for the general program, which included student participation through a Student Council.[11]

Each of the cottages elected two representatives and one alternate to serve for one month as members of the Student Council. At weekly meetings of the counseling team, comprised of all staff members working in a cottage, the Student Council representatives were voting members on all matters having to do with cottage rules. Meeting every two weeks with the superintendent, the council could introduce any topic and had the option of inviting any staff member to explain any matters not fully understood. Additionally, council representatives--three girls and three boys--served on a Commissioner's Council. Those six met with the commissioner twice a month in the central office in Hartford to provide feedback regarding conditions at the institution.

Currently, the Long Lane School treatment program is based on the principles of guided group interaction. Upon placement in a cottage each student is assigned to a cottage group. Normally, there are two groups of eight to twelve students operating in each cottage. Meetings are held daily in which the group focuses on one student's behavior. Group members present and evaluate more appropriate behavioral responses to those people, circumstances, or situations with which that student has had difficulty in the past. Based on its evaluation of alternative behaviors, the group develops a specific action plan to help the student effect positive behavior changes. The group, facilitated by a staff leader, has the task of helping the student, and the student the task of helping the group members, behave in a responsible manner.[12]

In addition to the guided group meetings, once a week there is a general meeting for all students within each cottage, led by the Cottage Coordinator and attended by other staff, to discuss issues such as maintenance/work details, cottage regulations, and planning special activities.

Notes

1. Information received from Commissioner John R. Manson, Department of Correction, Hartford, March 14, 1983.
2. *Ibid.*
3. Keathing, McArthur, Lewis, Sebelius, Singer, *op. cit.*, p. 38.
4. "Grievance Procedure," Policy and Procedures, Department of Correction, C.C.C. New Haven, Chapter 8.7, January 1, 1983.
5. *Ibid.*
6. *Ibid.*
7. Letter from Commissioner Mark J. Marcus, Department of Children and Youth Services, Hartford, October 18, 1982.
8. "Grievance Board," Proposed Policy, Long Lane School, Middletown.
9. *Ibid.*
10. "Long Lane Treatment Program." Monograph provided by Commissioner Mark J. Marcus, Department of Children and Youth Services, Hartford.

11. Baker, J. E., op. cit., p. 106.
12. "Long Lane Treatment Program" op. cit.

DELAWARE

The Department of Correction, created in 1974, administers all facilities for adult and juvenile offenders.[1]

Bureau of Adult Correction

The Bureau of Adult Correction administers eight institutions, including two facilities in Wilmington, the Pre-Trial Annex and the Multi-Purpose Criminal Justice Facility, both housing primarily persons in detention status awaiting either trial or sentencing.

Under the provisions of an Inmate Grievance Procedure established September 1, 1978, an inmate may, within four days following an incident, file a written grievance form with a staff grievance chairperson who will investigate the matter and present any findings to a four-member Resident Grievance Resolution Committee. This committee will hold a hearing at which staff members or inmates believed to be able to provide germane information may be requested to attend. Each housing unit elects two inmates to serve on the committee when an inmate of their unit is the grievant. Two staff persons appointed by the institution head serve as the other two members.[2]

A Department Inmate Grievance Officer is charged with monitoring the grievance procedure at each institution by making at least twice-monthly inspections of the records kept by the institution chairpersons. This officer may assist in the investigation of complaints and, following a final decision, is responsible for ascertaining that directed actions are taken. Additionally, this is a position of liaison with the office of the Attorney General to insure that appropriate steps are taken to avoid violations of inmates' rights.

The inmate may appeal the decision of the committee via the grievance chairperson and the Department Inmate Grievance officer to the institution superintendent, the Chief, Bureau of Adult Correction, or possibly the Commissioner, Department of Correction. While responses must be written, there are no time limits within which they must be made. There is no time limit for an appeal following a decision, but failure to appeal in a timely fashion may be construed as acceptance and render the decision binding. It is probable that a current revision of all administrative policies and procedures will effect changes in the grievance procedure.[3]

The Honor Court in operation at the New Castle Correctional Institution from 1921 to 1931 was reviewed in chapter I on Notable Early Experiences. That institution was closed in 1971.[4]

In late 1972, there were no inmate advisory councils in the institutions administered by the Division of Adult Corrections. However, the administration provided support to and assisted in the organization and functioning of various ad hoc committees elected by housing units to be concerned with specific purposes in matters of food, recreational programs, library services, rules and regulations, commissary, and special events.[5]

At the same time it was reported that work was progressing on the adoption of a Bill of Rights for prisoners based on that of the United Nations.

Another source indicates that in the aftermath of serious disturbances at the Delaware Correctional Center in September, 1971, shortly after it opened, the then Division of Adult Corrections, Department of Health and Social Services adopted a document, Rules for the Treatment of Inmates in Delaware Correctional Institutions, based on the United Nations' Bill of Rights for prisoners. The rules, written by a group of inmates, lawyers representing inmates, and staff of the Division of Adult Corrections, became effective February 1, 1972. However, the rules contained no provision for an inmate council or a grievance procedure.[6]

Nevertheless, inmate councils were established. The Medium Security Unit of the Delaware Correctional Institution, Smyrna, had an inmate council in 1973, designated as the Prisoners' Action Committee. Reportedly, the group worked with the administration on inmate complaints. Inmates in the Maximum Security Unit said at that time that they had attempted to form a council, but the administration refused to allow it. The administration said that rules provided for its approval of inmates elected to a council. In the case of the Maximum Security Unit, the administration did not approve of the persons elected to the council.[7]

It was reported that in 1973 the Women's Correctional Institution, Claymont, had an elected inmate council of eight members, four of whom comprised an executive council which worked with the institution staff, served as a grievance committee for inmates, administered the money earned by the commissary, and helped promote rehabilitation, education and recreational programs.[8]

At the present time there are no inmate advisory groups in Delaware adult institutions. However, the inmates have formed several service groups which, because of their credibility with the administration, can and do present inmate concerns to positive effect.[9]

Bureau of Juvenile Correction

The Bureau of Juvenile Correction provides residential care for committed juvenile delinquents in two facilities, and for detained youth in two others.[10]

The Inmate Grievance Procedure heretofore described is applicable to the juvenile facilities.

Information received in 1966 and 1967 indicated that an informally organized Planning Committee, which elected its own officers, had been in existence for about ten years at the Woods Haven-Kruse School for Girls, Claymont. The group was composed of five representatives from each of the two cottages, and reportedly was self-perpetuating in that incumbents elected the new members as vacancies occurred. The criteria of ability to show positive leadership and demonstrated good citizenship were used in this selection process. In addition to a role in coordinating social events, the group was a means of frank and open discussion with staff. In particular, the airing of program weaknesses and the need for special services to individual girls were cited as benefits of this communication. A staff coordinator was assigned by the administration from the clinical personnel.[11]

In 1973, information was received that a student council was organized at the Ferris School for Boys, Wilmington, in October, 1969, under a written procedure that provided for the secret ballot election of two representatives from each cottage to serve three-month terms of office. The group, which elected from the membership a president, vice-president, and secretary, met weekly with either the superintendent, the assistant superintendent, or a designate. Any topic could be discussed except that no verbal attack could be made upon any boy or staff member. All planning and programming decided by the council had to be consistent with the purpose, goals, and regulations of the school.[12]

Student councils no longer exist in the juvenile facilities. However, students participate in planning their treatment and placement programs, and recreational activities.[13]

Notes

1. Letter from Harold E. Stafford, Chief of Evaluation, Department of Correction, October 1, 1982.
2. "Inmate Grievance Procedure," Administrative Regulations, Section No. 1138, Adult Bureau, Dept. of Correction, September 1, 1978. (Also applicable to Juvenile Institutions.)
3. Letter from Midge Holland, Management Analyst, Dept. of Correction, April 8, 1983.
4. Baker, J. E., _op. cit._, p. 107.
5. _Ibid._
6. _The Delaware Prison System_, Report of the Delaware Advisory Committee to the U.S. Commission on Civil Rights, November 1974, p. 1.
7. _Ibid._, pp. 20-21.
8. _Ibid._, p. 46.
9. Letter from Harold E. Stafford, _op. cit._
10. Letter from Daniel Cox, Chief, Bureau of Juvenile Correction, Wilmington, October 5, 1982.

11. Baker, J. E., op. cit., pp. 107-108.
12. Ibid., p. 108.
13. Letter from Daniel Cox, op. cit.

FLORIDA

Department of Corrections

The Department of Corrections has jurisdiction over 26 major institutions, 25 community centers, eight road prisons, seven women's adjustment centers, nine probation and restitution centers and four vocational centers for adult offenders. The administration of these facilities, and probation-parole services, is divided into five regions, each headed by a director.

In 1975 the Department of Corrections initiated a multi-level Inmate Grievance Procedure applicable to all facilities.[1] An inmate may, within 30 days from the date on which an incident or action occurred, seek informal resolution by discussion with a staff member or the classification team. Should satisfaction not be obtained through such efforts, a request for administrative remedy form may be completed and tendered to the assistant superintendent (or the superintendent), who is responsible for investigating the alleged grievance and making a written response. An appeal may be made to the Regional Director (or the Secretary, Department of Corrections), which is the final level of consideration.[2]

A 30-day time limit for written responses at all levels of the procedure may be extended for a reasonable period not to exceed 30 days if it is evident that the initial time period is insufficient in which to make an appropriate decision. The inmate must be notified in writing as to the extension.[3]

If an inmate feels that filing of a written grievance within the institution may cause adversity, or the subject matter is of a sensitive nature, submission may be made directly to the Regional Director or the Secretary, Department of Corrections. However, a clear indication must be given as to the reason for by-passing the institution staff. Such a request may be returned to the inmate if the reason for not using normal channels is invalid.[4]

Regulations specify that inmates can be assured of no action being taken against them as a result of filing a grievance, unless facts show acts designed to render false or misleading statements.[5]

Currently there are no inmate councils.[6] The Glades Correctional Institution, Belle Glade, had a Dormitory Council in 1960 or 1961. The reason for its discontinuance is not known. For a period of time in 1971, the Florida State Prison and the Union Correctional Institution, both at Raiford, had inmate councils.[7]

Children, Youth and Families Program Office

The Children, Youth and Families Program Office, Department of Health and Rehabilitative Services, has jurisdiction over all training schools and community-based delinquency commitment programs.

Individually, or as a member of a group, a youth in a training school may file a complaint about the substance or application of any department policy, any of its program units, or about any behavior or action directed toward the grievant by either staff or other youths. Additionally, complaints may be filed regarding classification decisions and/or staffing recommendations.[8]

The grievance procedure has four levels: 1. Social Services Counselor; 2. Social Services Director; 3. Program Administrator; 4. Superintendent. At the first three levels, a grievance must be processed within 48 hours, and within 72 hours at the fourth, including a written response. Lack of response within the established time limits, including any extension (of which the grievant must be advised in writing), entitles the grievant to proceed to the next level of consideration. Following a response made within the time limits, any party to a grievance has 48 hours to appeal, except the superintendent.

If the grievance is of an extremely personal, confidential or emergency nature, the youth may inform the staff member or a member of the grievance committee that contact with the superintendent, assistant superintendent or duty officer is imperative. Such grievances must be processed within 24 hours.

Staff is required to counsel with a youth regarding a grievance. The counseling must include cautioning against willful use of the grievance procedure to slander staff or commit perjury. Attorney access is permitted a youth before, during or after completion of a grievance form.

If at any level of the procedure the respondent determines that the nature and scope of the grievance warrants a special review, a panel composed of personnel outside the facility, typically staff from the Department of Health and Rehabilitative Services, will be appointed. The youth has the option of accepting a panel review or proceeding to the next higher level. Recommendations of a panel are advisory only.[9]

There is no reference to a formally organized student council in the Florida State Training Schools Manual. The formation of a student council within the education program, since July 1, 1981, provided by local educational agencies under contract with the Florida Department of Education, is an issue subject to local decision-making.[10]

Information received in 1972 indicated that, although the

Division of Youth Services (now the Children, Youth and Families Program Office) had not issued directives on the implementation, purpose, and operation of student councils, each of the training schools had organized a student council on both the junior and senior levels, whose members were elected to represent their cottage of residence.[11]

Agenda topics at weekly staff-council meetings pertained to suggestions for policy or program changes and improvements, maintenance problems, leisure time activities, dress codes, and interscholastic athletics. Program and staff grievances were also aired. Community relationships were fostered by council participation in parades and pageants and assisting in clean-ups and giving help at other gatherings or activities. Liaison with the other Division of Youth Services facilities was maintained through inter-school council meetings.

A student council was organized in 1967 at the Arthur G. Dozier School for Boys, Marianna. Students prepared a constitution and by-laws. The council planned many school activities and was said to be responsible for presenting educational programs monthly to the entire student body. Members of the council were described as those students who had distinguished themselves in the program. In recognition of their efforts, and to motivate others to emulation, they were given additional privileges and permitted to wear a special insignia.[12]

Notes

1. Correctional Compass, Dept. of Corrections, Tallahassee, April 1975.
2. Policy and Procedure Directive No. 4.07.02, "Inmate Grievance Procedure," Dept. of Corrections, April 27, 1977.
3. Ibid.
4. Ibid.
5. Ibid.
6. Letter from Vernon Bradford, Information Services Director, Department of Corrections, Tallahassee, October 11, 1982.
7. Baker, J. E., op. cit., p. 108.
8. "Youth Rights and Discipline," State Training Schools Manual, (HRSM 175-4), Chapter 7, August 25, 1982.
9. Ibid., and letter from Richard E. Grimm, Program Staff Director, Children, Youth and Families Program Office, Tallahassee, March 31, 1983.
10. Letter from Richard E. Grimm, Program Staff Director, Children, Youth and Families Program Office, Tallahassee, October 8, 1982.
11. Baker, J. E., op. cit., p. 109.
12. Ibid., p. 109.

GEORGIA

Department of Offender Rehabilitation

The Division of Adult Facilities and Programs, Department of Offender Rehabilitation, administers 21 institutions and six transition centers (pre-release).[1]

An inmate grievance procedure established in 1974[2] defines a grievance as a problem which might hurt an inmate or a condition/situation that requires change or official attention. Each inmate is instructed to discuss a problem with the assigned counselor who, in most instances, would be able to resolve it. Should this not be possible, the inmate may then complete a grievance form. There are four levels of consideration with time limits for written reply as follows:[3]

1. Deputy Warden/Superintendent - 14 days.
2. Warden/Superintendent - 10 days.
3. Deputy Commissioner - 30 days.
4. Commissioner - 15 days.

Currently, offenders at the Georgia State Prison, Reidsville, serve on formal grievance committees which address a variety of operational and administrative concerns.[4] However, no indication has been received as to the role, if any, such committees play in the inmate grievance procedure.

Currently there are no formal inmate advisory councils.[5] Information was received in January, 1973 that offenders at the Georgia Diagnostic and Classification Center, Jackson, decided on a quarter-year basis which recreation programs should be implemented.[6]

In September, 1973, the department administration expressed skepticism as to the value of inmate councils, one concern being the possibility of certain strong inmates gaining too much control over the institution population. At the same time the then director of the Georgia Diagnostic and Classification Center, while evincing a similar concern, declared his intention to initiate a type of inmate council which would feature frequent rotation of leadership. At the Walker Correctional Institution, Rock Springs, small groups met weekly with counselors to discuss their problems.[7]

Division of Youth Services

The Division of Youth Services, Department of Human Resources, administers four Youth Development Centers and 17 Regional Youth Development Centers.

The four Youth Development Centers are large residential facilities for the treatment and rehabilitation of youths committed by Juvenile or Superior Courts for delinquent behavior for whom there is no alternate plan or placement.[8]

Youth in those four facilities have a right, under a grievance process, to file a complaint when in disagreement with the application of rules and regulations, expected standards of behavior, discipline actions (other than detention), or the dress code.[9]

A youth may discuss a complaint with the staff members involved. If there is no resolution, the youth will be provided a grievance form for submission to his/her social worker, who must, within five days, schedule a meeting with the staff involved. Lacking agreement, an appeal may then be made to the facility director. Consideration must be given and a decision made within five days by the director or a committee of one or two staff members or residents appointed by the director. Division regulations specify that residents should be, as often as possible, appointed for this purpose.

The final level of appeal is the Institutional Program Director of the Division of Youth Services for consideration and recommendation for resolution to the Division Director.[10]

Should the complaint allege discrimination, as defined by Title VI, Civil Rights Act of 1964, and the decision not be in favor of the grievant at the facility director level, appeal may be made to the Division Title VI Coordinator for referral to the Institutional Program Director and the Division Deputy Director.[11]

Although not within the grievance process as described, a youth may appeal an action regarding discipline, transfer, or referral for transfer to either the Specialized Treatment Program (located within the Center at Milledgeville) or the Intensive Care Unit (located within the Center at Augusta).[12]

There are no advisory councils in the Youth Development Centers.[13]

Notes

1. Letter from Ronald L. Powell, Deputy Commissioner, Division of Facilities, Dept. of Offender Rehabilitation, Atlanta, September 30, 1982.
2. Dillingham, David D. and Singer, Linda R., _op. cit._, p. 51.
3. "Orientation Handbook for Offenders," Department of Offender Rehabilitation, December 1980 (Revised).
4. Letter from Ronald L. Powell, _op. cit._
5. _Ibid._
6. Baker, J. E., _op. cit._, p. 109.
7. _Georgia Prisons_, report of the Georgia Advisory Committee to the U.S. Commission on Civil Rights, February 1976, p. 63.
8. _Annual Report, Fiscal Year 1981_, Division of Youth Services, Dept. of Human Resources, p. 13.
9. _Grievance Process_, Division of Youth Services Policy and Procedure Manual, March 22, 1982, Chapter 6, p. 11.
10. _Ibid._

11. Ibid.
12. Ibid.
13. Letter received September 24, 1982, from Alex Teel, Director, General Administration, Division of Youth Services, Atlanta

HAWAII

Corrections Division

All facilities for adult and youthful felony offenders and juvenile delinquents are administered by the Corrections Division, Department of Social Services and Housing.

An Administrative Remedy Process, established in November, 1970, revised in February, 1974, July, 1977, and lastly on July 13, 1979, delineates procedures through which inmates/wards may seek formal adjudication of complaints and grievances. A complaint is described as a specific allegation of wrongdoing, allegedly to have occurred within a facility, against another person or persons; a grievance is an injustice or unfair treatment an individual believes has been inflicted upon him/her as a result of inconsistent, coercive, or discriminatory application of a policy or rule by correctional personnel or the Adjustment/Program Committee.[1]

Within 14 days following an event or incident, an inmate may, after efforts at informal resolution through contact with staff have proved unsatisfactory, file a prescribed grievance form with the Unit Manager or Section Administrator (e.g., Programs). The inmate must be interviewed, investigations conducted as necessary to determining fully the circumstances of the grievance, and a written response made within 15 working days.

Following receipt of the decision, the grievant may appeal, within five working days, a Unit Manager's decision to the Section Administrator. The latter's decision may be appealed to the facility head, who will conduct an investigation and may hold a hearing. Whatever action is taken must be done within 15 working days and the grievant advised in writing. The facility head may either sustain, overturn, or modify the lower decision.

An appeal of the facility head's decision may be made to the Corrections Division Administrator not more than five working days later. The Division Administrator has 15 working days to provide a written response to the grievant. While this level is the ultimate recourse within the administrative remedy process, a grievant is free to invoke other remedies, e.g., writing to the Office of the Ombudsman, the State Attorney General, or a private attorney.

Grievances may be filed directly with the Corrections Division Director if the issue is of a sensitive nature, which if known could subject the grievant to punitive measures at the hands of facility staff or other inmates, or would otherwise adversely affect the grievant. Within five working days the grievant will be given a written decision on the merits of the issue, or both the grievant and the facility head will be advised that the issue is not appropriate for special attention and should be routed through normal procedural channels.

Time limits at all levels may be extended up to 15 working days if circumstances render the prescribed period insufficient to make an appropriate decision. The grievant must be advised in writing of any time extension.

A procedure for appealing disciplinary decisions requires that disciplinary measures be held in abeyance pending an appeal. On-the-spot actions are appealable to the Section Administrator or Unit Manager, the facility head, and the Corrections Division Administrator. Decisions of the Unit Adjustment team may be appealed to the Unit Manager, the facility head, and the Division Administrator. A decision of the Facility Adjustment Committee can be appealed to the facility head and the Division Administrator.

The procedure for appealing unit team or program committee decisions is the same as the process of disciplinary appeals. In both procedures the time limits and extensions and the requirement for written responses are identical to those of the administrative remedy process already described.

An Ombudsman Act was passed by the State Legislature effective June 24, 1967. The first Ombudsman was appointed on April 17, 1969 and assumed office in July, 1969.[2] Later the State Legislature enacted several laws affecting the rights and resources available to inmates/wards. The Ombudsman may investigate any complaint determined as an appropriate subject for investigation, or on his/her own motion may investigate if there is a reasonable belief that an appropriate subject for investigation exists. Inmate mail to the Ombudsman is considered privileged mail. Telephone calls to the Ombudsman are permitted except for those obviously initiated in bad faith for purposes of harassment.[3]

Inmates may contact the Ombudsman concerning acts of the Corrections Division which he/she regards as: contrary to law, unreasonable, unfair, oppressive, unnecessarily discriminatory, based on mistake of fact, improper or irrelevant grounds, unaccompanied by an adequate statement of reasons, performed in an inefficient manner, or otherwise erroneous.

Information received in 1966 was confirmed in 1972 as reflecting the situation then existent with regard to inmate advisory councils. However, the Corrections Division Manual as it pertained to councils was under study and due for some major amending. The following is the account prepared in 1966.[4]

The establishment of advisory councils is regarded by the Corrections Division as being a good institution management technique to facilitate staff-inmate communication. Directive No. 71 of the administrator describes the purpose, policies, and procedures of ward/inmate advisory councils. A constitution and by-laws drawn up by the inmates, reviewed by the facility superintendent, and approved by the administrator govern council activities. The superintendent attends the weekly meetings of the council members who are elected as representatives of their housing units. The term of office is limited to six months. Discussions concerning individuals, either inmate or staff, are not allowed. Prior to the establishment of a council the facility superintendent must interpret its purpose and objectives to both inmates and staff, stressing the advisory nature of the group. No authority over other inmates may be given to council members. All communication between the council and staff must be through the superintendent.

A Grand Council at the Hawaii State Prison, Honolulu, was organized around 1955. In 1962 a Ward Advisory Council was formed at the Hawaii Youth Correctional Facility, Honolulu. In 1956 the warden of the Hawaii State Prison reported on various activities of the inmate council there. For four years a committee had been responsible for developing and recording a 15-minute program of entertainment, discussion, and prison information which was broadcast regularly over a local radio station. In addition, a welfare committee raised funds to aid inmates and parolees in time of need; a teenage committee sponsored a community settlement swimming team, and another committee studied delinquency in the light of its own experiences, preparing radio programs and news articles. A public relations committee was credited with having played an important part in an effective community relations program. The inmate council of the Kulani Honor Camp at Hilo had a blood donor program under which they had agreed to supply blood to two young anemic boys.

Directive No. 71, originally issued in October, 1966, was reissued in October, 1973, under the title "Huki Like Advisory Councils," establishing a resident-staff advisory council in each facility, to be composed of an equal number of each group, with membership not to exceed 12. Resident members are elected to a term not to exceed six months by their peers. Employee members are selected by popular vote of the facility permanent staff to a term of not more than one year. The facility head is the chairman and must attend every council meeting, or assign an administrator alternate to do so.[5]

Office facilities and supplies are provided for the council. Through the office, residents and staff may present problems or communicate advice or suggestions for the betterment of institutional work and life.

Council meetings, required at least once a month, are conducted according to Robert's Rules of Order. No discussion of any individual, resident or staff, is permitted nor are matters which are the prerogative of the Governor, the Director of Social Services and Housing, the Corrections Administrator, the facility head, or the courts. The chairman explains why a topic is not within the scope of the council.

At no time and under no circumstances may the council be given authority to order other residents or employees to carry out projects, even those approved by the facility head. Council members may, however, obtain the assistance of others in carrying out approved projects.

At any time when the facility head is of the opinion the advisory purpose of the council no longer exists, the termination of the group may be ordered.

Huki Like? (Communication, cooperation and pulling together).

Notes

1. Policies and Procedures Manual, "Inmate Grievance and Appeals Process; Administrative Remedy Process," Corrections Division, July 13, 1979.
2. Weeks, Kent M. Ombudsmen Around the World. Berkeley, California: Institute of Governmental Studies, University of California, 1978, p. 158.
3. Policies and Procedures Manual, "Ombudsman, Access To," Corrections Division, July 13, 1979.
4. Baker, J. E., op. cit., pp. 110-111.
5. "Huki Like Advisory Councils," Corrections Division, October 1973 (originally issued October 1966).

IDAHO

Department of Corrections

The Department of Corrections administers two institutions for adult and youthful felony offenders.

Grievances of inmates, other than those arising out of actions taken within the adjustment process, are handled on an informal basis. The adjustment process provides a tri-level procedure in which the Director, Department of Corrections is the final level of review.[1]

Information was received in 1972 that a five-member Inmate Advisory Council was organized on October 8, 1969, and

> operates under the provisions of a constitution and by-laws whose preamble cites the purposes of the organization as the maintenance of high morale, the encouragement of participation in programs designed for personal accomplishment, and the propagation of inmate-administration cooperation and understanding.
>
> Elections are held in January and July. Any inmate who has been in continuous residence for six months may

> be elected to a six-month term, with tenure limited to two consecutive terms, to serve at-large. The council elects its own officers, with each member filling one of the following offices: chairman, vice-chairman, secretary-reporter, parliamentarian, and sergeant-at-arms. Unsupervised meetings are held the first and third weeks of each month, in a location chosen by the council, to prepare an agenda of no more than four major topics, each representative of a broad segment of the institution community, for discussion at a monthly meeting with the director. If it is believed they can more effectively present a proposal, one or two non-members may be asked by the council to attend this meeting. A councilman may be removed from office by a majority vote of the population provided he is given a written notice of the charges against him. Standing committees may be appointed by the council.
>
> A member of the Inmate Advisory Council attends meetings of the Adjustment Committee, Incentive Pay Board, and other staff committees, his role being described as basically that of a consultant. This arrangement has improved inmate-staff relationships.[2]

The Inmate Advisory Council stopped functioning in 1975.[3]

Department of Health and Welfare

The Youth Services Center, Saint Anthony, provides residential treatment services to youth adjudicated under the State Youth Rehabilitation Act, excluding status offenders. The department regulations govern all phases of the Youth Center operation, including grievances.[4]

The grievance procedure at the Youth Services Center provides for written grievances to be sent directly to the Administrative Director of the facility.[5]

Information was received in 1973 that a Student Council was involved in many aspects of facility government and behavior policies. A dress code and student possession of money were cited as results of council initiative.[6]

Current information indicates that the student council was an advisory group, not a formal governing body. The council is no longer in existence. The date of its demise is not known; reportedly it just gradually dissolved.[7]

Notes

1. Letter received September 27, 1982, from Eugene Larson, Dept. of Corrections, Boise; Dillingham, David D. and Singer, Linda R., op. cit., p. 51.
2. Baker, J. E., op. cit., pp. 111-112.

3. Letter from Eugene Larson, op. cit.
4. Letter from Linda Hagedorn-Guiles, Principal Planner, Division of Community Rehabilitation, Dept. of Health and Welfare, November 17, 1972.
5. Ibid.
6. Baker, J. E., op. cit., p. 112.
7. Letter from Linda Hagedorn-Guiles, op. cit.

ILLINOIS

Department of Corrections

The Department of Corrections has jurisdiction over all facilities for adult offenders and juvenile delinquents. In 1972, the department undertook a massive revision of its administrative regulations, which were subsequently enacted in 1973, in the form of a statutory unified code of corrections. The new regulations mandated that all institutions develop formal grievance mechanisms.[1]

Adult Division

The Adult Division administers 14 institutions for adult and youthful felony offenders over the age of seventeen. Two Correctional Centers, Vandalia and Dwight, also receive misdemeanants.

A 1974 description of the grievance procedure for inmates indicated that at each institution a staff member is assigned as a Special Counselor, with responsibility for the operation of the procedure ancillary to his/her primary duties. Also, in each institution there is a three-member Institutional Inquiry Board and a three-member Administrative Review Board, composed of two department employees and a person from the community.

Under the procedure an inmate with a problem approaches the Special Counselor. If that individual is not able to resolve the problem satisfactorily, the inmate then can prepare a written complaint for the Institutional Inquiry Board, which must give the grievant a hearing and deliver a response within ten days to the superintendent, who has five days to respond to the inmate. If still dissatisfied, the inmate can appeal to the department director. If the director decides that the complaint has merit, it is referred to the Administrative Review Board. The Board may conduct a hearing at the institution, then forward its recommendation to the director, who in turn responds to the inmate.

Any issue, including appeals of institution disciplinary panels, is grievable under the procedure. The 1974 description stated that at two of the largest Illinois institutions, the Administrative Review Board was then overturning approximately 70 per cent of the disciplinary decisions appealed to the director. One of the primary functions of the Board was to establish maximum punishments for institution disciplinary panels. By routinely reducing excessive punishments, the Board had changed policy without issuing a formal policy revision.

The procedure was begun in 1972 and a formal written procedure was issued in October, 1973,[2] under Administrative Regulation 845.

No current information has been received from the Department of Corrections regarding either inmate grievance procedures or inmate advisory councils.

The last information on inmate advisory councils was in October, 1966. At that time, although there were no advisory councils, the formation of such groups as a part of social education had not been entirely excluded from future planning.[3]

An attempt by Warden Hill to form an inmate grievance committee at the Illinois State Penitentiary, Joliet, was recounted in chapter I on Notable Early Experiences.

Juvenile Division

The Juvenile Division administers eight facilities for juvenile delinquents.

Following enactment of the Unified Code of Corrections, the Juvenile Division issued Administrative Regulation 613, Grievance Procedure for Youth, in 1972.

As a matter of policy, a youth's counselor assists in the preparation of a written grievance, which is processed in much the same way as described in the adult grievance procedure, i.e., throug a three-member Institutional Inquiry Board, before whom the grievant may appear, and whose report of findings and recommendations must reach the superintendent within ten working days. The latter then has five days to make a response in writing. If not satisfied, the grievant may appeal to the department director who may refer the case to a three-member Administrative Review Board, one member of which must be a person not employed by the department. Subsequent to receiving the board's report, the director will make a final determination and so advise the grievant in writing. No disciplinary action under any circumstances may be taken against a youth for using the grievance procedures.[4]

A 1973 report tells of a unique "court system" at the Illinois Youth Center-Valley View, St. Charles (then the Valley View School for Boys), related to the token economy at the school. (A current description of Valley View states that its program is a token economy system based on social learning principles.) Room and work assignments, privileges, and recreation were determined by the level of a resident's "bank account" in the token economy. Tokens were awarded and subtracted each week in a "court" session where every resident appeared before one of the two institutional "judges" with negative or positive reports from his counselors, teachers, and supervisors. A negative token value was levied for each disciplinary report, and awards of positive value were given for favorable behavior reports. Residents could appeal negative levies to another campus "judge" and could "sue" for grievance damages. At that time the "court" system was used more frequently than the formal grievance procedure. However, most of the residents then interviewed expressed serious disenchantment with the "court" system, viewing it as a disciplinary tool.

The same report speaks of the establishment of a Youth Advocate Office in Illinois juvenile corrections, patterned after the New York Division for Youth Ombudsman program, in February, 1974. As of September, 1974, the Youth Advocate program had replaced the grievance procedure entirely as a means of obtaining review of grievances at a higher level than the facility superintendent.[5]

No information was received regarding the current status of student councils. In February, 1973, it was reported that student councils or similar groups were active in seven facilities.[6]

A student council at the Illinois Youth Center, Hanna City (then the Hanna City State Boys' School), met weekly as teams with dormitory staff. A monthly meeting was also held with the superintendent and administrative staff. At the Illinois Industrial School for Boys, Sheridan (converted in 1973 to the Sheridan Correctional Center, an adult and youthful felony offender facility), an Administrative Call Line of key staff visited each housing unit weekly to discuss the delivery of services. Everyone was heard and all problems and suggestions were discussed.

Although the short length of time students were in residence before assignment to an institution precluded the establishment of a formalized student council at the then Reception and Diagnostic Center for Boys, Joliet, informal student input was provided in the Gemini program, and it was planned that students participate in procedure and program policy-making in a Bridge Learning Center being developed.

Four separate program units operated independently but shared the general facilities at the Illinois Youth Center, St. Charles (then the Illinois State Training School for Boys). All four programs had student councils in each cottage, meeting together as a student government. The councils were regarded as productive avenues in the decision-making process. The then Illinois State Training School for Girls, Geneva, operated as a coeducational facility. A Student Involvement Committee, representing all cottages, met with the superintendent and key administrative staff to develop program, projects, and activities, as well as to participate in the planning and implementation of rules.

The Illinois Youth Center, Napierville (then the DuPage State Boys' School), had group therapy programs, such as guided group interaction, the dynamics of which provided student input relative to daily living practices. Pre-parole groups met weekly with the administration to make recommendations pertaining to cottage life and program problems. A Student Involvement Council played an integral role at the Valley View School for Boys, St. Charles, in parole plans, token economy, reinforcement implementation, as well as reviewing rules on dress codes, dietary plans, and social activities. (The facility is now the Illinois Youth Center, Valley View.)

No information was obtained regarding the Jubilee Lodge, Brimfield, a 36-person facility which opened in 1972, or the eight school camps under the office of Forestry Camps and Schools, Springfield. In 1967 it was reported that a Student Advisory Committee was in operation at the Pere Marquette School Camps, Grafton (now the Illinois Youth Center-Pere Marquette). All nominees were required to make a speech setting forth their qualifications, after which open elections were held. Committeemen met with a staff member and were free to make recommendations on all subjects.

Notes

1. Illinois Code of Corrections, Chapter 38, 1003-8-8.
2. Keating, McArthur, Lewis, Sebelius, and Singer, op. cit., p. 39.
3. Baker, J. E., op. cit., p. 112.
4. "Grievance Procedure for Youth," Administrative Regulation 613, Juvenile Division, Dept. of Corrections, Springfield, (revised November 15, 1977; originally issued in 1972).
5. Keating, Gilligan, McArthur, Lewis, and Singer, 1974, op. cit., pp. 65-67. (Administrative Regulation 613, as revised in 1977, mandates that the Grievance Procedure be used for obtaining review of grievances at a higher level than the facility superintendent.)
6. Baker, J. E., op. cit., pp. 113-114.

INDIANA

Department of Correction

All facilities for adult and youthful felony offenders and juvenile delinquents are administered by the Department of Correction. Until the fiscal year 1982, there was an Adult Authority and a Youth Authority, each headed by an Executive Director.[1]

An offender grievance procedure was established in September, 1979, applicable to all institutions.[2] A grievance is defined as a complaint or allegation about departmental policy, administrative procedures, institution operations, staff neglect, abuse or misconduct.

Excluded from the procedure are parole board actions, clemency, disciplinary hearings, crediting of good time, pending civil or criminal litigation, and any matter in which procedure is provided for by law.

All grievances must be written on a specified form, and filed within 48 hours of an incident. However, an issue of a recurring nature may be submitted at any time.

An investigator appointed by the institution superintendent is responsible for conducting a fact-finding investigation in a ten-working-day period and forwarding a report to a grievance committee composed of both staff and inmates. A decision must be made in writing within ten working days. If not in agreement, the grievant may appeal to the institution superintendent and subsequently to the Commissioner, Department of Correction, the final level of review. Both of those levels are required to reply within ten working days.

Each institution is required to establish special provisions for responding to emergency or life-threatening situations. As an example, the procedure developed at the Indiana Girls' School, Indianapolis, requires that such situations be referred immediately to the superintendent, or designate. An emergency is defined as a situation which threatens the security, safety or welfare of offenders or staff, or poses a threat to the peaceful operation of the institution. A life-threatening situation is one which might affect the health or physical safety of offenders or staff unless remedied immediately.

Employees are forbidden to direct any reprisal against an offender who files a grievance.

Currently, the Indiana State Prison, Michigan City, is the only adult institution utilizing offenders in the grievance procedure. At least two offenders are members of the Grievance Review Committee.[3]

At the Indiana Girls' School one offender, a Campus Council Representative, acts as a member of the Grievance Review Committee.[4]

An Ombudsman program was established in 1974 which provided for written responses. Due to a lack of funding by the State General Assembly, the program was discontinued. However, an Ombudsman position was established within the Department of Correction in July, 1981, to provide prompt attention to a wide variety of offender grievances and complaints, including complaints by offenders' families directed to the Governor and the Department. Additionally, the Ombudsman regularly visits the institutions, serves on committees to audit and evaluate institution programs and objectives, reviews compliance with policies pertaining to operations, programs, and services, and assists in the drafting of policy and procedures and reviewing those proposed by institutions.[5]

Early in 1957, inmates at the Indiana State Prison, Michigan City, petitioned the warden to approve an inmate council. However, the warden questioned the request and it was subsequently formally disapproved by the Commissioner of Corrections.[6]

An Inmate Advisory Council was organized at the Indiana State Prison in June, 1969, with a membership of approximately 40. In January, 1973, the warden reported that upon taking office in August, 1969 he initiated a reorganization providing for two councils, one representing the main institution and the other representing the two prison farms and a trusty dormitory. To be eligible to run in the annual January election, an individual had to obtain 50 signatures endorsing his candidacy. The 12 members served until released from the institution. An agenda, prepared and submitted to the warden for his approval and additions, was discussed at periodic meetings which were taped for evening broadcast over the radio system. The council officers--president, vice-president, secretary, and committee chairmen--worked full-time in an office provided by the administration. The committee chairmen were permitted to visit their areas of responsibility during working hours to talk with inmates and to gather information for council meetings. The hospital, food service, and recreation were mentioned as service areas represented by council committees. Council accomplishments included the restructuring of diets, lowering the cost of certain food items sold in the commissary, and selection of recreational item purchases. Effectiveness of the council was questioned, as it was felt that those persons attracted to membership were not representative of the institution population.[7]

Sometime prior to 1935, a Cadet System was established at the Indiana Reformatory, Pendleton. Cadets were assigned to supervise groups of inmates as they marched to and from work areas and to assist in the cleaning and keeping of order in living quarters. When it was no longer felt to be a viable approach, the system was abolished in 1964.

While superintendent from May, 1961 to February, 1966, John Buck organized a Coordinating Committee of one representative from each inmate group, such as Alcoholics Anonymous and Jaycees, to assist in planning special programs. He found the participation of the group to be most helpful. Between 1967 and 1968 a group calling itself Inmate Committee for Better Relations came into existence. This group ostensibly meant to foster wholesome relations between staff and inmates. It defeated itself, however, by attempting to control job assignments and to set itself up as an official control force. Lack of administrative guidelines and controls added to the ineffectiveness of the group. The approach used by the group created new gulfs between staff and inmates and widened those already existent. During 1966 to 1968 there was sporadic discussion concerning the efficacy of inmate advisory groups.

In 1969, after discussion with both staff and inmates, then Superintendent George Phend initiated action to develop an Inmate

Council. The group met regularly and had the guidance of an assigned staff advisor. In January, 1970, a general election was held by the inmate population. A council of 48 men was elected to represent the population, and subsequently elected their own officers. The council had proven itself to be an effective communications medium for both staff and inmates. A number of projects proposed by the council were adopted--e.g., merit visits for inmates and more privacy during visits. The three-year operation of the council was enhanced by openness in discussions, promptness in investigating grievances, and observance of adequate controls relative to the function of the council. Council representatives were included in most discussions where the inmates were directly involved. Mutual openness between staff and inmates, the controlled, progressive delegation of responsibility to the inmates themselves, and the general acceptance of that responsibility by the inmates were cited as constituting a triad of reasons contributing to the acceptance and effectiveness of the council.[8]

In January, 1973, it was reported that the annual population turnover of four to five thousand misdemeanor offenders at the Indiana State Farm, Greencastle, had inhibited the organization of an inmate advisory council.[9]

At the Indiana Women's Prison, Indianapolis, an inmate council, composed of two elected members from each of the five cottages, was organized in October, 1968. In January, 1973 it was still active, holding meetings on call with the superintendent to present problems and discuss solutions, with other staff members attending should the topic pertain to their areas of responsibility.[10]

In February, 1973 it was reported that there was no council and no plans for one in the immediate future at the Reception and Diagnostic Center, Plainfield. This is a very short-term facility, which receives all male felons for study and assignment to an institution.[11]

There are no currently sanctioned inmate councils or similar groups functioning on a full-time basis in any of the adult institutions. Ad hoc committees are appointed for a specified time period to address and seek a solution to a particular situation. This approach has proven to be a successful communication mechanism and a positive force in the resolution process.[12]

At the Indiana Boys' School, Plainfield, a Student Council was established on July 1, 1969, and in February, 1973 was reported as being a member of the Indiana Association of Student Councils. Each cottage elected a member to the council. The president, vice-president, secretary, and assistant secretary were elected by the membership. The purpose of the group was to sustain a spirit of confidence and trust between the young men and the administration by providing for open communication. At the monthly meetings, any topic applicable to life at the school could be discussed. Several changes in policy were cited as originating through Student Council suggestion. All pertained to increased privileges.[13] The council has been discontinued. Students present grievances to their cottage teams or through the offender grievance procedure.

In 1967, a student council was organized at the Indiana Girls' School, Indianapolis. Each cottage elected one girl to serve a one-month term on the council which met weekly with the superintendent to discuss grievances and suggest changes. The group was described as being advisory in nature.[14] Currently, the Campus Council functions as a part of the Positive Peer Culture program. Each month a girl is chosen from her group of nine members to serve as a representative to the council. One representative participates in the due process hearings in the detention cottage. A representative serves, on a rotating basis, as a member of the Grievance Review Committee. The council spearheads all special events, e.g., the school prom, election days and use of the voting machine, and special presentations to visitors and community groups. The council has access to the superintendent to discuss or negotiate on institutional policies and procedures.[15]

A 1973 report stated that the Indiana Youth Center, Plainfield, had an inmate council whose constitution provided for the popular vote election of one councilman and two alternates to represent each housing unit for a six-months period, providing the candidate had been at the facility for at least 60 days and the date of his release was six months or more distant. A president, vice-president, and recorder-secretary were elected within the membership. Meetings of the council were held weekly. On alternate weeks, staff advisors met with the group to review actions. No resolution could be forwarded to the administration without advisor consent. The superintendent was given a monthly report on the progress of the council. No current information has been received.

Information regarding the Rockville Training Center, Rockville, indicates that with the exception of the Positive Peer Culture groups and the decision-making responsibilities each has, there are no groups which could be classified as inmate councils.[17]

Notes

1. Annual Report, 1981-82, Dept. of Correction, Indianapolis, p. 7.
2. Policy No. 02-01-401, "The Offender Grievance Process," Board of Correction, October 1, 1980 (supersedes Policy No. 6-09, September 7, 1979); Administrative Procedures Policy No. 02-01-401, "The Offender Grievance Process," Dept. of Correction, Indianapolis, October 2, 1980 (effective December 1, 1980).
3. Letter from John L. Nunn, Correctional Ombudsman, Dept. of Correction, Indianapolis, May 26, 1983.
4. Manual of Policies and Procedures, "The Offender Grievance Process," Indiana Girls' School, Indianapolis, December 1, 1980.

5. Letter from John L. Nunn, _op. cit._
6. Baker, J. E., _op. cit._, p. 114.
7. Baker, J. E., _op. cit._, pp. 114-115.
8. _Ibid._, pp. 115-116.
9. _Ibid._, p. 116.
10. _Ibid._, p. 116.
11. _Ibid._, p. 116.
12. Letter from John L. Nunn, _op. cit._
13. Baker, J. E., _op. cit._, p. 116.
14. _Ibid._, p. 116.
15. Letter by Supt. Thomas D. Hanlon, Indiana Girls' School, Indianapolis (to Deputy Commissioner Alfred R. Bennett, Dept. of Correction), October 12, 1982.
16. Baker, J. E., _op. cit._, pp. 116-117.
17. Letter by Supt. Walter E. Martin, Rockville Training Center, Rockville (to Deputy Commissioner Alfred R. Bennett, Dept. of Correction), October 4, 1982.

IOWA

Department of Social Services

The Department of Social Services has jurisdiction over all facilities for adult and youthful felony offenders and juvenile delinquents.

Bureau of Correctional Institutions

The Bureau of Correctional Institutions, Division of Adult Corrections, administers eight institutions for adult and youthful felony offenders.

In October, 1970, the Governor of Iowa created the office of Citizens' Aide, a state-wide ombudsman program to monitor state government agencies. In 1972, the Citizens' Aide Act was passed and funds appropriated to establish the Citizens' Aide as a separate state agency. In September, 1973, a Deputy for Corrections position was approved within the Citizens' Aide office to provide ombudsman services to three adult and three juvenile facilities and to 88 county jails.[1]

A 1974 description of the ombudsman office as it operated at the Men's Reformatory, Anamosa, stated that the scope of the program was primarily limited to individual grievances, although at times these led to recommendations for a change in policy or procedure.[2]

The Ombudsman got most of his complaints by mail. He also visited the two large male facilities weekly to see inmates and pick up complaints face to face. He conducted his investigations in person, by telephone, and through examination of records. He made an informal oral recommendation to the Warden, followed by a written recommendation if no action was taken within a reasonable period of time. He could appeal to the Commissioner of Adult Services, then the Commissioner of Social Services, and finally the Governor, if he was not satisfied with the response to his recommendation from the lower levels. Most of the grievances were handled within 30 days, although the law establishing the Citizens' Aide Office allows 60 days.

No current information has been received regarding either inmate grievance procedures or inmate advisory councils. A 1980 report indicates that a grievance procedure was established in 1973, which required written responses to be made within specified time limits. A formal hearing was given each grievant. The Commissioner, Department of Social Services, was the final level of review.[3]

In 1940, there was an unsuccessful experience with an inmate committee which helped operate an honor dormitory for a time at the Iowa State Penitentiary, Fort Madison. In 1972, while there was no inmate advisory council, three groups operated under staff sponsorship and procedures defined by practice or written constitution. They were: The Lainett Alcoholics Anonymous Group founded in 1948; a Gavel Club (Toastmasters International) organized on November 10, 1965; and the Pen City Jaycees, active since May 5, 1966.[4]

In 1934, at the Men's Reformatory, Anamosa (then the Iowa Men's Reformatory), an inmate committee of three members appointed by the warden was reported as assisting in the management of the prisoners' canteen. Another committee, known as the Athletic Board, was assisting in planning the athletic program, with particular emphasis on its intramural aspects.[5]

An Inmate Council was organized in 1956 at the Men's Reformatory. It ceased to exist in 1962, but was reorganized in 1964 and functioned under a constitution and by-laws which provided for the election of work-area representatives who met bi-monthly with a staff sponsor.

A 1972 description of the Men's Reformatory Inmate Council made no mention of a constitution, by-laws, or staff sponsor, but did give details of council procedures and areas of activity:

> ... serves to increase communications between residents and staff.... [A] vehicle which promotes the opportunity for a free flow of ideas and problems, providing an opportunity for understanding of the concerns of both.... [A]llows residents to take an active role in problem solving and exposes them to the varied expectations which are part of organizational activities found in the community.... [A]llows residents to demonstrate responsible behavior and utilize various skills in planning, organizing, and implementing constructive projects.

Any resident in the Men's Reformatory who, in the previous

three months, had no disciplinary report resulting in loss of good-time credits, could be elected by his fellow workers to represent a designated work area. A president and a services secretary were elected by the council membership.

Administrative and Correctional-Treatment Services personnel alternated at the staff-group meeting each week with the 17 council members. Other staff might be invited to discuss special problems or could attend on their own initiative. A typed summary of discussions was distributed to all residents and staff and written decisions were provided later by staff on all matters not resolved in the meeting. In order to provide for idea input by residents and to make them aware of departmental problems, the procedure provided for council appointment of subcommittees to meet with department heads. The council derived income from three sources, a movie screened twice a week, profits from visiting room vending machines, and donations from the community.

Expenditures of this income were determined by the council for the benefit of all residents. Interestingly, council members assisted housing unit staff in resolving interpersonal relationship problems, either resident-staff or resident-resident. Council members were assembled as a first move in coping with a possible disturbance. The overall effectiveness of the council at a given period was regarded as a reflection of its leadership.[6]

Information obtained in 1966 from the Women's Reformatory, Rockwell City (in 1982 this institution became the Medium Security Unit; the female residents were moved to the Iowa Correctional Institution for Women, Mitchellville, which until that time was the Iowa Training School for Girls), as presented herein, was reviewed by Iowa authorities in 1972 and returned with no changes. In order to provide the women an opportunity to express their concerns to the administration as well as to foster their involvement with the staff in program development, a Women's Council was organized in August, 1966. Three representatives from each cottage are elected by secret ballot to six-month terms. The superintendent is the chairman and secretary. The philosophy of the administration toward the council concept and an evaluation of council usefulness was made (in 1966) by the Acting Superintendent James E. Allen:[7]

> ... I think the most pressing need in adult institutions today is simply to be aware that women living in a group have concerns about the way they would like to live, and that the majority of their suggestions are fairly valid. The way in which the Women's Council is currently organized gives the top administrator the full advantage of purposefully involving the women in program planning, receiving an ongoing feeling of the tone of the institution, and an effective tool in group control since the members of the council are leaders in their units. The Women's Council is a semi-administration-inmate group that can serve many purposes. The group has been fairly effective both for the total population and for the staff....

A 1980 study indicated that a Staff/Resident Council was operative at Iowa Correctional Institution for Women, but no details were given.[8]

Bureau of Children's Services

The Bureau of Children's Services, Division of Community Programs, has jurisdiction over the single facility for juvenile delinquents, the State Training School, Eldora.

The Deputy for Corrections (Prison Ombudsman), Citizens' Aide Office, described in the foregoing section on the adult institutions, is applicable to juvenile institutions also.

A 1974 report described an internal grievance procedure designed in the period 1970-72, and revised and updated in 1973, at the Iowa Training School for Girls, Mitchellville (since 1982 this facility has been re-designated for female adult offenders and renamed the Iowa Correctional Institution for Women).[9]

The grievance procedure was activated when a girl filed a written grievance with the superintendant. There was no grievance form. Once the grievance was filed, a hearing was scheduled, usually for the same day or, at the latest, for the following day. The hearing panel was chaired by one of three staff persons: superintendent, treatment supervisor, or school principal, depending on the nature of the complaint. Two girls also sat on the panel; one was the elected grievance representative from the cottage where the complaint originated, and the other was a representative from one of the other cottages.

At the hearing, the complainant decided who would be present in the room during her appearance; if she wanted to confront any staff members involved in the grievance, she could do so. If she wanted to tell her story privately, then the panel later interviewed the others involved. Witnesses were called and testimony given, although the hearings were informal. After hearing testimony, the members of the grievance panel discussed the case. The chairman alone made and announced the final decision. A written report was then placed in the complainant's file.

A resident dissatisfied with the outcome could write directly to the Bureau Director. However, since anyone could write directly to the Bureau Director without going through a hearing, this hardly constituted a procedural appeal process. The principal explained that the procedure was designed especially for non-verbal girls who would not talk to the superintendent on a regular basis. The Advisory Council, later described, which formally met monthly with the superintendent, helped design the procedure. Complaints were filed by girls on an average of three times a month to voice personal complaints; youths did not use the procedure to advocate policy changes in the facility, according to the principal.

Staff interviewed at the time supported the grievance procedure, although they stated that it was not particularly important. They indicated that there had been no effort to educate staff about the procedure, although cottage manuals contained a written description. Staff also said that the Advisory Council no longer functioned, but that administrators got feedback from girls on an informal basis.

Residents at Mitchellville were not enthusiastic about the grievance procedure. Although some felt that serious personal problems might be resolved through the grievance procedure, most stated that residents rarely got favorable responses to their complaints and that it "was no good to complain because we always lose." This presumption seemed to be due, in part, to inadequate communications.

In March, 1938, a Student Council was organized in the high school program at the Iowa Training School for Girls, Mitchellville, as an experiment to be carried for the remainder of the school year. Each class elected two members who took care of the discipline in halls and lines between classes, and sponsored school parties. A vote taken in September, 1938, found that three-fourths of the girls favored continuance of the council. Additionally, council members tidied up the campus and sponsored initiation of the school freshmen, and sponsored Halloween and Thanksgiving dances, and were planning for the Christmas Holiday Season.[10]

Shortly after September, 1972, following the appointment of a new superintendent, a Superintendent's Advisory Council was organized at the Iowa Training School for Girls. As noted heretofore, the council helped design the grievance procedure. According to some staff members interviewed in 1974, the council no longer functioned.

The 1972 account of the Superintendent's Advisory Council indicated that each cottage elected a representative by secret ballot. An at-large representative was elected by all girls in the school. Meetings were held each Monday with the superintendent to discuss administrative policies only. The council also selected the weekly movies. Other program modifications were being considered to insure participation by girls in operations planning. A team approach was then being implemented which would provide twice-weekly meetings of team personnel and cottage residents.[11]

At the Iowa Training School for Boys, Eldora, a Student Council was organized among the boys in the discipline unit, which had undergone a physical, psychological, and philosophical facelifting. It was renamed Health Center and the philosophy was changed from punishment and suppression to medically oriented treatment of both physical and emotional disorders. The council operated from 1961 to 1965 as an integral part of the program. A president, vice-president and one representative from each wing of the building were elected by secret ballot. Weekly meetings were held with the staff, at which time the boys presented matters related to the unit program. The meetings were described in a 1964 article:

> Inmates are expected to bring up in the meeting factors disturbing to the general progress of the program; oftentimes considerable responsibility is shown in this area. Suggestions made in writing by inmates are read to the population by the council officers and they frequently lead to important discussions about one another's behavior. That the plotting of escapes has been reported on several occasions seems indicative of the strength of the council and of staff-council rapport. Comments about the personal shortcomings or successes of inmates are often introduced by their fellows for discussion, for example: "Why does Sam keep wiping his nose on the dish towel?"; "Joe has been slugging me and I want him to stop it"; "Jack did a nice job of planning the party last night." Staff members, too, must be strong enough to accept critical comments directed toward them.
>
> The activities of the student council are closely supervised and care is taken that it not degenerate into a kangaroo court. It serves a valuable function in providing a forum for the expression of inmate feelings. It teaches some measure of community responsibility and it has been especially helpful in the ego development of boys elected to official positions.

In December, 1972, it was reported that, since 1965, daily community meetings had been held which had eliminated the student council. Those meetings, attended by both staff and boys, were seen as more desirable than council meetings to meet the six objectives of: catharsis, problem solving, development of communication skills, development of self-awareness, development of ego strength, and staff development. In mid-1966 these community meetings were made a part of the program in all living units of the school.[12]

Currently, the only facility for juvenile delinquents is the coed facility, the State Training School, Eldora. In 1982, as previously mentioned, the Iowa Training School for Girls was re-designated as an institution for female adult offenders and renamed the Iowa Correctional Institution for Women, Mitchellville.

Participation by students is encouraged by the administration. Students from living units are selected to serve on the Superintendent's Advisory Council. The group meets with the superintendent to review operations and to allow for suggestions for improvements in services and physical plant.[13] Although it was not specifically stated, this council could be a continuation of the Superintendent's Advisory Council organized in 1972 at the Girls School when it was at Mitchellville.[13]

Another advisory group of students reviews menu selection with the dietician. A Detention Review Panel composed of two staff members and a student review detention admissions and impose sanctions as provided under established procedures. The student member is always from a living unit other than that of the offending student.

The superintendent believes this has been a good experience for most of the students.[14]

Notes

1. Keating, Gilligan, McArthur, Lewis, and Singer. Seen But Not Heard: A Survey of Grievance Mechanisms in Juvenile Correctional Institutions. Washington, D.C.: Center for Community Justice, 1974, pp. 44-45.
2. Keating, McArthur, Lewis, Sebelius, and Singer. Grievance Mechanisms in Correctional Institutions. Washington, D.C.: U.S. Dept. of Justice, 1975, pp. 40-41.
3. Dillingham, David D., and Singer, Linda R., op. cit., p. 51.
4. Baker, J. E., op. cit., p. 117.
5. Cox, William B., and Bixby, F. Lovell, Ph.D., eds. Handbook of American Prisons and Reformatories, West North Central States. Vol. I, First Edition. New York: The Osborne Association, Inc., 1938, pp. 44-45.
6. Baker, J. E., op. cit., pp. 118-119.
7. Ibid., p. 119.
8. Neto, Virginia V., and Bainer, LaNelle Marie, op. cit., p. 112.
9. Keating, Gilligan, McArthur, Lewis, and Singer, 1974, op. cit., pp. 46-47.
10. Cox, William B., and Bixby, F. Lovell, Ph.D., eds. Handbook of American Institutions for Delinquent Juveniles. Vol. I, West North Central States. New York: The Osborne Association, Inc., 1938, p. 69.
11. Baker, J. E., op. cit., pp. 119-120.
12. Ibid., pp. 120-121.
13. Letter from Superintendent James W. Hoy, State Training School, Eldora, March 28, 1983.
14. Ibid.

KANSAS

Department of Corrections

The Department of Corrections, established in 1974 to replace the Department of Penal Institutions, administers five institutions, two honor camps, and two work release centers, for adult and youthful felony offenders.

An Inmate Grievance Procedure was established in 1975 as was a State Ombudsman for Corrections position,[1] the latter as a result of a recommendation in December, 1974 by the Kansas Advisory Committee to the U.S. Commission on Civil Rights. The Ombudsman makes written responses within specific time limits to each grievant.

Should resolution of a complaint fail upon discussion of the situation with the housing unit team, or if no response is received, an inmate may file with the institution administrator a written grievance setting forth, on a prescribed form, the subject of the complaint; related dates and places; what effect the situation, problem, or person is having on the grievant which necessitates the complaint; the title and number, if possible, of any order or regulation involved;[2] and the action requested to resolve the matter. A response within 12 working days is required and must include the reason for whatever decision was made, together with notification that an appeal may be made. (Should the institution head realize that an adequate decision cannot be made within that time, the inmate must be notified within 12 working days and advised of the date a response will be made, which period cannot exceed 35 days from receipt of the grievance form.)[3]

Additionally, the institution head may designate, for a period not to exceed six months, two or more employees and a like number of inmates to participate in an advisory capacity in the making of decisions relative to complaints challenging general policy or practice. A particular inmate, or no inmates, may act in this capacity should the grievant object.[4]

The next level is the Deputy Secretary for Institutional Services who must respond in writing within 12 working days. An extension of this period may be made under the same conditions as heretofore described.[5]

An appeal may then be made to the Secretary, Department of Corrections, within 15 days, in which a request for outside review is permissible. The Secretary, at his discretion, may refer the complaint to the Ombudsman or some independent body outside the department. Within 30 working days[6] a complete investigation of the complaint and a recommendation for disposition will be made by the external reviewer, and a report given to the secretary, with a copy to the inmate. Actions recommended are not binding on the secretary. Following such a report, a response must be made to the inmate within 15 working days.[7]

Reprisals against inmates for good faith use of the procedure are forbidden. Personnel or inmates involved in the complaint may not participate in any capacity in the resolution process. Grievance proceedings files are confidential and only staff involved in the procedure may have access to records essential to resolution. Grievances of an emergency nature are forwarded immediately to the level at which corrective action can be taken.[8]

A 1975 report indicates that a Departmental Grievance Procedure was established in August, 1972 (approximate date). A description of the procedure as it operated at the Kansas State Penitentiary, Lansing, indicated that an inmate with any type grievance, "... including disciplinary appeals, writes a sealed letter to the Warden, who conducts an investigation and gives an answer. If the inmate is dissatisfied he writes to the Secretary of the Department who, in turn, investigates the complaint and delivers a written answer to the inmate. There are no time limits on the grievance procedure."[9]

Inmate councils as such are not used within the Department of Corrections at present.[10] In 1967, it was reported that councils in two honor camps had been disbanded as they were used by inmates as nothing more than a bartering agency which offered little toward resolving problems.[11]

Following a survey by the Osborne Association in August, 1937, the then Superintendent of the Kansas State Industrial Reformatory indicated that attention was being given to the establishment of an inmate council, based on that of the Federal Reformatory, Chillicothe, Ohio. No information has been obtained as to the fate of that intention.[12]

Reportedly, in 1973 an inmate council was formed at the Kansas State Penitentiary, Lansing, following a racial disturbance. When the goal of complete integration of the inmate population was not realized, the warden disbanded the council.[13]

In March, 1974, there were three "inmate-council type activities" active in the penitentiary. One group was working to effect desegregation of the cell houses; another was to "sort of supervise and help manage an art activity" which included music and inmate self-study; and the final one was helping administer the inmate welfare fund--managing the commissary (selecting merchandise and setting prices), and choosing movies.[14]

A study group recommended, in December 1974, that an inmate council be established at each adult institution, consisting of no less than five members elected at-large by the institution population to serve for six months, except at the Kansas Reception and Diagnostic Center, Topeka. Since the majority of inmates reside there for shorter terms, it was recommended that the institution administration establish a realistic length of service for its council members. In addition to an advisory role, it was also recommended that council members be empowered with reasonable decision-making responsibilities, specifically concerning the disposition of commissary profits placed in the inmate welfare fund.[15]

Youth Services

Youth Services, Department of Social and Rehabilitation Services, administers five facilities for juvenile delinquents. In 1973 the juvenile facilities were under the jurisdiction of the Division of Institutional Management, State Board of Social Welfare. In 1974, the facilities were placed under the Division of Mental Health and Retardation Services and so remained until mid-1982.

Youth Services directives require that each facility develop policies and procedures based on standards promulgated in accordance with those of the Commission on Accreditation for Corrections regarding human rights, discipline and the expression and resolution of grievances.[16]

At the Youth Center at Beliot a student may file a written grievance via a prescribed form with the Clinical Program Coordinator within five days following an incident or problem if attempts at resolution with the staff member involved and that person's supervisor are unsuccessful. The grievance is given to the three-member Grievance Committee which must schedule a hearing not later than five working days following receipt. Clinical staff members serve on a weekly rotating basis, coincident to service as chairperson of the Administrative Review Committee described later. The second member of the committee is a staff person mutually acceptable to both the student and the chairperson. The third member is a student member of the Campus Council (also described later). Campus Council members serve as grievance committee members on a weekly rotating basis.[17]

Following a formal hearing at which both the grievant and the staff involved present their position and answer committee members' questions, a written findings and recommendation must be made in the following three working days.

In the ensuing five days, an appeal may be made to the superintendent, who reviews the situation and may discuss it with any of the parties involved. Not later than five days following receipt of the appeal, the superintendent must render a written decision, which is final.

Should the issue be basically non-negotiable, the grievance committee is empowered to not hold a hearing but is required to make a written response to the grievant. If a grievance challenges the substance of a policy, not just its interpretation, the committee, if the members feel some basis for possible modification exists, may waive the three-day time limit while the issue is discussed with the superintendent and other administrative staff.

No student may be subjected to disciplinary action for discussing a complaint and/or filing a grievance with no intent to falsely attack or damage an employee.

Under an Administrative Review Hearing Policy, students referred for admission to a control cottage for security or seclusion status are entitled to read and to make a written comment on the reasons specified for such placement, and to a hearing within 24 hours, exclusive of week-ends and holidays. Although the student may opt in writing not to be present, the hearing will be carried out by a committee composed of the chairperson, the staff member who made the referral, and the control cottage supervisor. Following a structured hearing, the chairperson informs the committee of his/her decision to continue or terminate assignment to the control cottage.

If continuation of assignment to the control cottage is decided, a release plan must be established immediately and set forth in writing by the supervisor of the control cottage and the other committee members. The plan must delineate the treatment goals which must be accomplished by the student before release from the cottage may occur. The plan must be consonant with the reasons for referral.[18]

The student may file a written appeal of the decision to continue assignment to the control unit and/or the release plan within two working days of the hearing. The Clinical Program Director will rule during the next 24 hours as to whether the committee shall again consider the merits of the case. The student may appeal any ruling to the superintendent, who has a like period to make a written decision, which is final.[19]

In 1981, a Student Grievance Procedure was established at the Youth Center at Atchison. Any student is entitled to file a written grievance, via a prescribed form, regarding his care, treatment, or disposition of disciplinary action, with the guarantee that no reprisal will result from doing so. Upon receiving the written grievance, the superintendent appoints a Grievance Committee of three or more persons (including one each of supervisory and non-supervisory rank) to review, investigate and make a written report of its findings and disposition recommendation during the next ten working days. The superintendent then makes a written response including his decision and the reasons for it.[20]

A Student Appeals Policy provides an additional process for a student to appeal any decision by a staff member or a cottage committee which has the net effect of his losing one full week or more of progress in the institution.[21] The Center employs a five-level system, each of which includes sets of behavorial expectations or tasks which the student is expected to master before progressing to the next level and ultimately becoming eligible for release. The level system program is individualized by tailoring special tasks for each student according to his demonstrated needs.[22]

Within two weeks following an appealable disciplinary action, a student may file an appeal form with his treatment team, which will meet and render a decision within a week. The treatment team may uphold the assessed loss of time or reinstate all or any part of it. An appeal may be made to the Program Director who appoints a Student Appeal Board consisting of a psychologist, social worker, and the head youth service worker. Any member of the staff may be selected by the grievant as his advocate, whose duty it is to insure due process is accorded during the board hearing at which witnesses may be called. The board strives for consensus, but lacking agreement, majority vote prevails. The advocate explains the board decision and rationale to the grievant, then indicates on the written response an opinion as to whether or not the student received a fair hearing. If the opinion is negative, the Program Director convenes an Administrative Appeal Board composed of the superintendent, the Program Director, the appropriate division head, and the advocate.

Should a consensual decision not be reached by the board, the superintendent makes the final decision.[23]

In 1972, the superintendent of the Youth Center at Topeka (then the Boys' Industrial School), reported that shortly after he took office in 1969, he established a Student Advisory Council. The weekly meetings of 60 to 90 minutes provided a direct line of communication between the superintendent and the boys, facilitating his understanding of their program experiences and learning of their frustrations. Program changes resulted from those interchanges, giving the boys a sense of participation. Prior to 1969, small committees were utilized to plan cottage activities and recreation events, with the staff chairman having full veto power.[24]

A Student Government Program was initiated in August, 1966, at the Youth Center at Beloit (then the Girls' Industrial School), to provide opportunities for the girls to both plan and participate in extra-curricular activities and institutional policies. Initially, members were encouraged to assume responsibility in dealing with problems of inappropriate behavior and were given disciplinary authority. This was discontinued when the girls demonstrated a tendency toward unreasonable harshness and a frequent misuse of authority by aggressive acting-out and venting of anger on weaker students.

Each of the four cottages elected three officers, a president, vice-president, and secretary. These officers provided leadership in the one-hour weekly cottage meetings. The meetings were a medium by which all students could participate in decisions regarding group programs and activities, express dissent with cottage programs, and suggest changes. There was also a Campus Council, under the leadership of the director of Child Care Services, comprised of the presidents and vice-presidents of the four cottage councils. Staff utilized the meetings at each level to interpret the rationale for decisions and suggestions.

A 1972 report indicated that, although the original rather loose structure of the Student Government Program had been retained, operational experience had brought about the establishment of certain limits of function. More frequent behavioral difficulties and an increased rate of unresolvable conflicts were attributed to heightened anxiety levels engendered by the increased responsibilities placed on the students by the program. The administration believed that although the process might not be as democratic as initially conceived, the restructuring had resulted in a more therapeutic, beneficial, and generally constructive Student Government Program.[25] The program has continued to the present, essentially unchanged.[26]

The Youth Center at Atchison was established on July 1, 1887, as the Soldier's Orphans Home (orphans of Union Civil War soldier and sailor veterans). In 1909, the legislature changed the name to the State Orphans Home. The facility continued to function exclusively as an orphans home until 1943, when the name was once again changed to the Kansas Children's Receiving Home. During this time there were two major programs on campus. One program continued to serve the needs of orphans in the state, and a newer program was established as a psychiatric/psychological evaluative unit. Despite their being located on the same campus, the programs were administered separately until 1955 when they were combined under a single administration by the legislature. In 1965, the first program for rehabilitation of "wayward and miscreant" youth was established through the transfer of a program from the Youth Center at Topeka (then the Boys' Industrial School). The program was to serve as a halfway house for students from the Topeka facility. With the decline in the demand for institutional care of orphans, that component was phased out in 1972, and the facility was renamed the Kansas Children's Receiving Home/Atchison Youth Rehabilitation Center. The evaluation unit was phased out in 1977 and the facility became primarily a treatment and care program for delinquent youth under the administrative authority of the Topeka facility. As a result of a report and recommendation by the Talkington Legislative Commission in 1979, the Atchison facility became a separate entity administratively on July 1, 1980.[27]

A Campus Council was established at the Atchison facility in December, 1981. The first formal meeting occurred in February, 1982. Each of the eight living units has a student council from which a campus-wide representative is elected to serve as a member of the Campus Council. A chairperson is elected by the students. The group meets weekly with the Program Director, or, in his absence, another administrative official, whose position is best characterized as listener, note-taker, and secretary. Agenda items are brought to the attention of all administration authorities, who make program adjustments deemed necessary. Meeting minutes are posted throughout the campus to advise both staff and students of concerns and/or problems.[28]

The Center administration is seriously receptive to the remarks and comments of the population as represented by the council. The council has been an important channel through which to glean _real_ information. The administration insures that the council is provided a comfortable and constructive atmosphere in which to conduct its meetings.

Notes

1. Dillingham, David D., and Singer, Linda R., _op. cit._ p. 51; "Ombudsman," Inmate Rule Book, Article 44-15-203, Dept. of Corrections, Topeka (revised August 11, 1982). Ombudsman first authorized by KSA75-5251.
2. Departmental Regulations and Institution Orders applicable to inmates are available in the inmate library.
3. "Grievance Procedure for Inmates," Inmate Rule Book, Article 15, Rule 44-15-101, Dept. of Corrections, Topeka (revised August 11, 1982).
4. _Ibid._

5. This is a proposed additional level of review as of October 12, 1982.
6. This is a proposed shortening of the response time limit at this level from 45 to 30 working days.
7. "Grievance Procedures for Inmates," op. cit.
8. Ibid.
9. Keating, McArthur, Lewis, Sebelius, and Singer, op. cit. p. 40.
10. Letter from Bernard J. Dunn, Chief Legal Counsel, Dept. of Corrections, October 12, 1982.
11. Baker, J. E., op. cit., p. 121.
12. Cox, William B., and Bixby, F. Lovell, Ph.D., eds. Handbook of American Prisons and Reformatories, West North Central States. Vol. I, Fifth Edition. New York: The Osborne Association, Inc., 1938, p. 96.
13. "Inmate Rights and the Kansas Prison System," report of the Kansas Advisory Committee to the U.S. Commission of Civil Rights, December 1974, p. 75.
14. Ibid.
15. Ibid., p. 121.
16. Telephone conversation July 8, 1983, and letter from Benjamin S. Coates, Director, Juvenile Offender Programs, Youth Services, Topeka, July 12, 1983; Kansas Manual of Youth Services, Section 8000, Youth Center Standards, January 1983.
17. Procedural Memorandum No. 37, "Student Grievance Hearing Procedure," Youth Center at Beloit, April 1, 1982; telephone conversation with Dennis J. Shumate, Superintendent, July 8, 1983; Supt. Shumate said that an internal grievance procedure was first established about five or six years ago.
18. Policy Memorandum No. 82-46, "Administrative Review Hearing Policy," Youth Center at Beloit, June, 1982 (revised). Originally issued May 14, 1982.
19. Policy Memorandum No. 82-46(6), "Appeal Process," Youth Center at Beloit, May 14, 1982.
20. Letter from Mark S. Phelps, Superintendent, Youth Center at Atchison, July 18, 1983; Policy and Procedure Manual, "Student Grievance Procedures," Youth Center at Atchison, June 1983.
21. Policy and Procedure Manual, "Student Appeals," Youth Center at Atchison, November 1982.
22. Annual Report, Youth Center at Atchison, 1982; p. 5.
23. Policy and Procedure Manual, "Student Appeals," op. cit.
24. Baker, J. E., op. cit., p. 121.
25. Ibid., pp. 121-122.
26. Telephone conversation with Dennis J. Shumate, Superintendent, Youth Center at Beloit, July 8, 1983.
27. Annual Report, Youth Center at Atchison, 1982, p. 2.
28. Letter from Mark S. Phelps, Superintendent, Youth Center at Atchison, July 18, 1983.

KENTUCKY

Corrections Cabinet

The Corrections Cabinet administers ten institutions for adult and youthful felony offenders.

An ombudsman position was established in 1974 to provide an investigatory entity to facilitate the resolution of inmate and parolee complaints and to present recommendations to the administration to allay similar complaints. The ombudsman is empowered to investigate any actions alleged to be contrary to law or administrative regulations; or unreasonable, unfair or inconsistent with administrative policy or procedure.

Inmates may contact the ombudsman personally when he visits the institution, via letter, or by completing a prescribed form and placing it in a locked box whose contents are available only to the ombudsman. As a rule, complaints are accepted only after the inmate has exhausted all institution remedies, e.g., the inmate grievance procedure. If the ombudsman believes that a complaint has merit, he may recommend to the appropriate staff member an action to resolve or rectify the issue. If this informal overture is ineffective, a written recommendation may be made to the institution superintendent, who must respond within ten working days. Should that response be a rejection, the ombudsman may attempt a modified resolution or forward the original recommendation to the Secretary, Corrections Cabinet, who will render a written final decision.[1]

The ombudsman also monitors the inmate grievance procedure which was first established in 1977 on a pilot basis at the Blackburn Correctional Complex. The procedure is now in place at all institutions, each of which has developed a written policy and procedural guide.

The procedure is a four-level process in which an inmate clerk, elected by peers, attempts informal resolution of complaints, which must be made within five working days following an incident. If the result is not satisfactory, the grievant may file a prescribed form requesting a hearing by the grievance committee, composed of an equal number of inmates and staff. The decision of the committee may be appealed successively to the institution superintendent and the Secretary, Corrections Cabinet. An advisory outside review by the Young Lawyer's Section of the Kentucky Bar Association may be requested by the grievant. The Secretary may reject, accept, or modify that opinion.

Written responses are required at all levels following the initial one: ten working days at the grievance committee level, and 15 working days at subsequent levels. Following a decision, the grievant has five working days to appeal to the next level.[2]

The establishment of inmate councils and other groups is discretionary with the administration of each institution.

As of April, 1973, all of the five institutions under the then Department of Corrections,[3] except the Kentucky State Penitentiary, Eddyville, had an inmate council. Information was received at that time regarding two institutions.

The Inmate Advisory Council at the Kentucky State Reformatory, LaGrange, was composed of 36 members elected by secret ballot to serve a six-month term of office, to which an incumbent could once succeed himself. In the nine dormitories, each with four wings, one representative was elected by secret ballot. Inmates residing in a dormitory wing nominated candidates who were screened by the casework staff to insure that they met the criteria of no major disciplinary reports during the immediate prior three months, four-months' residency in the population, and a like period remaining to serve until tentative or actual release date. The Council elected from the membership a chairman, co-chairman, secretary, co-secretary, and five committeemen. These persons constituted an Executive Committee. A Racial Relations Committee, with four white and four black members, was mandated by the constitution which became effective in September, 1972. The Council met monthly with the superintendent, or his designee, to discuss a previously prepared agenda to which topics had been submitted by both the Council and the administration.[4] The Council ceased to function in 1977,[5] at which time the Inmate Grievance Procedure was being established.

Currently there is no inmate council at the Kentucky State Reformatory. However, a representative of each inmate organization, e.g., Jaycees, NAACP, Seventh Step, Inc., approved by the administration,[6] is designated as a member of the Inter-Club Liaison Group which meets monthly with the staff information manager and periodically with the warden.

Under a constitution and by-laws signed on March 5, 1973, a Resident Affairs Council of five members was established at the Frenchburg Correctional Facility, Frenchburg. The institution was opened in 1969 to provide residential treatment primarily for younger men undergoing a first confinement experience. Members were elected by secret ballot to serve a three-month term of office and could succeed themselves once. Elections were held each February, May, August, and November. Only residents who had a clear conduct record for the two months immediately preceding the election, and who had been at the facility for six weeks with at least two months remaining prior to a scheduled appearance before the Parole Board, could run for office. The Council presided at a monthly meeting of the population, and met each month with the superintendent to discuss an agenda whose topics had been contributed by both Council members and the administration. Council representation was present at weekly Treatment Committee meetings of the staff. The president of the Council could be present in an advocate/advisory capacity at meetings of the Adjustment Committee.[7] The institution was closed in 1978, reverting to the jurisdiction of the Federal Government, under which it had operated as a Jobs Corps Center.

At both the Kentucky State Reformatory and the Frenchburg Correctional Facility, the stipulation was made that the Council would have no policy-making powers. At the latter institution, however, the constitution stated that the Resident Affairs Council would have a distinct voice in some areas of the policy-making process. At each installation it was stressed that the superintendent was vested by law with both the authority and responsibility for institutional operations, and reserved the right to veto actions of the Council. However, the reasons for exercise of the veto power would always be explained in writing.

The superintendent of the Luther Luckett Correctional Complex, LaGrange (opened in 1980), meets with representatives of the eight inmate organizations at least once every 90 days to discuss changes in policies and procedures. The inmates have expressed an interest in organizing an inmate council.[8]

From 1895 until 1972, when jurisdiction was transferred to the then Kentucky Department of Corrections and the designation changed to Blackburn Correctional Complex, Lexington, that facility functioned as an institution for male and female juvenile delinquents. It was first named the Kentucky Houses of Reform, Greendale. Later it was renamed Kentucky Village.

In late 1972 an inmate advisory council was organized. Each of the three housing units then opened elected representatives for terms of specified length. In the Pre-Release Unit, several inmate committees were concerned with various programs and operational policies and procedures. Inmates sat as members of a Unit Adjustment Committee which considered minor disciplinary infraction reports. On an individual basis, newly arrived inmates were oriented to the unit milieu by council members.[9]

Administration-inmate discussions are being held (1983) regarding an inmate request to establish an inmate advisory council at the Northpoint Training Center, Danville. That institution was transferred to the Corrections Cabinet in 1983 by the Division of Residential Services, Department for Social Services, Cabinet for Human Resources, under whose jurisdiction it served as an institution for juvenile delinquents, and was designated the Danville Youth Center.

The president of each inmate club and an inmate representative of the grievance procedure meet quarterly with the warden at the Kentucky State Penitentiary, Eddyville.[10]

A Resident Advisory Council, established in April, 1972, is active at the Kentucky Correctional Institution for Women, Pewee Valley. The casework staff screens requests by residents to be nominees in a secret ballot general election supervised by the incumbent council and a caseworker. Those who meet the criteria of no major disciplinary action during the immediate prior three months, a residency of at least three months in the population, and a like period remaining to serve until tentative or actual release date, may stand for election to the at-large ten-member organization for a six-month term. From its membership, the council elects a chairman, co-chairman, and a secretary. The chairman may appoint members to ad hoc committees as needed. The council meets weekly in closed session to plan and promote programs to be presented, together with suggestions/grievances (not to exceed ten each month and all applicable to the entire population), at a weekly meeting with the warden or her designee. Such referrals must include a description of the situation, the difficulties or problems involved, and recommendations for resolution. The administration also presents topics for discussion. Minutes of all meetings are prepared and distributed.

Should a member receive disciplinary action, the council may make a recommendation as to continuance in office. Placement in segregation for disciplinary reasons mandates removal from office. Liability to a recall vote, subject to the warden's approval, may result should a member incur two consecutive unauthorized absences from council meetings or display an obvious lack of interest in council affairs.

The council has been useful as a barometer indicating population needs and moods. Since establishment of the inmate grievance procedure in 1977, the organization has not been as active or productive, but remains intact, with membership now at eleven.[11]

Division for Residential Services

All residential treatment facilities for juvenile delinquents are under the jurisdiction of the Division for Residential Services, Department for Social Services, Cabinet for Human Resources. The maximum capacity in any institution is 50.

The Service Program Grievance Procedure, an administrative complaint mechanism, was developed in the period 1971-1972[12] when the state began reorganizing the Department of Child Welfare which, until 1973, administered the institutions for juvenile delinquents. In 1973, the department was subsumed in the newly established Department for Human Resources, which is currently designated as the Cabinet for Human Resources.

Under the grievance procedure, a youth could file a written grievance with the institution superintendent, who attempted resolution. An appeal from the superintendent's decision could be made to the director of residential services. An investigation was then made by a departmental investigator who made a report to the director. After reviewing the report, a written decision was made by the director to the grievant. All of this was to occur within

40 days of the submission of the complaint. Within ten days after receiving the director's answer, the grievant had a final level of appeal available, a hearing before a three-party panel of correctional administrators appointed by the Department Commissioner. The grievant was entitled to enlist an attorney and to call and cross-examine witnesses at the hearing. The panel recommended a course of action to the commissioner who conveyed the final decision to the complaining youth.

In January, 1974, central office officials acknowledged that the grievance procedure was not widely used and cited a combination of causative factors. The major factor was the move to smaller facilities with a staff-to-youth ratio of near one-to-one, which facilitated communication between youth and staff at all levels, creating a milieu conducive to the handling of the vast majority of complaints on an individual basis. Additionally, there was a lack of understanding of the grievance mechanism on the part of staff and youth, some institution reluctance to "air dirty laundry" for the view of department officials, and a general presumption that youth complaints could be handled through informal means.

The departmental investigator who pursued a grievance once it had been sent to the director of institutional services, when asked why youths did not use the procedure, indicated that few knew of its existence. A further observation was that although staff were generally cooperative during the course of investigations, they felt threatened by the procedure. Site visits to three institutions tended to confirm, in varying degrees, the opinions given by the officials.

Currently, youth may file a prescribed form setting forth a grievance within 90 days following any action taken by the Department for Social Services, except those encompassing legal issues, which are processed through statutory procedures. A grievance is defined as a denial, reduction, exclusion from or termination of a service; dissatisfaction with service received, or failure to act upon a request for service with reasonable promptness.[13]

Prior to the filing of a complaint, personnel are directed to attempt resolution of conflicting situations. Appropriate personnel involved in a decision which has led to a conflicting situation, and their immediate supervisor, must meet with the youth. Following this, the youth may pursue the issue into the dual-level complaint process consisting of a local level evidentiary hearing conducted by a department hearing officer, and a de novo hearing or an administrative review.

All de novo hearings, defined as new hearings, are conducted in the department central offices. The hearing board is composed of three professional staff members who have no prior knowledge of the case. Following the hearing, an advisory report is made to the Department Commissioner, who has ten working days in which to give the grievant a written, reasoned decision.

An administrative review involves the review of the evidentiary hearing record by an employee appointed to do so by the commissioner. Within 40 working days from receipt of the appeal, the commissioner must advise the grievant in writing of the final decision.

At the Kentucky Houses of Reform, described in the foregoing section on the Corrections Cabinet, a 1939 survey found that, while there was no organized program of student government, the superintendent was experimenting with a form of student leadership for the boys. Under the plan, each cottage was to elect its own captain to be responsible for the cottage company and presenting complaints and recommendations at bi-weekly conferences with a committee composed of the captains and three staff officers appointed by the superintendent.[14]

Each of the dormitories for girls elected a monitor to supervise the dormitory. However, the monitor had no disciplinary authority. A one-month term of office was specified in order that a maximum number of girls could experience assuming responsibility.[15]

In December, 1972, when there were 14 facilities for juvenile delinquents under the then Department of Child Welfare, it was reported that the Youth Council concept had been a program element for an unknown number of years. The operating manual of the department described the process then in use in residential programs:

> Youth Council--In order for a youth to have a voice in the treatment program, there is set up on a bi-monthly basis a council that meets with the superintendent for the purpose of making recommendations about the program. A representative from each group brings suggestions and recommendations for discussion and consideration. Notes from these council meetings are typed up and posted on the bulletin board and also posted in the log for the entire staff to read. The youth also make suggestions for camp agreements during these meetings and also in a camp meeting relating to problems that affect the entire camp population in their living together as a group. These agreements are posted on the youth's bulletin board.[16]

Current descriptions of the programs of the facilities for juvenile delinquents make no mention of student councils.[17]

Notes

1. Information provided by Roosevelt Lightsy, Jr., Ombudsman, and Michael Bradley, Special Assistant, Corrections Cabinet, Frankfort.
2. Ibid.
3. In the latter months of 1973, the Dept. of Corrections became the Bureau of Corrections under the newly established

Dept. of Justice; in mid-1981 it reverted to department status; in 1982 it was redesignated as the Corrections Cabinet.
4. Baker, J. E., op. cit., p. 123.
5. Information provided by then Warden Stephen T. Smith, Kentucky State Reformatory, LaGrange (Mr. Smith is currently Director of Operations, Dept. of Adult Correctional Institutions, Corrections Cabinet, Frankfort).
6. Telephone conversation with Warden John D. Rees, Kentucky State Reformatory, LaGrange, August 26, 1983; Procedures Memorandum, KSR 08-009, Rev. 2. "Inmate Organizations," Kentucky State Reformatory, August 15, 1983.
7. Baker, J. E., op. cit., p. 123.
8. Telephone conversation with William Seabold, Supt., Luther Luckett Correctional Complex, LaGrange; July 15, 1983.
9. Conversations with Patricia Martin, Principal Assistant, Corrections Cabinet, Frankfort (Ms. Martin was Manager of the Pre-Release Unit at the Blackburn Correctional Complex, Lexington, from 1972 to 1976).
10. Conversation with Warden Al C. Parke, Kentucky State Penitentiary, Eddyville.
11. Conversations with Warden Betty Kassulke, Kentucky Correctional Institution for Women, Pewee Valley; Constitution and By-Laws, Resident Advisory Council, June 17, 1974.
12. Keating, Gilligan, McArthur, Lewis, and Singer, 1974, op. cit., pp. 55-61.
13. "Civil Rights Discrimination and Service Complaints," Chapter 1, Manual, Ky. Dept. for Social Services, April, 1982.
14. Cox, William B., Shelley, Joseph A., and Minard, George C., eds. Handbook of American Institutions for Delinquent Juveniles. First Edition, Vol. II. Kentucky-Tennessee. New York: The Osborne Association, 1940, p. 58.
15. Ibid.
16. Baker, J. E., op. cit., p. 124.
17. "Overview of Residential Treatment Programs," Ky. Dept. for Social Services (information provided by Commissioner Suzanne Turner).

LOUISIANA

Department of Corrections

The Department of Corrections administers all facilities for adult and youthful felony offenders and delinquent, neglected and dependent juveniles.

Information was received in December, 1972, that in October of that year the first scheduled mediation team meeting was held as a part of a plan to reactivate inmate representation at the Louisiana State Penitentiary. Team membership included inmates, ex-offenders, representatives of the Department of Corrections, the penitentiary, the United States Department of Justice Mediation Service, and a legal aid attorney appointed by the Federal District Court. Inmates were being given a voice in the formulation of rules and regulations and in making the problems of the prisoner population known to the administration. Results were described as promising and it was hoped that meaningful representation from inmates could be established and maintained on a permanent basis.[1]

A disciplinary procedure was adopted by negotiation teams for the Louisiana State Penitentiary, Angola, and prisoner representatives during federally mediated negotiation sessions held on December 5, 1972 and in March, 1973.[2]

A Prisoner Grievance Committee was established at the penitentiary effective March 7, 1973, providing for a General Assembly consisting of members elected by the residents of each housing unit and by each bona fide organization within the institution which had been in operation not less than six months, to serve a one-year term with indefinite succession possible. The Assembly in turn elects from its membership an Executive Committee of seven, who may serve no more than two consecutive terms, to be generally representative of the various areas and facilities of the institution. The purpose of the committee is to receive and categorize inmate complaints for presentation to an Administration Committee whose members include the warden, deputy warden, assistant wardens for custody and treatment, and the business manager. An employee, mutually acceptable to both committees, acts as a liaison between the groups.[3]

On standardized forms, the Executive Committee records the results of its investigation of a complaint; together with statements by supporting witnesses and any related documents, this information is then presented to the General Assembly for discussion and recommendation. In accordance with such recommendation, the Executive Committee then negotiates with the Administration Committee for a just resolution.[4]

A study published in 1980 indicated that an unwritten grievance procedure had been established in 1973 providing for a formal hearing of grievances in which inmates functioned in a decision-making role. Written responses within specified time limits were required. The final level of review was the Secretary, Department of Corrections.[5]

A Prisoner Grievance Procedure as described for the Louisiana State Penitentiary is evidently operative at all institutions. Recent information states: "Currently, this procedure is working well in the institutions."[6]

The Department of Corrections is planning a comprehensive inmate grievance procedure based on the provisions of Public Law 96-247, the Civil Rights of Institutionalized Persons Act.[7]

An Inmate Council was organized on December 10, 1955 at the Louisiana State Penitentiary, Angola. Written rules and procedures stated: "The Inmate Council is a privilege granted to the inmate population by the warden. The council and its members are given the privilege to negotiate with the warden or any member of his staff and to discuss in a proper manner any problem or situation affecting or of interest to the inmate body as a whole."[8]

A councilman was elected by majority vote in each dormitory and camp, as were two in each of the two cellblocks. The term of office was one year. An appointee of a councilman assisted him in his area of representation. This appointed representative was permitted to attend the regular monthly meetings with the warden at which items included on an agenda prepared at an unsupervised previous meeting were discussed. The written rules stated that councilmen should not attempt to discuss personal matters at council meetings. The administration of the State Penitentiary at that time regarded the Inmate Council as being helpful by bringing to the warden's attention reasonable requests and problems. Additionally, the council sponsored holiday inmate talent shows annually, initiated an eyebank, assisted with the yearly March of Dimes campaign, and began a fund to provide postage for indigent inmates. Successful operation of the council was attributed to an understanding by all concerned of its purpose and function.[9]

Information received in 1966 indicated that (a) inmate politics, which lessened the caliber of candidates; (b) administration apathy; and (c) loss of confidence in the Inmate Council by the inmate population were major factors contributing to a decreasing effectiveness of the council. These, together with a work stoppage, brought about the discontinuance of the group in August, 1965.[10]

It is assumed that, following the previously mentioned October 1972 meeting of the mediation team held as part of a plan to reactivate inmate representation at the Penitentiary, an Inmate Council was formed. This assumption is based on recent information: "... the council was not effective and has since fallen into disuse."[11]

In 1974, an inmate council was reported as having been established at the Louisiana Correctional Institute for Women, St. Gabriel, to provide some staff-inmate communication and to allow for the resolution of legitimate inmate grievances. Elected by other inmates, the council members assisted the administration in working up rules and regulations for the inmate population. Despite a claimed negative view by most inmates, one administrative official expressed the feeling that the council had been effective and responsible for bringing about some positive changes at the institute.[12] No current information has been received regarding this council.

In 1967, three of the institutions for juvenile delinquents, the Louisiana Training Institutes at Baton Rouge, Monroe, and Pineville, reported no present or past advisory councils, as did the Louisiana

Correctional and Industrial School, DeQuincy, an institution for young adult first offenders suitable for vocational and academic training.[13]

Notes

1. Baker, J. E., op. cit., pp. 125-126.
2. "A Study of Adult Corrections in Louisiana," report of the Louisiana Advisory Committee to the U.S. Commission on Civil Rights, May, 1976; pp. 119-124.
3. Ibid.
4. Ibid.
5. Dillingham, David D., and Singer, Linda R., op. cit., p. 52.
6. Letter from Martha Morgan, Attorney for the Secretary, Dept. of Corrections, October 19, 1982.
7. Ibid.
8. Baker, J. E., op. cit., pp. 124-125.
9. Ibid.
10. Ibid.
11. Letter from Martha Morgan, op. cit. (The letter then pointed out the inmate grievance procedure previously described.)
12. "A Study of Adult Corrections in Louisiana," op. cit., pp. 58-59.
13. Baker, J. E., op. cit., p. 125.

MAINE

Department of Corrections

The Department of Corrections, created effective September 18, 1981 by the Legislature as a cabinet level agency, is responsible for administration of all facilities for adult and youthful offenders and juvenile delinquents.[1] Formerly, the facilities were administered by the Bureau of Corrections, Department of Mental Health and Corrections.

According to a 1980 report, an inmate grievance procedure was established in the adult institutions in 1974, but there were no provisions for a formal hearing, written responses, or time limits for responses. Appeals were allowed, with the Commissioner being the final level of review.[2]

Currently, the Department of Corrections is designing a two-level Client's Grievance Procedure to be operative in all facilities.[3]

The Maine State Prison, Thomaston, does not have an active inmate council at present. Following a lockdown of the prison in April, 1980, the system for election of council members was redefined to provide for representation by housing units rather than at-large. The inmates have declined to participate under such a plan.

Until inmates express a wish to have a council or an inmate representative, the department intends to continue the inmate advocate and inmate grievance procedure.[4]

Reportedly, about 50 or 55 years ago an inmate council at the Maine State Prison used its privilege to meet in the evening within a cellblock to plan and execute an escape attempt. One of the guards was severely beaten. That episode ended the council.[5]

Information was received in 1966 that no self-government program existed at either the Maine State Prison or the Men's Correctional Center, South Windsor.[6] Inmates of the latter, now the Maine Correctional Center, a co-ed facility, have not requested an inmate council or collective representation group. Because of the high staff-inmate ratio, communication is facilitated since inmates have access to line officers for the purpose of expressing their concerns.[7]

A great deal of self-government among the inmates of the Women's Correctional Center, Skowhegan, was reported in 1966, but no details of the activity was received.[8] The institution is no longer in operation. Female inmates are housed at the Maine Correctional Center.

In 1967, the Superintendent of the Stevens School, Hallowell, a facility for female juvenile delinquents, who had been in the position a relatively short time, reported that a study made prior to her arrival mentioned a student "Gripe Council," the discontinuance of which was recommended because of the negative implications.[9] The school is no longer in operation.

At the Boys' Training Center, South Portland, there had been no inmate advisory council for at least two decades prior to a 1967 report. However, at that time there were informal student groups participating and expressing their ideas, under staff direction, in athletic and extra-curricular cottage life activities.[10] The facility, now co-ed and known as the Maine Youth Center, currently has an active inmate council whose members are elected to represent the various housing units. The council, which meets at scheduled times, advises the superintendent on general institutional policies and procedures.[11]

Notes

1. Letter from Commissioner Donald L. Allen, Dept. of Corrections, September 23, 1972.
2. Dillingham, David D., and Singer, Linda R., op. cit., p. 52.
3. Letter from Commissioner Donald L. Allen, op. cit.
4. Ibid.
5. Baker, J. E., op. cit., p. 126.
6. Ibid.
7. Letter from Commissioner Donald L. Allen, op. cit.
8. Baker, J. E., op. cit., p. 126.

9. *Ibid.*
10. *Ibid.*, pp. 126-127.
11. Letter from Commissioner Donald L. Allen, *op. cit.*

MARYLAND

Division of Correction

The Division of Correction, Department of Public Safety and Correctional Services, administers all facilities for adult and youthful felony and misdemeanor offenders.

An Inmate Grievance Commission was established on July 1, 1971 by the Maryland Legislature as a separate agency within the Department of Public Safety and Correctional Services. The Commission is comprised of five members appointed by the Governor, including at least two lawyers and two members with experience in corrections. An Executive Director and staff process the grievances that may be made by inmates of the Division of Correction institutions or those in the Patuxent Institution, Jessup, an autonomous correctional facility for selected adult offenders, directly under the Department of Public Safety and Correctional Services.[1]

An inmate may mail a completed grievance form to the Executive Director, who will investigate the allegations or the issue presented. (Since March 1, 1982, all complaints must be filed within 90 days from the date of an occurrence. However, for a grievance regarding a continuing problem, this time limitation may be waived.) Preliminary investigation consists of checking the dates and facts of the complaint with the institution Inmate Grievance Officer (an Assistant Managing Officer, a Classification Supervisor, or a Senior Correctional Officer appointed by the warden),[2] and making an initial determination about the validity of the complaint. If the complaint is considered to be wholly without merit, it may be dismissed. Cases deemed to be of special importance or concern may be selected for expedited disposition or hearing.

Any complaint arising as a result of disciplinary action within the institution must be processed through the institution adjustment procedure prior to submission to the Commission.

Formal hearings are held at such times and places as the Commission may direct and are open to the public to the extent that security considerations permit. The grievant may have counsel present and call such witnesses as the Commission agrees may have relevant testimony to give, and may request, with Commission approval, the production of documents and records useful and necessary to a determination of the merits of the complaint. The institution Inmate Grievance Coordinator attends all hearings.

If an employee of the Department of Correction is required

to appear before the Inmate Grievance Commission, department policy specifies that every effort must be made to comply. The employee may request representation by the office of the Attorney General.[3]

On the basis of the evidence presented at the hearing, the Commission writes its decision, including a statement of its findings, its conclusion and a recommended disposition, which is transmitted to the Secretary, Department of Public Safety and Correctional Services. The latter, within 15 days, may affirm, reverse, or modify the order of the Commission. The Secretary's action constitutes the final decision for purposes of judicial review.[4]

Within 30 days of the Secretary's order, the grievant is entitled to a judicial review, and proceedings may be instituted in the Circuit Court of the county in which the institution is located.

In the first two years of its operation, the Inmate Grievance Commission program reportedly lacked inmate confidence, primarily because of a time-lag between filing and receipt of the Commission's decision, ranging from five to seven months. However, within the third year, the time-lag was reduced to just under four months from receipt of a complaint to completion of the Commission's findings.[5]

Information obtained in 1960 indicated the existence of an Umpires and Referees Association at the Maryland Penitentiary, Baltimore, described as having many of the principles inherent in self-government. Under the direction of the Supervisor of Recreation, the Association inmate staff conducted instructional classes and gave examinations to aspiring arbiters. Suggestions made at weekly meetings were often accepted and adopted by the administration as recreation program policy. An Alcoholics Anonymous Program, also reported as being active, was sponsored by a member of a community Alcoholics Anonymous Chapter. There was also an Inmate Adoption Fund Plan sponsored by the Director of Education. Administered by a Board of Directors, the group met monthly, or at the call of the chairman, to discuss gifts, receive a financial report, and discuss means of continuing the fund. No other information was provided concerning the specific function or activities of the group except the unsupervised taping of a monthly radio program.

Another group, sponsored by the director of education, was the Colts Corral # 954, described as a professional football fan club which met monthly to view films of games, hear sports-figure speakers, and meet with various visiting professional teams and community sports reporters. Additionally, the group initiated drives to assist underprivileged children.

In late 1966, a Presidential Organizational Council was formed at the Maryland Penitentiary. The assistant warden for correctional treatment was administrative advisor to the council, whose membership was composed of the presidents and vice-presidents of the 13 inmate groups then active. Alcoholics Anonymous and the Maryland Penitentiary Umpires and Referees Association were cited as examples of the types of groups involved. The purpose of the council was to develop better communication between the inmate groups and to discuss organizational and institutional problems.

In April, 1973, information regarding the institutions administered by the Division of Correction revealed that the Maryland Penitentiary did not have an inmate advisory council. Only one of the nine self-help groups in existence prior to July, 1972 was active. Following a disturbance during that month, all groups with the exception of the Junior Chamber of Commerce rejected the conditions for their continued operation contained in a set of rules promulgated by the warden.[6]

As of December 30, 1982, 14 groups were active in the Maryland Penitentiary.[7]

There was also a disturbance in July, 1972 at the Maryland House of Corrections, Jessup. As a consequence, all self-help groups and the Inmate Advisory Council were suspended. However, in April, 1973 the council was again in operation, having been recently reactivated.[8] The council was reestablished on June 30, 1980, operating under a written constitution, which was replaced by an institution directive issued April 26, 1982.[9] One representative, and an alternate, is elected from each housing unit. Voting is by secret ballot, and the term of office may not exceed six months. Representatives are limited to two consecutive terms, but no such limitation applies to alternates. From its membership the council elects two co-chairpersons and a secretary.

In order to stand for election, an inmate must have been at the institution for 90 days, free of any disciplinary sanction for 30 days, have at least 90 days yet to serve, and be participating in an institution program or on a job assignment, or on volunteer status pending placement.

Placement in segregation, two or more disciplinary infractions, voluntary termination of program participation or job assignment, two unexcused absences from meetings, are causes for dismissal from council membership.

The council serves in an advisory capacity to the warden, who is the institution advisor and coordinator of the group. Meetings are held bi-weekly to consider items on an agenda prepared by the council five or six days previously. All suggestions and requests are responded to by the warden. Minutes of each meeting are distributed, and representatives are responsible for disseminating information about the issues discussed and decisions made.

As of early December, 1982, the council had been inactive for six months. However, elections had been held on October 20, 1982, and meetings were planned to commence in mid-December.[10]

An Inmate Advisory Council was reported in 1973 as meeting

monthly with pertinent institution personnel at the Maryland Correctional Institution, Hagerstown.[11] On January 1, 1980, an Inmate Advisory Council was established for the purpose of promulgating information pertinent to inmates, promoting administration-staff dialogue, providing a forum for inmates to air concerns and opinions, and discussing possible courses of action.[12]

Any inmate of sincere character, interested in the objectives of the council, is eligible to stand for election to a one-year term of office as a representative of his housing unit. From its membership, the council elects a president, vice-president, and a secretary. A Board of Directors and a parliamentarian are appointed by the president.[13]

The council holds a general meeting each week. Subject to the warden's approval, the secretary may call a special meeting at the request of four or more members.

The warden, assistant warden, and other staff meet once a month with the council to discuss items on a prepared agenda. Robert's Rules of Order are observed in the conduct of these meetings. Provision is made in the by-laws for the annual election procedures, suspension or removal from office for specified causes, and duties of all council members. Meeting minutes are prepared by the secretary.

The agenda for the November 23, 1982 meeting consisted of 39 items submitted from six housing units. The greater number were concerned with maintenance and procedural matters. None requested additional privileges. The list is reported as a representative one.[14]

A report in February, 1967 told of plans being contemplated to organize an inmate advisory council at the Maryland Correctional Training Center, Hagerstown, a 1,000-population institution then being opened. Shortly prior to April, 1973, the council was placed on inactive status pending the report of the superintendent's task force appointed to evaluate the whole concept of the council.[15] On October 4, 1979, an Inmate Advisory Council was established under a constitution and by-laws as a self-governing group deriving its powers directly from the warden.[16]

The governing body of the council consists of a chairman, assistant chairman, recording secretary, corresponding secretary, one representative from each of the six housing units, and ten staff members representing the following services: custody, food, education, classification, religious, medical, volunteer, and athletic. With the exception of those housing men in disciplinary status, each housing unit tier may elect a representative. However, that person is not a part of the governing body.

A five-member nominating committee composed of three residents and two employees conducts a secret ballot election to which any nominee approved by the warden may be elected to a one-year term of office to which he may once succeed himself. The election of governing body members, including staff members, is open to the general population.

Each housing unit representative meets weekly with his tier representatives. The governing body meets monthly, and more frequently if necessary, with the institution managing officers. Affairs of the council, including meeting minutes, are disseminated via the Village Life, the institution publication.

Any member of the governing body may be removed from office by a two-thirds vote following a due process hearing.

While no councilman may involve himself in another inmate's disciplinary problems, nor challenge the authority of a staff member in the discharge of his duties, the council may present to the administration a situation in which the majority of the population feels an injustice is inherent in a rule.

A review of eight 1982 council meetings indicates involvement in and concern with maintenance problems, recreational activities, food service, and slow response by staff to requests for interviews.

In 1940, the Maryland State Reformatory for Women, Jessup, was opened and admitted the 83 female prisoners who until then had been housed at the nearby Maryland House of Corrections. The facility was redesignated the Maryland Correctional Institution for Women on July 1, 1964. A 1967 report mentioned four annual meetings of the group to plan extracurricular activities such as variety shows and athletic events. An attempt was made to have a different cottage representative at each meeting. In April, 1973 an Inmate Advisory Council was in operation, meeting frequently with the superintendent.[17]

On March 30, 1981 an Inmate Advisory Council was established for the purpose of opening lines of staff-inmate communication and to serve in an advisory capacity to the warden. The requirements to stand for election are identical to those already described for the Maryland House of Correction, Jessup, as are the term of office and limits on succession, selection and number of offices. Causes for dismissal are similar.[18]

The council meets bi-weekly with the warden to discuss items on an agenda prepared by the group five or six days previously, and any issues added by the warden. Minutes of each meeting, upon approval by the warden, are distributed to council members who must post them in the housing units. Failure by the council to provide an agenda for or the lack of a quorum at two successively scheduled meetings with the warden are situations mandating suspension of all council meetings for the duration of the six-month term.

Currently, the Inmate Advisory Council is reported as having been active since June, 1982. The original meeting schedule is adhered to, and numerous issues have been discussed, e.g., institution policies, maintenance problems, Christmas packages, food, problems with visiting, commissary, and the allowance of additional personal property. If a committed group of representatives wins office at the next scheduled election, the administration intends to continue the council.[19]

Of the eight facilities in the Maryland Correctional Pre-Release System, only two have an inmate council type organization. At the Poplar Hill Pre-Release Unit, Quantico, the facility manager meets with selected inmates in a nonstructured situation to obtain input and feedback.[20]

A meeting of all inmates is held periodically at the Pre-Release Unit for Women, Baltimore, at which the facility head presides. At the meeting inmates may voice their concerns over facility matters and personal problems, provide input into facility policy, and engage in problem solving. Attendance at these meetings is mandatory. Inmate meetings, at which attendance is voluntary, are also held for general discussion and planning of activities. Staff attends by invitation only.[21]

Juvenile Services Administration

The Juvenile Services Administration, Department of Health and Mental Hygiene, administers ten facilities for juvenile delinquents.[22]

A Child Advocacy Grievance Procedure was established March 15, 1983, and was operative in all facilities by May 15, 1983. The procedure is not a substitute for existing policies on child abuse and sexual child abuse. Any child who has a grievance may, within three working days of the action or incident, initiate the five-level procedure.[23]

At the first level, a child informs the child advocate, directly or through a staff member, of a complaint. All child advocates are appointed by and report directly to the Juvenile Services Department Director. The child advocate reviews the complaint with the child to determine if it has merit. If the child does not accept a no-merit evaluation, or if the child advocate determines that the complaint has merit, the second step of the procedure is invoked. The child advocate discusses the complaint with any others, staff members or children, who may have been involved, and attempts to mediate a solution. Should all parties not be satisfied, the third step is undertaken: a conference presided over by the superintendent, who subsequently renders a written report delineating the facts and reasoning supporting his decision.

The grievant, or any other person affected by the third-level decision may appeal to the next level, the Assistant Director, Juvenile Services Administration, who reviews the cumulative file on the complaint and issues a written decision. If the Assistant Director consents, an appeal may be made to the Director, the fifth and final step of the procedure. The latter makes a written decision.

Should a child's complaint involve the child advocate, the superintendent appoints a staff member to assume that capacity. If a complaint is against the superintendent, the Assistant Director replaces him in the third level review, and the Deputy Director assumes the fourth level responsibilities.

There are time limits for response at all levels, none exceeding four days. All appeals to the next higher level must be made within three working days. A staff member involved in a complaint may appeal the superintendent's decision to the Assistant Director. Child advocate reports may not be placed in a staff member's personnel file.

A child has a right to seek legal counsel at any time. An attorney may represent a child at any stage of the grievance procedure. In such instances, the child advocate ceases to be involved.

In December, 1972 it was reported that only one of the ten juvenile facilities had an advisory council. The Montrose School for Girls, Reisterstown (now the Montrose School and co-ed), then received 12 to 18-year-old females adjudged to be delinquent and/or "children in need of supervision." (Since about 1975, children in need of supervision/assistance have been served by foster homes, group homes, and shelter care facilities.) The Advisory Council was composed of ten members, each elected by her cottage residents. The council met bi-weekly with the superintendent, and such other staff as might wish to attend, to discuss topics regarding cottage and institutional policies and procedures, with discussion of personal problems prohibited unless applicable to the cottage situation. Council members had no vote in determining overall school policy, functioning only as an advisory group with the objective of facilitating staff-student communication. The superintendent reported that his relationship with inmates was helped by the meetings. Additionally, the meetings resulted in positive changes in both girls and staff, producing significant program changes readily accepted by both groups.[24]

The juvenile institutions in Maryland do not have inmate councils at present.[25]

Notes

1. Division of Correction Regulation No. 180-1, "Inmate Grievance Procedure," Dept. of Correction, Baltimore, July 1, 1977 (rescinds DCR 180-1, March 22, 1974).
2. Division of Correction Regulation No. 180.2, "Inmate Grievance

Coordinator," Dept. of Correction, Baltimore, March 22, 1974.

3. Division of Correction Regulation No. 180-3, "Appearance of Staff Before Inmate Grievance Commission," Dept. of Correction, Baltimore, March 15, 1980 (rescinds DCR 180-3, January 1, 1977).
4. DCR No. 180-1, op. cit.
5. Keating, McArthur, Lewis, Sebelius, and Singer (Sept. 1975), op. cit., pp. 80-81.
6. Baker, J. E., op. cit., pp. 127-128.
7. Letter from Jon P. Galley, Commissioner, Dept. of Correction, Baltimore, December 30, 1982. (Within Maryland institutions the term "self-help group" is used interchangeably with "inmate organization." In some of the institutions, e.g., the Maryland Penitentiary, the Maryland Correctional Training Center, Hagerstown, and the Maryland Correctional Institution, Hagerstown, self-help group means a special type of organization which is authorized to conduct fund-raising activities. The size of the groups, frequency and length of meetings, the extent to which community volunteers participate, the group's status as "self-help," and authorization for the establishment and continuation of a group are within the discretionary authority of the warden.)
8. Baker, J. E., op. cit., p. 128.
9. Directive No. 300-1-1, "Inmate Advisory Committee," Maryland House of Correction, Jessup, April 27, 1982.
10. Memorandum from Dana V. Haskins, Administrative Liaison, Maryland House of Correction, Jessup, to Bruce Stout, Executive Assistant, Division of Correction, December 8, 1982.
11. Baker, J. E., op. cit., p. 128.
12. Institutional Directive "Inmate/Staff Communication," (Section V [C]), January 1, 1980.
13. "Constitution and By-Laws," Inmate Advisory Council, Maryland Correctional Institution, Hagerstown.
14. Memorandum from Gene D. Shives, Assistant Warden, Maryland Correctional Institution, Hagerstown, to Bruce Stout, Executive Assistant, Division of Correction, December 7, 1982.
15. Baker, J. E., op. cit., p. 128.
16. "Constitution and By-Laws," the Inmate Advisory Council, Maryland Correctional Training Center, Hagerstown, October 4, 1979.
17. Baker, J. E., op. cit., p. 128.
18. Institution Directive No. 400-la, "Inmate Advisory Council," Maryland Correctional Institution for Women, Jessup, March 30, 1981; Warden's Memorandum re addition to ID No. 400-la (regarding quorums).
19. Memorandum from Patricia Phelps Schupple, Assistant Warden, Maryland Correctional Institution for Women, Jessup, to Bruce Stout, Executive Assistant, Division of Correction, December 21, 1982. (The next election was scheduled for January, 1983.)

20. Memorandum from Eugene M. Nuth, Assistant Warden, Maryland Correctional Pre-Release System, Jessup, to Bruce Stout, Executive Assistant, Division of Correction, December 15, 1982.
21. Standard Operating Procedure 10-9, "Program/Services," Pre-Release Unit for Women, Baltimore, April 26, 1982.
22. Letter from James P. Casey, Assistant Attorney General, Baltimore, May 9, 1983.
23. "Child Advocacy Grievance Procedure," Juvenile Services Administration, Baltimore; Telephone conversation with James P. Casey, Assistant Attorney General, Baltimore, August 8, 1983.
24. Baker, J. E., _op. cit._, p. 129.
25. Letter from James P. Casey, _op. cit._

MASSACHUSETTS

Department of Correction

The Department of Correction, Executive Office of Human Services, administers all state institutions for adult and youthful felony and misdemeanor offenders.

In March, 1973 an inmate-staff committee was formed to handle a participatory grievance procedure at the Massachusetts Correctional Institution, Concord, following training provided by the Center for Community Justice and other outside groups. Appeal of the committee's decisions could be made to the superintendent and ultimately to an arbitration panel. Although the procedure began smoothly, by June, 1973 major personnel changes occurred in the correction system. The commissioner was replaced and the superintendent was transferred. With their departure, reportedly the entire grievance procedure became moribund.[1]

A grievance procedure was established on a pilot basis at the Massachusetts Correctional Institution, Walpole, in 1979. An employee was designated as coordinator of the procedure, which provided for written responses within specified time limits at all levels, with the final level being a review by some person or group outside the institution. Inmates participated in decision-making roles in the formal hearing level of review. However, the procedure was not implemented system-wide.[2]

An Inmate Grievance Procedure was established effective August 4, 1982, which is operating in all institutions. With the exception of medical decisions, and classification and disciplinary decisions for which separate appeal mechanisms exist, an inmate may make a written complaint, via a prescribed form, concerning an incident, condition of confinement, or the application of any department or institution policy, rule or regulation, within ten working days from the incident of complaint.[3]

An institution grievance coordinator investigates the factual basis of the complaint by interviewing the grievant or staff members, and prepares, within five working days, a written recommendation for either approval or denial, which is given to the superintendent. The latter has ten working days to notify the grievant as to affirmation, modification, or reversal of the coordinator's recommendation, with an explanation of the action.

If an inmate is dissatisfied with the superintendent's response, an appeal may be made to the Department Grievance Coordinator, who investigates the complaint, confers as necessary with other department officials, and makes a written response, within 30 days, specifying the reasons for denial, or the specific corrective action which is to be taken.

The time limits for filing a grievance or appeal or for response may be extended, but written notice must be given to the grievant.

Illiterate inmates, those who cannot write legibly, or who cannot speak English, may be assisted by other inmates if staff help is not available.

Grievances verified by the institution coordinator as being of an emergency nature are responded to by the superintendent within five working days.

Unless a complaint threatens the security or orderly operation of the institution, or contains statements knowingly false or misleading, no action may be taken against an inmate for submitting it.

There is no active inmate advisory council in any institution except at the Massachusetts Correctional Institution, Norfolk. No directives regarding councils have been issued by the department, leaving their establishment to the discretion of each institution superintendent.[4]

Information received in 1966 regarding inmate advisory councils is the basis for the following account:[5]

> The Correctional Institution at West Concord was built in 1878 to replace the State Prison at Charlestown. It served that purpose for six years until May 21, 1884, when legislation ordered return of the adult prisoners to Charlestown and establishment of Concord as the Massachusetts Reformatory on December 20, 1884. The present designation was given by the Acts of 1955. Concord is a maximum security institution. Prior to 1955 no one over the age of 30 could be committed there. While today there is no age limitation, the population is used mainly for the younger group.
>
> The administration at Concord reports that takeover by

aggressive individuals who controlled voting through intimidation and threat has been the cause for disbanding inmate councils organized in the past. A Self-Development Group which has been functioning for three years claims an impressive record of rehabilitation among its members. While believing this group has great potential, the administration voices concern that it may also be taken over by the wrong element. The constitution of the Self-Development Group cites its aim as being: 'to extinguish our anti-social habits by replacing them with new modes of behavior acceptable to ourselves and the community.' The only requirements for membership are a wish to stay out of prison and a willingness to help others do likewise. Using methods similar to those of Alcoholics Anonymous and Synanon, the group utilizes 'Seven Points' toward self-betterment.

The Correctional Institution at Framingham was the second in the country to be built exclusively for women prisoners. Opened in 1877 as the Reformatory Prison for Women, it lost the word prison in 1911 since it had become essentially a reformatory in spirit and operation. Attempts to form student councils have been made at different times but none has been significant in institution programming. In 1929 a council was organized following an escape regarded by the members as a slur on their efforts to uphold a high standard of citizenship throughout the institution. Records made no further reference to a council until 1956 when the Two-Side Club was formed. Approximately 40 girls were elected to represent the work departments, living areas and the institution clubs. Subject to approval of the superintendent, four officers were elected twice yearly by secret ballot. These four, president, vice-president, secretary, and historian, held monthly meetings at which arrangements were made for important functions, such as assemblies, holidays, fairs, and plays.

The Two-Side Club had no noticeable effect on policy changes made at the time. When the present superintendent arrived in 1958 there were no remnants of any inmate organization. The average period of confinement, of nine or ten months, is cited as the potential source of many difficulties in organizing a council.

The Massachusetts Correctional Institution at Bridgewater, housing over 2000 persons, contains in its four separate units alcoholics and drug addicts, the criminally insane, defective delinquents, and sexually dangerous persons. No attempt has ever been made to discourage the establishment of inmate councils. The availability of top-echelon staff to any patient has possibly eliminated the need for organizing such groups.

Following the national trends toward the construction of minimum security institutions, in 1951 the legislature authorized the construction of prison camps on land under the control of the Department of Natural Resources. The first of the Massachusetts prison camps was opened in 1952. Located near historic Plymouth in the Myles Standish Forest, this 14,000-acre institution is the only camp to have had an inmate council. The council functioned briefly in 1953, but it was found to be unnecessary in a population averaging only 50. The relaxed informal atmosphere of the camps, conducive to a positive staff-inmate relationship, negates the necessity for councils.

Department of Youth Services

In 1972-1973, all juvenile institutions in Massachusetts were closed. When a survey was made in 1966 and 1967, there were ten facilities in Massachusetts for the care of juvenile delinquents, all administered by a Youth Service Board. Information was received regarding two of these, the Industrial School for Boys, Shirley, and the Lyman School for Boys, Westborough. There was no inmate advisory council at the former and no definite plans to organize one.[6]

At the Westborough facility a Student Council had been organized in late 1965. Two representatives were elected by the boys in each of the nine cottages. Under by-laws drawn by them, these representatives elected a president, vice-president, and secretary, who directed council meetings under the supervision of the Clinical Department staff. A chronic understaffing of that department was given as the principal reason for the gradual dissolution of the council. The administration believed that the council was an effective advisory group and a beneficial experience to the boys, providing an opportunity to function in a group situation where they had a voice in policies and programs directly affecting them.

Notes

1. Denenberg, R. V., and Denenberg, Tia, "Prison Grievance Procedures," Corrections Magazine, Vol. I, No. 3, January/February, 1975, pp. 29-44 and pp. 61-62.
2. Telephone conversation with Robert M. Balboni, Grievance Coordinator, Dept. of Correction, Boston, June 9, 1983; Dillingham, David D., and Singer, Linda R. (1980), op. cit., p. 52.
3. Policy No. 491, "Inmate Grievances," Dept. of Correction, Boston, August 4, 1982.
4. Telephone conversation with Gail A. Darnell, Executive Assistant to Commissioner, Dept. of Correction, Boston, June 9, 1983.
5. Baker, J. E., op. cit., pp. 130-131.
6. Ibid., pp. 131-132.

MICHIGAN

Department of Corrections

The Department of Corrections administers 12 institutions and 12 correctional camps for adult and youthful felony offenders. A Reception and Diagnostic Center at the State Prison of Southern Michigan, Jackson, processes all committed male offenders.[1]

In March, 1973 the department developed a written grievance procedure to provide individual prisoners an administrative remedy for any condition of confinement, official act, or denial of rights. Institutional disciplinary decisions and parole board actions are excepted. Inmates and staff are advised to make reasonable efforts, within two days, to resolve grievances informally prior to an inmate's filing of a written complaint on a department form. The latter must be done within ten days following an incident, or not later than five days following rejection by the grievant of an informal settlement decision. The written grievance is given to the grievant's team manager, counselor, or camp supervisor, who must make a written reply within 15 working days. During that period grievances regarding health care, industries, and accounting are referred for comment to, respectively, the health care staff, the Michigan Correctional Industries institution staff, and the accounting staff.

If not satisfied with the response, the grievant has five days to appeal to the warden or superintendent (the deputy warden at the State Prison of Southern Michigan, Jackson, or the State House of Correction and Branch Prison, Marquette). The grievance is reviewed and the grievant interviewed within the following 15 working days, and a written decision rendered. This decision may be appealed in five days to the Regional Administrator who will reply in writing in the next 15 working days. The grievant may then send the grievance to the Legislative Corrections Ombudsman to whom progress reports concerning the administrative process of grievances are provided upon written request.[2]

Charges of discrimination, brutality, or corruption may bypass institutional levels of the grievance procedure and be sent directly to the department director. Reprisals for use of the procedure are forbidden. No copies of grievances are placed in the inmate's institutional file.

A 1980 report indicated that the Legislative Ombudsman Office was created by legislation in 1975. This independent office investigates inmates' complaints and disciplinary appeals.[3]

The first account of an inmate representative group, 1888-1891, at the Michigan State Prison (now the State Prison of Southern Michigan, Jackson), was recounted in Chapter I, Notable Early Experiences.

Since 1970, the Department of Corrections has recognized

the importance of establishing procedures to encourage communication by inmates of their concerns and views. Following an examination of the systems of other states, the formation of inmate advisory councils was the first method used to provide inmates an opportunity to share their views with prison staff on various aspects of institutional living.[4]

A directive issued March 28, 1972, entitled "Prisoner Representation," instructed that each institution establish procedures by which inmates may elect representatives to meet with the staff for the purpose of increasing inmate-administration communication. Guidelines for forming these advisory groups provided for secret ballot selection of volunteer candidates to serve a maximum tenure of six months as housing unit representatives. The number of representatives to be elected was to be determined by each institution, and must reflect the overall racial composition of the population. Representatives were to be encouraged to work closely with the housing unit staff in solving issues arising at that level. Other issues and problems could be discussed at a monthly meeting of the representatives and the head of the institution. Additionally, the representatives were to select two inmates to serve as voting members of the institution Benefit Fund Committee. Screening of candidates was also directed. Disqualification could result if reasonable grounds existed to believe that a candidate would prove irresponsible or disruptive to the work of the group. An appropriate official was to discuss the reasons for such action with any affected individual. As of mid-February, 1973, there had been no disqualifications.[5]

The State Prison of Southern Michigan, Jackson, formally instituted the council system in July, 1971, about nine months prior to the issuance of the "Directive on Prisoner Representation," after having experimented with the meeting concept in late 1970. Procedures established there provided for the secret ballot election of six representatives in each cell housing unit, including the hospital, and four representatives in each barracks housing unit. These Unit Committees met monthly, or more often if the need arose, with two Housing Unit Team members. Written minutes of those meetings were posted on the housing unit bulletin board.[6]

Each Unit Committee selected one member to serve on the Warden's Forum which met bi-monthly to consider institution-wide issues and problems. Recordings of these meetings were broadcast over the closed circuit radio system. Actions taken as a result of discussions at the Warden's Forum included the advancing of the evening count time to provide a longer recreation period, the option of keeping cell lights on all night, a change in the hours of several activities and programs to better accommodate the participants, the rewriting of the Resident Guide Book at a language level more generally understood by the intended readers, and the installation of telephone booths in all cell units for the placing of collect calls. On many occasions the successful resolution of the problems and concerns of an individual resident had resulted following presentation of his situation by staff to the housing unit committee.[7]

Staff also introduced at the Warden's Forum problems involving groups of residents. For example, two groups appeared determined to display discourtesy during the performance of entertainers from the community. Retaliation was threatened by other residents who resented the behavior of the two groups. Discussion of the situation at the Warden's Forum was followed by discussion at Housing Unit Committee meetings. The latter groups then held discussions with the individuals concerned. This procedure resolved the problem.[8]

By September, 1972, the other four institutions and the camps had implemented the directive under procedures similar to those established at the State Prison of Southern Michigan. At each facility other staff members, as deemed appropriate by the warden, also attended the monthly meetings. Usually these were the deputy wardens, the director of treatment, a counselor, or a psychologist.[9]

The concept of inmate unit representation was later defined in a department policy on "Clients' Right of Self-Determination," and is presently part of the department policy established in 1981 which combined the directives on inmate representation and inmate unit councils, and the Warden's Forum as previously described.[10]

The Policy Directive of November 23, 1981 states that each institution shall have elected representatives to act as an advisory group to the administration. Two representatives, one of whom represents a minority race, and one alternate, are elected by secret ballot in each housing unit to serve a six-month term to which reelection is prohibited until a like period of time has lapsed. Candidates must be volunteers free of misconduct during the six months prior to election. Removal from office may be effected by a two-thirds vote of the group or by administrative order for cause. Should the elected alternate not assume the office, the vacancy is to be filled by the inmate of the same race who was first runner-up in the last election. Should a special election be necessary, it will be arranged for by the administration. Staff are not permitted to select a needed replacement.

The housing unit representatives meet monthly with designated living unit staff, to consider items on a written agenda prepared at least three days previously. A written response to agenda items is prepared by the unit manager and distributed to each representative and the institution head.[11]

Unit representatives rotate as members of the Wardens' Forum, which meets monthly to consider items on an agenda prepared not less than one week previous to the meeting date announced two weeks in advance by the institution head. The latter, following the meetings, prepares written responses to the agenda topics for distribution to the representatives and the Department Office of Prisoner Affairs. In those institutions providing radio taping of the meetings, the tape is played on the closed-circuit radio system on the day of the meeting and the following day.[12]

Wardens' Forum duties may include selection of members to:

> Serve as voting members of the Inmate Benefit Fund.
> Participate in selection of movies.
> Perform inspection duties in the dining room.
> Establish radio-TV schedules.
> Serve on ad hoc committees for special purposes, as requested by the institution head, for an indefinite period within the term of office.[13]

Department of Social Services

The Institutional Services Division, Office of Children and Youth Services, Department of Social Services, is responsible for the operation of ten residential facilities for youth committed by a juvenile court for parental neglect and delinquency. One of the facilities, the Residential Detention Center, Flint, provides short-term regional detention services to youth upon court order until appropriate placement can be determined.[14]

A descriptive overview of current programs contains no reference to grievance procedures.

Student government is not used as a part of the management model of the division. However, extensive use is made of youth groups in the treatment/release process and in the day-to-day implementation of agency policies. Each staff team is responsible for two ten-youth groups. The degree to which the teams involve the groups in management is considered to be of utmost importance. An example of group involvement: the release of a youth to the community can be started only by a formal recommendation to staff from the youth's treatment group.

In 1973 it was reported that at the three training schools then in operation, basic youth treatment groups were very much involved in administering the programs. Youth groups of nine or ten students each were expected to cope with management-type problems in cooperation with a staff team. The latter routinely sought student recommendations on operational matters.[15]

The two youth camps then in operation were reported in 1973 as having a camp council in operation as a part of the administration. These were Camp Victoire, Grayling (now Camp Shawono), and Camp Nokomis, Prudenville. Information was received in 1967 that, upon their opening in 1963 and 1964, respectively, each facility immediately organized a camp council composed of six boys nominated and elected by secret ballot to a two-month term of office, to which they could succeed themselves. The purpose of the councils was to provide an official, direct, and uninhibited channel of communication from boys to staff. Although it was noted that council membership often altered a student's position with his peers, who perceived him as in effect being a part of the administration, this apparently did not inhibit the effectiveness of the councils in resolving problems. Racial conflict and scapegoatism were cited as illustrative of the type of problems resolved through council intervention.

To accomplish the goals of (a) stimulating positive leadership skills, (b) providing a quasi-official role in certain areas, (c) creating identification with program planning and structuring, (d) fostering the objective analysis of policies and issues, and (e) providing a means for staff to obtain insight into the boys' viewpoint, certain guidelines were established which provided the boundaries of council functions.

> (1) Planning decisions made by the group must be for the benefit of all and must take into consideration the purpose, goals, and regulations of the camp.
> (2) While discussion topics could cover any area, tone and approach must be constructive, realistic, and not involve character assassination.
> (3) Council discussions were to be handled confidentially.[16]

Notes

1. Letter from Carol R. Howes, Program Specialist, Operations and Policy Analysis Unit, Program Bureau, Dept. of Corrections, Lansing, October 27, 1982.
2. *Ibid.*, Policy Directive No. PD-DWA-62.02, "Grievance Procedure for Prisoners and Parolees," Dept. of Corrections, November 23, 1981 (supersedes Policy Directive No. PD-DWA-62.02, March 1, 1979); Procedure No. OP-BCF-62.01, "Prisoner Grievance Procedure," Dept. of Corrections, November 23, 1981 (supersedes OP-BCF-62.01, September 17, 1979).
3. Dillingham, David D., and Singer, Linda R., *op. cit.*, p. 66.
4. Letter from Carol R. Howes, *op. cit.*
5. Baker, J. E., *op. cit.*, pp. 132-133.
6. *Ibid.*, p. 133.
7. *Ibid.*, p. 133.
8. *Ibid.*, p. 134.
9. *Ibid.*, p. 134.
10. Letter from Carol R. Howes, *op. cit.*
11. Policy Directive ... Grievance Procedures ..., November 23, 1981, *op. cit.*
12. *Ibid.*
13. *Ibid.*
14. Letter from Vergil M. Pinckney, Director, Institutional Services Division, Office of Youth Services, Dept. of Social Services, Lansing, September 30, 1982.
15. Baker, J. E., *op. cit.*, p. 134.
16. *Ibid.*, pp. 134-135.

MINNESOTA

Department of Corrections

All institutions for adult and youthful offenders and juvenile delinquents are under the jurisdiction of the Department of Corrections. No directives regarding either inmate grievance procedures or inmate councils have been written by the department. Each institution has developed a policy to meet local needs as to both processes.[1]

Only the Minnesota Correctional Facility, Red Wing, has a student grievance procedure; it was established in 1980.[2]

An Ombudsman for Corrections was established through Executive Order No. 14 by the Governor in February, 1972, and subsequently by legislation on July 1, 1973. The Ombudsman, who reports to the Governor, took office in July, 1972, to serve the inmate population of all Department of Corrections institutions. Inmate complaints are processed through this mechanism rather than a multi-level procedure as used in other jurisdictions.[3]

At the Minnesota Correctional Facility, Stillwater (formerly the Minnesota State Prison), there was an inmate advisory council for about one year in 1960-61. Initially, elected members were quite stable persons. However, demands made upon councilmen by their constituents lessened the desirability of the office. Consequently, the caliber of candidates deteriorated, leading to the election of irresponsible persons whose unreasonable demands and threats to demonstrate and riot could not be tolerated. After attempts to create a sense of responsibility met with an unimproved response, the council was discontinued. In 1973 it was reported that a council was being organized.[4]

In October, 1977, Inmate Advisory Groups were established in each cell hall. Members are appointed by the cell hall director to a six-month term of office. Terms are staggered so that two new appointees assume office every two months in each six-member group. Membership is racially balanced in proportion to institution population percentages. The groups meet with the cell hall director once a month to discuss problems specific to the living unit. Twice a year representatives of all groups meet with the warden to discuss institution-wide concerns.[5]

In 1937, at the Minnesota Correctional Facility, St. Cloud (then the Minnesota State Reformatory and later the State Reformatory for Men), an athletic board whose membership included the vocational counselor, director of physical education, captain of the guard, and seven elected inmates, planned the recreational and athletic activities and scheduled games and tournaments.[6]

In 1967, the administration reported that inmate ad hoc

committees had been appointed from time to time to deal with specific problems.[7]

On October 7, 1974, at the St. Cloud institution, an advisory council was established to provide a representative board through which all the people who live and work at the institution could systematically consider, review, and make recommendations regarding policies, procedures, programs, and other matters relating to living-working conditions. The council is not a policy-making entity, but does provide staff and inmate input to the decision-making process of the administration.[8]

Eleven inmates and ten staff comprise the council membership. The latter are appointed by the superintendent. Each of four housing units elects a member and an alternate; a fifth housing unit elects two. Two members each are selected by the Indian Culture Group and the Black Brotherhood Cultural Development Organization, and one by the Chicano Culture Group. Elections and selections are held in June and December, supervised by the Ombudsman's office. Membership is limited to four full consecutive terms. A minimum of six months' residence in the institution and residency in the unit are the only qualifications to stand for election.[9]

The conduct of council meetings is based largely on Robert's Rules of Order. The meetings are held monthly to consider items on an agenda prepared in advance by an inmate and a staff member (both approved by the full council) from items suggested by other members.[10]

The council is considered by the institution superintendent to have operated quite effectively since its inception, and there has never been an instance in which serious consideration was given to its abolition. Inmate participation continues to be active and continues to grow in acceptance. The election process has never lacked candidates, and the culture groups have seldom failed to reappoint a representative when a resignation or release created a vacancy. Activities of the council are published monthly in the inmate newspaper, thus keeping the institution population informed.[11]

Currently, the council, through its chairman, recommends to the superintendent the yearly budget for the inmate Social Welfare Account. Some of the major contributions of the account to the institution are: cable TV; inmate telephones; referees for sports events; additional court yard space; and many changes in policy, e.g., inmate food, canteen items, staff-inmate relationships.[12]

The superintendent views the council as an integral part of the administrative functions of a major facility. He credits the council as having been instrumental in developing a better understanding of policies and procedures by both staff and inmates.[13]

Some form of inmate council has existed since 1970 at the Minnesota Correctional Facility, Shakopee (formerly the Minnesota

Correctional Institution for Women). At times the council has been suspended but has always resumed with a new format.[14]

The current inmate council, COED, was established in January, 1981. Two members are elected from each cottage. Prior to the monthly meeting with the superintendent, the residents in each cottage hold a meeting to express concerns deemed necessary to be presented to the council for consideration. The goal of COED is to address concerns, problems, and program recommendations relevant to the inmates and the staff. Additionally, council members may recommend policy and procedural changes and are responsible for keeping their cottage peers aware of council activities.[15]

In 1937, at the Minnesota Correctional Facility, Redwing (formerly the State Training School), each cottage elected one of its members to serve on an Activities Council which worked with the Director of Recreation in planning, scheduling, and carrying out a recreation program described as diversified and extensive. At that time, it was stated that several attempts had been made to install a system by which the boys could participate in the management of the institution but that staff reaction was generally unfavorable and the time did not seem ripe for it.[16]

A Student Council was operative at the institution for about six months, being discontinued in June, 1966. The group promoted several innovations described as worthwhile, including a student government day; student assistance in the selection of a new style of clothing; the liberalization of policies involving visiting and the wearing of jewelry; and a change in smoking policies. The council was discontinued upon the inception in 1968 of a Guided Group Interaction program, featuring individual cottage committees which gave the students a voice in parole readiness, home visits, cottage programs, administrative decisions, and presenting and discussing new ideas. The then administration firmly believed in student representation and would have continued the Student Council had the Guided Group program not evolved.[17] Currently the program is referred to as "Involvement Groups" and is similar to the original Guided Group Interaction program.[18]

Information was received in 1967 from the Minnesota Correctional Facility, Sauk Centre (formerly the Minnesota Home School) that a Student Council was operative but its establishment date was not given. Two elected students from each of the eight cottages formed the council which met periodically with the group living supervisor.[19] Currently, a Resident Council is reported to have been established April 9, 1981. One elected student from each of the open operating cottages saves on the council, which meets monthly on the first Wednesday. The present administration points out, as was true in 1967, that although the council is not a policy-making group, policy may result from the information it provides. Rated by the administration as a successful endeavor, the purpose of the council is to insure that residents have regular access to designated staff in order to present problems without delay or formality.[20] A policy-procedure statement provides for secret ballot elections monitored by cottage staff, special elections to fill vacancies caused by parole, and transmission of agenda items two days prior to the monthly meeting. Council members are required to report council discussions to their cottage peers.[21]

The Minnesota Correctional Facility, Oak Park Heights, Stillwater, dedicated and opened on March 4, 1982, is a maximum security institution designed to house primarily disruptive and high-risk inmates from the Minnesota Correctional Institution, Stillwater, and the institution at St. Cloud.

In line with the participatory management philosophy and style of the institution administration, a forum was established shortly after the facility began operating to provide for inmate involvement and input into the decision-making process on issues and concerns affecting inmates. Excluded, of course, are decisions on security functions.[22]

The forum implemented is the Inmate Representative Group. That name was chosen rather than advisory group or advisory council in order to designate specifically the purpose of the organization --representation of inmate concerns and issues rather than advice and counsel to the administration.[23]

Initially on a weekly, and currently on a bi-weekly basis, certain personnel meet with the group, comprised of staff-selected members within each of the 52-person living units, whose term of office is three months. Chaired by the unit Case Manager, the meeting deals with concerns, issues, and suggested changes presented in advance to the representatives by the other inmates in the unit. As requested by the inmates, other staff attend to respond to issues raised regarding programs for which they have responsibility; for instance, the Food Service Supervisor, Canteen Supervisor, or the Unit Lieutenant or other unit corrections staff. Meeting minutes are prepared by the Case Manager for the information of unit inmates and supervisory and administrative officials. Responses to all issues raised at the meetings are made within a week when it is possible to do so. Many changes made in institution operations and programs evolved from suggestions by the Inmate Representative Groups. Suggestions for change that are reasonable and rational and do not compromise security or staff management of the institution have been made. In the opinion of the administration, tangible evidence of their input is visible to the inmates.[24]

An Inmate Council was in operation for a short time but was discontinued in 1965 at the Willow River Camp, Willow River.[25] In July, 1972, a vocational-education program for adults was established for the total program of the facility, together with a Guided Group Interaction program featuring program committees, which is still operative. An elected representative system is not deemed necessary since the low census makes possible meetings with the entire population as needed. Staff-inmate communication is at a fairly high level due to the one to one-and-one-half ratio.[26]

In 1967, it was reported there was no student council at the Thistledew Lake Forestry Camp, Togo (now the Thistledew Camp). However, there had been experiences with such groups in the past; these produced only limited success. Apparently a departure from the original democratic purposes occurred in each instance and the group meetings became gripe sessions. One of the factors in the staff decision to discontinue councils was that participation did not result in any visible treatment value for the student.[27] Currently, there is no student council. The camp, now classed as a juvenile residential facility for boys ages 13 to 17, is geared for a short-term (three months) program designed to upgrade educational level and social living-learning skills.[28]

Because of the short-term nature of the program, the Minnesota Reception and Diagnostic Center, Circle Pines had never organized a student council, according to information received in 1967. Until the mid-1970s, it was a juvenile facility. Currently it is the Minnesota Correctional Facility, Lino Lakes, a medium-security institution for adult males. A staff/inmate council was organized several years ago. Under a constitution and by-laws, each cottage elects one member, and an alternate, who may serve two consecutive six-month terms of office. Staff members of the council are appointed by the superintendent. The council meets during the evening hours for 90 minutes on the first Tuesday of each month to consider an agenda of items submitted five days in advance. Discussion of any item is limited to 30 minutes, with debate time per member not to exceed five minutes. Recall and impeachment of members is provided for, as is a constitution amendment process.[29] The activity and interest in the council tends to fluctuate depending on the quality of the inmate members and the ideas or issues being considered.[30]

In the fall of 1965, a Student Council was formed at the Youth Vocational Center, Rochester. A constitution and by-laws were drafted providing for the election of representatives from the student body. However, the introduction of a Guided Group Interaction program in March, 1966, and shortly thereafter the activation of weekly Community Meetings, supplanted the need for the council.[31] This center is now closed.

The St. Croix Camp, Sandstone, had a student council from 1962 until 1965, when it was discontinued because of dominance by a few boys who used it to further their own interests. In September, 1966 a limited form of self-government was introduced through camp meetings held every two weeks at which the superintendent presided. Problems related to camp operations could be introduced either by staff or students. Should the discussion topic require it, only students could vote.[32] This camp is now closed.

Notes

1. Letter from Daniel P. O'Brien, Assistant to the Commissioner, Dept. of Corrections, St. Paul, September 21, 1982.

2. Letter from Supt. Gerald T. O'Rourke, Minnesota Correctional Facility, Red Wing, October 20, 1982.
3. Keating, Michael J.; McArthur, Virginia A.; Lewis, Michael K.; Sebilius, Kathleen Gilligan; and Singer, Linda R. *Grievance Mechanisms in Correctional Institutions.* Washington, D.C.: U.S. Dept. of Justice, 1975, p. 41.
4. Baker, J. E., *op. cit.*, pp. 135-136.
5. Letter from Warden Robert A. Erickson, Minnesota Correctional Facility, Stillwater, October 21, 1982.
6. Cox, William B., and Bixby, F. Lovell, Ph.D., *op. cit.*, p. 167.
7. Baker, J. E., *op. cit.*, p. 136.
8. Letter from Superintendent W. F. McRae, Minnesota Correctional Facility, St. Cloud, October 27, 1982.
9. "Constitution and By-Laws" Inmate Staff Advisory Council, Minnesota Correctional Facility, St. Cloud, October 7, 1982.
10. *Ibid.*
11. Letter from Superintendent W. F. McRae, *op. cit.*
12. *Ibid.*
13. *Ibid.*
14. Letter from Superintendent D. Jacqueline Fleming, Minnesota Correctional Facility, Shakopee, October 21, 1982.
15. "COED," Policy and Procedure Manual, Minnesota Correctional Facility, Shakopee, A-202.8, January 1981.
16. Cox, William B., and Bixby, F. Lovell, Ph.D., eds. *Handbook of American Institutions for Juvenile Delinquents, West North Central States.* Vol. I, First Edition. New York: The Osborne Association, Inc., 1938, pp. 147-148.
17. Baker, J. E., *op. cit.*, p. 136.
18. Letter from Superintendent Gerald T. O'Rourke, Minnesota Correctional Facility, Red Wing, October 20, 1982. (Also see: Dean, Charles W., and Reppucci, N. Dixon, "Juvenile Correctional Institutions," in Glaser, Daniel, ed., *Handbook of Criminology.* New York: Rand McNally College Publishing Company, 1974, pp. 878-879, re origins of the guided group interaction program at the facility.)
19. Baker, J. E., *op. cit.*, p. 136.
20. Letter from Superintendent Harvey C. Akerson, Minnesota Correctional Facility, Sauk Centre, October 21, 1982.
21. Policy-Procedure Statement No. 0108, "Resident Council," April 9, 1981.
22. Telephone conversation with Lieutenant Louis Stender, and letter from Warden Frank W. Wood, Minnesota Correctional Facility, Oak Park Heights, Stillwater, December 3, 1982.
23. *Ibid.*
24. *Ibid.*
25. Baker, J. E., *op. cit.*, p. 137.
26. Letter from Superintendent Ralph L. Nelson, Willow River Camp, Willow River, October 21, 1982.
27. Baker, J. E., *op. cit.*, p. 137.
28. Letter from Superintendent Derwood J. Lund, Thistledew Camp, Togo, October 22, 1982.

29. Constitution of Staff/Inmate Council (Rev. 5-78), and By-Laws of Staff/Inmate Council (Rev. 7-80), Minnesota Correctional Facility, Lino Lakes.
30. Letter from Bert R. Mohs, Programs Director, Minnesota Correctional Facility, Lino Lakes, March 23, 1983.
31. Baker, J. E., op. cit., p. 137.
32. Ibid.

MISSISSIPPI

Department of Corrections

The Institutions Division of the Department of Corrections is responsible for the administration of the Mississippi State Penitentiary, Parchman, for adult and youthful male and female offenders.

An Offender Grievance Procedure and an Ombudsman were established, respectively, in 1976 and 1978.[1]

When an inmate has a specific complaint which cannot be resolved or rectified through informal contact with the unit counselor or administrator, he/she may file a written complaint on a Request for Administrative Remedy form within 15 days following the incident giving rise to the complaint. A complaint may not be filed on behalf of another inmate or a group. Grievances involving or regarding disciplinary actions must first be filed through the disciplinary process.[2] (No mention is made of a current ombudsman).

Grievances must be logical and the requested or anticipated remedy must fall within the authority of the Department of Corrections. The written grievance is given to the Associate Warden (Program Administrator), who appoints a panel for review, investigation, and decision. Upon receiving a written response, the inmate may appeal the decision to the warden on a prescribed appeal form. The basis of the appeal must be specified as well as the points of the original decision which were unsatisfactory. The warden will make a written response within ten working days.

The regulation provides an alternate process in those instances when the issue is of a sensitive nature and the inmate has reason to believe he/she will be adversely affected should it become known at the program level that a complaint is being made. The grievance may be filed directly with the warden, from whose decision an appeal may be made to the Commissioner of Corrections.

If not satisfied with any response, an inmate may file suit in any appropriate court, but documentary proof must be attached to such petition as proof that remedies have been exhausted under the administrative remedy process.

Although a copy of the complaint and resulting decisions is

placed in the inmate's permanent record, the procedure specifies that no repercussions or oppression will obtain for filing a complaint.

In 1966, it was reported there was then no form of inmate self-government nor any knowledge of such a group ever having existed.[3] Currently, there are still no provisions for inmate self-government.[4]

Division of Juvenile Institutions

The Division of Juvenile Institutions, Department of Youth Services, administers four facilities for juvenile delinquents. None have student grievance procedures and no directives on the program have been issued by the Division.[5]

In 1967, there were two facilities for juvenile delinquents administered by the Central Office, Mississippi Training Schools. Information obtained indicated that there had never been an inmate council at the Columbia Training School, Columbia. The report of the Board of Trustees and Superintendent, Oakley Training School, Raymond, for the biennium 1963-65, received in February, 1967, contained no reference to a council.[6] There are no student councils currently.[7]

Notes

1. Dillingham, David D., and Singer, Linda R., op. cit., p. 52.
2. "Inmate Handbook and Rules and Regulations" (revised May 15, 1981), Mississippi Department of Corrections, pp. 100-113.
3. Baker, J. E., op. cit., p. 137.
4. Letter from Ken Jones, Public Relations Director, Department of Corrections, Jackson, March 11, 1983.
5. Telephone conversation with Charles Graham, Administrative Assistant to the Executive Director, Dept. of Youth Services, Jackson, June 23, 1983.
6. Baker, J. E., op. cit., p. 138.
7. Ibid.

MISSOURI

Department of Corrections and Human Resources

The Department of Corrections and Human Resources, Department of Social Services, administers the 11 state institutions for adult and youthful felony offenders.[1]

A 1980 report stated that an inmate grievance procedure had been established in 1974 which provided formal hearings on grievances filed by inmates, written responses within specified time limits and an appeal process of which the final level of review was the Department Director.[2]

Each of the institutions has an inmate council meeting twice monthly to discuss inmate complaints which are then referred to the institution administrator for action. At the co-ed Renz Correctional Center, Cedar City, the inmate dormitory council is involved in making recommendations on the budget, education and program content and similar activities. The councils are regarded as having been a valuable tool in the operation of the department.[3]

Although no dates were given as to when the inmate councils were established, information has been obtained indicating that the council at the Missouri Training Center for Men, Moberly, was formed in early fall, 1974. As of April 7, 1975, a constitution had been written and its acceptance by the institution administration constituted official recognition of the council as the representative body for the inmate population. Council membership was comprised of two men from each housing wing, a chairman, and a secretary. Plans at that time included future efforts to present specific proposals for the improvement of living conditions and to facilitate channels of staff-inmate communication.[4]

Information obtained in 1966 and 1972 indicated that while there were no formally structured inmate councils in any of the then seven facilities for adult and youthful offenders, ad hoc committees were appointed for special activities. At the Missouri Intermediate Reformatory, Jefferson City, an honor dormitory and two semi-honor housing units were regarded as self-governing in certain respects. The 150 young men who lived in the units signed themselves in and out and established their own rules for conduct and community living. To a large degree, the same was true at the Fordland Honor Camp (now the Ozark Correctional Center, Fordland).[5]

Division of Youth Services

Institutional services for juvenile delinquents are provided in four facilities administered by the Division of Youth Services, Department of Social Services.[6]

No mention is made of grievance procedures. However, a description of Positive Peer Culture, the treatment modality employed, appears to contain some of the elements essential to complaint resolution:

> The youngsters are placed into groups of ten. Each member is responsible for all the other members in his/her group. School classes, meals, and projects are attended as a group. Five nights a week group meetings are held to work on problems that have occurred during the day.

> These meetings are directed by a group leader who is part of the cottage team which includes three to four other treatment staff and school teachers. The cottage team is responsible for planning and implementing treatment of individual members and the group as a whole....[7]

There is no current reference to youth councils at any of the facilities. There were no councils according to information received in 1966 and 1973 when the facilities were administered by the State Board of Training Schools (a division of the Department of Corrections, but actually an autonomous body). At that time, a group counseling program was described as often stimulating the individual and the group toward an improved government of self. Each group member was responsible for recommending the release of each other group member as well as recommending other appropriate institutional changes.[8]

In 1937 a survey of the Training School for Boys, Boonville, found that certain boys were selected by the officers to exercise a measure of authority over other boys. The management style of the institution was the military model, with each of the eight housing units constituting a company. Boys were assigned to a company on the basis of age. The staff member in charge of a housing unit, the Captain, appointed boys, subject to approval by the superintendent, to the ranks of lieutenants, sergeants, and corporals. These boys were authorized to act as dormitory night monitors and represented the only supervision given. In the three companies of the youngest boys, a few of these appointees had been designated to exercise a measure of authority to deal with disciplinary problems to the extent they were able.[9]

At the State Industrial School for Girls, Chillicothe (later designated as the Training School for Girls; replaced in 1981 by the Chillicothe Correctional Center), in 1937 it was reported that each girl could place written suggestions in a box kept in the school building. A meeting of staff and students was held once a month to discuss and vote for the best suggestion. The winning contributor was awarded a prize of one dollar. It was claimed that all winning suggestions had been put into effect.[10]

Also in 1937, at the State Industrial Home for Negro Girls, Tipton (replaced in 1960 and designated as the State Correctional Center for Women, and currently the State Correctional Pre-Release Center), the girls in each living unit elected three of their members to be "Leaders," with the highest vote-getter being designated "First Leader." Leaders were in charge of the units, considered to be self-governing, and acted as assistants to the matrons in other units. They met each evening with the matrons and each Sunday with the superintendent to discuss unit and institution-wide matters. Although the scope of its activities included all aspects of institution life, including making disciplinary actions in some cases, the group's capacity was only advisory, with no authority to take action. The greater number of the girls considered the establishment of the council to have been the outstanding achievement at the institution in recent years.[11]

Notes

1. Letter from Lee Roy Black, Ph.D., Director, Dept. of Corrections and Human Resources, Jefferson City, Missouri, October 7, 1982.
2. Dillingham, David D., and Singer, Linda R., op. cit., p. 53.
3. Letter from Lee Roy Black, Ph.D., Director, op. cit.
4. From CONTACT, INC., Lincoln, Nebraska.
5. Baker, J. E., op. cit., p. 138.
6. Brochure: "Programs of the Missouri Division of Youth Services," Revised December, 1981.
7. Annual Report, Missouri Division of Youth Services, 1980, p. 14.
8. Baker, J. E., op. cit., p. 138.
9. Cox, William B., and Bixby, F. Lovell, Ph.D., op. cit., p. 219.
10. Ibid., p. 251.
11. Ibid., pp. 280-281.

MONTANA

Department of Institutions

Adult and youthful felony offenders are committed to the Department of Institutions, which places them in the Montana State Prison, Deer Lodge, the Swan River Forest Camp, or the Women's Correctional Center, Anaconda. Juvenile delinquents are committed to the Pine Hills School, Miles City, or the Mountain View School, Helena.

Corrections Division

The Corrections Division administers the five institutions mentioned above.

A 1980 report states that a grievance procedure was established in Montana in 1974. A formal hearing is provided and responses are made in writing within specified time limits. The final level of appeal is a review board outside the system.[1]

At the Women's Correctional Center, Anaconda, which opened on May 3, 1982, a Resident Grievance Procedure was drafted and had a proposed effective date of November 1, 1982. The procedure accepts any complaint except issues involving a disciplinary or classification process decision, or matters involving actions of the parole board. All complaints go directly to the head of the institution who may appoint a complaint investigator to receive, investigate, and make a report within five days. The institution head has 15 days to take action and notify the grievant in writing. In emergency cases involving food, health, or personal safety, every effort is to be made to expedite processing. Within five days following the institution decision, the grievant may appeal to the Administrator, Corrections Division, who must respond in writing within 15 days. That decision may be appealed to the final level of review, the Director, Department of Institutions, who has 30 days to make a written reply. No prejudicial action whatsoever may be taken against any inmate involved in the grievance procedure.[2]

At the Mountain View School, Helena, there is a resident grievance procedure available to all residents based on any disciplinary action by the administration. The opportunity to be represented in a disciplinary hearing by another resident or a staff member is optional with the grievant.[3]

An Inmate Council was operative from 1956 to 1959 at the Montana State Prison, Deer Lodge. Officers and representatives were elected by the general population. Cliques gained control and insured that only candidates acceptable to them were elected. The opinion that a council would be detrimental to internal organization was expressed by a previous administration (prior to 1972). However, no indictment was made of groups per se. Encouragement of organizations such as Jaycees and Alcoholics Anonymous was expressed.[4]

A Resident Advisory Council was established August 30, 1982, at the Women's Correctional Center, Anaconda, consisting of three residents elected by secret ballot to serve a three-month term of office. The group meets bi-weekly with the institution head to discuss resident concerns and to provide input to policies and programs. Meeting minutes are distributed to staff and all residents.[5]

In December, 1972, it was reported that a Camp Council had been in operation since the Swan River Youth Forest Camp opened in July, 1968. The five members, elected by secret ballot, held office until released or removed for certain disciplinary measures, or until they presented reasons for resignation acceptable to a majority of all boys in the population, which averaged 22 in 1971 within an age range of 16 to 18 years. In addition to a president, a vice-president, and a secretary who recorded notes of all meetings for posting on bulletin boards after transmittal to the staff, there was an Orientation Committee whose two members provided full orientation for all newly arrived boys. The goals of the Swan River facility Camp Council were to provide a means of boy-staff communication, develop an esprit de corps, and help boys learn to handle their responsibilities. The duration of weekly meetings was determined by the topics introduced for discussion and might range from a few minutes to several hours. Simplicity of operation, staff input, and a staff attitude of respect for the group were factors cited as having made the council effective and useful.[6] No current information has been received regarding the council.

The Mountain View School, formerly designated as the Vocational School for Girls, was established at its present site, seven miles north of Helena, in 1919 after operating from 1893 as a part of the Boys' and Girls' Industrial School, Miles City. A student government was in operation several years ago but no information is available regarding its procedures or reasons for discontinuance. Shortly after he was appointed in 1966, the superintendent, in 1972, initiated a Student Government program in which a president and council members were elected by the students. It was still operative according to information received in November, 1972.[7]

Currently, the Mountain View School is using a cottage representative form of government. Each of three cottages elects a representative. The group meets monthly with the superintendent and more often on an as-required basis. Content of the meetings includes all aspects of the school program. Many of the changes that have occurred over the last two years resulted from the meetings.[8]

In November, 1972, information was received that a Student Council had been organized in 1968 at the Pine Hills School, Miles City (formerly the State Industrial School). Two representatives were selected by the ten to 25 boys residing in each of the six lodges. Suggestions made at lodge meetings and presented by the representatives at weekly meetings with the superintendent and assistant superintendent resulted in constructive changes in program. Council members conducted tours of the school and sponsored activities both on and off the campus. In 1972 the superintendent initiated discussions with council members on rehabilitation concepts, lodge and student problems, and other topics they might wish to introduce, as a means of providing opportunities for both self-expression and learning about the philosophy and planning on which school operations were based.[9] No current information has been received.

Notes

1. Dillingham, David D., and Singer, Linda R., op. cit., p. 53.
2. "Resident Grievance Procedure," Proposed Policy to be effective November 1, 1982, Women's Correctional Center, Anaconda.
3. Letter from Superintendent William Unger, Mountain View School, Helena, Montana, September 29, 1982.
4. Baker, J. E., op. cit., p. 139.
5. "Policy and Procedure," Resident Advisory Council, Women's Correctional Center, Anaconda, August 30, 1982.
6. Baker, J. E., op. cit., pp. 139-140.
7. Ibid., p. 139.
8. Letter from Superintendent William Unger, op. cit.
9. Baker, J. E., op. cit., p. 139.

NEBRASKA

Department of Correctional Services

The Department of Correctional Services is responsible for all adult and juvenile correctional institutions. Until 1973, corrections was a division of the Department of Public Institutions.

Division of Adult Services

The Division of Adult Services administers and supervises four institutions for adult and youthful felony offenders.

A multi-level Inmate Grievance System was established in 1971 at the Nebraska State Penitentiary, Lincoln[1] (in 1963 the penitentiary and the reformatory were combined to comprise the Nebraska Penal and Correctional Complex; in 1979 the Lincoln Correctional Center was opened for youthful offenders and the complex name reverted to that of penitentiary). An inmate may register a complaint by completing a prescribed form, and the complaint will be investigated fully by a grievance officer who will recommend disposition to the warden. The grievance officer is empowered to carry out any action approved by the warden. Appeals may be made successively to the Director of Correctional Services and the State Ombudsman, State Capitol, Lincoln, an office established in 1973.[2]

In 1973 it was reported that the grievance committees within the then Penal and Correctional Complex consisted of four inmates--one white, one black, one Mexican-American, and one native American. The members were initially appointed by the administration, based on recommendations from correctional officers and other staff members. When a member left the institution or resigned from a committee, the successor was appointed by the remaining members. A staff coordinator met weekly with the committees to process written complaints. As of October, 1973, according to the coordinator, interposition by the committees had resulted in restoration of good time for an inmate, and the reduction of escape expenses charged to an inmate. Additionally, three correctional officers had been taken before a personnel review committee because of abusive treatment of inmates.[3]

Currently, offenders may voice their concerns and suggestions by using the Department of Correctional Services grievance system or by corresponding or speaking directly with correctional personnel.[4] It is assumed that the grievance procedure remains as described in a 1980 survey. Established in 1974, the procedure provides for written responses to grievances within specified time limits, and appeals, with the Director of Correctional Services as the final level of review. No formal hearing is provided.[5]

Offender councils are not permitted in either adult or juvenile institutions, but participation in club activities in which offenders elect their officers is allowed. A 1974 study of the Nebraska Prison system recommended the establishment at each institution of an inmate council having reasonable decision-making powers and a serious advisory role, with representatives elected at-large for a six-month term.[6]

In 1967, at the Nebraska State Penitentiary, an Athletics and Recreation Committee was reported as functioning under a constitution and by-laws providing for the ballot election of five members who met monthly with the warden to consider topics on an approved agenda. The favorable attitude of the warden in office at that time toward the organizing of advisory councils was well known to the inmates. (While warden at another institution he had had an advisory council that was able to accomplish a number of things.) The lack of sufficient interest among the inmates to warrant the development of an Inmate Advisory Council was cited as possibly being due to activities of the Athletic and Recreation Committee and a Junior Chamber of Commerce. The latter was involved in functions normally regarded as those of an advisory council. Other groups active at the time were Alcoholics Anonymous, Checks Anonymous, and a Gavel Club.[7]

In 1934 several committees were elected by inmates to confer with and make recommendations to the deputy warden relative to the various aspects of the athletic program. However, in 1937, the committees had been abolished. The deputy warden who had been appointed on January 1, 1937 stated that he conferred with inmates of his own choosing relative to such matters.[8]

At the Nebraska Center for Women, York (then the State Reformatory for Women), in 1972 each living area was administered in part by an Inmate Council. Representatives started as errand runners in the maximum security unit, progressing in responsibility in each living area. The three members elected in the Trusty Dormitory had almost all decision-making responsibility for that unit. In all instances final decision and actual authority rested with the staff and administration.[9]

Division of Juvenile Services

The Division of Juvenile Services administers and supervises two Youth Development Centers.

As previously mentioned, all offenders may voice their concerns and suggestions via the Department of Correctional Services grievance system. Offender councils are not permitted.

In 1967, a Student Council was reported as having been functioning since 1961 in the Youth Development Center, Kearney, then known as the Boys' Training School. The purposes of the group were to promote the students' general welfare and insure better student-faculty understanding. A constitution provided for the election of senators and congressmen from each cottage to serve a three-month term of office. Nominees must have been at the school for four months and in good standing. The council was regarded as an opportunity for pupil participation in government and not for so-called self-government. A feature was a Council Court which might hear a defendant's case and pass its decision to the superintendent. The president and vice-president of the council acted as judges, the senator from the defendant's cottage was the prosecuting attorney, with the defense being assumed by the congressman. The remaining councilmen formed the jury. The superintendent at that time met once a week with the council. Having been at the school only a brief time, he made no evaluation of the effectiveness of the group. In 1972, it was reported that the council was no longer active.[10]

In 1937, cottage monitors were appointed by the staff at the Kearney facility. Known as captain, first lieutenant, second lieutenant, and sergeant, these monitors in each cottage were supposed to exercise control over and prevent the escape of other boys. It was stated that the monitors "really ran the cottages" although they were not supposed to inflict punishments.[11]

According to 1967 information, there had never been an advisory council in the Youth Development Center, Geneva (then the Girls' Training School).[12]

In 1937, a monitor system was in effect which gave staff-selected girls official authority over others.[13]

Notes

1. "Inmate Grievances," Official Memorandum, No. 856.022, Nebraska Penal and Correctional Complex, Lincoln, December 4, 1974. (The preface to this memorandum indicates that an inmate grievance system had been operating successfully for three and one-half years.)
2. Ibid.
3. Report of the Nebraska Advisory Committee to the U.S. Commission on Civil Rights, August, 1974, pp. 58-59.
4. Letter from Laurie Smith Camp, General Counsel, Dept. of Correctional Services, Lincoln, September 22, 1982.
5. Dillingham, David D., and Singer, Linda R., op. cit., p. 53.
6. Letter from Laurie Smith Camp, op. cit.; Report of the Nebraska Advisory Committee to the U.S. Commission on Civil Rights, August, 1974, p. 96.
7. Baker, J. E., op. cit., p. 141.
8. Cox, William B., and Bixby, F. Lovell, Ph.D., eds. Handbook of American Prisons and Reformatories, West North Central States. Vol. I, Fifth Edition. p. 251.
9. Baker, J. E., op. cit., p. 141.
10. Ibid., pp. 140-141.
11. Cox, William B., and Bixby, F. Lovell, Ph.D. Handbook of American Institutions for Delinquent Juveniles, West North Central States. Vol. I, First Edition. pp. 309-310.

12. Baker, J. E., *op. cit.*, p. 140.
13. Cox, William B., and Bixby, F. Lovell, Ph.D., *op. cit.*, p. 336.

NEVADA

Department of Prisons

The Department of Prisons administers ten facilities for adult and youthful felony offenders, including two restitution centers.

Although no current information was received, a 1980 report indicated that in July, 1977, in response to prison unrest, a mediator was appointed by the Department Director to coordinate the complaint programs in all institutions and to handle directly complaints for some facilities. In some facilities, matters that cannot be settled informally are heard by an inmate/staff committee, with the mediator acting as chairman. Appeals may be made to the institution warden and the Department Director. Time limits for response exist at each level of review. The procedure was observed at the Northern Nevada Correctional Center and the Nevada Women's Correctional Center, both located at Carson City.

The same report told of an inmate grievance procedure established in 1978 in which inmates participate in decision-making roles in the formal hearing accorded a grievant, and written responses are made within specified time limits. The Director, Department of Prisons, is the final level of review.[1]

Information obtained in 1966 indicated that inmate advisory councils were first organized at the Nevada State Prison in 1955 and were originally called Inmate Committees. Three-member and six-member councils were reported as being operative, respectively, in a Reception-Guidance Center and a Minimum Security Facility. Candidates for election to the six-month term of office in each group were screened by the administration to insure their capability to serve the interests of other inmates. At the Minimum Security Facility, it was additionally specified that candidates must have a minimum of six months remaining to serve on their sentences, and a six-months' period of clear conduct.

These councils had an active part in presenting to the administration suggestions and grievances (the latter accepted from individuals only when they were felt to be indicative of popular opinion); presenting to the inmates those suggestions which the administration felt were in order; scheduling television and radio programs; coordinating holiday programs; and compiling information regarding potential purchases authorized under Inmate Welfare Fund provisions. No participation in custodial methods or procedures was permitted, nor were personal criticisms of staff.

In November, 1972, there was an inmate advisory council in

each of the three facilities of the Nevada State Prison complex at Carson City: a Maximum Security Prison, a Medium Security Prison, and the Women's Prison. (These are now designated, respectively, Nevada State Prison, Northern Nevada Correctional Center, and Nevada Women's Correctional Center.) The members were nominated and elected by the population, with the warden reserving the right to deny the nomination of any person. Otherwise, the Councils functioned in accordance with guidelines contained in the American Correctional Association Manual of Correctional Standards. Regarding as good his experience in having always worked with an inmate advisory council, the warden believed such a group was of primary importance as a vehicle of information exchange between inmates and administration. He stressed that a council should function only in an advisory capacity and not be permitted to assume administrative responsibility or authority.[2]

Whether the Inmate Advisory Council still exists at the Nevada State Prison, or the Nevada Women's Correctional Center, is not known, but a study made in 1980 reported councils at the Northern Nevada Correctional Center, and the Southern Nevada Correctional Center, Jean.[3]

The constitution of the Inmate Advisory Committee, established about 1980 at the Jean institution, provides that any inmate who has been in the Nevada prison system for six months, and has been at the institution for 90 days, may stand for election to a six-month term of office, with one succession permitted, provided he has had no more than one conviction for a minor disciplinary offense during the 90-day period prior to election. Each housing unit elects one representative. From its membership, the committee elects a chairman, vice-chairman, and secretary. The chairman, with the aid and approval of the committee members, appoints nine subcommittees, conducts all committee meetings, and is responsible for insuring communications between the inmates and the administration.[4]

The subcommittees are: 1. Grievance; 2. Hobby Craft; 3. Inmate Store; 4. Inmate Welfare Fund Finance and Payroll; 5. Culinary; 6. Movie and Recreation; 7. Laundry; 8. Health and Safety; 9. Orientation.

Removal from office may be by impeachment and a hearing by a committee of eight or more advisory committee members; by petition of 25 per cent of the institution population; or for being found guilty of two minor violations or for a general or a major violation. Minutes of all committee meetings are made by the secretary.

Department of Human Resources

The two facilities for juvenile delinquents are administered by the Youth Services Division, Department of Human Resources. Information was obtained in 1967 that neither had an advisory council.[5]

No current data have been received regarding either inmate councils or inmate grievance procedures.

Notes

1. Dillingham, David D., and Singer, Linda R., op. cit., p. 66.
2. Baker, J. E., op. cit., p. 142.
3. Neto, Virginia V., and Bainer, LaNelle Marie, op. cit., p. 111.
4. "Constitution, Inmate Advisory Council," Southern Nevada Correctional Center, Jean.
5. Baker, J. E., op. cit., p. 143.

NEW HAMPSHIRE

Adult Institutions

The Department of Corrections was established August 1, 1983. Until that time, adult corrections was managed by the New Hampshire State Prison, Concord, which operated a central maximum security facility and two community corrections centers.[1]

A 1980 report indicates that an inmate grievance procedure was established in 1977, in which written responses to complaints were required within specified time limits, with the warden as the final level of appeal.[2]

Presently, grievances are presented by inmates on request/complaint forms which are forwarded to the appropriate agency within the institution. The issue is investigated and a response is made. If appropriate, corrective or remedial action is taken.[3]

In 1960, information was received that there had never been any form of inmate council because of the small population census, then about 200.[4]

Inmate advisory councils were attempted in the mid-1970s. However, they became dominated by contentious, hostile, belligerent inmates who made unending demands. When the administration believed that no further concessions were in order, there occurred disturbances led by the council. No inmate advisory council is in operation now and none is planned.[5]

Juvenile Institutions

All juvenile detention services are administered by the New Hampshire Youth Development Center, Manchester (known as the New Hampshire Industrial School until 1973). A residential center, Friendship House, was opened in downtown Manchester in 1975.[6]

A resident grievance procedure was established in 1978 to insure that student complaints about policy, lack of policy, or actions directed toward a student are brought to the superintendent's attention. Each cottage elects a representative, by simple majority in a secret ballot system, to serve on a Student Grievance Committee. Meeting weekly and chaired by a staff member, the group considers complaints and, upon a determination that the issue is grievable, the complaint, and minutes made by a staff stenographer, are forwarded to the superintendent for resolution and written response. A decision of the superintendent may be submitted by the group to the Board of Trustees for review. A student may submit a complaint regarding any issue directly to the superintendent, via sealed envelope, and written and/or oral response will be made within three working days.[7]

In February, 1971, a new program of differential treatment was instituted at the Youth Development Center. Town meetings involving both staff and students were held weekly in each of five residential cottages, to discuss policies and procedures. Suggestions emanating from these meetings could be implemented after administrative clearance, the latter being regarded more as a means of communication than an administrative rein on the decision-making process. The overruling of a Town Meeting decision by the superintendent was reported as occurring rarely. Input into cottage operational procedures and programs increased student supportiveness. The Center, opened in 1858, is co-educational.[8]

At present, two residential cottages are operative. House or Town Meetings are still held. Clinical Treatment Coordinators, in conjunction with House Leaders, are responsible for the operation and management of their units. Rarely are their decisions countermanded by the administration.[9]

Notes

1. Letter from Warden Everett I. Perrin, Jr., New Hampshire State Prison, Concord, March 14, 1983.
2. Dillingham, David D., and Singer, Linda R., op. cit., p. 53.
3. Letter from Warden Everett I. Perrin, Jr., op. cit.
4. Baker, J. E., op. cit., p. 143.
5. Letter from Warden Everett I. Perrin, Jr., op. cit.
6. Letter from Superintendent John L. Sheridan, Youth Development Center, Manchester, October 5, 1982.
7. "Student Grievance Procedure," New Hampshire Youth Development Center Regulation 3903, February 12, 1980.
8. Baker, J. E., op. cit., p. 143.
9. Letter from Superintendent John L. Sheridan, op. cit.

NEW JERSEY

Department of Corrections

Until 1976, corrections was a division within the Department of Institutions and Agencies. The department is responsible for all adult and juvenile correctional institutions.

Division of Adult Correctional Institutions

The Division of Adult Correctional Institutions administers and supervises nine correctional institutions for adult and youthful felony offenders. One institution included in this counting is the Youth Reception and Correction Center, Yardville. The institution was opened in 1968 as a reception center for all youthful felony offenders. Currently, it is comprised of three reception units: one for adult felony offenders, one for youthful felony offenders, and one for juvenile commitments.

A 1980 survey reported that an inmate grievance procedure, established in 1978, was functioning in some of the institutions. It provided for hearings in which inmates participated in decision-making roles. Written responses within specified time limits, with appeals to the Director of Corrections (now Commissioner), the final level of review, were other features of the procedure.[1]

An Ombudsman office was established within the Department of Corrections in 1973. Currently, the office includes five professional and two secretarial staff persons. The Ombudsman may assist inmates in resolving problems and complaints which cannot be addressed within the institutions. Although the office cannot implement changes, policies, procedures, and regulations can be reviewed and, if indicated, recommendations made for change. Intercession in disciplinary matters is not within the purview of the Ombudsman, but referral can be made to determine whether a violation of due process has occurred.[2]

Inmate Liaison Committees may be established, under the provisions of a regulation issued in May, 1979 and revised a year later, for the primary purpose of providing a liaison between the institutional administration and the inmates. However, if an institution has developed an alternate method to accomplish that purpose, the method may continue if approved by the Commissioner. Each liaison committee may draw its own constitution and by-laws or some other written document subject to approval by the institution superintendent. Policies and procedures governing the operations of the group must be stated, including: the officers and their duties; duties of the committee members; the election process for officers and committee members, and the functions of standing committees. The superintendent is required to meet monthly with the committee. Other staff members are to attend the meetings when their presence is appropriate or necessary.[3]

In 1973, the then Director, Division of Corrections and Parole, Albert C. Wagner, provided descriptions of inmate councils in New Jersey institutions. While no written directives regarding the development of councils had been issued, it was evident that Director Wagner's favorable attitude had influenced the inclusion of such groups in institution programs.

The accounts of advisory councils which follow are based on information received in 1966, 1967 and 1973. Unless otherwise noted, the councils were active in 1973.[4]

Following a disturbance in the New Jersey State Prison, an Inmate Council was established on May 9, 1952. (See Chapter I, Notable Early Experiences, for reference to a 1923 inmate committee.) The first election resulted in the formation of a group not believed to be truly representative of the population. Another election was held. During a May 28 meeting the members announced they would not leave the room until they received definite information on Parole Board policy regarding the indeterminate sentences of some inmates. Additionally, they demanded that two committeemen be authorized to inspect the operation of the Inmate Council at the Rahway Prison Farm, some 40 miles distant. The attitude of the members was one of arrogance and defiance and their actions more akin to rebels making demands than to a representative group seeking redress of grievances. The sit-down strike continued until June 3, 1952, after the Commissioner of Institutions and Agencies and the Prison Board of Managers stated they would not meet with the group while it was in a state of rebellion. A meeting was held on June 10, 1952, at which rules were adopted to govern the relationship between the Inmate Council and state and institution officials. While there is no further official reference to the council, a staff member who was active as a staff-council liaison officer recalled that some of the councilmen became intoxicated, acted in a somewhat obstreperous manner, and brought about the demise of the group.

In December, 1971, an inmate congress-type organization, the Inmate Representative Committee, was formed for the purpose of establishing representation to consult with the administration and as an attempt to improve conditions in the prison for all concerned. Nineteen housing unit representatives were elected for terms of office of one year, secret elections being held at six-month intervals. The Inmate Representative Committee selected from the membership eight representatives to comprise the Inmate Council. Formal meetings were held between the administration and the Inmate Council twice a month to discuss items on an agenda submitted to the administration at least one week prior to the meeting.

Emergency meetings could be and were called by the superintendent. Housing Unit representatives attended in an observer capacity, with only the Inmate Council members having a voice. Still functioning actively in 1973, the Inmate Representative Committee was regarded as having played a vital role in improving the administration-inmate relationship at the Trenton institution.

Following a lack of success in implementing an inmate council in 1952 at the parent (Trenton) State Prison, no like effort was made at either the Leesburg or Rahway State Prison Farms. In early spring, 1964, Rahway State Prison ceased its farm operation and by legislative action in 1969 became known as New Jersey State Prison, Rahway. (See Chapter I regarding establishment of self-government in 1913.)

On the eve of Thanksgiving, 1971, a major disturbance took place, with inmates seizing control of two large housing wings and the auditorium. They took the superintendent and five correction officers hostage, and all received injuries. Two officers were released early during the disturbance. The superintendent and the remaining three correction officers were rescued by a faction of inmates who protected them throughout a major portion of the 24-hour siege. Negotiations with several of the inmate groups were attempted by the administration. Governor William T. Cahill, standing nearby the scene, agreed to select a committee to meet with elected inmate representatives to review the 14 grievances presented at the close of the disturbance on Thanksgiving night, 1971.

A 19-member committee was elected by the population, representing the 18 housing units and the Spanish-speaking inmates. The group met periodically throughout 1972 with a committee appointed by the governor as representative of the administration and the community. After response to the grievances was issued by the governor's office, both the inmate and governor's committees were dissolved, since their mission was considered accomplished.

During the first week of January, 1973, an institution-wide election was conducted and a 15-member committee was elected by the population. The function of this committee was to be of much broader scope than the group just dissolved. They were to meet each month with the institution administration to discuss any and all matters as they related to the general welfare of the residents. Every effort was being made by inmates and administration to firmly establish this means of communication.

The New Jersey State Prison, Leesburg, is divided into two units. A medium security unit and a minimum security unit each had an inmate committee, established January 8, 1971, and March 4, 1971, respectively, to provide greater communication between the inmates and the administration in matters affecting groups of inmates or the general inmate body. Individual complaints or grievances had to be resolved through personal interviews with individual staff members. The medium facility had six housing units, each of which had three representatives on the committee. The minimum facility had five housing units with two committee members each. No man who had had a serious disciplinary charge within the previous three months could serve as a committee member. A serious violation of the rules was sufficient cause for removal from the committee. All committee members were selected by secret ballot and each served for six months, not to be re-elected until off the committee for six months. Individual inmates could bring problems concerning groups or suggestions for improvement of the institution to the attention of any committee member in his unit. Each committee met with the superintendent, assistant superintendent, deputy keeper, business manager and other pertinent personnel once a month. Printed minutes of the meetings were distributed to committee members and posted on each housing unit bulletin board.

The past and present situation regarding Student Government at the Correctional Institution for Women, Clinton, is contained in Chapter I. The institution is now the Correctional Institution, Clinton, housing both female and male offenders, and juvenile delinquents.

An Inmate Congress was established at the Youth Reception and Correction Center, Yardville, New Jersey, shortly after the institution opened in 1968, to maintain a constant means of communication between the inmate population and the administrative staff. The Congress, composed of a president, vice-president, secretary and one elected representative and alternate from each of the 24 housing units, held one meeting weekly and met once a month with the superintendent, the business manager, the correction captain, and eight housing unit officers to discuss an agenda submitted a week previously to the superintendent. The 24 representatives and alternates, elected by secret ballot, in turn elected the Congress officers. Elections were supervised by members of the custodial and treatment staffs. Officers of the Congress usually served three months, with housing representatives elected as vacancies occurred through parole. A written constitution, containing provisions for the removal from office of any member found guilty of a serious disciplinary infraction, guided the actions of the Congress. A good disciplinary record for a period of 90 days then became a requisite to eligibility for re-election. Additionally, Congress representatives and their officers were responsible for communicating all proceedings to the inmate population and administration.

The Youth Correctional Institution, Annandale, was opened on April 16, 1929, as a minimum security institution for male first offenders between the ages of 15 and 26 who had not been incarcerated in a correctional or penal institution before. The trend of the era that followed, and the enactment of legislation, changed the age range to 15 to 21, resulting in a predominantly youthful population. Until 1970, the institution was designated as the New Jersey Reformatory.

Under the supervision of the Education Department in cooperation with the custodial and administrative staff, a Cottage Committee program provided a means of direct communication between the inmate population and administrative staff in matters concerning the general welfare of all. Each of the eight cottages had a committee of three elected by hand vote from staff-approved nominees who had resided in the cottage for at least one month, had good disciplinary records and good or better marks. The kitchen and several work details also had representation. Additionally, a nominee was expected to have the best interest of the cottage in mind. Committeemen had to attend all scheduled or special meetings, with one member from each cottage acting as recorder so that topics discussed could be conveyed to the cottage populations. Minutes were later printed and distributed to each cottage. No committeeman could have authority over other inmates under any circumstances, derive any special privileges from his position, nor succeed himself after serving a two-month term of office.

Weekly in each cottage a meeting of all residents was held to discuss questions pertaining to the general welfare. Twice a month the Cottage Committees met with the superintendent and department heads, at which time answers to specific questions were given, policies and procedures explained, and current problems discussed. The Attorney General's Survey of Release Procedures mentions a formal program of inmate participation at the Annandale institution:

> ... [T]he organization is much the same as at Norfolk, Massachusetts. The inmates of each of the eight cottages hold a weekly meeting, elect their own officers, and select a cottage committee. The cottage committee meets weekly with the cottage officer to discuss and help solve cottage problems. All cottage committees meet weekly with the superintendent, the director of recreation and the officer of the day to consider serious problems affecting the entire institution.

A report received in 1966 described a Cottage Committee program implemented on May 5, 1960. It was stated that a program of the same name existed prior to that date but that its purpose and functions were entirely different. It is not clear whether or not the latter program was the same one mentioned in the Attorney General's Survey of Release Procedures. Essentially the description of the organization, purpose, and function of the program as contained in the 1966 report is the same as that currently in operation.

The Youth Correctional Institution, Bordentown, was opened in 1937 as a prison farm and designated as the New Jersey Reformatory from 1948 to 1972. An Inmate Congress was organized in 1949 and operated under a constitution and by-laws. Secret ballot elections were held semi-annually to elect housing unit representatives. Nominees had to work inside the institution, live in the housing unit represented, and have sufficient time left to serve their three-month terms. The Bordentown Inmate Congress operated in 1973 in much the same manner as described in a 1951 account, except that meetings were being held weekly with a supervisory officer available to answer questions:

> Meetings of the representatives are held periodically without

officer participation or supervision. Some matters brought before it are settled immediately and discussed with the superintendent. These discussions range from "There are too many specks left in the potatoes when they are peeled" to a suggestion that the Congress assume partial responsibility for the cooperation of the men in taking counts.

It is necessary, if the institution is to have an effective inmate council, that the men be allowed free discussion of their problems, both among themselves and later when presented to staff. We must give their problems prompt and sympathetic handling. It is often necessary to take men into our confidence, explaining such items as budget limitations, public attitudes toward institutions, and the administration's need for insistence on security. It is, parenthetically, a constant surprise to find how easy it is to deal with the men at this level. A good many problems are turned back to the men for their own determination, with perhaps a word or suggestion on procedure. Actually, some of the best ideas for improvement of the institution have come from the Inmate Congress.

The objectives of the organization were framed by the men themselves, with only gentle hints from the staff. We feel that in some measure, at least, the objectives are being accomplished. They are: 1. To give official recognition to inmate expression, via the Congress, thus attempting to reduce the wide gap existing between the inmate population and the administration personnel; 2. To bring to the attention of the administration such problems as arise spontaneously from the population; and 3. To permit the men to govern to some extent their own affairs and, by discussing problems pertinent to the group, to aid them in eventually developing a sense of social responsibility.

In essence, inmate participation means free and easy access of inmate to staff and staff to inmate, the work staff including officers as well as professional people; an easy relaxed communication in the shops, the dining room, the housing units, even perhaps during mass movements. Such easy access of inmate to officer becomes a practical necessity where there is a good treatment program.

Division of Juvenile Services

The Division of Juvenile Services administers all institutions for committed juvenile delinquents.

The services of the Ombudsman office, described in the foregoing account of the Division of Adult Correctional Institutions, are available to residents of juvenile facilities.

The previously mentioned regulation of May, 1979, regarding the establishment of Inmate Liaison Committees, is applicable to juvenile facilities.

The accounts of inmate advisory councils which follow were obtained in 1973. Unless otherwise noted, the councils were active in 1973, as reported in a previous book.[5]

The Training School for Boys, Jamesburg (now the Training School for Boys and Girls), opened in 1866 to care for juvenile delinquents aged eight to 16, with maximum termination of care at age 21. A new institution was built to care for those aged eight to 12. Jamesburg continued to care for the 13- to 16-year-olds upon commitment. Most units had some form of self-government, such as the Explorer type programs in most cottages, and the Youth Council. The latter involved election by the resident body in each of the cottages. The Council met monthly with the administration. Problems that arose from the residents themselves were brought up for discussion, solutions found, and subsequent administrative changes effected. The Youth Council had been found to be a most positive program and had led the way to many changes helpful to the population and to the administration.

The Training School for Girls, Trenton, was established in 1871 and served court referrals of girls from eight to 17 years of age. A Campus Council consisting of one elected representative from each cottage met weekly with the superintendent. An alternate representative was also selected so that each cottage would always have a council member present at the meeting.

Representatives were selected by secret ballot. The only criterion was that a girl have the ability to speak for the cottage group. As a result, the indigenous leader was usually selected as the cottage representative. Council members had no authority over other students in the institution, but merely served as a means of communication between the inmate group and the superintendent. The meetings were usually positive and of mutual benefit to both the administration and to the students. The underlying theme in each of the discussions was related to positive goals and ideas which might improve the program.

Notes

1. Dillingham, David D., and Singer, Linda R., _op. cit._, p. 53.
2. Letter, and enclosures, from Ann Sanders, Assistant Administrator, Office of the Commissioner, Dept. of Corrections, Trenton, February 7, 1983.
3. "Inmate Liaison Committees" Standard No. 230, Dept. of Corrections; effective May 21, 1979; revised May 2, 1980.
4. Baker, J. E., _op. cit._, pp. 145-150.
5. Baker, J. E., _op. cit._, p. 144.

NEW MEXICO

Corrections Department

The Corrections Department administers all institutions for adult and youthful felony offenders and juvenile delinquents. The author was the warden of the penitentiary of New Mexico, Santa Fe, from August, 1967 through February, 1970, and during the last eight months of that period also directed the newly created Department of Corrections, serving as the first Secretary of Corrections.

Adult Institutions Division

The Adult Institutions Division, Corrections Department, administers six institutions for adult and youthful felony offenders.[1]

According to a study published in 1980, a grievance procedure was established in 1974 which provided for a formal hearing and written responses to grievances within specified time limits, with the Secretary of Corrections as the final level of review.[2]

Under a multi-level grievance procedure effective September 15, 1982, an inmate may file a written grievance--if attempts at informal resolution through discussion of the issue with the person or persons primarily responsible for the action complained of have been unsuccessful--within three working days of the alleged incident, and send it to the institution grievance officer. Within five working days the latter must determine if the complaint is subject to the grievance procedure; if it is not, the grievant must be notified of the reason in writing, and advised how resolution might be accomplished. If the complaint is accepted, the inmate is interviewed, witnesses and documents are examined, and a written response is made.[3]

Within three working days, an appeal may be made to the warden, who has five working days to review and make a written response. At the warden's discretion, a special grievance committee may be convened to provide additional points of view as to the disposition of the grievance. An extension of time not to exceed five working days may be granted when a committee is convened.[4]

If not satisfied with the warden's response, the grievant may appeal to the Secretary, Corrections Department via the Central Office Appeals Officer, who will present the issue at a monthly meeting of the Corrections Commission, within 45 days unless unusual circumstances prevent. The Commission makes a recommendation for resolution to the Secretary who will make a written decision within 15 days. Written materials concerning a grievance are not placed in the inmate's institutional file.[5]

By 1967, an Inmate Council had been in operation at the Penitentiary of New Mexico, according to staff statements, but there were no records available to determine its date of origin, procedures, or accomplishments. Reportedly, members were elected by secret ballot and the group met occasionally with the associate warden for treatment to discuss a variety of topics.

The idea of vitalizing the council was discussed with both staff and residents at periodic meetings. The consensus was that an attempt should be made to implement a group which could play a meaningful role in an advisory capacity to management. Accordingly, a Resident Advisory Council was established under a constitution whose provisions were similar to those of the 1963 Council reorganization at the U. S. Penitentiary, Terre Haute, Indiana.

Elections were held and several meetings took place, but the attention of both residents and staff became diverted and the council never completely fulfilled its intended role. During this time the institution was undergoing a metamorphosis from a custody institution to one of treatment-orientation, with a focus on the needs of both residents and staff. It was a dynamic period for all concerned. For some, it was a stressful time as they faced the challenge of perspectives new to their experience. However, most of the residents became involved in the various academic-vocational-social programs being implemented at many levels, and the majority of the staff plunged thoroughly into the newly established intensive in-service training and academic programs designed to aid them in redefining their individual roles from agents of custody to agents of care and treatment.

The Resident Advisory Council managed to retain its identity and from time to time it provided helpful feedback to the deputy warden and the associate wardens regarding the reaction of the resident population to the efforts to create a positive climate and a staff attitude of professionalism. A constitution dated March 3, 1972 was signed by the then warden of the Penitentiary of New Mexico, establishing a Resident Advisory Council for which the first elections were scheduled to occur on June 19, 1972. The provisions of the constitution were similar to those previously referred to. No information was received as to the actual operations of the organization.

The Penitentiary of New Mexico underwent many changes of leadership, as did the Central Office during the period from 1970 to 1980 (eight secretaries of corrections, five wardens). To this discontinuity of direction was added a withering away of the academic-vocational-social programs, growing tensions created by staff-inmate mutual distrust, a lowering of the entry-age of correctional officers to 18, and a slackening of employee training programs. The culmination was the holocaust of February 2 and 3, 1980, when for 36 horrible hours the inmates gained control of the institution and the staff on duty. The result was 33 inmates dead and many others wounded. Several of the staff were injured physically and psychologically.

Spurred by a change in Corrections Department and penitentiary leadership, several partial consent decrees and a final consent decree signed July 14, 1980,[6] many changes have been made, including the grievance procedure already described and administration efforts to establish meaningful communication modes with inmates.

There is now no inmate council nor any plan to implement one at the Penitentiary of New Mexico. The administration points out that the institution is operating under a partial consent decree and that they do meet with a representative of each housing unit on a fairly regular basis. During the meetings, inmates have the opportunity to bring up matters pertaining to the consent decree, or other concerns. In the warden's opinion, these meetings improve administration-inmate communications.[7]

At the Radium Springs Center for Women, Las Cruces, opened in 1978, there is a Resident Council of nine members, and two alternates, elected by secret ballot to represent the various program levels. Council by-laws set forth a number of requirements for continuing as a council member, with emphasis on knowledge of operations, regular attendance at meetings, and acting as an example for other residents by following all rules and regulations, being considerate to others, and accurately disseminating information. The council constitution indicated that residents who wish may present a grievance to the council for review and suggested resolution. Several programs and activities are sponsored by the group.[8]

The Roswell Correctional Center, Hagerman, invites resident participation during the twice-monthly dormitory meetings at which requests, complaints, and general discussions are recorded. These meetings are conducted by the dormitory case-manager, who acts as a mediator between the residents and the superintendent. All feedback, discussions and requests are recorded and forwarded to the superintendent for response and/or action. Follow-up is done on a one-to-one basis or collectively during the next dormitory meeting.

In addition, the residents have an Inmate Trust Account which is used, by majority vote, for purchases such as an ice machine for the dormitories, a micro-wave oven, and other items not provided by the state. Funding of the Inmate Trust Account is obtained from the interest paid on resident mandatory savings accounts. All residents who participate in the work release program are required to save 20 per cent of their gross income in an interest-bearing account. The interest earned is invested in a Certificate of Deposit which, upon maturity, yields further interest. All residents decide by majority vote what they wish to purchase.[9]

Some exploration of the feasibility of establishing an inmate council has taken place at the Los Lunas Correctional Center, Los Lunas, but no decision has been reached as yet. Considerable success has resulted from the appointment periodically of ad hoc committees, representing a broad cross section of the population, to meet with the administration for open, candid discussion of specific issues. The superintendent believes such exchanges have been beneficial to both staff and inmates.[10]

Camp Sierra Blanca, Fort Stanton, was originally opened in 1965 as a subsidiary to the New Mexico Boys' School, Springer. In 1976 it was redesignated as a minimum security institution for adult and youthful felony offenders. The Inmate Council is described as being a very active group which meets monthly with the superintendent to call attention to problems and make suggestions for the improvement of living conditions. The council is believed to be a very effective mechanism in the operation of the institution.[11]

Juvenile Institutions Division

The Juvenile Institutions Division administers five facilities for committed juvenile delinquents.

Under a grievance procedure at the New Mexico Youth Diagnostic Center, Albuquerque, established on July 1, 1970, when the facility was known as the New Mexico Girls' School, a student who cannot obtain resolution of a complaint at the cottage level may file a written grievance with the cottage program director, who is required to respond within two working days. An appeal from the decision at that level may be successively made to the following who must reply within the number of working days indicated:

Program Coordinator - 3
Director of Programs - 3
Superintendent - 4
Director, Division of Juvenile Institutions - 10
Secretary, Corrections Department - 10[12]

At the New Mexico Boys' School, Springer, a five-tiered grievance procedure was established on May 5, 1975, under which a student may complete a prescribed grievance form. If dissatisfied with the response at any level, the student may appeal to the next higher. The levels and the number of working days for reply at each are:

Lodge Correctional Supervisor - 4
Program Coordinator - 4
Manager of Lodge Programs - 4
Superintendent (or Assistant) - 4
Grievance Committee - 10

The Director, Juvenile Institutions Division, as chairman, and an employee designated by the Corrections Department form the membership of the Grievance Committee. After interviewing the grievant, a written decision is made. This is the final level of review.[13]

In late 1972 or early 1973, a six-member Student Advisory Council was organized at the New Mexico Girls' School, Albuquerque. The girls of each of the three cottages elected two representatives. Presiding leadership was rotated in order that each member might gain experience in that role. One of the first tasks of the council was to make suggestions on the structuring of cottage government. The plan submitted by the group was rapidly implemented by the administration. At cottage meetings, Student Council members obtained topics for discussion at their weekly meetings. A three-member staff committee provided direction and acted as resource personnel.[14]

At present there is no advisory council at the Youth Center. The small population of girls and the short-term diagnostic commitments appear, according to the Corrections Department, to operate better on an informal group basis with emphasis on positive peer culture.[15]

Between 1966 and 1969 there was some development of a cottage government structure at the New Mexico Boys' School, Springer.

At the present time a Student Advisory Council meets monthly with the superintendent. Each lodge (housing unit) nominates three candidates for council membership. The lodge classification committee appoints one of those three to serve a council term of three months duration.[16]

Notes

1. Letter from Roger W. Crist, Secretary, Corrections Department, Santa Fe, October 4, 1982.
2. Dillingham, David D., and Singer, Linda, R., op. cit. p. 53.
3. Procedural Statement No. CD-150501, "Inmate Grievances," Corrections Dept., September 6, 1982 (effective September 15, 1982).
4. Ibid.
5. Ibid.
6. Duran v. Apodaca, C.A. No. 77-721-C (D. N. Mexico).
7. Letter from Warden Harvey D. Winans, Penitentiary of New Mexico, Santa Fe, October 15, 1982.
8. "Resident Council Overview," Radium Springs Center for Women, Las Cruces (undated).
9. Letter from Superintendent Tom Newton, Roswell Correctional Center, Hagerman, November 9, 1982.
10. Letter from Superintendent Bob Marrs, Los Lunas Correctional Center, Los Lunas, October 15, 1982.
11. Letter from Superintendent E. B. Gutierrez, Camp Sierra Blanca, October 26, 1982.
12. Resident Rights Directive, "Grievance Procedures," New Mexico Youth Diagnostic Center, Albuquerque, revised January 25, 1982 (original issue: July 1, 1970).
13. Administrative Directive, Section IV-Program, "Grievance Procedures," New Mexico Boys' School, Springer, revised March 20, 1980 (original issue: May 5, 1975).
14. Baker, J. E., op. cit., p. 159.
15. Letter from Roger W. Crist, Secretary, Corrections Department, Santa Fe, November 5, 1982.
16. Ibid.

NEW YORK

Department of Correctional Services

The Department of Correctional Services administers 25 institutions for adult and youthful felony offenders, and six camps for young male offenders, of which three are for those age 16 to 25, two for age 16 and above, and one for those age 21 or older. Additionally, the department administers six community residential centers, all opened since 1972.

In 1972, a new division, the Department Inspector General Service, was established to investigate inmate complaints. The staff included three assistants, clerical support, and the Inspector General who was appointed by the Department Commissioner. It was reported that the Inspector General reported only to the Commissioner.[1] No information has been received as to the procedures, accomplishments or fate of this service.

In 1975, legislation was enacted requiring all Department of Correctional Services institutions to establish an inmate grievance procedure by early February, 1976. An Office of Inmate Grievances was set up to administer the grievance procedure system-wide. Both staff and inmates participated in the design and implementation of multi-level procedures at each institution. Extensive training of both groups in the techniques of mediation, resolution, fact-finding and conciliation was conducted by the Center for Community Justice and the Institute for Mediation and Conflict Resolution.[2]

An inmate who has been unable to resolve a problem through staff channels may file a grievance, using a prescribed form, with an inmate grievance clerk within six days of an occurrence. If representatives of the Inmate Grievance Resolution Committee cannot resolve the complaint within 48 hours, the full committee will conduct a hearing and must respond in writing during the following five working days. If not satisfied, the grievant may appeal to the institution superintendent, whose time limit for making a written reply is five working days. Not more than two days later an appeal may be made to the Central Office Review Committee, which will make written notification of its decision in 20 working days. That decision is appealable within three days to the Commission of Correction, which is a state agency responsible for inspecting and monitoring the level of care provided prisoners in all New York correctional facilities, municipal lockups, and county jails. The Commission may delegate its function of review and recommendation to an independent arbitrator. The recommendation by the Commission or arbitrator is given to the Commissioner of the Department, who must accept or reject it in writing in the next ten days.[3]

A grievance is defined as a complaint about the substance or application of any written or unwritten policy, regulation, or rule of the Department of Correctional Services or any of its program units, or the lack of a policy, regulation, or rule, or a complaint about any behavior or action directed toward an inmate. While the grievance procedure is the means of determining whether or not a complaint is within its jurisdiction, the following exceptions are noted for decisions made in those programs having an existing appeals process:[4]

Work Release.
Temporary Release Committee.
Media Review.
Superintendent's Procedures.
Individual Disciplinary Matters.
Any policy regulation, rule, or action of the Board of Parole.

However, the policy and rules of the Temporary Release Committee, the Media Review, and the disciplinary process, as generally applicable to inmates, may be the subject of a grievance.

According to statute, an Institution Grievance Resolution Committee must be a five-member body, consisting of two voting inmates, two voting staff members, and a non-voting chairman who may be an inmate, staff member, or a volunteer otherwise associated with the institution program. Additionally, there must be not less than two alternates for each staff or inmate representative. Four persons are designated to act as the non-voting chairman, as required.[5]

Inmate representatives and alternates are elected by secret ballot of their peers, to serve on the Committee for a period of six months. The superintendent appoints the staff representatives and alternates. Following their election, each group of representatives, staff and inmate, prepares a list of ten nominees to serve as non-voting chairmen. The groups then exchange lists and select two from each list. Non-voting chairmen also serve for six months. The Central Office Resolution Committee consists of the Deputy Commissioners and the Department counsel.[6]

Time limit extensions may be requested at any level of review, but only with the consent of the grievant. Without such extensions, complaints not decided within the time limits go automatically to the next level. No copies of a complaint may be placed in a grievant's file without his/her direct consent. Likewise, no copy of a complaint may go into an employee's file without the direct consent of the individual. No reprisals of any kind may be taken against either staff or inmate for using or taking part in the procedure.[7]

A report in 1966 indicated that the then Department of Corrections did not permit inmate self-government groups. Contacts made in 1966-67 with 13 major institutions in the state confirmed that neither self-government nor inmate advisory councils existed in 12 of them.

The Bedford Hills Correctional Facility, Bedford Hills, opened in 1901 as the Westfield State Farm. In 1933 the female population of Auburn Prison was transferred to Westfield. In 1967 the institution was reported as having three divisions under one superintendent: a Reformatory Division, a Prison Division, and the New York City House of Detention Annex. The women lived in cottages in the Reformatory Division and in wards at the Prison Division. Subject to staff approval, each living unit elected a representative called a chairman. A candidate was required to be a cooperative person, capable of leadership with the interest of others at heart, familiar with campus procedure, and with approximately six months yet to serve when elected. Disciplinary action for a serious incident during the six months preceding an election was disqualifying. Chairmen held weekly meetings in their units with the director of education and the recreation supervisor of each division, and periodic meetings with the superintendent.

Minutes of these meetings were circulated to staff and residents. In most instances the woman selected as chairman was favorably regarded and her counsel sought by the other women. This was regarded as usually being conducive to the personal growth and development of the chairman. On some occasions, staff had major reservations about the election of a certain individual, only to see her develop into a dependable leader. This was reported as applicable to both the aggressive personality and the shy, introverted woman. The program was reported as having been in operation since about 1929.[8]

On January 18, 1972, the Department of Correctional Services issued Administrative Bulletin No. 19, entitled "Establishment and Operation of Facility Inmate Liaison Committee." Guidelines attached to the bulletin directed the establishment of inmate liaison committees and contained a suggested format for constitution and by-laws to be submitted to the commissioner not later than March 1, 1972, with operational evaluation reports to be made quarterly, the first such being due during June, 1972. Additionally, it was directed that all personnel and inmates be informed of the objectives and the organization and function of the inmate liaison committees, the former through in-service training and the latter via appropriate means. The objectives of the program were stated as:

1. Effective communications with the inmates for accurate dissemination of information.
2. Consideration by management of worthwhile suggestions covering facility operations.

The guidelines specified that no grievances or gripes of individuals could be presented; the personality of individuals, either employee or inmate, could not be discussed; the committees were to serve in a liaison capacity only, with no disciplinary or administrative functions; and no committeeman would be granted special privileges because of his membership.

Each facility could define its membership qualifications, its voting districts or precincts, such as housing units and various work assignments, and its nomination system. Supervised elections provided for secret balloting on mimeographed lists of candidates to serve in any capacity for not more than six months during any 12. At his option, a superintendent was empowered to restrict from membership those inmates who had been recent or chronic disciplinary problems.

The superintendents felt that the inmate liaison committees were assets in that they provided channels through which grievances and problems were conveyed to the various administrations. Opportunistic use by individuals of a committee as a forum to advance personal causes or demands was mentioned as a major problem which had thus far emerged. Committees then functioned at almost all of the facilities and had been assisted by a Department of Correctional Services Lawyer in establishing their constitutions.[9]

The administrative bulletin was superseded on January 13, 1975 by a directive of the Department of Correctional Services entitled "Inmate Liaison Committee (ILC)." It is identical to the former with two exceptions: continued membership is restricted to two consecutive six-month terms, with reelection possible after the passage of another six months, and selection by the committee from its members of an Executive Committee composed of a chairman, vice-chairman, secretary, and sergeant-at-arms. Holding of an executive committee office is limited to a six-month term during a one-year period.[10]

Division for Youth

Since 1973 the Division for Youth, New York State Executive Department, has undergone a number of changes in response not only to the needs of youth placed in its care, but also to legislative mandates and court rulings; e.g., the Juvenile Justice and Delinquency Prevention Act of 1974, requiring the removal of P.I.N.S. (Persons in Need of Supervision, ages seven to 16) from training schools, and Article 70 of the Penal Law enacted in 1978, giving the Division specific responsibility for juvenile offenders (most serious offenders) ages 12-16 who may complete sentences in an adult correctional facility. Youthful offenders age 16 to 19 are placed with the division by adult criminal courts. Also placed are juvenile delinquents, ages seven to 16, who commit an act which would be a crime if committed by an adult. To address the wide spectrum of demands presented by the various offender groups, the division has developed and operates a number of diverse programs and facilities ranging from Secure Centers to Foster Care Services.[11]

In July, 1971, the Division for Youth Director ordered the design and implementation of the first Ombudsman program for juveniles in the United States. The program was activated in August, 1972 by the hiring of four young lawyers to serve the approximately 5,400 youths confined in New York facilities for juveniles. By 1973, two additional Ombudsmen had been hired.[12]

The purpose of the Office of Ombudsman is two-fold: to monitor the system to insure that legal rights of youth are not violated, and to provide a grievance mechanism under division jurisdiction, including, but not limited to, residents of secure facilities. Legal rights encompass anything to which a youth has a just claim because it is granted by statute, law, court decision, regulation, or policy.[13]

A 1973 description of the program stated that each Ombudsman was responsible for receiving and investigating complaints from institutions within one of four geographic regions.[14] Guidelines indicate that the Central Office Ombudsman Director shall provide administrative supervision to the regional Ombudsmen, but there is no indication as to the number of regions. In conducting an investigation of a complaint, the Ombudsman is entitled to access to any person, program, facility, or record which may have information regarding the alleged incident. After discussion with the facility or program director, the Ombudsman forwards a report to the Central Office Ombudsman Director, which is then disseminated to the Division Director, the Deputy Directors, the General Counsel, other appropriate personnel, and the Independent Review Board.[15]

The Independent Review Board is a Division Director-appointed committee of nine, but not more than 15 persons, not employed by the division and knowledgeable in the areas of juvenile justice and youth rights. The board meets at least bi-monthly with the Ombudsmen and the Division Director to review reports, make recommendations and seek information on the steps taken by the division to implement changes recommended by the board and/or the Ombudsman. The board is an advisory body and has no administrative duties. Additionally, the board makes an annual report to the director for guidance in formulating agency policy.

When he/she is a target of an investigation which might lead to disciplinary action or criminal prosecution, an employee may choose not to talk to the Ombudsman. An employee accused by a resident, another employee or any interested party, of violating a youth's legal rights may request investigation by the Ombudsman. Ombudsmen reports may not be placed or referred to in an employee's history file. Written notification of complaint disposition must be made promptly by the division to the Ombudsman Director and the grievant.[16]

A Youth Grievance Procedure is presently being implemented in the Division of Youth Secure Facilities, and will later on be established in the other facilities.[17] Other than two exceptions, the procedure includes all matters pertaining to the written or unwritten policies, practices, and procedures of the division. The exceptions: loss of good time as a result of a disciplinary hearing, and youth under division jurisdiction who have been placed in private agencies. Separate policies and procedures already exist in both instances.[18]

The procedure has four levels. If unable to resolve a complaint with the staff member concerned, a youth may file a prescribed grievance form within ten days of the incident out of which the complaint grew. A grievance coordinator, appointed by the facility director to monitor procedure activity and to assist youth participation, presents the complaint to the unit (housing) administrator who, after inquiry and discussion with the youth, must make a written reply within five days. As at all levels, the response shall include the rationale of the decision made.

If not satisfied with the level-one response, the grievant has five days to appeal to the Facility Review Panel, composed of an equal number of residents and staff and the grievance coordinator, who is a non-voting member. The grievant is granted a hearing before the panel within five days, and other witnesses or associated parties may be interviewed at the discretion of a panel. A written response is made by the panel not later than three days following the hearing. This response may be appealed to the facility director who has five working days to respond.

If the grievant is still not satisfied, an appeal may be made to the director of the Secure Facilities Management Unit, who will consult with the Central Office Ombudsman Director and reply not more than five working days later. The grievant may then appeal to the final level of review via the Director of Ombudsmen, who within five days must notify the Secure Facilities Management Director and the Director of Quality Assurance that the Director's Appeal Process has been invoked, and present to them in five days a written position statement. Not later than eight days following receipt of the position statement, the two officials mentioned must submit a written recommendation to the Division Director, who in turn has 15 days to make a reply. However, if the grievant requests that the issue be referred to the Independent Review Board (as mentioned in the foregoing description of the Ombudsman service), the Division Director has 60 days for response. The additional time is to allow consideration of the issue at the next regularly scheduled meeting of the Independent Review Board.

Occasionally a complaint may involve an institutional action which, unless it is stayed in its application, cannot be adequately remedied in the event the grievance is upheld. The definition of such a circumstance includes, but is not limited to, an action, situation, or condition in which a youth's or employee's health, safety, or welfare is in serious threat or danger, or where irreversible harm is imminent. Such instances are referred directly to the facility director.

No directives on student councils have been issued by the Division for Youth. Each facility is free to establish a council, if appropriate, for its population and program. Some facilities have established Camper Councils or have Town Meetings, the former meeting weekly or bi-weekly. Councils are composed of one representative from each housing unit and the facility administrators. Issues and concerns of residents are discussed, e.g., recreational activities and food services. The Town Meetings, which include all residents, staff, and on occasion the facility director, are held weekly and matters of interest or concern to all are explored.

At the Goshen Center, a Central Committee was established in April, 1982, as part of a bilingual program. Designed as a lesson in organizational skills, the group has five sub-committess: special events, photography, typing and reproduction, peer tutoring, and bulletin board management. (See later paragraph for 1973 report of Center Council at this facility.)

At the Harlem Valley Secure Center, Wingdale, opened in 1981, a Student Government was established in October, 1982, as a part of the academic program. With the faculty and other students the group plans school activities and is responsible for developing and implementing school programs. A facility newspaper has been developed by this group.

The present administration of the Division for Youth is of the opinion that a number of concerns and issues addressed by student councils in years past are now considered via other mechanisms, e.g., a Youth Rights Handbook issued in July, 1980, and the adoption of a Young People's Bill of Rights which is reproduced in Appendix C.[19]

The accounts which follow are of the situation regarding student councils as reported in January, 1973 by the Bureau of Children's Institution Services of the Division for Youth. Current information regarding the closing of certain facilities is also included.[20]

The Industry School, Industry, formerly designated as the School for Boys at Industry, and even earlier as the State Agriculture and Industrial School, had a Boys' Council for many years, but in 1973 operated without one. The recent development of a unit system with its built-in daily meetings had rendered it unnecessary. A Boy's Council started in January, 1957 provided a forum for the discussion of a wide variety of subjects including release, education, cottage adjustments, recreation, staff roles, and interpretation of administrative rules and directives. Initially, council members were prone to subjective discussions but as time went on they became more conscious of their role and personal problems gave way to group considerations.

Experience with the council indicated apprehension by staff at the outset. To offset this a close line of communication was established to inform staff of the content of council discussions. In addition, cottage staff members and community representatives were also invited to participate in the meetings. Community representatives sometimes included Youth Bureau personnel, legislative representatives, and Job Corps staff.

In March 1956, the first Student Congress was established at the Otisville School for Boys, Otisville, under a constitution and by-laws. Constant turnover of students, the average length of stay being about eight months, was a major contributing factor to discontinuance of the group shortly after. Reorganized again in October, 1959, the Congress in 1973 was regarded by the administration as an important feature in communication within the school and had made a substantial contribution to improving programs and maintaining an atmosphere of shared responsibility among boys and staff for the life of the institution community.

All residents of each cottage were members of a cottage congress, each group electing its own officers, a president, vice-president, and secretary. The president and secretary of each cottage attended the monthly meeting of the Institution Congress. The assistant superintendent served as chairman of this group, the functions of which were to promote program participation, suggest new programs, and solve problems together. In addition to the general cooperation of all staff, specific assistance was required from particular areas for a successful Student Congress. No staff member was expected to be at cottage congress meetings for the purpose of supplying direct answers to problems brought up for discussion, but staff were there to help the students find their own answers. No staff member was expected to force a cottage to prolong a meeting which it decided it did not want or need; the philosophy was that each Cottage Congress should be an opportunity for the students, not a burden. The school, first named the State Training School for Boys, is now closed.

The Goshen Center for Boys, Goshen, now the Goshen Center, which opened on January 6, 1947, occupying two buildings in the former New York City Reformatory at New Hampton, was originally designated as the Annex of Boy's Training Schools. Its present facilities, completed in the fall of 1962, have a maximum capacity of 100 boys. A boy government in council had always been a part of the program, continued by succeeding directors. Called Center Council, each of its five members was president of his wing council, sponsored by the head child care worker and the recreation director. Wing council meetings were held monthly, with the Center Council meeting held every four to six weeks to consider an agenda derived from the wing meetings. Examples of programs either initiated or expanded through the Center Council included a weekly honor roll system, a seasonal recreation program, off-campus sports and other activities, personal clothing, home visits, a personal hygiene and health program, and canteen services. The administration, in 1973, planned to continue the councils, stating that programs operated more successfully when boys had had a hand in their implementation.

The Director's Council at the Brookwood Center, Claverack, formerly the Brookwood Center for Girls, and earlier the Brookwood Annex of the Training School for Girls, Hudson, originally formed in January, 1967, was no longer in operation in 1973. During the time it was, two representatives from each of the four wings were elected by secret ballot to serve until released. Nominees had to meet several qualification criteria, including desirable personal traits, good deportment, and average or above academic grades. Weekly meetings with the director were followed by informal wing meetings.

The Warwick School for Boys, Warwick, in 1973 had no student advisory council but had had such groups in the past. However, students were involved in policy-making decisions through frequent consultations. Although there had never been an advisory council at the South Kortright Center for Boys, South Kortright, in the past known as the Branch of the Boys' Training Schools, there had always been a weekly town hall forum since the facility opened in 1963. These meetings involved the total population of 50 juveniles and served as a combined group interaction program as well as a forum for student expression.

At the Hudson School for Girls, Hudson, originally the Training School for Girls, each of the cottage units elected by secret ballot a representative to serve a two-month term of office on the Superintendent's Council. Weekly meetings were used to disseminate information to the students, who also presented questions and problems from their cottages. Minutes were distributed for review by staff and students. This facility is now closed.

The Student Council at the Tyron Secure Center, then the Tyron School for Boys, Johnstown, was formed on October 27, 1971. The purpose of the Council was to have boy representatives meet with department heads and administrative staff to review all phases of the program. Student Council representatives were selected by the boys of each cottage. Originally, the council met on a weekly basis; however, it was found that more time was needed between meetings to follow up on suggestions and questions raised. Meetings were held thereafter on a bi-monthly basis. From its inception, the Student Council met with various administrative and program staff members, including the assistant superintendent, business officer, recreation supervisor, food services manager, clinic director, and principal child care worker. A sampling of matters discussed in Student Council included: daily activity schedule, church requirements, phone calls, group incentive, family visits, off-grounds activities, and hair policy. An administrative review of the function of Student Council suggested that boys attending Student Council were not truly representative of the rest of the boys in their cottage, but more often presented their personal opinions, although tempered somewhat by the known views of other boys in the cottage. It was agreed that in reality Student Council was a sampling of opinion, but it was considered worthwhile even in that form. Plans included reviewing the organization of Student Council early in 1973 in order to update procedures and make the council more meaningful. However, there is no longer a council.

Although the Highland School for Children, Highland, formerly known as the State Training School for Boys, which served children under age 13, did have a Student Council in its early years, it was discontinued because of the age of the youngsters. The Overbrook

Center for Children, Red Hook, established in 1966 and serving youngsters age seven to eleven, had no student council. The Wynantskill Training School for Girls, which closed in 1971, held weekly meetings in each cottage to discuss matters of common concern, but did not have an organized Student Council.

Notes

1. Warehousing Human Beings, report of the New York Advisory Committee to the U.S. Commission on Civil Rights, December, 1974, p. 27.
2. "Prevention and Control of Conflict in Corrections," Final Report, Center for Community Justice, Washington, D.C., April 15, 1979. (LEAA Grant ED-99-0009, October, 1975-December 31, 1978).
3. "Inmate Grievance Program," Directive No. 4040, Dept. of Correctional Services, August 8, 1976.
4. Ibid.
5. Ibid.
6. Ibid.
7. Ibid.
8. Baker, J. E., op. cit., p. 153.
9. Ibid., pp. 153-154.
10. "Inmate Liaison Committee (ILC)," Directive No. 4002, Dept. of Correctional Services, Albany, January 13, 1975. (Supersedes Administrative Bulletin No. 19, January 18, 1972, and Supplement No. 1, November 7, 1974.)
11. Letter from Robert L. Maul, Director, Program Utilization and Management Assistance, Division for Youth, Albany, March 21, 1983; Brochure: "Functions of the New York State Division for Youth"; Brochure: "Rehabilitative Services Program Level System: Summary," New York State Division for Youth.
12. Keating, Gilligan, McArthur, Lewis, and Singer, op. cit., p. 22.
13. "Office of the Ombudsman Guidelines," Division for Youth, Albany (Statutory References: Executive Law, Sections 500 and 515a); Undated.
14. Keating, Gilligan, McArthur, Lewis, and Singer, op. cit., p. 23.
15. "Office of the Ombudsman Guidelines," op. cit.
16. Ibid.
17. Letter from Robert L. Maul, Director, Program Utilization and Management Assistance, Division for Youth, Albany, March 30, 1983.
18. "Youth Grievance Program," Item 3444, Policy and Procedures Manual, Division of Youth, Albany, November 19, 1982.
19. Ibid.
20. Baker, J. E., op. cit., pp. 155-158.

NORTH CAROLINA

Department of Correction

The Department of Correction has jurisdiction over all facilities for adult and youthful felony, and some misdemeanor, offenders through a Division of Prisons and a Youth Services Complex.

Division of Prisons

The Division of Prisons, Department of Correction, administers the facilities for felony offenders over 21 years of age.

A formal Inmate Grievance Procedure is in operation at all institutions. An inmate seeking procedural review of a disciplinary action may appeal directly to the Inmate Grievance Commission, an autonomous agency associated with the Department of Correction, which provides for the administrative review and redress of inmate grievances. Operational procedures of the Commission are codified in the general statutes of North Carolina (Chapter 148) and have been reduced to administrative policy in the Department of Correction Policy-Procedure Manual.[1]

A grievance is defined as a formal complaint concerning an incident, policy, or condition within an institution or within the Division of Prisons. Grievances may be individual, e.g., the unexplained exclusion from a vocational program for which the inmate feels qualified; or institutional, e.g., the failure to include a course on physical hygiene in the institution school curriculum.

No grievance other than one seeking procedural review of a disciplinary action may be appealed to the Inmate Grievance Commission until internal institution procedures have been exhausted. Those procedures encompass three levels.[2]

On a prescribed form, an inmate sets forth the specifics of a complaint. The form is given to the officer in charge of the housing unit. An investigation is made by that officer or another staff member knowledgeable of correctional policy and having a sensitivity to the personal dilemmas of confined persons. Within 24 hours a written response will be made. If not satisfied, the inmate may appeal to the three-staff member Institution Grievance Evaluation Board. The function of the Board is not to determine fault or impose sanctions, but to make an evaluative investigation and give a personal hearing to the grievant. The Board may send a proposed resolution to the superintendent, or refer the grievance to a higher level board. This must be done within five days.

The Higher Level Grievance Evaluation Board is composed of the superintendent, a psychologist or other appropriate staff member, and, if possible, an interested person from the community, preferably someone with a legal background and a concern for local prison policy.

This Board meets at least every two weeks. At its option, the Board may conduct further investigation, seek the advice of legal counsel available to the Department of Correction, and interview the grievant. A written response must be given to the inmate within five days.

An appeal may then be made to the Inmate Grievance Commission. The five members of the Commission are appointed by the Governor from a list of ten persons recommended by the Council of the North Carolina State Bar. Two of the five must be attorneys, and at least two of the remaining three must be persons of knowledge and experience in one or more of the fields under the jurisdiction of the Secretary, Department of Correction. An Executive Director, appointed by the Commission with the approval of the Governor, may appoint hearing examiners.

A preliminary review of the grievance is made to determine whether the record is a sufficient basis for decision. If so, a decision will be rendered in writing. The Commission may also dismiss a grievance without a hearing or specific findings of fact if it is determined to be wholly lacking in merit, or is outside the scope of Commission authority. Such an order of dismissal will be provided the grievant, and for the purposes of any judicial review constitutes the final decision of the Secretary, Department of Correction.

If, following the preliminary review, the Commission finds a grievance deserving of examination, an examiner will conduct a hearing as promptly as practicable, and present a finding of facts, conclusions, and recommendation which will, within 30 days, by majority vote, be accepted or rejected by the Commission.

In those instances in which the preliminary review finds that a grievance is not wholly lacking in merit, the Commission will hold a hearing. An order of the decision reached, including a statement of the findings of fact, conclusions, and disposition, is sent to the Secretary, Department of Correction, who within 15 days must affirm, reverse or modify it. The Secretary may order the institution superintendent to accept the Commission order in whole or in part, or may take whatever action is deemed appropriate in light of the Commission findings. The order of the Secretary is final.

In a hearing before an examiner or the Commission, the grievant has the right to call a reasonable number of witnesses, and to be represented by an employee of the Department of Correction-Division of Prisons.

Following the final decision of the Secretary, the grievant is entitled to initiate proceedings for a judicial review.

No current information concerning inmate advisory councils was received. In December, 1972 there were no councils, but various planning, steering, and guidance committees had been organized.[3]

In 1974, it was reported by inmates that at one time there had been an inmate council under the guidance of the program director at Mecklenburg II, Huntersville. Although the nine members were elected from each of the nine housing groups, the council was ineffective because of poor direction and apathy.[4]

Also in 1974, the warden of the Correctional Center for Women, Raleigh, stated that an inmate council tried there was not effective.[5]

Youth Services Complex

Youthful offenders under the age of 21 who are committed to the Division of Prisons are placed in the Youth Services Complex, in which institutions they are placed according to age and custody classifications.

The Inmate Grievance Procedure previously described is available to the residents of the Youth Services Complex institutions.

No current information concerning inmate advisory councils was received.

At the Umstead Youth Center, Butner, an advisory council was formed shortly after the official opening in 1949. At last report, in 1972, the organization, known as the Mayor and His Council, was still in existence. By secret ballot the boys elected a mayor, from a slate of four nominees, to hold office for six months. Any boy was eligible for nomination provided he was not on restriction or extra duty. There was a provision for his removal should he violate a major rule or the staff deemed such action necessary. Regulations prescribed that the mayor should be a boy of high moral character, definitely interested in helping others. In addition to presiding at twice-monthly meetings of his council, the mayor was expected to set a good example for others, encourage them to obey orders, work willingly and to make good use of their time.[6]

Additionally, seven group leaders were elected to four-month terms to serve as members of the Mayor's Council. Any boy not on restriction or extra duty could stand for election. Those elected were expected to work closely with the staff counselor to insure observance of rules and regulations by their constituents, offer informal counsel to other boys, supervise recreational activities, and work as leaders on clean-up details or other work assignments.[7]

Division of Youth Services

The Division of Youth Services, Department of Human Resources, administers five facilities for juvenile delinquents.[8]

A Student Grievance Procedure establishes the right of a

student to appeal major and moderate infractions that significantly affect level status. Within 24 hours following imposition of a sanction, a student may make a written appeal which is given to the social worker. If unable to present a written report, the student may ask the cottage representative to the Student Council, or the Student Advocate, to do so. A hearing is held at the next scheduled meeting of the Treatment Team, or is handled within five working days. The staff member who issued the infraction may be called to testify or submit a detailed justification of the incident at issue. Should the student not be satisfied with the Treatment Team decision, appeal may be made to the Treatment Committee.

A copy of the appeal is given to the head of the department to which the employee who issued the infraction is assigned. Within five working days, the department head may settle the issue on the basis of the findings of the Treatment Team, or can pass the appeal to the Treatment Committee, which is the final level of review.

Grievances other than those directly concerned with Mainstream (a treatment program utilizing a levels system) are sent to the facility director, whose decision may be appealed to the Division Assistant Director for Institutional Services who will make a final decision within five working days.[9]

A basic Due Process Procedure is also in effect at each of the five facilities, in which a student has a right to a hearing when his/her status is changed to a more restrictive one.

In 1941, at the Eastern Carolina Industrial Training School for Boys, Rocky Mount, it was found that some leadership was permitted the boys in the school chapel exercises and the cottage prayer meetings. On March 18, 1943, the superintendent reported that the older boys had organized a Red Book Club. All boys on the honor roll every week in a month received a Red Book at a ceremony held in the chapel. The institution was opened in 1925, and the first building was occupied in January, 1926.[10] The name of the institution was later changed to the Richard T. Fountain School, then to the Richard T. Fountain Reception and Diagnostic Center, and is currently the Richard T. Fountain Youth Center, one of the institutions of the Youth Services Complex.

The State Training School for Negro Delinquent Boys, opened on January 5, 1925, was redesignated the Morrison Training School in 1939, and later as the Cameron Morrison School, Hoffman. In 1941, student monitors, appointed by staff, assisted in maintaining order in the dormitories, school lines, and on work details. They were expected to report boys for misbehavior. The officers of a Garden Club, supervised by the social case worker, took part in orienting new arrivals to acquaint them with the facility program and to ease the initial pains of confinement.[11] This institution is no longer listed among the five facilities administered by the Division of Youth Services.

Grace M. Robson was appointed superintendent on July 1, 1934, at the State Home and Industrial School for Girls (Samarcand Manor), Eagle Springs. She established, in January, 1936, an honor system that reportedly permeated the entire life of the facility, affecting discipline, cottage government, and all campus activities.[12]

Any cottage whose members agreed to an honor code was granted a charter by the superintendent which permitted a form of self-government. After having been at the facility for three months, with a good conduct record, a girl could, by three-fourths vote of the cottage population, be approved for honor club membership. A staff referee met weekly with the cottage honor group to discuss a previously prepared agenda. A major responsibility of the honor group was orientation of newly arrived girls. Honor group privileges included walking unescorted on the campus, attendance at a movie and a girls' dance each month, and the option of staying up for one hour longer.

After having been an honor group member for one month, a girl could be elected to the Council which met with the cottage staff counselor to prepare the agenda already mentioned.

A banner system provided for the awarding of a green banner containing one star to any cottage from which there had been no runaways by honor girls. Awarding of the banner meant that members of the honor group could write one additional letter each month. A cottage which kept the Goldstar Banner for six months was allowed to select a present, not to exceed 15 dollars, for the living room. At the end of each six months of banner possession, an extra letter privilege was granted. The cottage honor group appointed girls as counselors to supervise house duties and to plan for parties, dances, and other entertainment.[13]

At the Stonewall Jackson School, Concord (formerly the Stonewall Jackson Manual Training and Industrial School), opened on January 2, 1909, surveys made in 1941 and 1943 indicated that staff-appointed boys were used as lieutenants or monitors to assist cottage and work detail officers in supervising other boys. These appointees were expected to pursue runaways.[14]

In January, 1973, a student council had been developed during the prior two years in seven of the eight facilities for juvenile delinquents then administered by the Office of Youth Development.[15] At the Dobbs School for Girls, Kinston, a Campus Council had been in existence since the school opened in 1944. The organizing of student councils was perceived by the administration as a means of providing students a voice in day-to-day activities. Since there had been no such prior involvement of students except at the Dobbs School for Girls, the process of planning and implementation, including the orientation of both students and staff, required much time. The rate of progress varied among the facilities.

Student council members were elected to represent cottages.

Officers, including a president, vice-president, secretary, and parliamentarian, were elected by the entire student body. Committees were appointed to be concerned with matters such as cottage planning, dress code, philosophy, orientation, food services, recreation, and social activities. Council members were assigned as chairmen of the committees, membership of which was composed of both council members and appointees. Each school had an administrator's advisory council whose members included both staff and students.

Additionally, in 1972 there was developed what appeared to be an innovative plan to obtain meaningful participation in program planning by those most directly affected. Three "recipient of services committees" were organized in three schools. The dozen members of each group represented six former students who had received discharges and over whom the Office of Youth Development had no authority, three students in the community under conditional release status, and three students currently enrolled at the school. One-day meetings were held semi-annually at each school or in the vicinity. A representative of the Commissioner of Youth Development and five officials of the school met with that school's committee. The latter included the school director or assistant director, director of social services, director of cottage life, principal of the academic and vocational programs, and the chief vocational counselor. Evaluations of current or proposed programs were made to determine the degree to which there had been, or was a potential for, meaningful assistance to students in both residential and community programs. The administration felt that maximum services delivery depended on knowing what had been, or could be, of optimal value to those who received the services. Suggestions made by those still in the various stages of recipiency and those who had successfully been reintegrated into the community were regarded as a valuable resource.

"Recipient of services committees" at the other five schools were scheduled for activation by mid-1973.

In November, 1978, the establishment of Student Councils by January 1, 1979 was mandated by the Division of Youth Services. Each facility director was required to develop procedures to assure the proper functioning of a Student Council. A constitution specifying election method, term of office, frequency of meetings, specific duties and responsibilities of the council and of each member, and the appointment of staff advisors, is required. It must meet with approval of the facility director and the Division Assistant Director for Institutional Services.[16]

Notes

1. Letter from William A. Dudley, Executive Director, Inmate Grievance Commission, Raleigh, April 14, 1983.
2. "Inmate Grievance Procedure," Policies Procedures, No. .0300, Dept. of Correction, Division of Prisons, Raleigh, February 1, 1976. (Procedure initiated in 1975.)

3. Baker, J. E., op. cit., p. 158.
4. Prisons in North Carolina, report of the North Carolina Advisory Committee, to the U.S. Commission on Civil Rights, February 1976, p. 53.
5. Ibid., pp. 53-54.
6. Baker, J. E., op. cit., pp. 158-159.
7. Ibid., p. 159.
8. Letter from L. Michael Cayton, Chief of Field Operations, Division of Youth Services, Raleigh, April 21, 1983.
9. "Student Grievance Procedure," Division of Youth Services, Raleigh (undated).
10. MacCormick, Austin H., ed. Handbook of American Institutions for Delinquent Juveniles. Vol. IV, First Edition. Virginia-North Carolina. New York: The Osborne Association, Inc., 1943, p. 458.
11. Ibid., pp. 538-539.
12. Ibid., p. 609.
13. Ibid., pp. 604-614.
14. Ibid., p. 696.
15. Baker, J. E., op. cit., pp. 159-160.
16. "Youth Leadership Development," Executive Directive No. 17-78, Division of Youth Services, Raleigh, November 1, 1978 (the Directive stipulated that Student Councils must be organized and functioning by January 1, 1979).

NORTH DAKOTA

Office of Director of Institutions

The three facilities for adult and youthful felony offenders, misdemeanants, and juvenile delinquents are under the jurisdiction of the Director of Institutions.

An Inmate Grievance Procedure was established in 1972[1] at the North Dakota Penitentiary, Bismarck, and is also applicable to the North Dakota State Farm, Bismarck, located approximately six miles from the penitentiary. The farm is under the management of the penitentiary.

A grievance is defined as a circumstance or action considered to be unjust and grounds for complaint. An inmate may, within 30 days from the date the incident occurred, seek resolution through informal contact with staff. If this approach is unsuccessful, the inmate may complete a prescribed form for administrative review. A Grievance Committee, composed of staff members not involved in the grievance issue, has 15 days to investigate the complaint, hold a hearing with the inmate present, and draft a reply subject to review by the warden. If not satisfied, the inmate may appeal during the 15 days following to the Director of Institutions, the final level of review.[2]

Time limits at all levels of review may be extended for a like period if an appropriate decision cannot be made within the prescribed period. The grievant must be advised in writing of any time extension.

If an inmate believes the grievance issue is of a sensitive nature and fears possible adverse effects if known at the institution, the complaint may be made by mail to the Director of Institutions.

Regulations point out that an inmate may mail a complaint or file a law suit directly with the appropriate court. However, inmates should be advised that courts frequently require evidence that grievance procedures have been exhausted before ruling on a complaint.

Status offenders, misdemeanants and juvenile delinquents are committed to the co-educational North Dakota Industrial School, Mandan. The State Youth Authority, Department of Human Services, provides treatment services. Youth may appeal disciplinary committee actions to the superintendent and if not satisfied with the decision may, within the 30 days following, appeal to the Director of Institutions.[3]

The Director of Institutions determines the release date of juvenile delinquents. Decisions of a hearing officer in that regard may be appealed within two working days to the superintendent, who will render a decision during the subsequent three working days.[4]

Appeals may be made by youth of treatment decisions by completing a Request for Administrative Review form and mailing it to the Children and Family Services unit, State Youth Authority, Bismarck. If not satisfied with the response, the youth may file a request for a Fair Hearing form with the Social Service Board of North Dakota.[5]

A survey in 1937 reported that an athletic manager, selected by the inmates, cooperated with the Deputy Warden in arranging athletic activities.[6]

Information was received in March, 1973 that, because of a relatively low census of usually less than 150, good inmate-staff rapport, and the existence of inmate organizations which represented various segments of the inmate population, no need was felt for any kind of inmate council or self-governing group at the North Dakota Penitentiary.[7] There is still no formal inmate council at the institution, the administration relying chiefly on various established inmate organizations for feedback on inmate concerns and activities. However, an appointed inmate advisory committee has been established to provide an inmate perspective to the architect during a remodeling project at the institution.[8]

The North Dakota State Farm, Bismarck, a state misdemeanor facility under the management of the penitentiary, has an elected inmate committee which provides information, suggestions, and solutions on the overall operation and management of the facility. The group also participates actively in the orientation of new inmates, and is considered by the facility administrator to be a valuable and viable administrative tool.[9]

In 1937, it was reported that student monitors were appointed by the superintendent of the State Training School, Mandan (now designated as the North Dakota Industrial School), to assist cottage officers from time to time when there was some special need for it.[10]

In 1966, information was received that, prior to 1965, a Student Council which functioned similarly to a high school group was in operation at the North Dakota Industrial School. Demand on staff time was a factor in its discontinuance. During the 1965-66 school year, a Campus Council was formed, with representation on the basis of classes as well as living units. Meetings with a staff supervisor provided an opportunity for the expression of negative feelings about institutional programs, and served as a sounding board for the staff.[11]

In July, 1973, a report stated that in recent years the Campus Council had been renamed the Policy Making Committee, with student representation from each of the living units and staff representation from the work areas. The group, usually numbering 12, had authority to review and modify all policies. Active during 1971 and 1972, the Committee had ben inactive in 1973 largely because of administration planning for procedural changes designed to provide increased student interaction. The administration believed that this type of involvement was important and meaningful to students.[12]

Currently, the North Dakota Industrial School has an Advisory Committee composed of five representatives. Each of the five living units elects a member. The group meets once a month.[13]

Notes

1. Dillingham, David D., and Singer, Linda R., op. cit., p. 54.
2. "Inmate Grievance Procedure," Administrative Regulations, Section No. 517, North Dakota Penitentiary, Bismarck, February 12, 1982.
3. "Student Residents Rights," Discipline Committee Regulations, North Dakota Industrial School, Mandan (undated).
4. Detention Hearing Appeal Form, North Dakota Industrial School, Mandan.
5. Forms: Request for Administrative Review; Request for Fair Hearing.
6. Cox, William B., and Bixby, F. Lovell, Ph.D. Handbook of American Prisons and Reformatories. Fifth Edition, Vol. I, West North Central States. New York: The Osborne Association, 1938, p. 303.
7. Baker, J. E., op. cit., p. 160.
8. Letter from Edwin F. Zuern, Legal Counsel, Office of Director of Institutions, Bismarck, May 31, 1983.

9. Ibid.
10. Cox, William B., and Bixby, F. Lovell, Ph. D. Handbook of American Institutions for Delinquent Juveniles. First Edition, Vol. I, West North Central States. New York: The Osborne Association, 1938, p. 365.
11. Baker, J. E., op. cit., pp. 160-161.
12. Ibid., p. 161.
13. Letter from Edwin F. Zuern, op. cit.

OHIO

Department of Rehabilitation and Correction

The Department of Rehabilitation and Correction administers ten institutions and four subsidiary facilities for adult and youthful felony offenders.

A Departmental Ombudsman was appointed in August, 1972, under Department Administrative Regulation 847, whose three primary responsibilities were:

> Investigate inquiries or complaints of departmental staff or inmates;
> Monitor administrative practices to ensure that they comply with Ohio law and department regulations;
> Self-initiate investigations into problems brought to the office from whatever source.

The Ombudsman and his staff monitored the grievance procedure which is later described. At the end of January, 1975, the chief Ombudsman retired and the program was terminated. Cited as a principal reason for the termination was the fact that inmates used the Ombudsman to bypass local management personnel with their problems, thereby circumventing institutional review of grievances where most problems could be resolved most efficiently and effectively.[1]

Administrative Regulation 845, issued in August, 1972, established a Grievance Procedure for Residents, applicable to all institutions. A 1974 description indicated that a full-time Resident Liaison Officer had been appointed at each institution to operate and monitor the procedure. Also, an Institutional Inquiry Board of three members was appointed by each warden to conduct hearings on inmate grievances.[2]

The grievance procedure was initiated by an inmate contacting the Resident Liaison Officer, who had the option of investigating and resolving the grievance and making recommendations to the warden or referring the case to the Institutional Inquiry Board. The Board would conduct a hearing at which the grievant had a right to appear. The Board had ten days to submit its recommendations to the warden, who advised the grievant within five days of any action to be taken. If dissatisfied with the warden's response, an appeal could be made to the Department Director. The procedure was non-specific as to any action the Director might take. The scope of the procedure was not defined.[3]

Administrative Regulation 845 was revised in August, 1974. The apparent principal changes were to broaden the powers of the Resident Liaison Officer, and specify that all requests by inmates for assistance in solving a problem or for information must be replied to within ten working days by the addressee staff member. Lacking a response within the time specified, the inmate was authorized to file a formal grievance.[4]

In 1976, Administrative Regulation No. 845 was replaced by Rule No. 5120-9-31, Inmate Grievance Procedure, which was revised February 10, 1978, and again on July 10, 1980. In its preamble the procedure states:

> The grievance procedure outlined herein is designed to give inmates in Ohio correctional institutions a method for presenting complaints and problems relating to the conditions of their incarceration. It is intended to be the mechanism to which inmates may turn after they have attempted to resolve the problem or complaint with the staff member(s) most directly responsible for the aspect of institutional life in question.

Exclusions from grievable issues are decisions on disciplinary infractions (for which there is a separate process), and issues not within department jurisdiction, e.g., legislative action, adult parole authority policies and decisions, and judicial proceedings. The principal difference from the former procedure is that the Resident Liaison Officer has been replaced by an Inspector of Institutional Services, who is the sole decision-maker in the institution, except that issues not within the scope of authority of that office are referred to the warden. The final level of appeal is the Chief Inspector. Time limits for written responses are: Institution Inspector, ten working days; warden, ten working days; chief inspector, 20 working days. The grievant must be advised in writing when additional time is required at any level.

Any grievances to which the warden or the institution inspector are a party are sent directly to the Chief Inspector.

No documents regarding a grievance may be placed in any inmate file available to the adult parole authority, unless such documents contain a false accusation or statement made by an inmate in a knowing, deliberate, and malicious attempt to cause significant injury to another party and the potential for such injury is substantiated.[5]

In April, 1872, the department issued Administrative Regulation

846 directing that elected inmate advisory councils be established in each institution. The regulation, which was revised on August 9, 1972, specified that for each council the constitution and by-laws, approved by the Director of the Department, must specify an electoral process of nominations, free elections, and a secret ballot voting system. Representation could be by either work assignment or housing unit, as approved by the superintendent of the institution concerned. The superintendent had the right to remove from office any member he considered unsuitable to represent the population in a constructive and adaptive manner. Instances occurred where removal had been necessitated, e.g., violation of institution regulations and conduct of such type as to render the individual unsuitable to represent properly those who had elected him. Those elected to a six-month non-successive term of office met at least monthly with the superintendent or his designee to discuss an agenda submitted a week in advance. Each institution was to provide a convenient place, furnished with equipment and related supplies, where its council would have the right to meet weekly. Honor dormitories and honor camp units located outside a main institution could also establish councils. Under procedures established in another regulation, the council could represent individual inmates in grievances through an institution liaison officer. Otherwise, councils were to function in a liaison advisory capacity only, with no authority to establish or administer institution policy.

As of February, 1973, all of the institutions within the Department of Rehabilitation and Correction had implemented the regulation regarding the establishment of inmate advisory councils, with varying degrees of success. As a result of certain activities and involvement, some councils were not then functioning. There had been a mixed reaction at various staff levels to the establishment of councils, ranging from complete cooperation to some resistance.[6]

In July, 1973, it was reported that, early in 1972, the London Correctional Institution, London, established an elected inmate council as a result of inmate proposals made during a sitdown strike. According to statements made in 1973, the inmates had high praise for the council and claimed that about 80 per cent of its proposals had been enacted by the institution administration. In July, 1972, administrators abolished the council on the grounds that it had been undemocratically elected and was serving as a vehicle of unrest. In lieu of the council, ad hoc advisory committees of administration-appointed inmates were established for specific areas such as food, clothing, and entertainment. According to some inmates, those committees were unproductive, unknown to the inmate population, and therefore unrepresentative of inmate concerns.[7]

At the present time (1983) there are no central office directives regarding inmate councils. The decision to establish a council is at the discretion of the institution head. Three institutions are reported to have inmate councils: the Marion Correctional Institution, Marion (established and operated pursuant to the court order in the case of <u>Taylor v. Perini</u>, 455 F. Supp. 1241); the Lebanon

Correctional Institution, Lebanon; and the Ohio Reformatory for Women, Marysville. The councils in the last two institutions consist of members elected to represent housing areas.[8]

Department of Youth Services

The Department of Youth Services (formerly the Ohio Youth Commission), established November 23, 1981, by HB 440, Ohio State Legislature, administers nine facilities. Only felony or capital offenders are committed. Sentences are for mandatory minimum lengths of time, either six or 12 months, depending upon the seriousness of the offense. At the present time, there are no student councils or grievance procedures in any of the facilities. Superintendents of the facilities believe that the ready accessibility of staff to discuss student problems makes such formal programs unnecessary.[9]

In February, 1973, various forms of student councils existed in the nine facilities then in operation. The following accounts of past experiences, projected plans, and current thinking toward such groups are presented as written in 1973.[10]

Although the Zanesville Youth Camp, Zanesville, has no student council, the superintendent does occasionally receive indication of the need for some policy changes through discussions arising in group therapy sessions conducted with students by social workers. Since the number of students is small, usually about 35, the superintendent is accessible to both students and staff to hear problems.

Currently, there is no student council at the Training Center for Youth, Columbus, a special treatment unit for boys aged ten to 17. Here again, open communication and ready access to the superintendent and staff is enhanced by a student body whose census averages 90 to 100. The establishment of a student council will be considered at the Juvenile Diagnostic Center, Columbus, upon completion of the planned conversion to a treatment facility where the students will remain for a much longer period of time. It is assumed that the brief time students spent at the Center has heretofore made organization of a student council impractical. (The facility is now designated as the Buckeye Youth Center.)

At the present time, the Fairfield School for Boys, Lancaster, does not have a student council. However, the administration hopes that one will be developed with the expansion of a program, now in its initial stages, referred to as a Zone System. The administration of the Maumee Youth Camp, Liberty Center, recognized the value of student opinion input in the preparation of its program, but in early 1973 had no crystallized plans as to the optimum method of utilizing this resource in the operational structure (now the Maumee Youth Center).

The discontinuance of a student council program at the

Mohican Youth Camp, Loudonville, approximately two years ago, is attributed to problems such as the low motivation of students, the difficulty of maintaining active involvement by the assigned teacher representative, and scheduling conflicts with other activities. Two students are currently involved in the planning of menus, one from the educational program, the other from the work training program. Evaluation is being made of the feasibility of establishing an advisory board composed of students in the Orientation-Prerelease Cottage to insure the opportunity of participation by school and work training students under staff direction and supervision. (The facility is now the Mohican Youth Center.)

All students at the Riverview School for Girls, Powell, are involved in groups which are given considerable responsibility in the formation of policies concerning group routines and in planning and organizing group functions and programs. The ultimate goal of this group program approach is to have girls involved in truly meaningful and critical decisions--for instance, the readiness of a girl to return to the community. (The facility now houses males: the Riverview School for Boys.)

A Campus Council was initiated recently at Scioto Village, Powell, to encourage students to participate in activities and to better familiarize themselves with all aspects of living at the facility. A representative is elected by each cottage, and membership on the Council is reported as being a prestigious position. A girl who has been at the facility for at least eight weeks, has a minimum time of three months remaining until release, and who is doing reasonably well in the academic, vocational, or on-job training may be nominated to stand for election provided she can obtain: (1) the endorsements of one youth leader in her cottage, her guidance counselor, and one other staff member from any department; and (2) the endorsements of at least five students from her cottage. The Council is the official body which provides communication between students and staff. The group meets monthly under the direction of the recreation leader to discuss the ways in which the operations of various departments affect the life of the students.

The Training Institution Central Ohio, Columbus at one time had a Boy's Committee, described below. The present administration has invited students to meet with staff to provide their viewpoints, such as at budget meetings. Currently, two to four student representatives visit all cottages and invite inquiries and opinions, later meeting with a Volunteer Council to discuss views so obtained. This procedure provides feedback to both the Volunteer Council and the student body.

The Boy's Committee, organized in the latter part of 1965, was discontinued in early 1967, after members began to be negative and anti-authority. Information obtained in 1966 regarding the Boy's Committee indicated that each of the eight cottages selected a representative to meet weekly with the superintendent. The agenda to be discussed could include almost any topic the members chose. There were two strictures: no individual names were to be mentioned when discussing a complaint, and no use of offensive language was allowed in reference to any staff member. Discussions at the meetings were occasionally instrumental in formulating or modifying facility policy. An example was cited of changing the bedtime from ten to ten-thirty p.m. The original precipitating reason for organizing the Boy's Committee centered around a rumor that the deputy superintendent insisted that every boy remain at the institution a minimum of 18 months before being considered for release. Through the Committee, the superintendent hoped to forestall such rumors and to clarify whatever misunderstandings regarding institutional policies existed among the boys. The net evaluation was that the meetings had proven to be useful in at least a limited way, especially in the area of communication.

Notes

1. Keating, McArthur, Lewis, Sebelius, and Singer, _op. cit._, p. 43.
2. _Ibid._, p. 42.
3. _Ibid._, pp. 42-43.
4. "Grievance Procedures for Residents," Administrative Regulation No. 845, Dept. of Rehabilitation and Correction, Columbus, August 1, 1974 (revised).
5. Rule No. 5120-9-29, "The Office of Inspector of Institutional Services," February 10, 1978; Rule No. 5120-9-30, "Office of the Chief Inspector," effective July 10, 1980 (had been revised February 10, 1978); Rule No. 5120-9-31, "Inmate Grievance Procedures," effective July 10, 1980 (had been revised February 10, 1980).
6. Baker, J. E., _op. cit._, pp. 161-162.
7. _Protecting Inmate Rights: Prison Reform or Prison Replacement?_ Report of the Ohio Advisory Committee to the U.S. Commission on Civil Rights, February 1976, pp. 51, 106.
8. Letter from Thomas J. Stickrath, Chief Inspector, Dept. of Rehabilitation and Correction, Columbus, November 4, 1982.
9. Telephone conversation with Mary Irene Moffitt, Chief, Office of Communications, Dept. of Youth Services, Columbus, June 3, 1983; Letter from Mary Irene Moffitt, June 3, 1983.
10. Baker, J. E., _op. cit._, pp. 162-164.

OKLAHOMA

Department of Corrections

The Department of Corrections administers 11 correctional centers for youthful and adult felony offenders, and eight minimum security community treatment centers for offenders nearing release.[1]

An Offender Grievance Process was established on May 1, 1978. Under the process as last amended effective March 1, 1983, an inmate may file a grievance regarding all policies, conditions of confinement, actions by employees and other inmates, and incidents occurring within the jurisdiction of the department that affect the grievant personally. Grievances about a disciplinary hearing may be made following completion of a disciplinary appeal process. Inmates are advised to seek informal resolution prior to filing a written grievance via a prescribed form, which must be done within 15 calendar days of the aggrieved incident. However, the reviewing authority may extend the filing time to 60 days.[2]

In actions brought under 42 U.S.C. 1983, where a court has stayed an action for a period not to exceed 90 days in order to require an offender to exhaust the offender grievance procedure, the grievant must attach a copy of the court order to the grievance report form and submit it to the warden within ten days of the order. The warden is responsible for establishing deadlines to insure the appeal will be completed at the Director's level within the court-ordered period of stay. All other grievances are to reach final disposition within 120 calendar days after original filing unless the grievant agrees in writing to an extension for a fixed period of time.

The procedure is a three-tier arrangement (Warden, Deputy Director or Medical Director, Director) which provides for written responses within 15 days at each level. An additional 15 days is possible provided the grievant is given a written notification.

Should an inmate feel that the complaint is of a sensitive or emergency nature, or that he/she would be adversely affected by submitting it at the institution level, it may be sent directly to the Deputy Director or Medical Director. Reprisals, specified as any action or threat of action against anyone for the use of or participation in the procedure, are strictly prohibited. Any such reprisal may be the basis for a grievance.

The Director, Department of Corrections, meets annually with a committee of his appointment, representing staff and inmates to review grievance procedures and data on grievances.[3]

In 1966, information was received that, at the Oklahoma State Penitentiary, McAlester, two inmates served as members of the Inmate Welfare and Recreation Board, a statutory organization of seven members: the warden, two state employees, and two inmates selected by the warden, and an appointee each of the State Board of Public Affairs and the Commissioner of Charities and Corrections.

Although it was stated in late 1972[4] that an Ombudsman position was being established as a means of effecting inmate-staff communications, subsequent surveys did not find such a position.[5]

No directives have been issued regarding inmate councils.[6] However, a policy statement first issued in 1976 states: "To the extent that the practicalities of corrections permits, the Director of the Department of Corrections will encourage the provision of opportunities for the inmate to participate in the penal process and decisions concerning his/her care and treatment while in the custody of the Department of Corrections."[7]

Recently an Inmate Advisory Council was established by the warden of the Joseph Harp Correctional Center, Lexington. Council members are elected to represent each housing unit. The group meets each Saturday night to review suggestions submitted by other inmates. Those having merit are proposed to the warden at one of his two monthly meetings with the Council. A Warden's Advisory Committee composed of selected staff members reviews the suggestions and either approves or disapproves them. The warden then advises the Council of the decisions. Some changes attributed to Council proposals involve visiting procedures, canteen operations, inmate dress codes, and the ordering of authorized items from outside merchants.[8]

Institutional Services Unit

The Institutional Services Unit, Department of Human Services, administers three facilities for juvenile delinquents.[9]

A juvenile may convey a grievance in writing directly or through the aid of the Student Defender/Representative to the superintendent. Those two, together with other staff and juveniles as required, attempt resolution of the grievance within ten days. Grievances which remain unresolved are reviewed periodically. Complaints may be about:

> Care or omission of care or other staff actions directed toward a juvenile.
> Arbitrary or incorrect application of policies and rules.
> The substance of department policies or institution rules a juvenile believes are contrary to State law, or regulations, or are unreasonable.[10]

In 1966, development was underway of a Student Advisory Council for recreational services and programs at Girls' Town, Tecumseh (now the Central Oklahoma Juvenile Treatment Center), and a cottage committee plan at the other facilities for juveniles. In 1973 it was stated there were no student councils in the three juvenile facilities. Various group-process techniques were being utilized but were not regarded as systems of self-government.[11]

Current information indicates there is a student council in one of the three facilities for juvenile delinquents,[12] but no details of its operations were received.

Notes

1. Letters from Michael Avant-Pybas, General Counsel, Dept. of Corrections, Oklahoma City, March 23, 1983; Bob Faulkner, Senior Case Manager, Planning and Research, Dept. of Corrections, Oklahoma City, May 27, 1973.
2. Policy Statement OP-130201 (revised), "Offender Grievance Procedure," Dept. of Corrections, Oklahoma City, December 12, 1982 (effective March 1, 1983). Offenders and employees were afforded an advisory role in the formulation and implementation of this procedure. This Policy Statement cancelled OP-130201, "Inmate Grievance Process," dated July 23, 1980, and OP-160110, "Inmate Medical Grievance Procedure," dated March 4, 1982.
3. Ibid.
4. Baker, J. E., op. cit., p. 165.
5. Corrections Compendium, CONTACT, Inc., Lincoln, Nebraska, August 1977; and Dillingham, David D., and Singer, Linda R. Complaint Procedures in Prisons and Jails: An Examination of Recent Experience. Washington, D.C.: National Institute of Corrections, U.S. Dept. of Justice, July 1980, p. 54.
6. Letters from Michael Avante-Pybas, and Bob Faulkner, op. cit.
7. Policy Statement P-030200 (revised) "Inmate Involvement in the Penal Process," Dept. of Corrections, Oklahoma City, January 12, 1979. (The purpose of this policy: "To improve relations between correctional staff and residents and to alleviate many of the tensions that are associated with being confined in a correctional institution.")
8. Letter from Bob Faulkner, Planning and Research, Dept. of Corrections, May 27, 1983.
9. Letter from Jack Campbell, Supervisor, Institutional Services Unit, Dept. of Human Services, Oklahoma City, April 1, 1983.
10. Policy Manual, Institutional Services Unit, Dept. of Human Services, Section 1725.9, revised March 1, 1983.
11. Baker, J. E., op. cit., p. 165.
12. Letter from Jack Campbell, op. cit.

OREGON

Department of Human Resources

All facilities for adult and youthful felony offenders and for juvenile delinquents are under the jurisdiction of the Department of Human Resources, established in 1971.

Corrections Division

The Corrections Division administers three institutions for adults and youthful felony offenders.

An institution Ombudsman position was established in 1971 by the warden at the Oregon State Penitentiary, Salem. There was no written statement of the Ombudsman's scope of work. He operated primarily as a trouble-shooter, to cut red tape. Circulating throughout the institution, the Ombudsman would make notes of problems presented by inmates who stopped him for discussion. Investigations were made in person and by telephone. Most of the problems appeared to be individual matters. Two staff members were fired after the Ombudsman's investigation confirmed that they were physically abusing inmates.[1]

Subsequently, the Ombudsman position was elevated to the Corrections Division central office, then transferred to the Department of Human Resources, and finally to the Office of the Governor. Budget limitations forced deletion of the position circa 1981. The majority of the concerns formerly handled by the Ombudsman have been returned to handling by the Corrections Division staff and/or through a formal grievance procedure.[2]

A Grievance Complaint Review system was established in 1977[3] for all adult institutions. A grievance is defined as an unresolved complaint about the substance or application of any written or unwritten policy, regulation, or rule of the Corrections Division or any of its functional units; the lack of a policy, regulation, or rule, or any behavior or action directed toward a client. Individual disciplinary matters are not grievable, but policies and rules of the disciplinary process, as generally applicable to clients, may be the subject of a grievance. Other exclusions from the procedure are: Parole Board policy, regulation, rule or action; incidents or actions for which there is a separate appeal process and final decisions of such processes, and class actions. Additionally, only those clients directly involved in an incident or problem may file a grievance.[4]

If, after 14 days, during which discussions with staff have failed to bring about resolution, a client may, within seven working days, file a completed grievance form with the supervisor of the staff member involved in the subject matter or area of grievance. The supervisor must personally contact the grievant and attempt resolution within five working days. This decision may be appealed to the superintendent who has a total of five working days to make any further investigation necessary, including a hearing if appropriate, and render a written decision.

An appeal to the Administrator, Corrections Division, may be made. A review and response will be made no later than ten subsequent working days. No reprisals are permitted should a client seek review of a complaint outside the Corrections Division.

Material obtained in surveys made in 1966-67 and 1972-73 was reviewed by the present administration and updated.[5]

The first Inmate Council of record at the Oregon State Penitentiary, Salem, was formed in 1951 following several weeks of tension in the institution. Two general inmate assemblies were called to permit nomination of candidates and discussion of procedural methods. By secret ballot six councilmen and two alternates were elected to serve six-month, non-successive terms of office. The group met with the warden a week later, electing a chairman and vice-chairman. Sixteen topics were presented for discussion, most being acted upon favorably by the warden. A council on recreation was scheduled to be formed in November, 1951, although there is no evidence to indicate that either the Inmate Council or the Recreational Council ever became a voice in the institution. Two groups periodically held meetings in the recreation yard, but minutes are not available nor is it known if they were ever made. Staff members recall that successive administrators ignored the existence of any council. The groups met, talked over their grievances, and then adjourned. Apparently the councils were neither listened to nor instructed to disband. It is indicated that both groups were abolished the night of July 10, 1953, when a riot began.

Following a riot in March, 1968, a demand for the development of an inmate council was met by the administration. During the ensuing months the council thus formed became increasingly militant and demanding, moving from a representative to a leadership role. A series of assaults on staff, two strikes, and the death of a correctional officer appeared attributable to council activities and the organization was disbanded by the superintendent in April, 1969.[6]

The present warden of the Oregon State Penitentiary recently affirmed the foregoing account as reflecting the current situation.[7]

The Oregon State Correctional Institution, Salem, was opened in May, 1959. A new unit was completed and occupied in October, 1966, raising the capacity to 500, most of whom are first felony offenders. An Inmate Relations Council was organized in October, 1960 and continued in operation until about 1964. Inmates whose conduct record had been clear for six months and who had demonstrated a constructive attitude toward institutional goals, if proposed by at least five fellow housing unit residents, could stand for election by secret ballot to a six-month term of office. The four-man council chose a secretary and chairman from its membership. The minutes of monthly meetings were reviewed by the superintendent who then met with the council officers to give his decisions on suggestions or questions. While the Inmate Relations Council was a means of advising the superintendent of matters inmates were interested in, for the most part the latter's suggestions were predominantly oriented to creature comforts. Lack of interest on the part of individuals whose leadership could have been positive in nature, pressure tactics on weaker men by candidates at election time, and the shallowness of council referrals combined to weaken the image of the group in the eyes of both inmates and staff. Resistance on the part of a few self-styled operators to the manner in which an election was held precipitated discontinuance of the council.[8]

There has not been an inmate council at the Oregon State

Correctional Institution since 1964 and none is planned. Inmate input into management and operations is solicited through encouraged individual suggestions and, when indicated, through ad hoc bringing together of inmate club leadership, e.g., Jaycees president, Indian Club chief, and Black Culture presidents.[9]

At the Oregon Women's Correctional Center, Salem, the superintendent meets on request with any inmate who submits a request for information or identifies a problem. Resolution of issues or problems may be sought through the grievance procedure. Inmates also have unrestricted correspondence access to the Administrator of Corrections and the Governor. A telephone service has expanded inmate access to attorneys and the courts.[10]

Children's Services Division

The Children's Services Division, created in 1970, administers the two facilities for juvenile delinquents.

A Grievance-Appeal Procedure for students was established January 1, 1982. The procedure is in full effect at the MacLaren School, Woodburn, and in process of adaptation at the Hillcrest School of Oregon, Salem.[11]

Any student who believes he/she has been dealt with unjustly, is dissatisfied with the program, staff, conditions at the school, or who has any other kind of grievance not resolved to his/her satisfaction after discussion with the staff most directly involved, may file a written grievance with the Student Case Review Committee. The three members of the committee are the student's cottage counselor who is the chairman, and a representative each of the education and group life staffs.[12]

If the grievance concerns initial placement by the Reception Committee, it is sent directly to the superintendent, whose decision is final.

For other than appeals of disciplinary action, the Student Case Review Committee informally reviews the grievance, adopting in each case whatever methods are appropriate for the student to fully present his/her side of the matter. If the student is not satisfied with the decision, which must be made within five working days, an appeal may be made to the Unit Case Review Committee, composed of the Unit Director (chairman), the Principal of Education, and the Section Director. The latter is responsible for supervising the non-casework activities of cottage staff.

The Unit Case Review Committee, following the same procedure as the Student Case Review Committee, must review the grievance and render a decision no later than five working days after the hearing. If still dissatisfied, the grievant may appeal to the superintendent, the final level, who will either review the issue personally or appoint an impartial person to do so and to make a recommendation for resolution. Within ten days following receipt of the appeal or receipt of the impartial person's report, the superintendent makes a written response.

If a grievance concerns a disciplinary action, the Student Case Review Committee conducts a formal hearing at which the grievant is entitled to be represented by a staff member mutually acceptable to him/her and the superintendent. Confrontation and cross-examination of adverse witnesses, either staff or students, the presentation of documentary evidence, and the calling of defense witnesses are rights accorded to the grievant. Appeal may be made to the Appeals Committee whose membership includes the warden's executive assistant as presiding officer, and two supervisory level employees not directly involved in campus program activities. The next level of appeal is the superintendent, whose decision may be appealed to the Court of Appeals as provided by State statute.

In 1940, girls were chosen by the staff to assist in supervising the washroom, kitchen, and other details at the Oregon State Industrial School for Girls, now the Hillcrest School of Oregon.[13] In 1967, it was reported that several years earlier, in an effort to gear policy and program to the expressed needs of the girls, biweekly luncheons were held to stimulate communication between staff and representatives of each housing unit. The program was discontinued in 1966, at which time it was planned to establish a student council to be composed of two representatives from each cottage, one to be elected by the girls, the other to be selected by cottage staff. As of early 1967, the council had not been organized.[14]

In May, 1973, it was reported that through a long and difficult participatory process involving both staff and students, a constitution and a bill of rights had been recently written at the Hillcrest School, and that a similar process had been going on for the past year at the MacLaren School, Woodburn. The constitution established the Robert S. Farrell High School Student Body Council, declared membership open to any student enrolled in the Farrell High School, and provided for three elected representatives, and alternates, from treatment team groups who elected from the membership a president, secretary-treasurer, and sergeant-at-arms, all to serve until released from the facility or removed from office for absence without permission, violence, or non-attendance at meetings. The school counselor was designated as advisor, together with a teacher and a cottage staff member each selected by the group to serve for a period of six months. Twice weekly meetings were scheduled and special meetings could be called by the council president, the school principal, or one of the advisors. These three could also call a student assembly to be conducted by the council.

A Black Student Union had been organized and functioned under a constitution which limited membership to Black students, but allowed non-voting participation by others. The membership elected a chairman, secretary, and treasurer who served until released.

A teacher was elected as sponsor. Both the Student Body Council and the Black Student Union adopted the "Student Bill of Rights" signed on October 20, 1972, reproduced here in its entirety:

STUDENT BILL OF RIGHTS

The Constitution of the United States of America explicitly guarantees the freedoms of speech, press, assembly, self-identity, personal appearance, and religion. Along with these, we have the right to be secure in personal effects and against unreasonable search and seizures without probable cause, and also to have fair representation and due process in matters involving discipline or suspension from school. The enumeration in the constitution of certain rights does not mean one can deny others the rights retained by the people.

1. Students have the freedom of verbal expression. This freedom cannot be restricted unless its exercise interferes with orderly conduct and work.

Students and staff or students and students should not violate the first right which is the freedom of speech. If a person harasses another person, they have violated their freedom of speech. An example of this would be calling another person a name with malicious intent which causes the other person to lose their temper and become disorderly. This example would be a violation of the freedom of speech because it is designed for the harassment of an individual instead of the expression of an idea.

2. Students are entitled to a free press. This does not give the license to slander or abuse individuals. Students must be able to defend what they write with logic and evidence. Students have the freedom of the press as long as they do not violate the guidelines established by the journalism class.

3. Students have the right to self-identity. This identity may be sought and expressed in any of the following arenas: political, cultural, racial, individual, or religious. This expression can be perpetuated in appearance (grooming, dress) and should not be limited unless these present a clear and present danger to health and interfere with work or order.

4. Students have the right to assemble with or without supervision according to choice. The assembly is to be conducted in an orderly manner. It is understood that to assemble for the purpose of overthrow of the institution or conducting a riot will not be condoned.

5. Students have the freedom to participate or not participate in religion or religious activities of their choice.

6. Students have the right to possess personal property. This does not pertain to articles which have been proven harmful. These problems should be decided upon by a group of staff and students.

7. It seems necessary that in order to maintain due

process and fair representation in relation to the school program that a judicial review board would be created and implemented. This review board would be composed of staff and students.

8. To be searched as a matter of routine (being stripped upon return from a home visit) is an example of disrespectful treatment of students. The time and reason for searching or seizing, if it is necessary, should be a mutually agreed upon process between student and staff.

9. Students have the right to be treated with respect at all times.[15]

The MacLaren School, Woodburn, was originally opened in 1891 as the State Reform School, located seven miles from Salem. In 1927, the facility was moved to its present location and renamed the Oregon State Training School for Boys. Subsequently, the name was changed to MacLaren School for Boys, and within the past decade, to the current designation.[16]

A survey made in 1940 reported that each cottage had student monitors, known as sergeants or squad bosses, appointed by the cottage manager to act as assistants. Detail officers also appointed boys temporarily from day to day to assist in supervising the work details. Monitors were authorized to order around and, for misbehavior, slap those over whom they had been placed.[17]

In 1967, information was received that boys were playing a significant role in the development and evaluation of policy and procedures through their representation and participation in the Youth Council which was organized May 8, 1962. Two boys who had lost no privileges were chosen from each living cottage, one by secret ballot and one by the cottage manager, to participate in weekly council meetings with the superintendent or a staff advisor. By majority secret ballot the members elected among themselves a president, vice-president, secretary, and two board directors. Members could be removed by the superintendent or by a two-thirds vote of council members in attendance, by reason of parole or other permanent assignment off-campus, or the loss of full privileges. The council was popularly known as the JC-YC since it was sponsored by the Woodburn, Oregon, Junior Chamber of Commerce. Boys were able, via the council, to present suggestions and recommendations to the staff and make significant contributions to the Woodburn community by assisting in various civic projects.

The then superintendent, under whose administration the Youth Council was organized, reported experience with such groups for many years. He expressed his belief that it is essential that all humans have an opportunity to feel that they have some voice in decisions that affect them, and that persons involved in decision-making become more responsive to rules, regulations, policies, and procedures. He was also firmly convinced that inmate councils should not become governing bodies nor should they have responsibility for treatment plans or discipline.

In its then less than five years of operation, the Youth Council was credited with several important accomplishments. For example, boys were formerly permitted to have only one home visit a month; as a result of YC action, boys with 60 consecutive days of full privileges were entitled to two home visits each month. Other changes provided for unsupervised movement from cottages to school and return; unlimited mailing privileges to parents and girlfriends; the wearing of personally owned clothing; and the consultation with Youth Council members by the administration prior to the purchase of new institutional clothing.[18]

No information was received regarding student councils at the present time, nor is any mention made of student councils in Chapter 412, Oregon Administrative Rules, Children's Services Division, dated January 1, 1982.

Notes

1. Keating, McArthur, Lewis, Sebelius, and Singer (1975), op. cit., pp. 43-44.
2. Letter from O. R. Chambers, Executive Assistant, Corrections Division, Salem, May 17, 1983.
3. Dillingham, David D., and Singer, Linda R. (1980), op. cit., p. 54.
4. "Rule Governing Grievance Complaint Review System for Corrections Division Clients," Corrections Division, Salem, January 29, 1982 (supersedes Rule dated January 17, 1979).
5. Letter from O. R. Chambers, Executive Assistant, Corrections Division, Salem, October 4, 1982.
6. Baker, J. E., op. cit., pp. 165-166.
7. Letter from Supt. H. C. Cupp, Oregon State Penitentiary, Salem, September 28, 1982.
8. Baker, J. E., op. cit., pp. 166-167.
9. Letter from Supt. G. E. Sullivan, Oregon State Correctional Institution, Salem, October 1, 1982.
10. Letter from Supt. Patricia R. Tuthill, Oregon Women's Correctional Center, Salem, September 29, 1982.
11. Letter from Malcolm Tabor, Executive Assistant, Office of Juvenile Corrections and Community Services, Children's Services Division, Salem, April 18, 1983.
12. "Grievance-Appeal Procedures for Students," Juvenile Corrections Services, Children's Services Division, Oregon Administrative Rules, Chapter 412, Section 412-44-030, effective January 1, 1982.
13. Cox, William B., and Shelly, Joseph A., eds., op. cit., p. 239.
14. Baker, J. E., op. cit., p. 167.
15. Ibid., pp. 167-168.
16. Cox, William B., and Shelly, Joseph A., eds., op. cit., p. 245.
17. Ibid., p. 262.
18. Baker, J. E., op. cit., p. 167.

PENNSYLVANIA

Bureau of Correction

The Bureau of Correction is currently a part of the Office of General Counsel. Prior to 1980 the Bureau was a component of the Department of Justice which was replaced by the Office of the Attorney General coincident to a changeover from an appointed to an elected Attorney General.

The Bureau of Correction administers nine institutions for adult and youthful felony and misdemeanor offenders, and 15 community service centers. Of the institutions, one houses adult women, one houses both adult and youthful offenders, and the remaining seven are for adult males. Two of the seven are designated as regional correctional facilities. Only offenders with maximum sentences of at least six months and not more than two years are admitted to each.[1]

An Inmate Complaint Review System was established in March, 1976. It was a two-level procedure, institution and Bureau of Correction, through which nearly 6000 complaints were processed by March, 1978.[2]

A Consolidated Inmate Grievance Review System replaced the aforementioned on January 10, 1983, which provides a tri-level procedure for the resolution of inmate complaints not covered by other Bureau directives or policies. The latter includes incoming publications, disciplinary and restricted housing procedures, and policy and procedure for obtaining a pre-release transfer. These exceptions are accorded only a two-level review.[3]

Via a prescribed form an inmate may file a written grievance within 30 days following the event upon which a complaint is based. No group complaints are permitted. An institution Grievance Coordinator will conduct an investigation of the issue during which interviews with other persons and the grievant may be held. Within ten working days a written response will be prepared, including a brief rationale and a summary of conclusions, and any action taken or recommended to resolve the issue will be specified.

If not satisfied with the initial review decision, the grievant has five working days to appeal to the superintendent, who will respond in writing within ten working days. The superintendent is the final level of review for the exceptions previously noted.

A grievant has seven calendar days to appeal for a final review by the Central Office Review Committee, composed of the Commissioner, Deputy Commissioner, and Chief Counsel. The committee may require additional investigation before making a decision. A written response will be given to the grievant no later than 15 working days following receipt of an appeal.

None of the institutions have inmate advisory councils. However, each has a variety of organizations, e.g., Jaycees and Lifers. Reportedly, these groups have a positive impact on the overall institution program by suggesting improvements for daily living procedures. Additionally, inmates at each institution participate in the management of the Inmate General Welfare Fund. The fund is principally derived from sales of craft shop items and donations from the community. Expenditures are made for the purchase of athletic and musical equipment, entertainments, movies, and books. Some institutions have inmate committees involved in the selection of movies.[4]

In the summer of 1971, a Resident Advisory Council was organized at the State Correctional Institution, Muncy, a facility for female offenders. For the first several months the superintendent attended the bi-weekly meetings; during this time the purpose and scope of the council's responsibilities were determined. The principal obligation of council members was to provide a liaison between population and administration; they had no responsibilities for institutional programming and security. In February, 1972, the deputy superintendent for treatment was designated as staff representative to attend all bi-weekly and emergency meetings. Through council representation all residents were provided an opportunity for input into the formulation of rules and regulations.

Revamping of cottage security rules and leisure time programming were examples of council-administration activities. The council had an active part in dealing with unacceptable behavior of other residents in the Behavior Clinic. Factors cited as determining council continuation were the responsibility demonstrated by the population in the quality of representation elected, the evident high calibre of performance of those representatives, and the insight into resident concerns provided to the administration.[5]

The council was discontinued in 1977. Apparently some cottage representatives had begun using their position for personal advantage. Unauthorized meetings of the group had been held which tended to have an inflammatory effect, causing problems for the administration.[6]

Bureau of Group Residential Care

The Bureau of Group Residential Care, Office of Children and Youth, Department of Public Welfare, administers all facilities for juvenile delinquents, consisting of secure institutions, residential facilities, and forestry camps.

Although no central office directive has been issued on the subject, each institution has developed an internal student grievance procedure.[7] Information on two was received.

A Review Board was established in 1974 at Youth Forestry

Camp No. 3, James Creek (former address: Aitch). If a student believes that an action taken against him violates his rights of safety, security, food, clothing, shelter, worship, medical assistance, or correspondence, he may lodge a complaint with his dormitory supervisor. If the latter ascertains that one or more of the listed rights was violated, the complaint will be referred to the Review Board composed of a camp administrator as chairman, and two other personnel, one from the academic school and one dormitory staff member, and two members of the Student Advisory Council, which is later described. All parties involved in the complaint have the right to be heard and to call witnesses. The action of the Review Board is final.[8]

At the Weaversville Intensive Treatment Unit, Weaversville, any student who does not receive a satisfactory answer to a complaint from a staff member may arrange to meet with that person's immediate supervisor, and ultimately with the Project Manager. (The Unit is operated by the RCA Service Company/Government Services, under a State contract.)[9]

In 1966, a survey made of the nine facilities then directly under the Office of Children and Youth, Department of Public Welfare, revealed that five had councils, two had discontinued them recently, and two utilized ad hoc committees for specific events. Although the superintendent of one of the last mentioned had never had experience with a council, he was convinced of the validity of the criticisms of such groups and preferred not to organize one.[10]

At the Youth Development Center, Canonsburg, with a population of 239 (of which 102 were girls), a Student Council operated from 1958 until 1966, when it was discontinued because of a reorganization of the staff. Several methods of membership selection were tried, the principal two being popular vote and selection by staff as an earned privilege. Despite various problems, including a tendency of some council members to misuse their office, the staff felt the group was a desirable activity and planned to reactivate it.[11] The Center was closed in 1966 or 1967.

In October, 1966, there had been no student council among the 147 boys at the Youth Development Center, Warrendale, for more than a year. Individual cottages intermittently had attempted to organize a student council or a staff approved "junior counselor" role. Although the staff was not in favor of the council idea, it did utilize the emerging leadership abilities of the boys through the use of ad hoc committees to plan special events.[12] The Center was closed in 1981.

In the North Philadelphia Youth Development Center, with a population then of 223, a student council was organized October 13, 1965, to provide a modified experience in democratic living and the opportunity to discover the close relationship between privilege and responsibility, and to serve as a means of developing leadership qualities. As of October, 1966, it was reported that expectations had been realized.[13] The Center was closed in 1980 or 1981.

A Student Council was reestablished at the Youth Development Center, Bensalem (former address: Cornwells Heights), in September, 1982, composed of two representatives and one alternate from each of the six living units. Meetings are held twice weekly to give the students an opportunity to share in some of the administrative processes involved in program activities and provide some understanding of the parliamentary procedures of organization formation and governance. The office of chairman is rotated periodically to allow each representative the experience of presiding. While the group has no power to make policy decisions, the members have been instrumental in interpreting administration positions on AWOL's, weekend passes, and campus activities. Student participation as a part of the clinical process will be continued.[14]

The Youth Development Center, Loysville, with an October 1966 population of 105, established a Student Council in May 1966 that operated under a constitution stipulating that the organization has no policy-making powers and citing among its purposes cooperation with the administration, the promotion of programs fostering the welfare of the students, the recommendation of conduct and behavior norms, and the opportunity to obtain experience in democratic practices. Two representatives of each living unit were elected for six-month terms of office. These members elected their own president, vice-president, and secretary who conducted the monthly meetings. A staff advisor was appointed by the superintendent.[15]

At the present time there is no formal council at the Loysville Center. A weekly meeting is held in each group living unit, composed of 16 students and staff, to discuss unit problems and happenings of the week, and to make plans for future leisure time activities. Various committees composed of peer-elected students from each living unit meet with staff to provide input which the administration regards as helpful and as having an impact on the decision-making process in areas affecting the on-going climate of the facility, e.g., the Food Committee which meets monthly, and the Clothing Committee which meets annually.[16]

The 28-bed North Central Secure Treatment Unit, Danville, an annex of the Youth Development Center, Loysville, does not have a student council. However, the same general philosophy is employed to enable students to have an impact upon the decision-making process.[17]

The South East Secure Treatment Unit, Embreeville, also an annex of the Youth Development Center, Loysville, employs a high degree of student participation. During the past year, a student council representative position was established. The students select a student representative, and an alternate, to act as an advocate in disciplinary hearings and to present student concerns in staff meetings. In disciplinary hearings, the advocate has a role in determining the discipline and the amount of point fines to be assessed under the token economy system.[18]

The Youth Development Center, Waynesburg, opened in 1960 and replaced in 1969, was originally for girls only. A Girls' Council of six members was established in December, 1961. In June, 1966, a Junior Council of four girls was formed as a source from which to fill vacancies occurring on the Girls' Council. The fact that many girls sought Council status for the prestige and privileges involved was the main reason for creation of the junior group. The Girls' Council met regularly with the superintendent and was directly responsible to her. In addition to planning special activities, discussions were held on the behavior of particular girls which might be detrimental to the others.[19]

Council members were chosen on the basis of good adjustment, sense of responsibility, and a demonstrated ability to work toward realistic goals. Each was expected to set a good example. A Council girl decided for herself whether or not to share her observations of the behavior of others for the protection of all. The staff believed the Girls' Council had a definite and significant place in the program of the Center, and cited two reasons for its successful operation: members receive added privileges, which serves as an incentive to good behavior in order to attain membership; and members are not required to report on the behavior of others, which enables them to retain their peer group status.

The aid of the Girls' Council might be sought in situations where the administration is concerned about a potential absconder, in which instance the Council girls may volunteer to talk with the girl or keep her under surveillance; and in the case of a girl's illness, in which two members might be asked to sit with her until medical help becomes available.

The Center became co-educational in 1978. The administration encourages participatory management which has included the involvement of students. It is believed that this has increased student identification with the goals of the facility, which has resulted in the enhancement of service quality.[20]

Each of the six cottages, including a secure unit, has a daily maintenance group in which all students are directly involved in the formation of rules and regulations. Additionally, there are three committees whose policies are based on student participation.

Members of the Steering Committee of the Narcotics Anonymous Group are selected by their peers after consultation with the staff advisor, a certified drug/alcohol-abuse therapist. The group, initiated, organized and operated almost entirely by students, plans educational and entertainment movies for its members and arranges symposiums in which professionals in the field of chemical substance abuse are invited to make special topic presentations.

The group drafted its own by-laws and assumed full responsibility for conducting its meetings. In January, 1983, the group was granted a charter recognizing it as a chapter of the national organization.

A Student Recreation Advisory Council composed of elected representatives of each cottage meets monthly with the recreation director to provide input into the assessment and development of recreational programs.

A Sex Education Committee operates primarily on the same premise as the Narcotics Anonymous Steering Committee. Members are directly responsible for the operation of the group, which meets weekly, with the cooperation and guidance of a staff advisor.

A Student Advisory Board was initiated on May 9, 1977 at the Youth Development Center, New Castle. Each cottage elects a representative and an alternate. A president and vice-president are elected within the membership. The group meets each month with a staff coordinator. Since its inception, the group has provided input into all program areas, e.g., dietary, volunteer resources, tours, and the purchase of student clothing. Short stay, large turnover of students, and the attitude of some personnel that students should have no input into programs or operations have created problems in the functioning of the group.[21]

A student serves on the Canteen Committee with full voting rights as to the operation of the canteen and allocation of its revenues for various programs. Students have also served on other major committees, e.g., the Open House Committee, various recreational committees, and a committee responsible for selecting movies. At the cottage and unit level, students are currently involved in unit beautification and recreation committees. Students also officiate intramural basketball games.

At Youth Forestry Camp No. 1, Hookstown, a Campers Activities Council was formed in May, 1966, to plan and coordinate social and recreation activities for the 51 students. Members of the Council met with similar groups from other institutions regarding such joint activities as dancing, dinners, and outings. The superintendent believed that the Council provided a positive experience which could be the basis for inculcating feelings of trust and responsibility. It was planned to utilize the Council concept in other areas of the camp life program as staff became more skillful in its administration.[22] The Student Council process faded out because the students were generally more interested in using their leisure time for activities other than meetings concerned with student activities. Subsequently, ad hoc committees have been appointed as needed to make decisions regarding campus and off-campus monthly activities, selection of clothing purchases, food selection, discipline policies and procedures, and movie selection. The administration believes the ad hoc committee process is an improvement over the campus council because more students can be involved in matters of special interest.[23]

Youth Forestry Camp No. 2, White Haven (Hickory Run State Park), organized a Camper's Committee in March, 1958, when a poor climate of staff-camper relationships made the need for a participating group apparent. This group was reported as being successful in promoting the achievement of common goals. As with most organizations, it fluctuated in its effectiveness among the 50 boys. Its value was summed up in the superintendent's observation that the most turbulent moments of the camp occurred during the times the Camper's Committee was at its weakest.[24] The Camper's Committee is still in existence, being regarded by the administration as an integral part of both the treatment and operational aspects of the overall program. The most important function of the group is to ascertain both complaints and innovative ideas from the constituency of each member. Such feedback is presented for staff review, from which program and operational changes may be made. Members have provided support and advice to problem students, under staff guidance, when it was believed that such students would respond more positively to peer influence, particularly those peers holding a position of leadership status. Committee members are also active participants in food selection meetings and assisting in directing other students in clean-up activities.[25]

In October, 1966, it was reported that ad hoc committees concerned with craft and recreational programs for the twenty boys were utilized at Youth Forestry Camp No. 3, James Creek (former address: Aitch). A rapid turnover of population was given as the principal reason for preferring that arrangement to a permanent council.[26]

In 1974, a Student Advisory Council was developed at Youth Forestry Camp No. 3 as part of the social studies activity, with the instructor as group advisor. Representatives are elected by the classroom groups and projects to serve a two-month term of office. Qualifications for office are: a minimum of 42 days already served at the camp, and good academic standing. Elected representatives are provided a two-week period of orientation prior to assuming office. The council meets weekly with the administration to consider an agenda of items suggested during the twice-a-week meetings each representative must hold with his constituents and approved for listing at the weekly meeting of the council members. Removal from office is provided for consistently negative behavior, attempting to use council membership as a position of power from which to harm other students, compiling more than ten hours of discipline, fighting, using or smuggling drugs, AWOL, and missing a council meeting without a valid excuse.[27]

Having served on the council for more than 25 days entitles a member to an extra hour of home pass and to off-campus walks of 30 minutes duration, either alone or with another committee member.

While there is no student council at the Weaversville Intensive Treatment Unit, Northampton, there are informal, non-structured methods which provide for student input and participation, principally through discussion groups. The internal grievance procedure previously described also provides a means of expression.[28]

Notes

1. Letter from Kenneth G. Robinson, Press Secretary, Bureau of Correction, Camp Hill, May 11, 1983.
2. "Inmate Complaint Review System," Bureau of Correction, Camp Hill, March 2, 1976; Dillingham, David D., and Singer, Linda R., op. cit., p. 54.
3. Administrative Directive 804, "Consolidated Inmate Grievance Review System," Bureau of Correction, January 10, 1983.
4. Letter from Kenneth G. Robinson, op. cit.
5. Baker, J. E., op. cit., p. 171.
6. Letter from Kenneth G. Robinson, op. cit.
7. Telephone conversation with Carl J. DiVincenzo, Asst. Director, Bureau of Group Residential Services, Harrisburg, August 11, 1983.
8. Letter from Ray T. Coffman, Jr., Director of Education, Youth Forestry Camp No. 3, James Creek, to Carl J. DiVincenzo, March 24, 1983.
9. Monograph "Response to Request for Information on Student Involvement in YDC/YFC Administration," Joseph I. Abraham, Caseworker, and Thomas P. McArdle, Manager, Rehabilitation Services, Weaversville Intensive Treatment Unit, Weaversville, April 20, 1983.
10. Baker, J. E., op. cit., pp. 171-172.
11. Ibid., p. 172.
12. Ibid., p. 172.
13. Ibid., pp. 172-173.
14. Memorandum from Tommy L. Head, Supervisor of Clinical Services, Youth Development Center, Bensalem, to Carl J. DiVincenzo, April 4, 1983.
15. Baker, J. E., op. cit., p. 172.
16. Memorandum from John R. Williams, Director, Residential Services, Youth Development Center, Loysville, to Robert V. Dieck, Director, Office of Field Operations, Bureau of Group Residential Services, Harrisburg, March 25, 1983.
17. Ibid.; Memorandum from Thomas R. Jenkins, Director, North Central Secure Treatment Unit, Danville, to Carl J. DiVincenzo, March 28, 1983.
18. Memorandum from Fred D. McNeal, South East Secure Treatment Unit, Embreeville, to Carl J. DiVincenzo, April 6, 1983.
19. Baker, J. E., op. cit., p. 173.
20. Statement re Student Involvement in the Administration of the Youth Development Center, Waynesburg, April 6, 1983.
21. Memorandum from Robert D. Waddington, ACSW, Director, Youth Development Center, New Castle, to Carl J. DiVincenzo, April 5, 1983; Manual, Code 130, "Student Advisory Board," May 9, 1977 (revised April 14, 1980).

22. Baker, J. E., op. cit., pp. 173-174.
23. Memorandum from Richard W. Coles, Director, Youth Forestry Camp No. 1, Hookstown, to Carl J. DiVincenzo, March 21, 1983.
24. Baker, J. E., op. cit., p. 174.
25. Monograph "Student Involvement in YDC/YFC Administration," Paul H. Gavala, Youth Development Counselor II, Youth Forestry Camp No. 2, White Haven, April 1, 1983.
26. Baker, J. E., op. cit.
27. Letter from Ray J. Coffman, Jr., Director of Education, Youth Forestry Camp No. 3, James Creek, to Carl J. DiVincenzo, op. cit.
28. Monograph "Response to Request for Information on Student Involvement in YDC/YFC Administration," Joseph I. Abraham, Caseworker, and Thomas P. McArdle, Manager, Rehabilitation Services, op. cit.

RHODE ISLAND

Department of Corrections

The Department of Corrections administers seven facilities for adult and youthful sentenced felony offenders and pretrial detainees.

A multi-level grievance procedure was established on January 8, 1980. It is in operation at all facilities. Within three days following an incident and/or actual knowledge of the origination of a problem, any inmate, sentenced or awaiting trial, who is directly affected may prepare a written grievance on a prescribed form, and file it with the Grievance Coordinator. An investigation will be made to determine the validity of the grievance. The Coordinator may review any files, interview any persons who may be able to furnish pertinent or relative information, and make conclusions based on the findings within five working days, exclusive of weekends and holidays. If the complaint is against a specific staff member, a representative of the Rhode Island Brotherhood of Correctional Officers will be immediately notified for assistance in the investigation. The grievance, with the investigation report, is submitted to the Associate Director of the institution who must respond in writing within ten working days.[1]

Within three working days an appeal may be made to the Deputy Assistant Director for Adult Services, who is required to make a written response within ten working days after investigating the issue.[2]

If dissatisfied with the decision of the Deputy Assistant Director, the grievant may, within three working days, appeal to the Assistant Director for Adult Services. An investigation is again conducted in which, if possible, the grievant will be personally interviewed.

In any event, a written decision must be made within ten working days.[3]

Should the grievant be not yet satisfied, a final appeal may be made within three working days to the Director, Department of Corrections. A review based on all previous decisions and any collateral information that may be obtained will be made by the Director, and a written response issued within 20 working days.[4]

Decisions not grievable are those made by qualified medical personnel regarding an inmate's health, and unlawful acts committed by an inmate. A disciplinary appeal process exists for considering grievances of Disciplinary Board decisions. Unless an inmate demonstrates a pattern of abuse of the grievance procedure by making clearly frivolous or repetitious complaints, punishment or disciplinary actions will not result from filing a complaint.[5]

Since department policy is to deal with inmate grievances on an individual basis, via the multi-level procedure, no inmate advisory councils are allowed.[6] Information was received in 1966 that no councils had been established in the adult institutions.[7]

Division of Institutional Services

The Division of Institutional Services, Department for Children and Their Families, is responsible for the Rhode Island Training School for Youth, a co-ed facility at Cranston. Until January 1, 1980, the Division of Youth Services of the Department of Corrections had this responsibility.

A tri-level Resident Grievance Procedure was established on July 1, 1979, to provide residents with a means to express dissatisfaction with any matter, excepting disciplinary board actions, regarding the substance or application of any written or unwritten policy, rule, or regulation of the Division or any decision, behavior, or action by an employee, agent, or contractor, or by other persons committed to the Division. Staff are enjoined from acts of retaliation against residents for having used the procedure and from discouraging or inhibiting attempts to do so.[8]

Within five working days of an alleged incident or event, a resident may file a grievance form with the Unit Grievance Chairperson who has been elected to that post by the housing unit population. The Chairperson must attempt, within 48 hours, to resolve the issue through discussions with the Unit Manager and/or other appropriate staff. The grievant may be present during any discussion. Lacking a resolution to the satisfaction of the grievant, an appeal may be made to the Grievance Committee.[9]

The Grievance Committee consists of five six-month term members: two residents, two staff members, and a non-voting chairperson. Staff members are nominated by staff and resident members by residents, each with an alternate, from which pool members are randomly selected as needed. The committee chairperson is selected by the Deputy Assistant Director, Division of Institutional Services. Upon receiving an appeal, the committee must hold within five working days a hearing which the grievant and the Unit Grievance Chairperson may attend. Following a hearing, the committee makes a written recommendation, within three working days, to the Deputy Assistant Director. In turn, that official must make written response within a like time frame. Should that response contest the committee recommendation or if the grievant is not satisfied, a referral for outside review ensues.[10]

Outside Reviewers are named, as needed, by the Division Director on the basis of recommendations and reputations as decision makers and community leaders. A Reviewer must conduct a hearing within ten working days and make a written recommendation during the following two weeks to the Assistant Director, who then has three working days to send a written notification to the committee and the grievant, setting forth what action will be taken. The Assistant Director will adopt the decision of the Outside Reviewer unless it is in violation of law, would result in physical danger to any persons, would require expenditure of funds not reasonably available, or, in the Assistant Director's judgment, would be detrimental to the public or to the proper and effective accomplishment of Division duties.[11]

The Division of Institutional Services does not feel the need for an inmate advisory council because of the grievance procedure, which is described as being very active.[12] Previously, information had been received that no councils had ever been established.[13]

Notes

1. "Procedure for the Filing and Disposition of Inmate Grievances," Administrative Policy Statement No. 1.20.01, January 7, 1980, Department of Corrections, Cranston.
2. Ibid.
3. Ibid.
4. Ibid.
5. Ibid.
6. Letter from Anthony Ventetuolo, Jr., Assistant to the Director, Dept. of Corrections, Cranston, September 20, 1982.
7. Baker, J. E., op. cit., p. 174.
8. "Resident Grievance Procedure," Policy Statement No. 831, July 1, 1979, Residential Facilities, Youth Services Division, Dept. of Corrections, Cranston.
9. Ibid.
10. Ibid.
11. Ibid.
12. Letter from Michael Morello, Ed.D., Assistant Director, Division of Institutional Services, Dept. for Children and Their Families, September 20, 1982.
13. Baker, J. E., op. cit., p. 174.

SOUTH CAROLINA

Department of Corrections

The Department of Corrections administers 27 institutions for adult and youthful felony offenders and misdemeanants.

An Ombudsman Office was established in August, 1972, to serve all inmates in Department of Corrections institutions. To initiate a complaint, an inmate usually requests an interview with the Ombudsman, although the latter may initiate an investigation of problems. All complaints, whether about individuals' problems or policies and procedures of the Department, are within the Ombudsman's jurisdiction. After investigating a complaint, the Ombudsman makes recommendations to the proper Department officials. If the action taken is inadequate, the Ombudsman makes a recommendation to the Department Director.[1]

In 1976, the Department of Corrections began planning for the establishment of a multi-level inmate grievance procedure by providing that 20 middle managers attend a week-long seminar in dispute resolution and mediation. The seminar prepared the personnel to participate in future development of mechanisms in the state. The Kirkland Correctional Institution, Columbia, a medium-security institution opened in 1975, was chosen as the site for a pilot procedure. In August, 1977, the procedure commenced operation in only two of the seven dormitories, and expanded to the remaining five dormitories following a favorable evaluation after 90 days of operation. The procedure was begun at the Women's Correctional Center in November, 1977,[2] and currently is in operation at some, but not all, of the department institutions.[3]

Under the Procedure, an inmate complainant goes first to an inmate clerk who attempts to work out an informal resolution, then to a hearing before a committee composed of staff and inmates. Appeals can be made to the warden, the Commissioner of the Department, and finally, to a private group independent of the department. The independent review is not binding; the Commissioner makes the final decision. Time limits exist at each level of review. All responses are written.[4]

The following information, received from the Director, Department of Corrections regarding inmate advisory councils in 1973, was referred for updating to the Department in 1982. The reply, which was principally addressed to the inmate grievance procedure and the Departmental Inmate Advisory Council, also stated: "For the sake of brevity, this paper will not recapitulate inmate representation information contained in the update request." The accounts are restated here as written in 1973.[5]

An Inmate Council was organized in March, 1968, at the Central Correctional Institution, Columbia. Constructive suggestions, as well as complaints, are brought to staff attention through the

Council, whose authority is limited to the making of recommendations. Sections established within the institution may each elect one representative and one alternate who, after final approval by the warden, serve a one-year term of office. Representatives may succeed themselves once. No prerequisites for membership have been established. The Council, meeting twice a month with the warden or his representative, has proven to be a useful method of communication and has provided the staff with constructive criticism. An example is the modification of the twice-daily count process. As a result of the interchange of views within the Council meeting framework, more efficient and mutually agreeable procedures were devised.

The Givens Youth Correction Center, Simpsonville, Inmate Council was organized in 1970. Its activities declined, however, and it was reorganized in February, 1972, with a membership of five elected to represent the dormitories. In July, 1971, an Inmate Council was organized at the Goodman Correctional Institution, Columbia. The warden, chief correctional supervisor, and all inmates attend the meetings.

Two members are elected from each of three housing areas as representatives to the Inmate Council formed in December, 1972, at the Maximum Security Center, Columbia. The Wateree River Correctional Institution, Rembert, Inmate Council was begun in August, 1970. Two representatives, one white and one black, are elected from each of the seven wards. Each ward elects its own representatives to the six-member Inmate Council, in existence since August, 1971, at the Manning Correctional Institution, Columbia.

The Inmate Council at the Harbison Correctional Institution for Women, Irmo, dates back to November 27, 1964. The membership of six is composed of three elected representatives from each of the residential buildings. (This institution is not listed on a July, 1982 organizational chart of the Department of Corrections.) A six-member Inmate Council selected from the wards was formed in January, 1971 at the Walden Correctional Institution, Columbia. An elected representative from each of the five dormitories is a member of the Inmate Council organized in July, 1971, at the MacDougall Youth Correction Center, Ridgeville.

A report of a 1974 site visit to the Central Correctional Institution, Columbia, to review the operation of grievance mechanisms, described the Inmate Advisory Council there:

> Twenty inmates are elected annually to represent living units. Each representative has an elected alternate. The departmental ombudsman attends every weekly meeting, the warden every other meeting.
>
> The Council meets every Friday morning. In meetings with the ombudsman alone, the Council discusses problems and decides which ones to present to the warden in the following week's 'open' meeting. The warden attempts to have a response to every request ready by the

time of the next 'open' meeting two weeks later. Once every quarter the Director attends an 'open' meeting. He also attempts to respond to all requests within two to three weeks.

Minutes are prepared of every open meeting and within a week to ten days are distributed to CCI inmates.

The Council restricts its efforts to problems of concern to larger numbers of inmates. Individual complaints are rejected.

A review of several copies of minutes suggests that anywhere from five to 15 problems are brought up in every open meeting. Some of these are repetitions of earlier issues not yet resolved.

Modification of dress regulations to allow inmates to wear their own colored shirts, and extended hours for use of the athletic field were cited as illustrative results of the Council program.[6]

The first meeting of the Departmental Inmate Advisory Council was held on November 14, 1974. Representation is provided on institutional, regional, and division bases. For administrative purposes, there are two correctional regions, Appalachian and Coastal, and two institutional operation divisions, Minimum Security and Medium /Maximum Security. Institutions that have a present emergency operating capacity of 500 or more have individual representation, but small institutions within a region are collectively represented by an at-large representative. Exceptions to this arrangement are the Women's Correctional Center, Columbia; the Midlands Reception and Evaluation Center, Columbia; and the Wateree River Correctional Institution, Rembert.[7]

A representative, and alternate, for each institution/region/ division is elected by a majority vote of the elected Inmate Advisory Councils. A nominee must have no less than six months remaining of his/her confinement term. From its membership the Council elects a chairman, vice-chairman, and a secretary. The chairman is empowered to appoint such committees as may be necessary to investigate particular matters and in order to accomplish the duties and responsibilities of the Council.

The purpose of the Council is to create and encourage a direct line of communication between inmates and Department of Corrections officials; to call attention to outstanding problems in order that solutions may be aggressively pursued; assist in the development of policies and procedures, and act as a conduit of grievances concerning Department policies and procedures for those institutions where formal grievance procedures do not exist.[8]

The Council meets formally each month, the meetings being held alternately at the Central Correctional Institution, Kirkland Correctional Institution, and Manning Correctional Institution, all located in Columbia. A quarterly meeting is held at Department headquarters with the Commissioner and senior staff members, to consider an agenda whose items were sent to the Commissioner two weeks prior. Basic rules of parliamentary procedure are observed. Minutes are kept of each meeting and are widely distributed. Minutes of the quarterly meeting held on August 31, 1982 reveal that fully responsive answers were provided by staff, and of the 15 issues presented, seven were approved outright, one was denied, and the remaining seven were to be explored and, if feasible, granted.

According to the department administration, the dual systems through which an inmate may voice concerns at any time, and through their representatives bring group concerns to the attention of top administrators, function very well. Additionally, inmates are comforted to know their concerns are heard, and upper management has an opportunity to acquire first hand information concerning conditions from an inmate point of view.[9]

Department of Youth Services

The Office of Institutional Programs, Department of Youth Services, administers four facilities for juvenile delinquents, including the William J. Goldsmith Reception and Evaluation Center, all located in Columbia.[10]

No grievance procedures exist other than the ombudsman, previously described, who responds to inquiries from students and their parents.[11]

Information received in 1972 mentioned an existing Student Advisory Committee at the John C. Richards School for Boys, Columbia, but contained no details of its organization and procedures.[12]

There are no department written policies regarding student councils at this time.[13]

Notes

1. Keating, McArthur, Lewis, Sebelius, and Singer, 1975, op. cit., p. 45.
2. "Prevention and Control of Conflict in Corrections," Final Report, April 5, 1979, LEAA Grant No. 77-ED-99-009, Center for Community Justice.
3. Information narrative received from Dept. of Corrections, Columbia, October 14, 1982.
4. Dillingham, David D., and Singer, Linda R., op. cit., pp. 66-67.
5. Baker, J. E., op. cit., pp. 175-176.
6. Keating, McArthur, Lewis, Sebelius, and Singer, 1975, op. cit., pp. 45-46.
7. Information narrative, op. cit.
8. By-laws, Departmental Inmate Advisory Council, Dept. of Corrections, Columbia, August 31, 1982 (revised). (The

by-laws were previously revised January 4, 1977, and February 28, 1978.)
9. Information narrative, op. cit.
10. Letter from Susan M. Durst, Executive Assistant, Dept. of Youth Services, Columbia, October 4, 1982.
11. Ibid.
12. Baker, J. E., op. cit., p. 176.
13. Letter from Susan M. Durst, op. cit.

SOUTH DAKOTA

Board of Charities and Corrections

The Board of Charities and Corrections administers five institutions for adult and youthful felony offenders and juvenile misdemeanants.

A Client Grievance and Appeals Procedure was established in 1977.[1] A grievance is defined as a written complaint or recommendation about the substance or application of any written or unwritten policy procedure, rule, or regulation of the Board of Charities and Corrections or any of its institutions, or the lack of same, and any behavior or action directed toward a client. Grievances may not be filed on any issue for which an existing appeal mechanism is available, e.g., classification and disciplinary actions, or actions of agencies not under the jurisdiction of the Board.[2]

If a client cannot obtain a satisfactory decision or action after discussion of a grievance with staff, a written grievance may be made to the immediate professional staff member primarily responsible for his/her day-to-day program and treatment services, within 14 days after the grieved action or incident. That person has 14 days to render a decision and offer a written solution.

If not satisfied, the grievant may, in the next ten days, appeal to the institutional grievance committee which consists of at least three staff members appointed by the institution head. Within ten days, the committee chairman may take either of two actions: submit the grievance to the committee for action without a hearing and provide a written explanation to both the client and the institution head, or schedule a hearing date no later than 20 days following receipt of the appeal; the client must be advised of the date at least 48 hours prior to the hearing. If deemed necessary, the chairperson may appoint an investigator to assist in ascertaining the validity of the grievance.

At the hearing, the client may call witnesses, as may the chairperson, and introduce relevant documentary evidence. Although the committee hearing is not presumed to be a court of law, a client may, at personal expense, be represented by legal counsel. Within ten days, the committee must submit a written decision. Should the remedy or resolution be accepted by the client, it is to be initiated as quickly as time and resource constraints allow.

Appeal of the committee decision may be made in the following five days to the institution head, who will conduct an impartial investigation and make a written response within seven days. The final level of review is the Board of Charities and Corrections, to which an appeal may be made, via the Executive Director, no later than ten days subsequent to the decision of the institution head.

A grievance believed to be of an emergency nature may be reported orally or in writing to the grievance committee chairperson. If the chairperson determines that routine processing would obviously result in serious harm to the grievant or constitute a threat to the safety or security of the institution, the issue will be immediately presented to the institution head, or designee, for expeditious handling.

Time limitations for responses at any level of review may be extended upon the written mutual agreement of the institution head and the grievant. However, failure of a client to comply with time limits constitutes an automatic withdrawal of the grievance. Failure of staff to respond within the time limits is tantamount to a waiver of the option to review the grievance, freeing the client to pursue the next step. Failure of the Board of Charities and Corrections to comply with the time limits is considered to be a settlement in the client's favor only if there is a reasonable relationship between the grievance and the requested remedy.

Acceptable forms of relief may include, but are not limited to: monetary award, restitution of property, program reassignment, correction of institutional records, personnel actions, a change in institutional policy or practice, or agreement by staff to remedy an objectionable condition within a reasonably specific period of time. No formal or informal adverse action, or threat thereof, may be taken against a client for having invoked or participated in the grievance procedure.

In December, 1972, it was reported there was no inmate advisory council at the South Dakota Penitentiary, Sioux Falls. However, approximately five or six years previously, a Jaycees Chapter had been organized and was regarded as a good medium of communication, supplementing almost daily contacts with the population by the administration.[3]

A 1980 survey reported the existence of an inmate council at the Women's Correctional Facility, Yankton, but gave no particulars of its operations.[4]

In November, 1966, a Student Council at the South Dakota Training School, Plankinton, functioned principally in the areas of planning recreational activities and the conducting of tours. By December, 1972, Guided Group Interaction was the treatment technique in use, the administration believing that such a method of involving students in their own treatment provided them with more possibilities to participate in the formulation of rules and procedures.[5]

Also in December, 1972, the Nils A. Boe Youth Forestry Camp, Custer, then known as the Youth Forestry Camp, established in 1967, reported that while there was no council, participation was required in peer groups of four to seven campers from which recommendations could be made through a counselor regarding camp procedures.[6]

There are no councils at any of the South Dakota institutions at this time. The current administration, while recognizing that client participation does work reasonably well in other state correctional systems, does not believe that correctional clients should be involved in administrative issues, e.g., policies and procedures, grievance resolution, and treatment decisions.[7]

Notes

1. Dillingham, David D., and Singer, Linda R., op. cit., p. 55.
2. "Client Grievance and Appeals Procedure," Board of Charities and Corrections, Pierre, South Dakota.
3. Baker, J. E., op. cit., p. 176.
4. Neto, Virginia V., and Bainer, LaNelle Marie, op. cit., p. 111.
5. Baker, J. E., op. cit., p. 176.
6. Ibid.
7. Letter from Brian L. Wallin, Deputy Director, Board of Charities and Corrections, Pierre, May 9, 1983.

TENNESSEE

Department of Correction

The Department of Correction has jurisdiction over all facilities for adult and youthful felony offenders, misdemeanor offenders, and juvenile delinquents.

Adult Services

The Adult Services administers 11 institutions for adult and youthful felony offenders.

According to a 1980 report, a grievance procedure was established in 1976 which required responses in writing within specified time limits, with the Director of Corrections as the final level of review.[1]

Any complaint can be made on any issue within seven days

following the occurrence on which it is based, except disciplinary decisions, inmate pay, decisions or actions of the Board of Paroles or any agency outside the Department of Correction, and classification decisions, e.g., institutional placement and security designation. Complaints regarding continuing practices or policies must be filed within one week following their effect on the individual.[2]

Each complaint, prepared on a prescribed form, is given to an inmate clerk, appointed by the warden to serve a term of one year, subject to reappointment. The chairperson of the grievance committee attempts resolution by contacting persons concerned, and through any investigation believed to be necessary. An appeal may be made within five days to the grievance committee which will hear presentations by the grievant and his/her advocate, another inmate. A written decision must be made no later than five days following the hearing.

The next level of appeal, within five days, is the institution warden, who will respond in writing in ten days. The final level of review is the Department Commissioner, who may either hear the case or appoint a designee/committee to conduct a review and make recommendations. A response at this level is required within 20 days, and is final.

The chairperson of the grievance committee, appointed by the warden to a nine-month term, subject to reappointment, is a non-voting member whose function is to facilitate group consensus.

If the institution population is more than 200, the grievance committee will have four members (two staff and two inmates) other than the chairperson; otherwise there are two additional members (one staff and one inmate).

Staff committee members are elected to six-month terms by the inmates from a list of nominees submitted by the administrative staff. The same procedure obtains in the selection of the inmate members who are selected by the administrative staff from a list of nominees prepared by the inmates.

Provision is made for the accelerated processing of a grievance judged by the chairperson to be an emergency situation in which the ordinary time factor of the grievance procedure could thwart the meaningful resolution of the grievance. Emergencies are reviewed by the warden, whose decision is appealable to the Commissioner.

Grievances must be responded to within the prescribed time limits unless the grievant agrees, in writing, to an extension.

As part of a settlement between the Department of Corrections and a group of inmates who, on April 7, 1975, held hostages for nine hours until officials agreed to consider their list of grievances, a Review Board was established at the Tennessee State Prison, Nashville. Two inmates were elected to the Board by their peers. Twelve other members were appointed, representing the penitentiary, the Federal Prison System, higher education, ex-offenders, state government, the medical profession, and private attorneys. The Commissioner, Department of Corrections, was the chairman.[3]

The establishment of inmate councils at all adult institutions was mandated in January, 1982. Council members are elected by simple majority vote of the inmates, except those representing the Hospital Housing Unit who are appointed by medical personnel, as are those representing units housing punitive and/or administratively segregated inmates. Term of office for all council members in six months, subject to one consecutive term. The council meets once a month with the warden, or associate warden/captain. Minutes of each meeting are distributed to the warden and associate warden. Regulations specify that an inmate council shall not be involved in the inmate grievance procedure. Council discussions, recomendations, and proposals have no binding effect on the operation of the institution.[4]

Guidelines on the establishment of other inmate organizations are provided in a policy statement issued on January 1, 1982. Inmates wishing to form an organization are required to submit organizational by-laws for approval by the warden. All approved organizations are supervised by a staff coordinator. Membership cannot be denied on the basis of race, religion or creed. Ideally, membership size should be no more than ten per cent of the inmate population. Regular programs and special activities are subject to administration approval. All organizational funds must be maintained and monitored by the warden or the associate warden for administration. Suspension of an organization may be ordered by the warden should the group fail to observe its own by-laws or institution policies and procedures, or for inappropriate conduct or poor attendance.[5]

In 1973, it was reported that a program designed to provide residents with a large measure of responsibility for their personal behavior had been established in a housing unit at the Tennessee State Penitentiary, Nashville. A resident who had maintained a clear conduct record in the general population for 12 months, been employed in his present position for a minimum of six months and earning incentive time credits in the immediate past three grading periods, and whose work supervisor was of the opinion that he could function in a minimum supervision situation, could be referred to a three-member staff selection board representing treatment, security, and industry. If approved by that group, the resident could then be assigned to the special unit where he would continue to reside as long as he continued to earn incentive time credits. Other than a requirement to be present in his cell at the nine p.m. daily count, a resident had the freedom of the unit. While present in the unit he had possession of the key to his cell. He was responsible for the cleaning of his cell, and could be selected by the staff in charge for other clean-up assignments. A Rules Committee, selected by the residents, submitted suggestions on governing the unit for consideration by the administration.

In August, 1973, a Self-Government Group, organized about three years before at the Tennessee Prison for Women, Nashville, was composed of residents who had been rated as above average in work or training in the dormitory. The Group reviewed all applications for membership, referring acceptances to a staff committee for final approval. Members were given additional privileges. They were allowed to have their own food, keep later hours, and visit in each other's rooms. The Group also disciplined its members if rules were broken. Additionally, members operated a snack bar on weekends, assisted in the orientation of new admissions to the institution, and engaged in community projects such as visiting nursing homes and sending Christmas baskets to needy families.

For an unspecified period of time between February and September, 1960, there was an elected inmate committee at the Brushy Mountain Penitentiary, Petros. However, the members used their position for personal gain and some members became agitators. The organization was permitted to expire of its own accord.[6]

A 1980 study listed an established council only at the Turner Center for Youthful Offenders, but no details of its operations were given.[7]

Youth Services

The Youth Services administers five facilities for youthful felony and misdemeanor offenders and juvenile delinquents.

A Student Grievance Procedure was established in 1979 at the Highland Rim School for Girls, Tullahoma. A grievance may be filed regarding policies, procedures, disciplinary decisions, and actions of staff or other students. Written responses within specified time limits are required at each of the four levels of the procedure, which are: the institution director, a grievance committee, the assistant commissioner, Youth Services, and the Commissioner, Department of Correction. The grievance committee includes student members. A grievance procedure is being developed at the remaining four facilities.[8]

In July, 1973, it was reported that each of the five facilities had or was organizing a student council to serve as an advisory group. Generally the councils were composed of one or more representatives from each dormitory and a president elected at large, and held weekly meetings.[9]

Information was received in 1966 and 1967 that a Student Council was in operation at the Tennessee Youth Center, Joelton. Organized in 1965, just three years after the Center opened, the Council was composed of one representative from each vocational course. Members were selected by the students and held weekly meetings with a staff advisor at which criticisms of program and suggestions for modification were made. The president of the Council, a student elected by the membership with no staff involvement, was a member of the staff discipline committee which also included two vocational instructors and the academic school principal. This student member had freedom of expression regarding the situation of any disciplinary case and usually entered into all discussions. He could offer any suggestion for disposition and staff often acceded.[10]

Currently, there are no student councils.[11]

Notes

1. Dillingham, David D., and Singer, Linda R., op. cit., p. 55.
2. "Inmate Grievances," Administrative Policies and Procedures, Index No. 501.01, Dept. of Correction, Nashville, January 1, 1982.
3. Corrections Digest, Annandale, Virginia, May 28, 1975, p. 7.
4. "Inmate Councils," Administrative Policies and Procedures, Index No. 503.04, Dept. of Correction, Nashville, January 1, 1982.
5. "Inmate Organizations," Administrative Policies and Procedures, Index No. 503.01, Dept. of Correction, Nashville, January 1, 1982.
6. Baker, J. E., op. cit., pp. 177-178.
7. Neto, Virginia V., and Bainer, LaNelle Marie, op. cit., p. 111.
8. Telephone conversation with Sheryl Bransford, Executive Aide, Division of Youth Services, Nashville, May 6, 1983.
9. Baker, J. E., op. cit., p. 178.
10. Ibid.
11. Telephone conversation with Sheryl Bransford, op. cit.

TEXAS

Department of Corrections

The Department of Corrections administers 22 institutions for adult and youthful felony offenders.[1]

Under a grievance procedure established July 14, 1975, applicable to all institutions, an inmate who cannot resolve a complaint with staff may complete and forward to the warden a grievance form. Ordinarily, the filing must occur within 30 days from the date on which the complaint occurred, unless it is not feasible to do so in that period. The warden must respond in writing within 15 working days. A complaint of an emergency nature which poses a threat to the inmate's immediate health and welfare must be answered as soon as possible.[2]

If dissatisfied with the warden's response, the grievant may appeal, within 30 days, to the Director, Department of Corrections, who will make a written reply within 30 working days. If still not satisfied, the grievant is free to file suit in an appropriate court, including documentary proof that the administrative remedy has been fully pursued.[3]

There is no mention in the directive establishing the procedure of any issue as being excluded. If a complaint is of a sensitive nature and the grievant believes he/she would be adversely affected should it be known at the institution, the complaint may be sent to the Department Director, who will rule on it and respond within 30 working days. Inmates are assured no disciplinary or punitive action will result from use of the procedure, unless statements made are proven false.[4]

Inmate councils are not utilized in any of the institutions.[5]

Texas Youth Council

The Texas Youth Council administers all facilities for committed juvenile delinquents. The Council has 14 Community Advisory Councils, which serve every facility; they are composed of about two dozen knowledgeable persons local to each community in which a program is operated.[6]

A Student Grievance and Appeals System was established about February, 1976, to assure students that a process operates to resolve problems affecting their health, safety, and welfare. Through the process, the Texas Youth Council assumes some measure of accountability to its students. A grievance may be filed about placement decisions, allegations of mistreatment, problems with other students, problems with staff, and problems with rules, programs, policies and procedures. The grievance is sent to those persons who can provide the quickest and surest resolution to the problem; e.g., placement problems to the Executive Director, Texas Youth Council; mistreatment allegations to the superintendent of the facility; and other problems to the facility staff or staff/student committees.

All resolutions of grievances may be appealed to the Executive Director level.[7]

A student's complaint alleging abuse or neglect, whether made orally or in writing, must be reported promptly to the superintendent who, within 24 hours, is required to notify the Office of Youth Care Investigation. The superintendent must also appoint a staff member to investigate the complaint, unless the superintendent requests the legal department to conduct the investigation, or the latter assumes the investigation at the direction of the Executive Director (or assistant) or on its own motion. When neither of the conditions arise, the staff investigator makes a report of findings to the superintendent within seven working days, or ten days if the superintendent approves an extension of time because of unusual circumstances of the situation. The superintendent has three days to take any corrective action needed and to notify the student of the right to appeal to the Executive Director. When the complaint alleges a serious violation of the criminal law, the local District Attorney is notified.[8]

To file a complaint on any issue other than mistreatment, a student completes a prescribed form and gives it to one of the student grievance clerks or alternates who have been elected by their peers. The grievance is then given to a superintendent-appointed grievance coordinator who will determine to whom it should be referred. Placement complaints are forwarded to the Executive Director, following a discussion between the grievant and a caseworker.[9]

Each institution selects an equal number of staff and students to serve on a Staff/Student Grievance Committee. The grievance coordinator selects the members and serves as a non-voting moderator. The committee is the second level of the procedure for grievances concerning a rule, policy or program. The process differs somewhat depending on whether the grievance involves a student problem or a staff problem, but in all situations the right to appeal is provided.[10]

Appeals to the Executive Director require that specified documentation be furnished by the institution staff, e.g., the names of persons who made the decision being appealed, a statement of the evidence relied on, and reasons for the decision. Usually the appeal is given to the Assistant Executive Director for Child Care, whose staff will conduct any necessary research and draft a proposed decision within ten days. An Appeals Committee comprised of the Executive Assistant for Child Care, the Director of Hearings, and either the Director of Institutions or Director of Community Services as appropriate will informally review all appeals decisions to determine the appropriateness or consequences of such decisions. If an appeal raises questions about or consequences for Texas Youth Council programs, policy or procedures, the Appeals Committee may meet for a formal review of the issue and submit findings to the Executive Director. Should a student or his/her representative or attorney request oral arguments on the appeal, the Appeals Committee will convene for that purpose.[11]

At each facility there is a student council composed of one representative from each cottage elected democratically. The council meets monthly, or more frequently if required, with the superintendent or his appointee. The purpose of the council is to provide for student input to staff on current student issues, institution policy affecting the student body, and to develop special student projects.[12]

Notes

1. Letter from Terry Wunderlich, Management Services, Dept. of Corrections, November 30, 1982.
2. "Administrative Remedy of Complaints Initiated by Inmates of the Texas Department of Corrections, effective date: July 14, 1975.

3. Ibid.
4. Ibid.
5. Letter from Terry Wunderlich, op. cit.
6. Letter from Joan Timmons, Information Specialist, Texas Youth Council, Austin, March 29, 1983.
7. "Student Grievance and Appeals System, General Information," 90.45.010, Texas Youth Council General Operating Policies and Procedures Manual, February 1983.
8. "Student Grievance and Appeals System, Suspected Mistreatment, 90.45.020, Texas Youth Council General Operating Policies and Procedures, February 1983.
9. "Student Grievance and Appeals System, Grievance Procedures," 50.45.010, Texas Youth Council Institutions Manual, February 1983.
10. Ibid.
11. "Student Remedies, Appeal to the Executive Director," 90.45.05[illegible] Texas Youth Council General Operating Policies and Procedures, March 1980.
12. "Student Council," S 89.313-.133, Texas Youth Council Official Rules Manual.

UTAH

Division of Corrections

The Division of Corrections, Department of Social Services, administers the Utah State Prison, six community centers, and a diagnostic unit for adult and youthful felony offenders. The institution is comprised of five facilities (units) administered by a Program Director directly responsible to the warden: Women's Facility, Maximum Security Facility, Medium Security Facility, Minimum Security Facility, and Special Services Facility.[1]

An Inmate Grievance Procedure was established at the Utah State Prison, Draper, in 1972. If an issue cannot be resolved informally through discussion with the staff primarily responsible for it, and with the social service worker, an inmate may file a written grievance, via a prescribed form, with the program director of the facility in which he or she is housed. There are no time limits for such filing. In the ensuing ten working days the program director will personally investigate the complaint, or assign a staff member or any standing prison committee to do so, and give written notification of the decision made and the reasons therefor.[2]

If the grievant is dissatisfied with the decision of the program director, an appeal may be made within five days to the warden. After a personal or delegated investigation by a staff member or a standing committee, the warden will reach a decision and transmit it in writing, including its rationale, to the grievant. The warden has ten working days to make a response.

In the following ten working days, the grievant may appeal to the final level of review, the Director, Division of Corrections. While no time limit is specified in which the Director must make a written response, the procedure does state that reasonable haste will be taken to investigate and resolve the issue.

The filing of repetitive complaints on the same set of circumstances is not permitted. A recommendation, at any level of the procedure, involving the expenditure of state funds is subject to final approval by the State Board of Examiners.

If the program director or warden fails to respond within the prescribed time limits, an appeal may be made to the next level of review without delay. Absent mitigating and extenuating circumstances, failure of a grievant to act within the time limits constitutes a withdrawal of the complaint.

The Community Corrections Centers have a separate, but similar, grievance procedure.[3]

In September, 1966, information was received that the first Inmate Advisory Council was organized in the main institution in October, 1957, and another later in the Minimum Security Facility which was regarded as being more effective. The opinion was expressed that a more pressurized situation existed among the types of inmates housed in the main institution, enabling the more aggressive and assaultive persons to gain election to office.

Under the provisions of a Constitution and By-Laws, each representative to the Inmate Advisory Council was required upon taking office to sign a pledge to "represent my constituents, and the inmate body as a whole, honorably and to the best of my ability ... observe all requirements of the Constitution and By-Laws, and ... refrain from engaging in personalities at the meetings. I will do nothing to embarrass the Council ... [and] will not abuse the privileges that go with membership...." Two members from each housing unit were elected by secret ballot to six-month terms of office. The Council selected a chairman and vice-chairman from the membership. The Secretary was chosen by the warden from a slate of three persons nominated by the Council. Robert's Rules of Order governed the conduct of the weekly unsupervised meetings and the monthly meeting with the warden.[4]

At the present time (1983), there is no Inmate Advisory Council. It was found by the administration that inmate lack of interest lessened the feasibility of the council. When there is a need on the part of either inmates or administration to discuss policy changes and problems, a meeting is held with inmates chosen by their peers. After discussion of issues, the inmate representatives attempt to develop a consensus among their constituents, which forms the basis for a later problem-resolution meeting. The administration has found this approach a more effective means of communication with inmates.[5]

Division of Youth Corrections

The Division of Youth Corrections administers the State Youth Development Center, Ogden. The facility was established in 1888 as the Territorial Reform School. In 1896, the name was changed to the Utah State Industrial School. Until circa 1977, the facility was co-educational. At that time the present designation was adopted.

Under a two-level institution grievance procedure a student may first lodge a complaint with his cottage administrator, whose decision may be appealed to the superintendent. Any complaint against a staff member is referred to the Ogden, Utah, city police.[6]

For approximately 30 years there has been a Student Council program. In the early years, the Council was operative only during the school year. Membership included a president, vice-president and secretary elected by the students, and representatives of each home room. In March, 1965, a Group Living Student Council was organized in addition to the school group. Since 1970, there has been a single Student Council program to accomplish the purposes of developing treatment programs appropriate to student needs through student-staff communication, and to provide Council members and the student body with a series of developmental educational and social experiences. The program is under the supervision of the assistant superintendent and the director of education. No criteria for Council membership have been established. Each cottage selects representatives by popular vote, and the leadership--president, vice-president, and secretary--is chosen by vote of the Council members.

Student Council members meet on occasion with the executive staff and the superintendent, and attend other meetings concerned with the management and the life style of students in residence. In December, 1972, a plan was under consideration to establish for the Student Council members a daily social science laboratory-type program designed to develop an understanding of the relationship between the regulations involved in the management of a Student Council and regulations at all levels of government. The administration strongly advocated the student council system in facilities for juvenile offenders, commenting that perhaps growth in social responsibility is one of the greatest gains to students as they participate in the management of others.[7]

The Student Council is still in operation. It is discontinued each year for a three-week academic school vacation.[8]

Notes

1. Information received via telephone from office of Administrative Assistant, Utah State Prison, Draper, August 11, 1983.
2. "Inmate Grievance Procedures," Utah State Prison, Draper; Dillingham, David D., and Singer, Linda R., op. cit., p. 55.

3. Information received via telephone, August 11, 1983, op. cit.
4. Baker, J. E., op. cit., p. 179.
5. Letter from Jim Gropp, Administrative Assistant, Utah State Prison, Draper, March 18, 1983.
6. Telephone conversation with Dick Scadde, Youth Development Center, Ogden, Utah, August 11, 1983.
7. Baker, J. E., op. cit., p. 180.
8. Telephone conversation with Dick Scadde, op. cit.

VERMONT

Department of Corrections

The Department of Corrections, Agency of Human Resources, administers six institutions for adult and youthful felony and misdemeanor offenders.

A Grievance Procedure was established in 1978 and revised in 1980 and again on February 26, 1982, to provide offenders with a formal channel to file written complaints concerning an incident, policy, or condition which affects them.[1]

If unable to resolve a problem by personal contact with staff, an inmate may submit a grievance via a prescribed form to the institution superintendent. The latter will assign a non-involved employee to investigate and make a report. Within the following two weeks the superintendent makes a written response which may be appealed in a week to the Commissioner, Department of Corrections.[2]

At the discretion of the Commissioner, evidentiary hearings may be conducted, witnesses and other parties interviewed, and records and documents examined. A copy of the Commissioner's written decision is sent to all concerned persons.

Any grievance may be held in abeyance at the institution or department level if the issue is being litigated in court, after coordination with the State Attorney General. The latter will notify the grievant of such action.

In instances of a confirmed emergency nature, e.g., health, personal tragedy, or financial crisis, the time constraints will be waived and a written response made to the grievant within 24 hours.

Any grievance filed against the institution superintendent is forwarded to the Department central office.

The Department disciplinary policy has a somewhat parallel method by which an offender may appeal actions generated by that process.[3]

In September, 1966, it was reported that an Inmate Council

was in operation several years previously for about one year at the Vermont State Prison and House of Correction for Men. In addition to becoming a "gimme" group, the Council began analyzing the situations of various inmates and demanding the right to correspond with social agencies to express views on the handling of social problems of certain individuals.[4]

In December, 1972, a Liaison Committee, composed of five residents elected by the population and the institution head, was in operation at the Windsor institution which had been renamed the State Correctional Facility.[5]

The last warden at the State Correctional Facility assumed office in August, 1974. An inmate-elected Liaison Committee was organized. (No information has been obtained regarding the fate of the committee reported as being in operation in 1972.) The group was allowed to exercise veto power over applications for a furlough program. Reportedly, a third of the population was released over Christmas (all returned). Inmates were made a part of the disciplinary process. Such initiatives, combined with the charisma of the warden, brought about "... a dramatic improvement in the emotional lives of nearly all inmates." The institution was closed in August, 1975.[6]

At present there are no inmate councils in the institutions and the development of such groups is not anticipated.[7]

Juvenile Services

Vermont has no state facility for juvenile delinquents. All juvenile delinquents are under the administration of the Director of Social Services, Department of Social and Rehabilitation Services, Agency of Human Services. Community placements are used for juveniles.

Notes

1. Letter from Dennis F. DeBevec, Research and Planning, Dept. of Corrections, Waterbury, May 27, 1983.
2. Policy and Operating Procedures, "Grievance Procedures" (953), Dept. of Corrections, February 26, 1982.
3. Letter from Dennis F. DeBevec, op. cit.
4. Baker, J. E., op. cit., p. 181.
5. Ibid.
6. Fried, William. "The Limits to Reform," The Prison Journal, The Pennsylvania Prison Society, Vol. LV, No. 2, Autumn-Winter, 1975, pp. 41-47.
7. Letter from Dennis F. DeBevec, op. cit.

VIRGINIA

Department of Corrections

The Department of Corrections has jurisdiction over all institutions for adult and youthful felony and misdemeanor offenders, and juvenile delinquents. Prior to 1978, all institutions were under the Department of Welfare (Division of Corrections and Division of Youth Services).[1]

Division of Adult Services

The Division of Adult Services administers 13 major correctional facilities and 27 field units through five geographic regions.

An Inmate Grievance Procedure was first established in February, 1974. However, it has been superseded by another which conforms to the minimum standards for Inmate Grievance Procedures specified in the Civil Rights of Institutionalized Persons Act, Public Law 96-247, 94 STAT. 349 (42 U.S.C. 1997). (See Appendix A.) Virginia is the first state in the nation to have a grievance procedure conditionally certified by the U.S. Attorney General.[2]

The procedure is a four-level arrangement providing for responses within fixed time limits at all levels. At the first level, inmate-employee participation is mandated and must take one of the following forms:

1. Formally established inmate-employee grievance committees in which the inmates have some choice in the selection of inmate members. All employee appointees, by the warden, must be persons having regular contact with inmates, of which one must be at line level.
2. Review by existing Inmate Advisory Committees, as well as by a committee of employees whose composition must be as cited in the previous paragraph.
3. Review by an ad hoc committee of inmates and employees empaneled solely for review of a particular grievance and chosen as indicated in (1) above.
4. Solicitation of comments in general population meetings and in employee meetings.
5. Solicitation of written comments by inmates and employees on posted or published abstracts of grievances, with adequate time for review and response.

All recommendations at the first level must be forwarded to the second level (the warden) within 15 days following receipt of the grievance. The warden must then respond within eight days. Should the grievant so wish, he may, within five days, appeal to the Regional Administrator or to the Assistant Director for Classification and Parole Administration if the issue involves classification decisions or policies. A reply in 20 days is required. This is the last level except for those grievances questioning or challenging general policy or procedure of the Division of Adult Services or emergency grievances. Such issues may be appealed to the Deputy Director. Grievances concerning general policy or procedure of the Department of Corrections may be appealed to the Director. The time limit for response at this level is 15 days.

No copies of grievances or any adverse reference to any grievance may be placed in an inmate's institution or division file. Regional Grievance Coordinators are required to monitor the procedure regularly at all institutions.

Although a 1980 report[3] indicates that an ombudsman position was established in 1977 and written responses were to be made within specified time limits, no mention was made of the position in information recently obtained.

In 1973 it was reported there were no inmate advisory councils in the institutions administered by the then Division of Corrections, Department of Welfare and Institutions.[4]

In 1966, information was received about a short-lived inmate council at the Southampton Correctional Center, Capron (then the Southampton Correctional Farm), a facility for youthful first offenders. A council was organized in February, 1965 under a constitution and by-laws providing for the secret ballot election of two representatives from each housing unit, with terms of office varying from two to six months. After endorsement by at least ten others in his housing unit, an inmate who had been in the institution not less than two months with a clear conduct record, and with a minimum of six months left to serve, could stand for election if approved by a Staff Committee which included the superintendent, assistant superintendent, and department heads. Twice monthly meetings during working hours were authorized to discuss matters relative to the general welfare of the population. No problems of individuals were to be discussed except when it was apparent that they could affect other persons generally. A like situation was provided for in relation to matters covered by state statutes, discussion being allowed if it was believed the statutes were being ignored to the detriment of inmate welfare. Despite these rather liberal and permissive conditions, lack of inmate interest brought about the demise of the council late in the same year.[5]

At the present an inmate advisory committee may be organized, under policy guidelines established in 1974, at the discretion of the institution administration. Membership on a committee is regarded as a privilege to be won by responsible inmates rather than a right to be demanded.[6]

At those institutions having a population in excess of 200, the committee membership is nine; at institutions where the population is 100 to 200, there can be seven members, and five members may be chosen at those in which the population is less than 100. Any inmate not in segregation who has served a minimum of six months on the current sentence and who has a like period of time yet remaining to be served may be nominated for office. The 15 nominees receiving the highest number of votes become candidates for election at-large by secret ballot, presided over by both staff and inmates, to serve a six-month term of office, at the completion of which re-election may not be sought until a period of 90 days has elapsed.[7]

The advisory committee may meet in a designated location twice a month to conduct its internal business, and will select from its membership a chairman, vice-chairman, and secretary. In its twice-monthly meetings (or more frequently if needed) with the warden and other officials, committee members may present the opinions and suggestions conveyed to them by their constituents on matters pertaining to any institution program or procedure. An issue of individual concern may not be introduced except as it may point up a problem of broad implication. Additionally, the committee is charged with cooperating to maintain a state of institution cleanliness. Minutes of meetings, with the superintendent's approval, are posted throughout the institution. The guidelines emphasize the advisory nature of the committee.[8]

While no listing of institutions having an inmate advisory council was obtained, a 1980 study mentioned such a group being in operation at the James River Correctional Center and the Powhatan Correctional Center, both located at State Farm, Virginia.[9]

Division of Youth Services

The Division of Youth Services administers eight facilities for juvenile delinquents.[10] The Division is initiating a grievance procedure for the eight facilities, involving staff and youth participation in its design, implementation, and operation.[11]

In 1941, at the Bon Air Learning Center, Bon Air (then the Virginia Home and Industrial School for Girls), older girls were used on occasion as counselors for the more unsteady or depressed girls. In 1943, following a change of superintendent, a Student Council was organized, composed of two members from each cottage, with a president elected by the membership. Elections were held every three months.[12]

In 1966, none of the juvenile facilities had a student council. By 1973 all of the facilities except the Pinecrest Center, Richmond, had a student council or a similar organization. No information was received at that time regarding the Bon Air facility (by then known as the Bon Air School for Girls).[13]

At the Hanover Learning Center, Hanover (then the Virginia Manual Labor School for Colored Boys), some youths were appointed as monitors to supervise new arrivals until they became assimilated into permanent working details. Military drill furnished some opportunity for leadership to a few youths.[14]

A 1973 survey found that a student government had been in existence since 1968 at the Hanover facility (at that time designated as the Hanover School for Boys). Prior attempts to organize such a program had been made, but no details were available. Two representatives were elected by the boys in each of the eight cottages. Weekly cottage meetings were held under the direction of counselors. Later a campus Student Government meeting was held to which representatives brought complaints and suggestions made in the cottage meetings. Staff sponsors were a counselor and an academic teacher who acted as liaison with the administration. During the prior 18 months the success and effectiveness of the Student Government had been generally poor. Since there had been few actions taken by the administration on suggestions channeled through the group, a belief had grown among many of the boys that making suggestions was a waste of time. This reaction was also manifested by representatives choosing to participate in other activities rather than to attend the Student Government meeting. The scheduling of Student Government meetings concurrently with other group meetings had been recognized as a factor contributing to the lack of attendance. Reorganization of the Student Government in the near future was hoped for.[15]

A Student Council was organized in 1968 at the Beaumont Learning Center, Beaumont (then the Beaumont School for Boys), and functioned for several years with some success. It was found that the comparatively short stay of a student at the school--at that time it was six months--resulted in more time being spent in election of representatives and officers than in constructive activity. Since discontinuance of the council, several other methods had been found to involve the students in school function and administration, of which two were cited. A Positive Peer Culture program required groups of students to assume responsibilities for improving their daily living situation, and to play a major role in deciding when individual group members were ready for release. Also, an atmosphere of accessibility was developed in which students could freely approach staff of any level with the realization that their complaints, suggestions, and recommendations, involving only self or the entire facility, would be listened to.[16]

Several attempts to form a student council at the Appalachian Learning Center, Honaker, from the time it opened in October, 1967 (as the Juvenile Vocational Institute) to March, 1973, were unsuccessful. The major difficulty cited, in addition to lack of staff experience with such groups, was an organizational structure which permitted the negative element among the student body to gain control. Using the experience of past errors, development was underway by the administration of a new organizational structure for a student council.[17]

The lack of success in attempts to establish a student government at Pinecrest Center, Richmond, was attributed basically to the age of the boys, none being over 12, and their concern with personal and immediate goals rather than with a group program.[18]

In the Honor Cottage at the Virginia Industrial School for Colored Girls, Peaks Turnout, a form of youth representation was reported in operation in 1941. Three group leaders elected by the girls met with the superintendent to present suggestions as to how the cottage life might be improved and made more entertaining. In an assembly on each Monday Morning, the girls were asked by the superintendent to take part in a general discussion of school life. An attempt, the year before, to develop group leaders in another cottage was dropped because the staff lacked enthusiasm for the idea.[19] So far as can be determined, this facility, which opened originally on January 1, 1915 as a private institution designated as the Industrial Home for Wayward Colored Girls and deeded to the state in 1920, is no longer in operation.

A Student Advisory Committee has been required in all juvenile facilities since 1975. Composed of youth from each cottage, with a staff advisor, the committee meets monthly with the superintendent to make known the concerns of the population, make suggestions and recommendations, and develop projects and activities. Minutes of meetings are maintained. Twice a year the committee members from each facility meet with the Assistant Director of Youth Institutional Services to discuss concerns, rules and policies.[20]

Notes

1. Letter from Gilbert B. Miller, Public Affairs Office, Dept. of Corrections, Richmond, September 22, 1982.
2. Department Policy No. 4-4, "Inmate Grievance Procedures," Dept. of Corrections, Richmond, July 23, 1982; "Monday Morning Highlights," Federal Prison System, June 20, 1983, p. 2.
3. Dillingham, David D., and Singer, Linda K., _op. cit._, p. 55.
4. Baker, J. E., _op. cit._, p. 181.
5. _Ibid._, pp. 181-182.
6. Letter from Gilbert B. Miller, _op. cit._
7. "Inmate Advisory Committee," Division Guidelines, No. 848, Division of Corrections, Richmond, February 28, 1974.
8. Ibid.
9. Neto, Virginia V., and Bainer, LaNelle Marie. _Offenders Participation in Corrections: Methods for Involving Offenders and Ex-Offenders in the Correctional Process._ National Institute of Corrections, U.S. Dept. of Justice, 1981, p. 111.
10. Letter from Raymon J. Cowans, Dept. of Corrections, Richmond, March 21, 1983.
11. _Ibid._
12. MacCormick, Austin H., ed. _Handbook of American Institutions for Delinquent Juveniles._ First Edition, Vol. IV. _Virginia-North Carolina._ New York: The Osborne Association, Inc., 1943, p. 242.
13. Baker, J. E., _op. cit._, pp. 182-183.
14. MacCormick, Austin H., _op. cit._, p. 311.

15. Baker, J. E., _op. cit._, p. 182.
16. _Ibid._, pp. 182-183.
17. _Ibid._, p. 183.
18. _Ibid._, p. 183.
19. MacCormick, Austin H., _op. cit._, p. 379.
20. Letter from Raymon J. Cowans, _op. cit._

WASHINGTON

Department of Corrections

The Department of Corrections administers 13 institutions for adult and youthful felony offenders.

An inmate grievance procedure was established in 1976, according to a 1980 survey, in some institutions which indicated that a formal hearing, in which inmates participated in a decision-making role, would be granted to a grievant. No details are given as to the levels of the procedure, except that appeals were permitted and the warden was the final level of review. There was no requirement for written responses or specific time limits in which a reply was to be made. However, a survey made in 1977 received a negative response to the question: "Does your state have a prison ombudsman, grievance committee, or arbitration process?"[1]

On August 3, 1981, all institutions implemented an inmate grievance mechanism, except the Washington State Penitentiary, Walla Walla, which followed suit on December 1, 1981. A manual was published in November, 1981, to provide information and guidance required to develop and maintain an effective inmate grievance mechanism. The standards set forth in the manual are consistent with those of the Commission on Accreditation for Corrections and the 1980 Civil Rights of Institutionalized Persons Act (see Appendix A). The Department intends to apply for certification by the U.S. Department of Justice of each grievance sub-system.[2]

Grievable issues are defined as institution or department policies, rules, and procedures; actions by employees, volunteers, contract staff, or other inmates; reprisals for filing a grievance or participating in an inmate grievance procedure, and any lack of policy, regulation, rule or procedure which affects an inmate's institutional living conditions.

Nongrievable items are State and Federal law; decisions by the Board of Prison Terms and Paroles; court decisions, and decisions of the disciplinary and classification committees, for which there is an existing appeal process.

For all grievances, except those alleging staff misconduct, an inmate may complete a prescribed form and give it to the institution staff member designated as the coordinator, who will investigate and make a written response within seven working days. If dissatisfied with the decision, the grievant has two working days to appeal to a staff committee. In a hearing conducted by the committee, the grievant may be assisted by an advisor. The committee must reply in writing in ten working days. The further levels to which the grievant may appeal are the superintendent and the Department of Corrections via the Department coordinator. The time limit for a response at each of these levels is, respectively, ten and 20 working days.

Any grievance alleging staff misconduct is sent directly to the superintendent who directs the grievant's immediate supervisor or other staff to investigate and make a report within ten working days. The superintendent then reviews the investigation results and prepares a written response. This is the final level of review for this type of grievance.

A grievance of any emergency nature is sent directly to the superintendent after the institution coordinator has attempted to resolve it. The superintendent expedites resolution of such a grievance. An "after the fact" review is made by the Director, Division of Prisons. An emergency grievance is defined as a matter posing a serious threat to the security or safety of the inmate or institution unless its resolution is expedited.

A Corrections Standards Board is responsible for reviewing the development and functioning of the grievance procedure. Together with the Secretary of Corrections, the Board is required to visit and inspect annually each institution in which the population is 150 or more. A single Board member may be designated this duty for smaller institutions.

In the aftermath of the riots and disturbances that swept over the United States in the early '50s, the State of Washington made a general reorganization of its adult correctional institutions. Inmate advisory councils were authorized by the then Department of Institutions in a 1954 directive for the purpose of promoting good will and to provide free and efficient inmate-staff communication. Through council activities it was believed that inmates might become more sympathetically aware of the problems of prison administration and, conversely, staff might become more acutely aware of the psychological stresses and strains of prison life. Although council members were to be granted considerable leeway in the selection of topics for discussion, it was stipulated that none was to be given authority to implement administration-approved suggestions or to involve others, either inmates or staff, except as directed by the superintendent.[3]

Despite the mandatory provisions of the first paragraph in the directive--"There shall be established at each correctional institution an Inmate Advisory Council consisting of seven to 15 members" --a survey made in 1966 found only one advisory council in existence. Another institution had discontinued a council, and the small population at each of the honor camps allowed such a high degree of staff-inmate interaction that councils were felt to be unneeded. Ad hoc committees were in use at the Reformatory and the Corrections Center to deal with the blood bank, movie selection, inmate talent shows, and athletic events, each committee being disbanded upon completion of the activity.

A directive was issued in 1970 to supersede that of 1954. Under its provisions each of the six institutions, including two honor camps, had a resident governmental council composed of members representing housing units or program areas, elected by secret ballot and limited to a six-month term of office. Procedures were governed under a constitution prepared by the residents and approved by the superintendent and the central office. It was regarded as essential that all residents understand how and by whom they were represented on the councils and have the opportunity to participate in the open elections. Community representatives could attend meetings of the councils.[4]

At the Washington State Penitentiary, Walla Walla, the Inmate Advisory Council was organized in 1956, composed of 11 members limited upon election by secret ballot to a single six-month term of office. Although elected by the residents of his housing unit, the scope of each councilman's responsibility was institution-wide. To be eligible for office, a candidate must have had his minimum sentence set by the Parole Board, a suitable conduct record, and at least six months to serve if elected. A chairman and a secretary were chosen from the membership to conduct and record the semimonthly meetings, one of which was attended by the superintendent or his representative.

As a result of the 1970 directive, the name of the Walla Walla institution council was changed to Resident Governmental Council in November, 1970, and a new constitution was drawn up and published in April, 1971. The 11-member composition was retained. However, the franchise of each voter was enlarged so that he could cast 11 votes to be distributed as he chose. Council members elected from their ranks a president, vice-president, and executive secretary. Each of the other members was assigned to head ad hoc project committees as needed. Interesting features were the publication of a newspaper by the Council under a five-member resident-staff Editorial Review Board, the Council privilege to contact the news media provided the superintendent had been given a courtesy copy of the communication, and a Citizens' Advisory Committee. This latter group had six members selected by the superintendent and the council president from civic, fraternal, and service organizations, and individuals who were permitted access to all institution residents and areas at any time. The Committee advised the Resident Governmental Council and the administration on matters of mutual concern, and might invite officials from all levels of government and private citizens to observe, participate in discussions, and offer advice at Council meetings. The constitution was under revision late in 1972.[5]

Resident Governmental Council representatives participated in staff meetings, adjustment committee hearings, and classification committee meetings as well as staff-resident committees. Results of this participation were evaluated in 1972 as being productive of both positives and negatives. It was hoped by the administration that experience would increase the former and eliminate the latter.[6] Alas, this hope was never realized.

A 1974 description of the Walla Walla Resident Governmental Council cited as the group's biggest project the design of a new constitution and planning for a realignment of all institution councils into a new state-wide organization to be incorporated as a non-profit corporation with a proposed first year budget of $550,000. A subgroup had developed, the People's Action Committee (PAC), which handled individual complaints. The PAC met weekly to discuss handling of individual problems its members had dealt with in the living units. The Citizens' Advisory Committee was mentioned as still alive, meeting once a week. Two illustrative program results of the council were given: an extension by two hours of telephone use time, and a liberalization of visiting procedures.[7]

A new constitution was ratified in October, 1974, containing some new features which it was hoped would revive interest in the Resident Governmental Council. These included the use of a two-stage electoral process (primary and general) and the establishment of a "House of Representatives" as a consultive organ made up of five "permanent" members representing the three racial-ethnic organizations, Blacks, Indians, and Chicanos, and the two largest specialized groupings, "Lifers with Hope" and the Motorcycle Club, plus two "non-permanent" representatives to be chosen by the original five from among the numerous smaller clubs and organizations. By this time the Council had come to lack inmate credibility and was no longer looked to as the major channel of communication with the administration.[8]

As of April 1, 1975, the Resident Governmental Council was disbanded. The announcement was made jointly by the council president and the institution superintendent. Three months later, in June, 1975, a restructured Residents Council was inaugurated, with its constitution defined as "Guidelines."[9]

At the present time (1983) there is no inmate advisory council at the Walla Walla institution.[10]

An Inmate Advisory Council was established in 1954 at the Washington State Reformatory, Monroe. Operating under the directive of the Department of Public Institutions, the organization was never fully accepted by line employees, who from time to time expressed considerable hostility towards its philosophy and function. This presented the Council with a dilemma--the expectations of their constituents pressed them squarely into the face of the disapproval of the keepers. In February, 1965 it was determined that an inmate boycott of the dining room had been carried out by Council, and it was disbanded following the transfer of its members to the penitentiary. Investigation suggested that the boycott was a retaliation against the superintendent for not approving as many proposals as the Council wanted.[11]

On August 10, 1981, a Resident Advisory Committee was established to replace an organization designated as the Resident Reform Council. No information was obtained as to the origin and procedure of the latter group but it was, on the date mentioned, summarily disbanded and declared to be no longer sanctioned or recognized as an inmate organization at the Washington State Reformatory. The new organization is composed of the president/chairman and vice-president/chairman of the Black Prisoners Caucus, Los Mexicanos, Indians of all Tribes, the Awareness Project, the Asian Alliance, Lifers, and the Multi-Service Center.[12]

The purpose of the Resident Advisory Committee is to represent the population in general and their respective organizations individually regarding matters of policy and program in correspondence or meetings with the administration. The committee meets monthly with the administration to consider an agenda of items submitted five days prior to the meeting. Additional meetings may be held if approved by the superintendent.[13]

At the McNeil Island Correctional Center, Steilacoom, which was ceded to the State by the Federal government in 1981, resident representatives are elected to serve as members of the housing unit teams which are responsible for daily programming and living conditions. Any inmate who has been at the institution a minimum of 90 days and has a like period of good conduct may stand for a staff-supervised election to a five-month term of office. Representatives are required to provide communication between the unit team and residents by presenting at weekly meetings suggestions or complaints relating to programs and procedures. Meeting minutes are posted in the unit upon review by the unit supervisor. Provision is made for removal of any representative who is found guilty of a major disciplinary infraction or misses two consecutive or a total of three meetings without advance approval. A member of a unit team or a resident constituent of a representative may file charges calling for his recall. Such a petition must be in writing and specify the charges. The associate superintendent is the reviewing authority.[14]

At the Purdy Treatment Center for Women, Gig Harbor, the 11 members of an Inmate Council, including an Executive Board consisting of a chairperson, vice-chairperson, and secretary, are elected by secret ballot to serve a one-year term of office. A candidate for an executive board position must not have incurred a major disciplinary infraction in the six months prior to election, have a like period of time left to serve, and must reside in one of three specified units (presumably honor housing).[15]

The monthly meetings of the council are open to all inmates. The Executive Board meets each Monday afternoon with the superintendent. It is specified that the role of the council is advisory.

The council provides a means of inmate input into the development of institution rules, policies and programs.[16]

At the Cedar Creek Correctional Center, Little Rock, an inmate who has been there for at least 60 days and has a like period of time remaining to be served may be elected to a three-month term of office as a member of the Resident Advisory Committee, to which a one-term succession is possible. Each program is entitled to elect three members. Minutes of the twice-a-month meetings are given wide distribution. Supervisory and program personnel attend the meetings. The superintendent meets with the committee every other month, or at his discretion. The duties and responsibilities of the members include the formulation of new proposals for the betterment of the institution, orientation of newly committed inmates, serving as a role model for other inmates, and acting as a means of two-way communication between inmates and the administration.[17]

An organization designated as the Climate Control Committee was established on May 5, 1981 at the Clearwater Corrections Center, Forks. The three members of the committee are elected by secret ballot to serve a six-month term of office to which there is no succession. A requirement to stand for election is a record of no major disciplinary infractions for the 60 days prior, and none during the term of office. A lieutenant meets weekly with the group at which are aired concerns and complaints arising out of institution policies, rules, practices and procedures.[18]

An Inmate Advisory Council has been established at both the Washington Corrections Center, Shelton, and the Olympic Correctional Center, Forks. Each operates under written procedures outlined in either a constitution, by-laws, or both.[19]

There is no Department of Corrections policy statement regarding inmate advisory councils.[20]

Division of Juvenile Rehabilitation

The Division of Juvenile Rehabilitation, Department of Social and Health Services, administers five institutions and seven group homes for juvenile delinquents.[21]

A Youth Complaint-Appeal Procedure was established on July 1, 1982, as a means of resolving youth complaints about institution policies or the actions of staff. A youth completes a prescribed form to enter a complaint into the tri-level process consisting of: Program Committee, Superintendent, and Administrative Review.

No time limits are specified within which a response must be made at the first level, but the superintendent must make a written reply within five working days. A person outside the institution will conduct the administrative review upon appointment by the Division Director, and makes recommendations to the Director, whose ruling is final. This level of review is not applicable to complaints of staff misconduct which, if true, could result in disciplinary action or criminal charges against the employee.[22]

At the Green Hill School, Chehalis (opened in 1891 as the State Reform School, receiving both boys and girls; redesignated as the Washington State Training School for Boys in 1914 when the girls were moved to a new institution at Centralia), it was found in 1939 that a system of student officers was in operation. To be selected as a captain, lieutenant, or guard, a boy must have earned half the minimum number of points required for placement (release),[23] and, in the opinion of staff, possess the ability to manage other students. In the absence of supervising staff, the student captains and lieutenants were authorized to submit written disciplinary reports. Any student engaging in a fist fight with a student officer was ineligible to ever become an officer. Unless the reason was self-defense, a student officer participating in a fight forfeited his position, but could later be reinstated by the superintendent.[24]

At the Maple Lane School, Centralia (opened in 1914 as the State School for Girls), a program committee was appointed in 1939 as the beginning of a plan to organize a program of student cooperation. Early in 1940, the plan was expanded to a Student Council. To be eligible for a three-month membership, a girl was required to have an academic average grade of C, be of, or near, honor roll caliber, and possess a reputation for honesty and integrity. The group was in charge of assemblies and planned programs, and received and introduced visitors. A creed was written stressing the need to be of service to others at all times. Monitors were appointed by the council to assist in keeping the halls and bathrooms orderly. Arrangements were reported as being underway for council members to supervise the recreation areas as they were then supervising swimming sessions.[25]

Information was received in 1967 that a council program organized in 1950 was then in operation under a constitution and bylaws amendable by a two-thirds majority vote and staff advisor approval, which provided for the election of a council in each cottage, the presidents of each comprising the Campus Council. When a girl was regarded as ready to handle responsibility her name was placed on a Cottage Council membership eligibility list. Chosen by a simple majority on a secret ballot, a member was elected to an indefinite term of office from which she could be removed for failing to assume necessary responsibility. Each Cottage Council elected a president, vice-president, and secretary. Those groups met weekly with a staff member present. Suggestions, requests, or complaints could be referred to the Campus Council which met every other week with a staff advisor from the Cottage Life Department to consider suggestions for referral to the staff. Suggestions could be only on facilities, programs, or special projects. Recommendations of a disciplinary nature or pertaining to the physical or mental health needs of an individual were excluded. Chairmanship and secretary functions were rotated weekly.[26]

Currently the Maple Lane School houses male juvenile delinquents.

According to 1967 information, the Camp Council of the Youth Camp, Naselle, was organized November 1, 1966, just two weeks after the first students were received at the facility. The four living units were called lodges. Each lodge council chose three of six staff-selected boys to run for a two-month term of office. Voting was by secret ballot and the nominee receiving a majority vote was declared lodge chief. Two other councilmen were elected to one-month terms. Two bay chiefs were appointed by the staff to two-month terms. Qualifications for council membership included two months' camp residence for bay chiefs and councilmen, three months for lodge chief, and a willingness and ability to handle the job in a manner beneficial to the camp, with a further consideration of what benefits the particular council member might gain by being in office. Lodge councils met weekly with a staff leader. At all Camp Council meetings, held on an irregular basis, the lodge chiefs and their staff leaders might plan athletic, recreation, and social activities as well as community projects, discuss relationships between lodges, and consider suggestions on camp policies and procedures.[27]

The same 1967 source reported that the Cedar Creek Youth Camp, Little Rock, had student councils in operation in both its Timberline and Alpine programs, the latter being a subsidiary facility. Each council was representative of the student population and met with a member of the counseling staff to discuss policy and procedure, make recommendations for modifications of procedures, assist in planning and evaluating recreational activities, participate in the integration of new students and, under staff supervision, work with students who were experiencing difficulty.

In the original Cedar Creek program, Timberline, a Student Council was organized in 1954 with a membership of ten. Six of these were work program crewleader or foreman positions designated as "Colored Hats." To be eligible for a colored hat, a boy must have been in the program a minimum of three months. He was appointed by staff on the basis of his work ability and leadership qualities. One member of the Council was the "Camp Kick," a representative of the student population elected by secret ballot to a one-month term. A candidate for this office must have been in the program a minimum of four months and in good standing. The remaining members, representing the three dormitories, must have been in the program two months. Election was by secret ballot and tenure of office continued until paroled. The Council had no officers or constitution and by-laws.

In the Alpine program, a Student Council was developed in December, 1959, but was discontinued in 1961 because of a drop in the age level of the boys to 14-15 years. In the latter part of 1963, when the camp again began to receive older boys, the Council was reinstated and was functioning well according to the last information received in 1967. Its membership was composed of two staff-appointed crewleaders, a Camp Kick, and two elected crew representatives. Qualifications, tenure, and organization were similar to those in the Timberline program.[28] This camp was converted to an adult facility in 1980, and renamed the Cedar Creek Correctional Center.

The Student Council at the Spruce Canyon Youth Forest Camp, Colville, also known as "Colored Hats," was established in 1961 and was functioning well according to the last information received in 1967. The positions of colored hats were one camp kick (red), two crew leaders (green), and five squad leaders (yellow). The first position was filled by secret balloting on a nominee slate selected by the staff from boys who had demonstrated outstanding work ability and above-average peer and authority relationships to serve a term of one month. The other positions were filled by staff appointment. Potential for positive leadership and personal improvement were primary selection criteria. The Council met bi-monthly with the supervisor of student life to consider suggestions for betterment of camp living.[29]

When the Woodinville Group Home opened in 1965, a Student Council was organized to give the boys an opportunity to express their feelings toward operations and the development of programs. All boys took part in the twice-monthly meetings with staff. A president, vice-president, secretary, and master-of-arms were elected by majority vote to serve until released or asked by staff to step down because of poor behavior. Disbursements from a student fund financed by a ten per cent contribution of each boy's earnings were determined at Council meetings.[30]

In 1967, it was reported that the Pioneer Group Home at Tacoma had had group participation since shortly after the facility opened in 1962, the purpose of which was to establish rapport between students and staff regarding program and goals. Additionally, the group made decisions on expenditures of student funds and group recreational activities. Due to the small population, membership in the group was automatic.[31]

The Fort Worden Treatment Center, Port Townsend, was opened in 1958 and closed in 1972. In 1967, information was received that a group of boys and girls, elected from the cottages, met with the recreation staff to plan coeducational activities. The group was not regarded as being a student council, however.[32]

At the present time, none of the Division of Juvenile Rehabilitation facilities have formalized systems which involve the residents in a student council function or other form of participatory administration. However, in most of the facilities, solicitation is made of student ideas and suggestions regarding recreational activities and use of resident welfare funds.[33]

Notes

1. Dillingham, David D., and Singer, Linda R., <u>op. cit.</u>, p. 55;

Corrections Compendium, CONTACT, Inc., Lincoln, Nebraska, August 1, 1977.
2. Grievance Manual, Institutions and Community Services. Dept. of Corrections, Olympia, November 1981.
3. Baker, J. E., op. cit., pp. 183-184.
4. Baker, J. E., op. cit., p. 184.
5. Baker, J. E., op. cit., p. 185.
6. Ibid.
7. Keating, McArthur, Lewis, Sebelius, and Singer, op. cit., p. 46.
8. Tryner-Stastney, Gabrielle, and Stastney, Charles I. "The Changing Political Culture of a Total Institution: The Case of Walla Walla," The Prison Journal, Pennsylvania Prison Society, Vol. LVII, No. 2, Autumn-Winter 1977, pp. 43-55.
9. Ibid.
10. Letter from Dick Paulson, Public Information Chief, Dept. of Corrections, Olympia, Washington, November 18, 1982.
11. Baker, J. E., op. cit., pp. 185-186.
12. "Resident Advisory Committee," Memorandum, Superintendent, Washington State Reformatory, Monroe, August 10, 1981.
13. Ibid.
14. "Resident Representatives to Unit Teams," McNeil Island Correctional Center, Steilacoom, Undated.
15. "Inmate Council," Policy and Procedures, Section 1.90.00, Purdy Treatment Center for Women (as revised April, 1982).
16. Ibid.
17. "Resident Advisory Committee," Policy No. 7-20, Cedar Creek Correctional Center, Little Rock (as revised August 1982).
18. Climate Control Committee By-Laws, Clearwater Corrections Center, Forks, May 5, 1981.
19. Letter from Dick Paulson, op. cit.
20. Ibid.
21. Letter from Director Jerome M. Wasson, Division of Juvenile Rehabilitation, Dept. of Social and Health Services, Olympia, October 11, 1982.
22. "Youth Complaint-Appeal Procedure," Bulletin 13, Division of Juvenile Rehabilitation, Olympia, July 1, 1982.
23. The school operated on a credit marking system. On admission a boy received 1000 merits toward a total of 2000 required for release. With a good record a minimum of six merits could be earned daily. Student captains received 35 extra merits each month for satisfactory services rendered; first lieutenants, 30; second lieutenants, 25; and boy guards received 20.
24. Cox, William B., and Shelley, Joseph A., eds. Handbook of American Institutions for Delinquent Juveniles. First Edition, Vol. III. Pacific Coast States. New York: The Osborne Association, Inc., 1940, pp. 367-368.
25. Ibid., pp. 310-311.
26. Baker, J. E., op. cit., p. 186.
27. Ibid., p. 187.

28. Ibid., p. 188.
29. Ibid.
30. Ibid.
31. Ibid., p. 188.
32. Ibid., pp. 188-189.
33. Letter from Director Jerome M. Wasson, op. cit.

WEST VIRGINIA

Department of Corrections

The Department of Corrections administers four institutions for adult and youthful felony offenders and three facilities for delinquents.[1]

Under a grievance procedure established in 1977,[2] an inmate may make a written complaint, on a prescribed form, to the warden about food quality, mistreatment by staff, cell and living unit conditions, work assignments, classification decisions, storage of property, supervision of visitation, and problems with mail and telephone calls. Complaints about institution policy are excluded. A personal interview, if requested, may be granted at the warden's discretion.[3]

A written response will be made within seven days by the warden. However, should he decide to conduct an investigation of the issue presented, he will so notify the grievant. A final reply will then be made within 30 days following the date the form was received.[4]

If dissatisfied with the warden's reply, the grievant may, within seven days, appeal to the Commissioner, Department of Corrections. Unless the Commissioner decides to order an investigation, he will make a written response within 21 days. Following an investigation, a response will be made within 60 days following the original receipt of the appeal.[5]

There are no advisory councils in West Virginia institutions.[6] In 1966 it was reported that although there were no councils, the administration then was seriously considering experimenting with such groups.[7]

Notes

1. Letter from Roger A. Bias, Administrative Assistant, Office of the Commissioner, Dept. of Corrections, Charleston, October 21, 1982.
2. Dillingham, David D., and Singer, Linda R., op. cit., p. 55.
3. "Grievance Procedure," West Virginia Penitentiary, Moundsville (this procedure is indicative of those in all West Virginia Dept. of Corrections facilities).

4. Ibid.
5. Ibid.
6. Letter, and enclosures, from Roger A. Bias, op. cit.
7. Baker, J. E., op. cit., p. 189.

WISCONSIN

Division of Corrections

All facilities for adult and youthful offenders and juvenile delinquents are administered by the Division of Corrections, Department of Health and Social Services.

Wisconsin was one of the first states to enact and have functioning a grievance mechanism. Known as the Inmate Complaint Review System, it went into operation in November, 1972.

The system is an administrative procedure involving three levels of review. Written complaints, which may be of any nature, are initially reviewed by the institution superintendent. If the inmate is dissatisfied with the decision at that level, an appeal may be made to the Administrator, Division of Corrections. If the inmate is still not satisfied, an appeal is possible to the final step of the system, the Secretary, Department of Health and Social Services.[1] At the institution level an appointed Institutional Complaint Investigator screens all complaints within 24 hours to spot emergency cases. In each instance, an investigation report is made to the superintendent within five days. The superintendent has 17 days to act and make a written response to the inmate and others involved. During that time, the superintendent may refer the complaint to a Complaint Advisory Board, consisting of two staff members and two inmates. The Board, whose members serve for three months, must make a recommendation to the superintendent within seven days. An appeal to the Administrator, Division of Corrections, is directed to the Corrections Complaint Examiner, an Assistant Attorney General, who has 45 days to act, with a possible extension of 30 days. At the discretion of the Assistant Attorney General, a hearing may be held. A recommendation is then sent to the Division Administrator, who has 15 days, with a possible extension of ten days, to respond in writing. The Secretary, Department of Health and Social Services, has 30 days to make a response, with a possible extension of 30 days.[2]

In the early 1940s an inmate council was in operation at the Wisconsin State Prison, Waupun. Reportedly, individual complaints were given undue weight when handled by the council rather than through ordinary procedures, resulting in unwarranted attention to many minor and ridiculous matters. The elections of representatives of the major departments soon resulted in the formation of committees whose membership was drawn from aggressive nonconformists. It was felt that the council was a factor in a major disturbance in 1944; this led to its abandonment.[3]

In March, 1973, Inmate Participation Advisory Committees were developed as a project in four of the adult correctional institutions: the Waupun Correctional Institution (then the Wisconsin State Prison), the Green Bay Correctional Institution (then the Wisconsin State Reformatory), the Fox Lake Correctional Institution (then the Wisconsin Correctional Institution), and the Taycheedah Correctional Institution (then the Wisconsin Home for Women). The project was a cooperative venture between the Wisconsin Council on Criminal Justice and the Division of Corrections, in response to a recognized need to develop, establish and maintain a mechanism to involve citizens, offenders, and implementers in program development and review.[4]

Each committee had an equal number of inmate and staff members. The original charge to each committee was to review and make recommendations to the Wisconsin Council on Criminal Justice, a state planning agency funded by the Law Enforcement Assistance Administration, on grant requests pertaining to the institution it represented. Both the reduction of available federal funds and recognition of the potential value of committee contributions led to an expansion of the charge to include the development of innovative programs, to which was added later the function of reviewing programs or evaluation procedures developed by others within the Division of Corrections.[5]

However, a lack of formal coordination, consistent support and clearly defined guidelines caused the committees to flounder for the first three years. As a remedy, specific guidelines were drawn, and a central office coordination staff of four was established. The project name was changed to Reintegration Advisory Planning, and the project was expanded to include, by 1978, six adult institution committees and one juvenile committee. Elected inmates, volunteer institution and Community Corrections staff comprised the adult institution committees. The juvenile committee was composed of juvenile residents, volunteer institution and Community Corrections staff and community volunteers, juvenile ex-offenders and parents of juvenile ex-offenders.[6]

During the period from 1976 to mid-1978, the committees suggested and developed 45 innovative programs, of which 16 were implemented or approved for implementation, and the remainder were in some stage of review, the only exceptions being three which were not approved. The low rejection rate was indicative of the caliber of the proposals. Some examples of approved proposals:

Family visit program to maintain and strengthen family ties.
Job-seeking skills training program.
More direct involvement of Community Corrections agents in institution pre-release preparation programs.
Paralegal program.
Inviting citizens into institutions to discuss criminal justice issues with residents and staff.[7]

In the area of program and evaluation review, on nine occasions committees were asked to review new or existing programs affecting division clients or to provide feedback on evaluation procedures for division programs. Some examples:

> A request from the Wisconsin Council on Criminal Justice to comment on the effectiveness of its Affirmative Action Grant.
> A request from the League of Women Voters to assist in developing and implementing a survey of the impact of the National Guard on the correctional institutions during the State Employees' strike.
> Requests from the Corrections Division to: assist in developing procedures to evaluate the Mutual Agreement Program and the Purchase of Services system; review the Model Probation Project.

In 1978, the Division of Corrections established a policy mandating review by the Reintegration Advisory Planning committees of all new services affecting adult institution clients.[8]

Due to statewide budget reductions, the Reintegration Advisory Planning committees were discontinued in August, 1980. Some independent efforts were made by institutions to maintain the concept, but so far as is known, no committees are operating now.[9]

Prior to 1973, ad hoc advisory councils had been appointed from time to time for special activities. Some were functioning in that year.

In 1967, at the Kettle Moraine Boys School, Plymouth (now the Kettle Moraine Correctional Institution, for adult males), representative groups from the various cottages could confer with the superintendent regarding problems not solved in the group counseling programs conducted in all living units by a psychiatrist, psychologist, or social worker.[10]

In 1967 it was reported that the therapeutic community program at the Wisconsin School for Girls, Oregon, featured Community Meetings and Cottage Representatives. In the former, all girls of a cottage met together for one hour daily with a counselor and a social worker. The content of the meetings varied, as did the function: the focus might be on the problems of one girl; the determination of appropriate disciplinary action for an individual or a group; or the solution of everyday cottage living problems. The social worker might ask for recommendations or decisions, reserving the right to overrule either. Any conclusions reached were subject to staff approval. The Cottage Representatives program provided for an informal weekly meeting of the superintendent and the elected representatives of the ten cottages. Representatives reported on the progress of programs, and could give their views on contemplated modifications or innovations.[11]

Notes

1. Inmate Complaint Review System, Annual Report, 1981. Division of Corrections, Madison.
2. Keating, McArthur, Lewis, Sibelius, and Singer, Grievance Mechanisms in Correctional Institutions. Washington, D.C.: National Institute of Law Enforcement and Criminal Justice, U.S. Dept. of Justice, 1975, p. 47.
3. Baker, J. E., op. cit., p. 190.
4. "The Reintegration Advisory Planning Project: An Issue Study," Division of Corrections, July 1978.
5. Ibid.
6. Ibid.
7. Ibid.
8. Ibid.
9. Letter from John G. Stoddard, Chief, Program Services, Bureau of Adult Institutions, Division of Corrections, Madison, October 4, 1982.
10. Baker, J. E., op. cit., p. 190.
11. Ibid.

WYOMING

State Board of Charities and Reform

The five facilities for felony and misdemeanor offenders and juvenile delinquents are administered by the State Board of Charities and Reform.

An inmate grievance procedure was first established at the Wyoming State Penitentiary, Rawlins, in 1977. It provided for written responses, a formal hearing, and an appeal process of which the State Board of Charities and Reform was the final level of review.[1]

The Administrative Grievance Procedure now in effect is applicable to both the penitentiary and the Wyoming Honor Farm, Riverton.[2] The procedure was recently certified as meeting the criteria established under the Civil Rights of Institutionalized Persons Act (see Appendix A). The U.S. Attorney General, William French Smith, congratulated Wyoming officials on becoming the first jurisdiction to be certified.[3]

A grievance is defined as any complaint against the Wyoming State Penitentiary involving a rule or policy; the manner in which a rule or policy is applied; an action or inaction by any staff member, employee, or administrator; an exercise of authority by an employee; classification or reclassification decisions; disciplinary action, and any other good-faith complaint.

If unable to solve a problem by discussion with a counselor or supervisor, an inmate may file a formal complaint with the warden on a prescribed form within 30 days following the occurrence giving rise to the complaint. The warden assigns a supervisory level employee, who is not directly or indirectly the subject of the grievance, to investigate the complaint, including consultation with the grievant and others involved. If the complaint challenges a general policy or practice, it is also reviewed by a Grievance Procedure Review Committee composed of three inmates and four employees appointed by the warden.[4] The investigating employee makes a written report to the warden for determination as to whether or not there is any factual basis for the grievance, and any appropriate remedy action. If it is believed that further facts are needed, the warden may require a hearing. In any event, the warden must respond in writing within 30 days after receiving the grievance.

If dissatisfied with the warden's decision, the inmate may, within ten days, appeal to the Board of Charities and Reform. The Board will reply within 45 days. This is the final level of review. Appeals of emergency grievances will be answered within ten days.

Emergency grievances are expedited and replied to within 72 hours. An emergency is defined as an unforeseen combination of circumstances, or the state resulting from such. If the warden decides that disposition of the grievance according to the specified time limits would subject the inmate to a substantial risk of personal injury, or cause other serious and irreparable harm, the grievance is considered to be an emergency.

No employee or inmate who appears to be involved in a grievance may participate in its resolution. Time limits may be extended if the grievant agrees in writing. Expiration of a time limit without response entitles the inmate to move to the next level of the procedure. It is contemplated that resolution of a grievance be made within 85 days, or less. The dispositional time from filing to final resolution must not exceed 90 days.

No formal or informal reprisal may be taken against a user or participant in the grievance procedure. Any reprisal may be the issue of a grievance.

A tri-level grievance procedure at the Wyoming Women's Center, Evanston, provides that inmates may file formal complaints on a broad range of issues, from which are excluded actions by the disciplinary and classification committees, the Board of Parole, the Board of Charities and Reform, and violations of law.[5] This procedure has been approved by the Attorney General and the Board of Charities and Reform, and follows American Correctional Association guidelines.[6]

Within 72 hours following an occurrence, an inmate may file a formal complaint on a prescribed form. If discussion with a staff member does not result in a satisfactory resolution, the grievance is routed to the Grievance Committee composed of two staff members and two inmates. The latter are elected by secret ballot.

Inmates standing for such election must be able to read and write at the fifth grade level, have resided at the institution for not less than 120 days, be free of a disciplinary report for the same length of time, be able to present themselves in an adult, responsible manner, and possess the ability to communicate verbally with inmates and staff. Term of office for inmate committee members is six months.

The Grievance Committee has seven working days to hold a hearing or effect an informal resolution. Within that period a written response must be made to the grievant. The committee action may be appealed to the warden who will make a written response within three working days.

Not satisfied with the warden's response, the grievant may request an "outside review." The three-member review board is chaired by a person who is not a member of the institution staff. One member, selected by the grievant, may be a staff member, inmate, or an approved volunteer. The third member is selected by the warden. Within ten days following the board's meeting, the chairman will advise the warden and the grievant in writing of the group's recommendations. The latter are advisory and not binding on the warden. No later than five working days after receiving the board's recommendations, the warden will advise the grievant of the final decision.

Any grievance against a staff member which might result in disciplinary action is sent directly to the warden for investigation. The warden will advise the grievant, in writing, if appropriate action will be taken. However, the warden is not obligated to tell the grievant of any specific action taken.

Grievances of an extremely personal, confidential or urgent nature are referred to the warden, deputy warden or program coordinator immediately upon request by the grievant, and will be heard within two working days.

The Wyoming Girls School, Sheridan, has an informal grievance procedure. The resident housemother makes the decisions on specific grievances, and these decisions may be appealed to the superintendent. Records are kept of all complaints and their resolutions. A procedure identical in nature is in operation at the Wyoming Industrial Institute, Worland.[7]

The Wyoming State Penitentiary, Rawlins, had an Inmate Advisory Council for a brief period in 1955. It was abolished because of unreasonable demands by the members. In July, 1966, a three-member popularly elected Inmate Council was formed. It met twice a month with the warden to discuss topics relating to the health and welfare of the population. There were no written rules or regulations governing its function.[8]

There is currently no formal council at the penitentiary. Inmates are selected to participate in decision-making regarding severa matters, e.g., incentive pay. The participants are chosen at random; however, their wish to participate is considered.[9]

During the early 1960s, student government was tried at the Wyoming Girls School, Sheridan. Variations in structure and changes in rules and regulations did not produce results warranting documentation of methodology. In 1973, it was reported that student participation in affairs of the facility was an integral part of the organization dynamics, brought about through group meetings which were regarded as both therapeutic and functional. All group meetings were subject to staff approval or veto.[10]

Since 1973, the Wyoming Girls School has employed certain aspects of positive peer culture in the everyday life of the students. Each is responsible first to and for herself, and second to her assigned group. The group is the setting for solving personal problems as well as day-to-day functioning throughout the period of residence. Each group aids in decisions regarding an individual's campus status, home visitation, off-campus employment, extra-curricular activities, and requests for release.[11]

In 1967, it was reported that, although the administration was favorably disposed toward the idea of an inmate advisory council and during the prior two years had given consideration to organizing one, no council then existed at the Wyoming Industrial Institute, Worland.[12] No formal council exists at this time. However, students are involved in decision-making on recreational and athletic activities.[13]

At the Wyoming Women's Center, Evanston, opened in 1977, a four-member council is involved in minor rule-making decisions. Two student activity coordinators are involved in decision-making on recreational and athletic activities.[14]

An inmate council was established in March, 1983 at the Wyoming Honor Farm, Riverton, to function as a self-governing entity for the inmates and to be utilized by the administration as both a management and therapeutic tool.[15]

The council is composed of eight inmate members and the superintendent or his designee. Five members are appointed by the superintendent and two are elected by their peers at a general meeting. The eighth position, selected from the population, provides for a rotation at each meeting to insure that each inmate has an opportunity to participate.

From its membership the council elects a president, executive secretary, and a treasurer, whose term of office is six months. Each is eligible for reelection.

The council meets each Tuesday and Thursday at midday, and special meetings may be called as needed. All meetings are open to the population except necessary executive sessions and disciplinary hearings. Minutes of each meeting are posted throughout the facility and are the topic of discussion and interpretation at weekly meetings with the population.

Council duties include recommending of policies and regulations to the superintendent, after each has been posted for three meetings, read at each of three meetings with the population, and revised by input from inmates and staff. Council members are required to enforce all rules and regulations set forth in the inmate handbook.

The council provides a general information class for all newly arrived inmates, and is required to evaluate inmates recommended by the penitentiary staff for transfer to the honor farm. Additionally, the council is authorized to conduct inmate Incident Hearings, under the supervision and direction of the superintendent, and to recommend consequences to the superintendent. Each inmate has the option of appearing before a staff committee at the facility or the penitentiary. Following a hearing before the inmate council, an inmate may accept the council's action or return to the penitentiary for a disciplinary hearing. Actions which the council may recommend are:

- -Return to the penitentiary for disciplinary action.
- -Levy fines in accordance with rules contained in the inmate handbook (all fines are deposited to the Inmate Welfare Account, from which disbursements are made for inmate activities as approved by the population, the council and the superintendent).
- -Suggest consequences related to the particular violation, i.e., visits, phone calls, and excursions. Agreement is required by the inmate involved and the superintendent.

In cooperation with the correctional officers, the council acts as a general governing force within the facility. Council members may be contacted by a member of the security force regarding a real or potential problem. A minimum of four council members may handle a situation, but must advise security and the superintendent of the situation. Councilmen must immediately report to security any instance of escape, physical violence, or drinking (of alcoholic beverages).

Council members may recommend actions to the superintendent regarding:

- -Complaints by inmates of a staff member's behavior.
- -Complaints by staff of an inmate's behavior.
- -Complaints by inmates of another inmate or group of inmates.

As of May, 1983, the Honor Farm Inmate Council, although relatively new, is, in the opinion of the administration, fulfilling its expected purpose. Refinement and expansion of its policies is anticipated with further experience, as evidenced by the following administration commentary:

The concept of the Inmate Council is expanding, and as it is now functioning it has created a more controlled and yet relaxed environment than we have ever had at the Farm. By involving the entire population we develop a much stronger sense of the inmate having some control and responsibility for his life, and thus a much stronger sense of community has developed. The inmates who have agreed to appear before us have for the majority reported they felt the members of the Council were fair and truly concerned. The Council asks many questions, offers much advice, and overall are usually very encouraging to the inmate.

There is always the fear of "kangaroo court," but there has been no indication of such behavior whatsoever. Every inmate member of the Council, regular and rotating, has sweated blood to be as fair and considerate as possible, not only for the inmates, but also for any staff involved, no matter what their role. It is a new situation for the inmates to assume responsibility for others, but the effect it has had on everyone is astounding. The few inmates who wish to keep the inmate-staff separation, and who attempt to advocate the "snitch code," find it very difficult to live in this environment, and a few have requested to return to Rawlins [the penitentiary].

The lack of "power trips" and the increased communication and cooperation is very encouraging. By having the Inmate Council assume a more active role has allowed the Correctional Officers more opportunity to plan other activities, counsel with inmates, or just interact more with the general population.

This concept could not have started everywhere, but we were lucky enough to have a unique combination of seven experienced inmates who had the courage and were willing to take the risk to create a better community for everyone, both staff and inmates. The strength of the program is the fact it is based on cooperation and communication. To be at the Honor Farm is a privilege, and participation in this program is entirely voluntary.

One final point that is crucial regarding the authority of the Council to make recommendations to the superintendent on consequences for rules violations is the fact that members of the Council who must play "cop" know that they will have the opportunity to treat the man fairly at the Incident Hearing if the inmate so desires. This fact allows the members of the Council to see themselves in a teaching role, and not in the typical "rat" role, because then it becomes the responsibility of the accused inmate as to what his final outcome will be. The Council is based on the democratic model of government and judgment by peers.

Notes

1. Dillingham, David D., and Singer, Linda R., *op. cit.*, p. 56.
2. Administrative Grievance Procedure, Wyoming State Penitentiary, Rawlins.
3. "Monday Morning Highlights," Federal Prison System, Washington, D.C., June 20, 1983 issue; p. 2.
4. The Grievance Procedure Review Committee also periodically reviews the effectiveness and credibility of the procedure. Any participation on an individual grievance must occur before the initial adjudication (by the warden) of the grievance, and is limited to advisory comment on policy questions raised or implied in a grievance. Individual names or specific facts of a grievance are not identified. No inmate may participate in a case over the objection of the grievant.
5. "Grievance Procedure," Wyoming Women's Center, Evanston.
6. Letter from Anthony T. Malovich, Corrections Administrator, State Board of Charities and Reform, Cheyenne, May 19, 1983.
7. *Ibid.*
8. Baker, J. E., *op. cit.*, p. 191.
9. Letter from Anthony T. Malovich, May 6, 1983.
10. Baker, J. E., *op. cit.*, p. 191.
11. Letter from Anthony T. Malovich, May 6, 1983.
12. *Op. cit.*
13. Letter from Anthony T. Malovich, May 6, 1983.
14. *Ibid.*
15. "Creation and Authority of Wyoming Honor Farm Inmate Council," Memorandum, Supt. James M. Gamble, Wyoming Honor Farm, Riverton, March 1983.

CHAPTER IV

THE FEDERAL PRISON SYSTEM

The Federal Prison System, established in 1930 and known as the Bureau of Prisons until recently, administers a complex of facilities for persons sentenced to confinement for violations of federal laws. These facilities range from close custody penitentiaries to minimum security camps and community half-way houses, including institutions for juvenile offenders, youthful offenders, and a medical center to care for the mentally ill and those with serious medical disorders that cannot adequately be treated in the other institutional hospitals.

In 1974, the administration of federal facilities was divided into five regions, with regional directors located in Atlanta, Georgia; Dallas, Texas; Kansas City, Missouri; Philadelphia, Pennsylvania, and Burlingame (near San Francisco), California.

An Administrative Remedy of Complaints policy took effect on October 18, 1974 at all Federal Prison System institutions, subsequent to a pilot-test beginning in September, 1973 at the U.S. Penitentiary, Atlanta, Georgia, the Federal Correctional Institution, Danbury, Connecticut, and the Federal Correctional Institution, Tallahassee, Florida.[1] The policy was revised, effective November 1, 1979, as the Administrative Remedy Procedure for Inmates.[2]

All types of complaints relating to any aspect of imprisonment may be made through the tri-level procedure, with the exception of tort claims, inmate accident compensation claims, freedom of information or privacy act requests, or complaints on behalf of other inmates.

An inmate first discusses the problem with staff who attempt to resolve the issue informally. If the result is not satisfactory, the inmate may file, within 15 calendar days following the date on which the basis of the complaint occurred, an administrative remedy form with the staff member designated by the warden to coordinate the procedure. Upon receipt of the form the warden has 15 calendar days to complete the response portion and return it to the inmate. Investigation of alleged misconduct of staff may not be made by the person complained about, nor may members of an institution disciplinary committee review appeals of disciplinary decisions.

If an inmate believes the complaint is sensitive and he/she would be adversely affected if the complaint became known locally, the complaint may be filed directly with the Regional Director. If the latter agrees that the complaint is sensitive, it is accepted and responded to. Counterwise, the inmate is informed in writing of that determination, without return of the complaint. The inmate may pursue the matter by filing the complaint with the warden.

When the warden's response, due within 15 calendar days, is not satisfactory to the inmate, an appeal may be made to the Regional Director, who must reply within 30 calendar days. If still not satisfied, the inmate has 30 calendar days to appeal to the General Counsel located in the Headquarters Office; he has a like period of time to respond. Appeal to the General Counsel is the final level of review.

Extensions of institution, regional, and headquarters time limits may be extended once by the same amount of time originally allowed for response, if the allowed time is insufficient to make an adequate response. This decision is unilateral, but must be conveyed to the inmate in writing. A time limit that expires without a reply is deemed a denial.

Should a complaint be determined to be of an emergency nature which threatens the inmate's immediate health or welfare, the warden must respond within 48 hours of its receipt.

So far as the author is aware, an ombudsman position was established at only one institution, the Federal Correctional Institution, Englewood, Colorado (then the Federal Youth Center), which is later discussed.

Guidelines on the organization of inmate groups were first provided by a Policy Statement in May, 1972, which affirmed the previous policy of leaving the approval and supervision of organized inmate groups to the discretion of each institution administrator.[3] That policy statement was superseded by a Program Statement, effective August 1, 1979.[4]

Inmates wishing to form an organization are required to obtain written approval of the institution head prior to becoming active. A tentative constitution and by-laws defining the organization's purpose and operation must accompany the request for organization. All organizations approved must be coordinated by a designated employee. Meetings may be held at times which are not competitive with regularly scheduled work and treatment programs. All activities and projects sponsored by an organization must be approved by the institution head. Fund-raising projects are limited to those not requiring staff time beyond the capability of resources available to the institution and those not in competition with the commissary or interfering with the orderly operation of the institution.

While membership dues and a method of collection may be

authorized provided guidelines are established for an appropriate bookkeeping system including an annual fiscal audit, no inmate may be excluded from membership in an organization solely on the basis of lack of funds for dues.

Federal Penitentiaries

There are six United States Penitentiaries.

The U.S. Penitentiary, Atlanta, Georgia, in 1972 was using ad hoc inmate committees in a variety of programs. Staff members have mentioned an inmate council as having existed at one time, but there is no official record of it.[5] In 1940 an Inmate Publication Committee was reported to be developing into a permanent organization which might eventually include all inmates in the scope of its activities.[6] There is no inmate council at present.[7]

In 1940, shop committees had been organized at the U.S. Penitentiary, Leavenworth, Kansas. An Inmates' Advisory Council was in operation in February, 1944, but the actual date of its formation is unknown. A constitution, revised January 1,1947, provided for the secret ballot election of one representative for each of 22 work details to serve a one-year term of office. Candidates, chosen in a primary election, must have had at least a year remaining to serve. Representatives selected a chairman and a secretary from their membership or from the population. If selected from the population, neither was permitted to vote in council deliberations. The council met monthly in closed session to determine the agenda to be presented to the monthly meeting with the warden or his representative. The constitution stipulated the advisory nature of the group, expressly prohibiting concern with individual problems. The election of all representatives and all proposals by the council were subject to approval by the warden. Operation of the council was discontinued on July 2, 1951, after it had apparently become only a sounding board for petty gripes and grievances. The Sports Committee of the Inmate Advisory Council at Leavenworth continued to function after disbandment of the parent group and was reorganized under its own constitution on February 2, 1953, as the Recreation Advisory Committee. This group was dissolved in July, 1954 at the request of the members, as they believed it no longer had a part to play in the organization.[8] There is no inmate council at present.[9]

There has never been an inmate advisory council at U.S. Penitentiary, Lewisburg, Pennsylvania. For a few years there was an Inmate General Welfare Committee whose purpose was to provide financial aid to inmates, their families, former inmates, and worthy community welfare programs. This group was discontinued in January, 1965, primarily because of the demands on staff time. Information received in 1972 indicated that ad hoc committees were being utilized extensively to deal with special matters.[10]

In 1959, the former Army Disciplinary Barracks at Lompoc, California was transferred to the Federal Prison System and classified as a Federal Correctional Institution. In 1981 the institution was redesignated as a U. S. Penitentiary. A Policy Statement dated December 7, 1972 established an Inmate Advisory Council. Each officially recognized inmate group designated a member as its representative to the Committee. There were 14 organizations at the time of the Policy Statement issuance, representing ethnic, racial, hobby and self-help groupings. The Committee met monthly for 60 to 90 minutes with an administrative group composed of the two associate wardens, chief correctional supervisor, chief of case management, and the group activities coordinator. Other staff members were invited when discussion topics fell in their areas of responsibility. Minutes of the discussions held on the items listed on the previously prepared agenda were distributed to meeting participants and posted on housing unit bulletin boards after approval by the associate wardens. The Committee was not a decision-making group, but the Policy Statement reflected the possibility of staff decisions based on discussions presented by the Committee.[11]

In 1977, an Inmate Advisory Council was established at the Lompoc institution, but was discontinued in 1979 upon the transition of the facility from medium security to a penitentiary. Town Hall meetings are held monthly in each housing unit, providing a forum for inmates to express concerns and for staff response and announcements of items of interest.[12]

The Lompoc institution has a satellite minimum security camp in which the Inmate Advisory Council established in 1977 continues to operate under local guidelines. Three representatives are elected by secret ballot to serve a six-month term of office. The operational details are much like those described heretofore regarding the Council established in 1972.[13]

The Inmate Advisory Council was organized at the Terre Haute, Indiana, penitentiary in 1941, less than one year after the institution opened under the administration of Warden E. B. Swope. The author observed the development of the Council except for the periods of December, 1943 through June, 1946, and October, 1953 through July, 1959, while respectively in the Army Air Force and assigned as Chief, Classification-Parole at another institution. From August, 1959 until May, 1964, the author was the associate warden for treatment at the Terre Haute institution and provided the principal liaison between the staff and the Council.

While election by secret ballot was always a feature of the Terre Haute procedure, in the beginning years the elections were actually nominations subject to approval by the administration. This resulted in a membership of more mature and intelligent men. Meetings were held regularly at monthly intervals. In accordance with a constitution, the agenda for each meeting was approved in advance by the warden and minutes were subsequently submitted to him. In 1947, the associate warden for treatment was designated as staff liaison officer with the group.

The Inmate Advisory Council was disbanded in the early 1950s, largely because of staff disinterest. Attempts to revive it met with little success until 1956 when a new constitution was drawn which provided for a representative and alternate to be elected in each housing unit by secret ballot to a six-month term of office. Qualifications for candidacy were 90 days residency in the institution and a minimum of six months' time yet to be served.

The newly activated Advisory Council sought to function on what has been described as a forensic level--that is, the administration conveyed plans and policies to the representatives as a means of enlisting inmate aid in realizing institution goals. According to the then associate warden for treatment, there was a respectful interchange between the administration and inmates, with the latter accepting responsibilities earnestly and with no secondary motives. Although matters presented for discussion by Council members often included those described by the staff as trivial, the administration avoided in any way minimizing the importance of any topic. As an antidote to the practice of a member withholding action on a matter simply to provide himself with an item for discussion at the next meeting, a plan was initiated to have members report on improvements accomplished since the last meeting.

As with other such groups, the history of the Terre Haute Council is a series of highs and lows. By the late 1950s, the image of the Council was not favorable in the eyes of many staff and inmates. In 1960, although no modifications were made in the constitution and by-laws, a change did occur that overshadowed all other considerations. The Inmate Advisory Council was accepted as being truly representative of the institution population. Warden T. Wade Markley, who had only recently assumed the position, advised the inmates that they were to be regarded as members of the institution operating staff and that Council members, as their representatives, would be advised of financial and other records relevant to management. The successful results of that approach are evident in the excerpts of a 1961 report by Warden Markley:

> The Inmate Advisory Council has been in existence at this institution for several years. Organizationally it has remained about the same. However, in the past year we have drastically changed its orientation and functions.... We have communicated with the council extensively, tried to keep responsible inmates as members and have tried with considerable success to orient them toward providing leadership in establishing and maintaining a decent place to live. They have assumed this responsibility to the best of their abilities and have contributed to the establishment of the good climate we have achieved....
>
> We are advising the entire inmate body of our allotments and how we allocate them. We have had some interesting sessions in which we allowed smaller groups such as the Inmate Council to study our allocations and try to find a source from which additional funds could be

made available for food or clothing. They have been unable to find a better solution and usually give up in a short time when the effect of any transfers are pointed out. They have even developed insights into the needs for personnel and of the effect on them of personnel shortages. They also develop some understanding that the unfavorable publicity of their own acts has much to do with the lack of public acceptance, which in turn is responsible for much of the limitations of appropriations.

As a result of the understanding developed from these communications, the level of expectation was lowered considerably. Many even express surprise that the food can be so good. Thus we are able to attain a position whereby to the inmate body the food is as good as can reasonably be expected under the circumstances and it has become acceptable. There is a second dividend that is even more important. A toe-hold for the development of an acceptance of group responsibility is furnished. They begin to see that if they steal or waste food, or fail to take care of clothing or maliciously damage bedding or equipment they are hurting only themselves. They cannot control the situation as individuals, but must act as a group. It has prompted spontaneous campaigns to control waste and has actually reduced losses.... They are conducting sanitation campaigns and participate in the weekly inspections. Also, they are conducting programs aimed at preventing waste and malicious damage, controlling homosexuality and theft, and against the use of vulgarity and inmate slang.

In addition to setting an example and taking individual actions in the housing units, the council as a whole has sponsored newscasts, issued leaflets and posters, and prepared articles and a series of cartoons for the Terrescope (the inmate bi-weekly publication). The cartoons are humorous but directed toward improving behavior. The two characters depicted are So Seedy, the typical inmate rationalizer who contaminates himself and others, and Preston Forward is the hero who always wins while So Seedy is made to look ridiculous and the weakness of his position is evident. Another interesting innovation in the council-administration relationship was the development of agenda for the monthly meetings held with various staff members. These agendas are issued prior to the meeting and allow the staff member to consult with others if necessary and the council to discuss and consider items before entering the meeting.

The desirability of inmate councils has been debated for years. We feel that ours is a positive force and that it increases program effectiveness. Perhaps, desirability hinges upon approach and attitudes.

Council operations continued on this level until late 1962. A boycott of the dining room then occurred and investigation determined that it was encouraged by a small group, two of whom were council members. The council then went into a period of limbo during which time a complete review was undertaken of the Inmate Advisory Council program. One thing was clearly evident: the program was not attracting the men most qualified to represent others. The question was how to encourage such men to participate and at the same time leave the selection of their representatives to the men themselves.

Finally, in late March, 1963, procedures were established based on the recommendations of a staff committee chaired by the author. A man wishing to be a candidate would so inform his caseworker who would then forward his application to the Adjustment Committee, provided that his file reflected an adequate institutional adjustment, a minimum of 90 days served at Terre Haute, and a minimum of six months to be served beyond the next election. The Adjustment Committee, in turn, would confirm the applicant as a candidate if it was believed he had the potential for carrying out the duties of a councilman as indicated by his ability, adjustment, attitude and leadership. Prior to an election the Adjustment Committee appointed a three-man nominating committee in each affected housing unit. That committee selected a slate of four candidates from the list of eligibles already certified as candidates.

The result of this innovation was to heighten the desirability of Council membership. The process involved approval by significant staff members, which gave prestige to those qualifying. In turn, it insured that thugs and clowns, clearly incapable of meeting councilmanic responsibilities, would not be elected. The actual selection of those who were to stand for election was left in the hands of the inmates through the nominating committee, and final selection was still that of the general electorate via the secret ballot.

As it was desired to bring about a broad-based staff interest, custodial supervisors were later designated to select the persons to serve on the nominating committees in each housing unit. Additionally, a staff-inmate coordinating committee was appointed to provide the closest possible liaison between the administration and the inmate population. Chaired by the associate warden for treatment, the membership of this committee included the Council president, the secretary and a third councilman appointed by the president, plus five staff members who served for six-month periods. Appointments were made by the associate warden from all departments and included line personnel as well as supervisors.

The name of the council was changed to Resident Advisory Council and all men were thereafter referred to as residents rather than inmates. Emphasis was placed on the individual responsibility of each councilman in effecting an improved staff-resident communication. Each was given an opportunity to learn about institutional policies, procedures and goals, and encouraged to disseminate that knowledge to others. Councilmen became involved in the admission-orientation program for newly arrived men, being scheduled as speakers in what had been heretofore exclusively a staff function. Councilmen were appointed as members of staff committees on services, such as food and laundry. In addition, members attended staff planning committees on budget and vegetable gardens. A handbook on councilmen's duties and responsibilities was prepared.

This new approach was received enthusiastically by the residents and after some initial reservations the staff accepted it. The significant thing about it was that it accomplished its purpose of a more meaningful communication. The base of this communication was broadened by having inmate workers participate in departmental staff meetings. The views of residents were obtained in developing plans for the enrichment and strengthening of programs.[14]

Information was received in 1972 that the Terre Haute Resident Advisory Council had ceased to operate in 1964. In its stead, ad hoc committees were appointed for specific purposes.[15] There is no council at present.[16]

At the U.S. Penitentiary, Marion, Illinois, a Residents' Council operated for three years under procedures similar to others already described. In July, 1972, it became necessary for the administration to disband the group.[17] Currently, there is no council.[18]

The U.S. Penitentiary, McNeil Island, Washington, was administered by the Federal Prison System until 1981 when it was ceded to the State of Washington. The institution was originally a territorial jail constructed during the period of 1872-1875, and was under the control of the U.S. Marshal until turned over to the U.S. Attorney General in 1907.

An Inmate Advisory Council was organized circa 1936, with representatives selected by the inmates from their own group in each employment unit, including the farm. Elections were held semiannually. Term of office was six months, with no limitation on succession. The council selected from its membership a president and secretary. Tenure of these officers was limited to one term. The editor of the inmate publication, The Island Lantern, was an ex-officio, non-voting member of the group. Failure to obey institution rules could cause a representative to be dismissed from the council. The council met monthly in the library to consider suggestions made by the inmate population. No institution employee was permitted to attend the meetings. Occasionally the warden would visit for a short time but did not attempt to influence the proceedings in any way. Meeting minutes were forwarded to the warden for consideration. Subcommittees were appointed on special activities, such as athletic programs, entertainments, radio programs, and movies.[19]

In 1960, a Men's Advisory Council was formed to promote the general welfare of the inmates by providing a liaison with the staff. A constitution and by-laws, revised effective January 1, 1965, stated that any inmate of average intelligence and with an educational level not less than sixth grade could be a candidate to represent his housing unit for a six-month term of office provided he had been in the institution six months and had not incurred a record of major misconduct for the six months immediately prior to election. The 12 members were elected by secret ballot and selected from their membership a chairman, vice-chairman, secretary-reporter, and parliamentarian. The Council met twice a month to prepare an agenda of topics to be discussed by the Executive Committee, composed of the four officers, at its monthly meeting with the warden. The agenda was limited to five topics. Minutes of all meetings were disseminated via bulletin boards. Standing committees on blood bank, education-recreation, entertainment, publicity, rules and safety-sanitation were appointed by the Council, the chairman of each being selected by majority vote. Ad hoc committees were formed for specific purposes.

R. W. Meier, warden at the McNeil Island Penitentiary from October, 1966 until mid-1970, continued the Men's Advisory Council essentially as described. Monthly meetings were utilized as forums of information exchange between staff and residents. Management input included, for example, discussions on the need for efficient operations by effecting economies in electrical power use, food, and clothing items.

In 1972, the administration reported being in an experimental stage in inmate communications. While no directives or policy statement had been issued, a number of inmate organizations and clubs were in existence and the administration met regularly with them to discuss items on a previously drawn agenda. Consideration was being given to resuming the procedures followed by the Men's Advisory Council organization from 1960 to 1966.[20]

Federal Correctional Institutions

There are 24 federal correctional institutions, of which three are for youthful offenders sentenced under the Youth Corrections Act of 1950.

The Federal Correctional Institution, Alderson, West Virginia, was opened in 1927, and until the past several years was designated as the Federal Reformatory for Women. The first superintendent, Mary B. Harris, reportedly established a form of student government based on her experiences while superintendent in 1918 at the Clinton, New Jersey Reformatory for Women. Inmate cooperative clubs, intended as an experiment in self-control, self-government, and citizenship, were established in 1928. A club existed in each cottage, and members were elected to electorate, committee, or council status. Membership was strongly encouraged by the superintendent, and by the granting of additional privileges such as three outgoing letters per week or chevron badges for each term of service. Members were responsible for cottage management in matters such as fire drills, escorting newcomers on campus, and for policing behavior. When severe problems arose, the superintendent called upon the councils and committees for help. In 1936, the superintendent commented on her support of the groups:

> Whenever we have had a situation which was ... detrimental to the morale of the institution, this ... body of inmate representatives has thrown its weight on the side of law and order and proved its efficiency.[21]

In 1973, it was reported that a representative resident group had been in existence intermittently for many years. Reactivated in March, 1965 as the Community Council, the group was predicated on the belief that residents and staff should share responsibility for the general welfare and management of the community (institution) and that improved communications provided through the organization would add to the insight of all in mutual expectations. Realizing that success of the program could be assured only by staff support, the reorganization was preceded by several meetings in which the nature and potential of an inmate council was discussed. Management expectations of the staff role were incorporated into the operational procedures for each cottage housing unit. Although it was regarded as not without problems, the Council was believed by the administration to have more positive than negative aspects. Additionally, the administration believed that if the Council was to be really effective, the expenditure of much high-level staff time was necessary.

The associate warden was staff advisor to the community council, which operated under a constitution revised on September 20, 1966, and again on August 26, 1970. A woman who had been in the institution for at least 90 days, and had a year remaining to serve from the date of election, could be nominated from the floor or by a three-member nominating committee to stand for election by secret ballot to be a representative of her cottage, provided she had resided there for 60 days. Two representatives of each cottage were elected to serve one-year terms of office. The Council elected a chairman, vice-chairman, and a secretary, who together with five other Council representatives selected by them, composed an Executive Committee. This group prepared background material on matters to be discussed so as to facilitate the monthly Council meetings. Items on the agenda were compiled by the secretary from reports of monthly cottage residents' meetings conducted by the two council representatives and the officer-in-charge. In addition, there was a Coordinating Committee of four members, appointed by the Council chairman, whose function was to inquire into any questions arising about Council representatives and to act as arbitrators in the event a problem could not be resolved at the cottage level.[22]

A Warden's Council, established on April 6, 1979, is currently operative at the Alderson institution.[23] The constitution is similar to the one described in the foregoing paragraph. Notable differences are:

> -The Executive Committee is composed of the chairperson, vice-chairperson, secretary, three other council representatives appointed by the chairperson, and the Spanish representative.
> -The chairperson is an ex-officio member of all committees

which may be appointed, with the warden's approval, as deemed necessary to carry out the work of the Council.
-An Inmate Emergency Fund is sponsored by the Council.[24]

An Advisory Council was in operation at the Federal Correctional Institution, Ashland, Kentucky (then the Federal Youth Center), for approximately a year, beginning in early 1962. It was revived on two or three occasions for brief periods. Reportedly, it was difficult to maintain a membership that was representative of the entire population rather than just of the more aggressive elements. The Council was regarded as negative with reference to staff-inmate relationships. It was planned to organize an inmate council within a few months. The activities of several inmate committees on programs, commissary, and food, to name a few, together with a treatment-team approach which encouraged evaluation by inmates, were indicative of administrative concern with inmate-staff communication.[25] Currently, there is no council.[26]

A Program Advisory Committee was established at the Federal Correctional Institution, Butner, North Carolina, in May, 1977, one year after the opening of the facility in May, 1976. Composed of five inmates elected by peers in their housing units, and five staff members, the Committee meets each month to discuss items on an agenda prepared two days in advance. The purpose of the organization is to provide an additional channel of inmate-staff communication, to discuss proposals for institution programs and activities, and to make recommendations thereon.[27]

At the Federal Correctional Institution, Danbury, Connecticut, an Advisory Council in existence for several years was discontinued in early 1963. An Inmate Communications Committee was organized in March, 1972, under an institution policy statement for the purpose of improving inmate-administration communications on matters of general concern. It was specified that there was no intention of replacing individual inmate-staff communications. The two elected representatives of each housing unit served until released or transferred to another unit. Minutes were prepared and posted on bulletin boards following each of the two 90-minute meetings held monthly with the administration.[28] Currently, there is no inmate council.[29]

An Advisory Council was organized in July, 1940, shortly after a serious disturbance, and continued until some time in 1960, at the Federal Correctional Institution, El Reno, Oklahoma (then designated as the Federal Reformatory). The development of new classification procedures apparently opened up channels of staff-inmate communication which supplanted those provided by the Council.

An Inmate Advisory Group was established at the El Reno institution on August 18, 1972, to function as a communicative and advisory group between the residents and the administration. Two representatives were chosen by secret ballot from each housing unit and one representative was selected from each of the recognized cultural or civic groups such as Jaycees, Black Heritage, and Indian

Culture, to serve a three-month term. Regularly scheduled meetings were held twice monthly with a staff coordinator in attendance.[30] There is no council at present.[31]

A Resident Community Council was organized in October, 1972 at the Federal Correctional Institution, Englewood, Colorado (then the Federal Youth Center), creating a formal channel of communication between staff and residents. Among the goals established for the Council were the promotion of mutual action in problem solving, insuring the reception by appropriate staff of the existence of resident concerns, and the development of better resident-resident understanding. Nominees for Council membership were permitted to campaign by addressing their housing unit peers in regularly scheduled weekly sessions designated as Town Hall Meetings. Two representatives and one alternate were elected by secret ballot to serve an unspecified term. There was a limitation of two terms, consecutive or otherwise, during any three-year period. The twice-a-month meetings held with a staff ombudsman were so scheduled to insure minimal interference with other programs. The Council was encouraged to act as an advisory group with the realization that it had no power to dictate to staff. Additionally, there was an expectation that staff, through the ombudsman, would respond to the Council in an honest, expeditious manner.[32] It is not known how long this Council was in operation. However, when the institution became a Youth Corrections Act facility in May, 1982, an inmate council, reportedly in existence for two years, was done away with.[33]

In early 1972, the warden of the Englewood institution recognized a need to demonstrate administration concern with legitimate complaints of the youth population by appointing an ombudsman. A youth was expected to attempt resolution of grievances at the unit level, first by discussion with a counselor and the unit manager. If the complaint was still unresolved, the youth could make an appointment with the ombudsman.[34]

Although established to investigate and make recommendations for actions on all kinds of complaints, including unit and institutional policies, the ombudsman program reportedly became, at best, a means to review the decisions of unit managers in individual cases. Although the program achieved some measure of success in resolving personal problems of youths, it was not viewed by staff or youths as a means of reviewing unit or institutional policy. Part of the explanation for this attitude may have been the Resident Community Council already described. The Council discussed and presented institutional policy recommendations on behalf of the population to the Advisory Committee on Treatment, composed of seven staff members and one voting youth, and described as the major policy committee of the institution.[35] No information has been received as to the fate of this program.

Believing that effective correction in an institutional setting requires an adequate forum for expression of resident views to administration, and that if given appropriate opportunities residents will make positive contributions to the improvement of operations, especially in areas immediately involving them, the administration of the Federal Correctional Institution, Fort Worth, Texas, established several resident representative councils in April, 1972. Three groups mentioned in a policy statement were a Consumer Council, a Programs and Operations Council and a Residents Council on Corrections. In the first mentioned group, the membership was composed of one representative from each housing unit elected by secret ballot to serve a three-month term. The group met monthly with the Warden's Executive Assistant and the Chief of Client Management to discuss and recommend changes in procedures on commissary, movie selection, release clothing, and community entertainment groups.

Each established program unit selected by secret ballot a representative to serve a three-month term of office on the Programs and Operations Council. That group met monthly with the associate wardens to present recommendations regarding institution programs and operations, other than those areas reserved for the Consumer Council.

The Residents Council on Corrections at the Fort Worth institution was interesting, and although not novel, was certainly not widely employed. Council members were selected for 90-day periods to meet with the warden to discuss philosphies, and to contribute their views on the status of contemporary corrections. Selection of members was based on an assessment of the individual's capacity for serious discussion. Consideration was also given to maintaining a proper representation based on ethnic origins, criminal sophistication, and sex. The institution had facilities for both males and females.[36] There is no council at present.[37]

A Resident Communication Committee was organized in August, 1972, under an institution policy statement, at the Federal Correctional Institution, Milan, Michigan, as one effort to fulfill a policy of facilitating communication. In December, 1972, results were rated as successful. Members and alternates were elected by secret ballot to represent their housing units for not more than two terms of four months duration. The Committee had no decision-making power regarding the issues presented at monthly meetings with staff members. Saliency of proposals by the Committee was regarded as the basis for its effectiveness and influence. After six months (by March, 1973) the administration planned to evaluate the program and, in cooperation with the Committee, make modifications believed to be necessary.[38] There is no council at present.[39]

The Federal Correctional Institution, Morgantown, West Virginia, was opened as the Robert F. Kennedy Youth Center in 1968, with facilities for juvenile and youth offenders of both sexes. In June, 1970, a Student Advisory Committee was established, consisting of elected representatives from each cottage who met each week with the Program Management Committee, which consisted of the Case Management Supervisor, Education Supervisor, Chief Psychologist, and Administrative Officer. Once a month the director also attended the meeting. The weekly meetings with the Program Management Committee primarily served three purposes: (1) for students to seek review and clarification of existing policies and programs pertaining to them; (2) for students to propose changes or additions to program; and (3) for the administration to discuss with students programs and policies currently under development or review, or matters needing student support.

Organizationally, each cottage had two elected representatives on the Student Advisory Committee; an exception was the Pre-Release Cottage, which had one. There were no restrictions as to who could serve on the Advisory Committee. Representatives were expected to reflect the views of the students in their cottage and to report back in their cottage town meetings the results of their meetings with the Program Management Committee. The representatives selected one of their members to serve as the chairman of the Advisory Committee and another as vice-chairman. There was also a staff member who assisted them in developing a weekly agenda in their preliminary meeting and who prepared the minutes of the regular Student Advisory Committee and the Program Management Committee. Agenda items could be submitted by either staff or student, the only stipulations being that the item pertain to a matter of general institutional concern and that it not involve individual personalities. In actual practice, most agenda items were advanced by students. Once a month the meeting between the Committee and the Program Management Staff was held in a large room and all interested students were encouraged to attend. The director attended periodically, but kept a low profile. He regarded the process as workable and well worth the time involved.

Early in 1972, the administration commenced appointing students to serve with staff on special task forces. The initial step was to include students on the Task Force concerned with the revision of the Student Advisory Committee by-laws. This was followed by student inclusion on the Task Forces on Grooming and Student Behavior. Reportedly, the students involved performed fairly responsibly.

Additionally, each cottage had a weekly town meeting involving all students and staff on duty at that time. The meetings were primarily informational in nature with staff using the time to make administrative announcements, and for discussion of living unit problems and rumors. Students, in turn, were able to raise whatever questions or complaints they might have regarding the operation of the cottage or program. Town meetings were regarded as contributing to the successful operation of the institution.[40] There is no committee at this time.[41]

For several years the Federal Correctional Institution, Petersburg, Virginia, then designated as the Federal Reformatory, utilized two inmate advisory groups. One group, formed in late 1966, whose membership was appointed by the administration, met with the warden quarterly. The other group, whose members were appointed by the housing unit officers, met with the Assistant Supervisor of Education to select television and radio programs. In April, 1972, an institutional directive was issued which changed the structure and procedures of the program at the Petersburg institution, providing for one group to be known as the Inmate Representative Group. A representative from each housing unit was elected by secret ballot to a three-month term of office. Meetings were held monthly with the warden and various staff members to discuss an agenda composed of topics suggested by inmates or staff. The directive specified that "representatives will alternate between the Black and Caucasian races from quarter to quarter." Although the program was relatively new, the administration, in December, 1972, believed that the group served as a valuable vehicle of inmate-staff communication.[42] There is no inmate representative group now.[43]

At the Federal Correctional Institution, Pleasanton, California, a coed facility opened in July, 1974, each housing unit may establish an Inmate Advisory Group. Each of the three units elects three representatives and two alternates to serve a six-month term of office on the Institution Inmate Advisory Group (Inmate Council), a staff-inmate organization. The associate wardens for programs and operations, unit managers, superintendent of industries, the leisure time activities coordinator (who is also the liaison person), and department heads serve as management representatives. The council meets once a month to consider agenda topics which must be clearly concerned with general welfare and problem areas. Personal problems regarding either staff or inmates may not be discussed. Meeting minutes are distributed to management staff and posted on all unit bulletin boards.[44]

Inmate representatives must maintain good conduct and act in a responsible manner at all times. One major or three minor disciplinary reports will result in removal from the council. An ethnic balance of representation is required. Inmates are restricted to two consecutive terms of office. The administration is pleased with its council relationship, pointing out that it has not only brought about better administration-inmate communication, but has been the catalyst for significant improvements in institution operations and programs.

During the period from 1948 to 1959, the Federal Correctional Institution, Sandstone, Minnesota was used by the State of Minnesota as a medical facility. When it reverted to the jurisdiction of the Federal Prison System in 1959, Ray W. Meier was assigned there as warden. During his administration (1959-1964), a Men's Advisory Council was organized. A nominee approved by the administration could stand for election to a six-month term of office as a representative of his housing unit. Tenure was limited to one term. An unsupervised meeting of the Council was held each month to prepare an agenda for the monthly meeting with the warden. The agenda was limited to five topics and the duration of the meeting with the warden could not exceed one hour. Minutes of the meeting were posted on the bulletin boards in all housing units.[45]

According to information received in 1967, an Inmate Council was organized at the Sandstone, Minnesota institution on November 19, 1964. Meetings held monthly with the warden, associate warden, and other concerned personnel were regarded as being productive. A constitution provided for the secret ballot election of a representative from each housing unit to serve a six-month term of office with one succession possible. Only those persons who had been in the institution for six months and who had a like period remaining to be served could stand for election. A disciplinary report during the six-month period prior to election disqualified a nominee applicant.

It is not known how long the Inmate Council organized in November, 1964 lasted. An institutional policy statement established an Inmate Council in June, 1972, to improve inmate-administration communications on matters of mutual concern in order to facilitate improved institution operations for staff and inmates. It was specified that there was no intention that the Council supplant individual inmate-staff communications. A representative of each housing unit, chosen by secret ballot, together with representatives elected by minority groups, comprised the membership and two-hour meetings were held twice each month, one of them being attended by the warden or his representative. Minutes of the latter meeting, after approval by the warden, were posted on all bulletin boards.

Six months served and six months remaining to be served, no disciplinary reports for a like period, and three months residency in the Sandstone institution were the qualifications for any man wishing to be elected to serve a six-month term of office, to which he could once succeed himself. Council members chose among themselves a chairman, vice-chairman, and a councilman-at-large, the latter acting in the dual capacity of sergeant-at-arms at Council meetings, and as a mediator among housing units. A secretary was appointed by the chairman from either the elected membership or the population.

The preamble to the constitution of the Inmate Council at the Sandstone institution cited the purposes of the organization as being the fostering of effective idea exchanges, the development of a harmonious atmosphere, and the enhancement of inmate morale. It further stated that councilmen were both expected and required to so conduct themselves as to avoid criticism personally or of the Council. Members must never act to impair the Council or to negatively influence their peers.[47] At the present time there is no inmate council.[48]

On January 20, 1959, the Federal Correctional Institution, Seagoville, Texas organized an Inmate Advisory Council. Under procedures established in a constitution, a representative from each housing unit, and one alternate, could be elected to a six-month term of office by secret ballot. There was no limitation on succession. Any man who had attained an eighth-grade education, or its equivalent, and who had been in population for 90 days could run for office provided he had a six-months clear conduct record and more than 90 days remaining to serve. A meeting was held each month with the warden and associate warden to discuss various activities. In some instances the Council was helpful to the administration in regard to management problems. Line staff, in general, had few favorable comments on the function of the Council.[49]

The Inmate Advisory Council at the Seagoville institution was discontinued around June, 1969. When a Unit Management System was adopted in April, 1972, various types of town hall meetings were initiated in each of the five 80-man units. On June 15, 1973, an institution policy statement established a Staff-Resident Communications Committee, culminating discussions held during the prior year on the need to reestablish such a group to facilitate interchange between the population and the administration.

Membership of the Staff-Resident Communications Committee consisted of the warden, associate warden, chief of correctional programs, the executive assistant to the warden, who was designated as the staff coordinator, the supervisor of education, and two representatives from each of the five living units. Following secret ballot elections, each unit manager listed the names of the three residents receiving the highest number of votes. From these lists the warden selected two persons to serve six-month terms as official committee members. The third person was designated as an alternate member. Tenure was limited to two consecutive terms. The Committee met once a month to discuss the items on an agenda prepared and published the previous week at a meeting of the executive assistant and one representative from each unit. Matters involving institution security, orderly operation, and facility emergencies were stated as being staff prerogatives. Discussion topics were limited to those clearly definable as program or general welfare concerns, with no inclusion of a resident's personal problems.[50] There is no inmate council at this time.[51]

An Inmate Advisory Council was organized in October, 1951 at the Federal Correctional Institution, Tallahassee, Florida. The constitution provided for secret ballot election to a six-month term of office as a representative of his housing unit for any man with a clear conduct record who had been at the institution at least 90 days and who was regarded as acceptable for membership by the associate warden. At the twice-monthly meetings, councilmen considered suggestions tendered by their constituents. These suggestions, by majority vote, could be forwarded to the administration. Each councilman assisted the housing unit officer in disseminating pertinent information and was responsible for television program scheduling. Additionally, the councilman played an important role in orienting new men to the unit. The then administration viewed the council program as being mutually beneficial to staff and inmates by promoting better communication and by offering an opportunity for the latter to develop leadership qualities as well as civic pride. The warden who took office in June, 1972 reported that the Inmate Council was not functioning at that time. A committee whose members were chosen by popular vote selected movies and television and radio programs.[52] There is no council at present.[53]

The Federal Correctional Institution, Terminal Island, California, was opened on July 1, 1938. The original population included a small group of females transferred from the Federal Correctional Institution, Milan, Michigan. In 1940, ad hoc inmate committees were used to plan entertainments and athletic activities. One committee was especially active in organizing a schedule and tournament of softball teams.[54]

In December, 1941, the institution was turned over to the Navy. In May, 1955, it reverted to the Federal Prison System. The institution was comprised of a Men's Division and a Women's Division until the mid-'70s when the female prisoners were transferred to the Federal Correctional Institution, Pleasonton, California, which was opened in July, 1974.

The last inmate council was discontinued in 1980 because of the high turnover in population.[55] In the past several years, the institution has had a Federal Detention Center component.

In 1958, an Advisory Council was organized in the Men's Division and thereafter functioned on a sporadic basis. The Advisory Council, Women's Division, originally known as the Inter-Relations Council, was organized in March, 1962. Both groups functioned under a constitution similar to others already mentioned. While the author was Associate Warden of the Men's Division from May, 1964 through July, 1967, the group was redesignated as the Terminal Island Council. Occasional enthusiasm by a few members would lead to short-lived periods of activity. In October, 1965, staff attention and effort were directed to implementing the Work Release Program. The Council continued to function, meeting on an irregular basis.

During the period 1967 to 1969, Council activity was quiescent, reactivating only occasionally. In December, 1972, it was reported as having been quite active since 1969. Representation was by housing units, ethnic groups, and social groups, all elected, and meeting at least once a month with various staff members. Communication between Council and staff was credited with limiting a November, 1971 work stoppage to a one-day duration.[56]

Federal Prison Camps

There are six Federal Prison Camps.

The Federal Prison Camp, Boron, California, opened in 1979. The present superintendent reports that, prior to his arrival in September, 1980, there was a semi-council which did not succeed, primarily because of the short sentences of the population.[57]

Sometime during 1979, an attempt was made to establish an inmate council at the Federal Prison Camp, Safford, Arizona. The turnover in population resulted in a lack of continuity and the repetitive resurfacing of the same problems, which was frustrating to both inmates and staff. The group lasted approximately 18 months and was dissolved because of a lack of interest and participation.[58]

In December, 1972, the then superintendent reported that organization of an inmate council was anticipated in the near future.[59] There is no council at present.[60]

Former Institutions

The Federal Reformatory at Chillicothe, Ohio, was opened in 1926 and ceased to operate as a federal institution in December, 1966, when it was ceded to the state of Ohio. An Inmate Advisory Council was organized there on November 7, 1933, under a constitution whose preamble proclaimed its purpose to be to effect a closer cooperation among inmates and the administration, and to promote the general welfare of the inmate body. The group attracted national attention a few months later when a leading periodical reported its formation. "Inmates of the U. S. Industrial Reformatory at Chillicothe, Ohio, now have an advisory council of 65 members, one to every ten of the dormitory population, with an executive committee of 15, to bring matters of general welfare before the administrative officers. Early proposals concerned recreation facilities and suggested means for cutting down electric light bills."

From the long experience at the Chillicothe institution with advisory councils, in May, 1966 the 101st Resident Advisory Council was elected and there developed several observations: good representation is of mutual benefit to the population and administration; an advisory group must be limited and controlled to avoid its ultimate downfall; domination by councilmen who place their own wishes ahead of the good of the group is detrimental to the viability of the council. This last observation created guidelines for a listing of characteristics which should be applicable to all councilmen:

1. Does his best to reflect the honest views he represents.
2. Possesses true leadership qualities and seeks ways to improve programs and rehabilitation efforts.
3. Has the stature to stand up for the right things and assists his Quarters Officer and the administration in eliminating thievery, sex play, obscenity, and gambling.
4. Is a tactful person who is effective through intelligent persuasion and example.
5. Counters rumors and distortions with facts.
6. Does his best to make his quarters as decent and wholesome a place to live as he knows how.
7. Realistically and conscientiously tries to find ways and make suggestions for improvements in the institution.
8. Is always polite, courteous, appreciative and considerate of others.

9. Makes it a point to learn and know of the efforts and improvements being made in the institution and attempts to instill some degree of appreciation in other inmates.
10. Is considerate of the difficult job an officer has, and does his best at all times to foster and improve good staff-inmate relationships.
11. Is able to work out most of the problems in quarters with his Quarters Officer.

Dinner meetings were held after each election at which the outgoing officers were honored and newly elected officers welcomed. The guidelines for elections called for a 90-day clear conduct record, a four-month term of office, and a willingness to remain in the same quarters (state-of-promotionlessness) during term of office. Voting was by secret ballot with allowances for first, second, and third choices. All elections were subject to the final approval of the administration. In addition to representation for quarters, there were members elected whose constituency and concern reflected the various industrial areas, such as chair factory, machine room, foundry. The original constitution and by-laws were drawn up on November 7, 1933; the by-laws were amended on February 7, 1938, and a completely revised and amended constitution and by-laws was published on March 3, 1941. J. A. Mayden, who was warden at the Chillicothe institution from 1965 until 1966, classified advisory council activities as occurring at three levels.

1. Forensic Level--The advisory council is an organization utilized by the administration to convey information to inmates, and possibly to receive information from inmates.
2. Administration Aid Level--At this level, the advisory council is charged with responsibility in specific activities, such as the planning of radio, television and movie schedules, and arranging holiday events. In the housing unit, the councilman's duties revolve primarily around helping to maintain a smooth operation.
3. Policy Level--The advisory council at this level is included by the administration in discussions and decisions on policy.

Warden Mayden believed that the forensic level would be difficult to maintain, since there is little to sustain the interest of the participants. He cited the administrative aid level as being the simplest in terms of management in that it obtained the aid of inmates with no danger of encroachment on the authority of the administration.

The third level was emphasized by Warden Mayden as being the most productive to all concerned. One of the gravest problems this level of advisory council operation holds is the threat felt by personnel. Before council operations at this level can be successful and valuable several ground rules must be established. These rules should include active participation by the warden or a representative who can take action; sincerity of intent in participation by the staff, even when faced by challenges to cherished traditions; open and direct lines to high-level staff for ready consultation; and the inclusion in council membership eligibility of varied behavioral types in order that the administration may effectively approach the turbulent element in the population. Warden Mayden stated that some of the most productive councilmen had been of that element. He also compared participation in council activities to group therapy.

The Chillicothe Councils functioned principally on the administrative aid level as described by Warden Mayden. The organization was used effectively by the supervisor of education in recreational programming. On the housing unit level the correctional officers and councilmen worked cooperatively. As the population of the institution was being reduced by the transfer of residents to other institutions in anticipation of ceding the facility to the state, the council was of considerable assistance to the administration.[61]

The National Training School, Washington, D.C., was turned over to the Federal Prison System in 1939. In January, 1967 a Student Advisory Committee was formed. The superintendent met every two weeks with the members who were selected by the housing unit officers for three-month terms. That communication was helpful to the administration, leading to some minor changes in several programs. The school was closed in 1968 upon the opening of the Federal Correctional Institution, Morgantown, West Virginia.[62]

Notes

1. Keating, McArthur, Lewis, Sebilius, and Singer, op. cit., p. 36.
2. Program Statement 1330.7, "Administrative Remedy Procedures for Inmates," Federal Prison System, October 12, 1979 (effective November 1, 1979).
3. Policy Statement 7300.15, "Inmate Organizations," Federal Bureau of Prisons, May 4, 1972.
4. Program Statement 5381.2, "Inmates Organizations," Federal Prison System, July 16, 1979 (effective August 1, 1979).
5. Baker, J. E., op. cit., p. 208.
6. The Attorney General's Survey of Release Procedures. Vol. V, "Prisons," June 1940, p. 335.
7. Letter from D. W. Hasty, Executive Assistant, Southeast Regional Office, Atlanta, Georgia, November 8, 1982.
8. Baker, J. E., op. cit., p. 208.
9. Letter from R. L. Phillips, Executive Assistant, North Central Regional Office, Kansas City, Missouri, October 14, 1982.
10. Baker, J. E., op. cit., pp. 208-209.
11. Ibid., pp. 225-226.
12. Letter from Warden Robert J. Christensen, U.S. Penitentiary, Lompoc, California, November 18, 1982.

13. Ibid., and "Inmate Advisory Committee," Institution Supplement No. 5381.2, Federal Prison Camp, Lompoc, California, April 26, 1982 (supersedes No. 7312.2-1, April 27, 1979).
14. Baker, J. E., op. cit., pp. 210-214.
15. Ibid., p. 214.
16. Letter from R. L. Phillips, op. cit.
17. Baker, J. E., op. cit., p. 214.
18. Letter from R. L. Phillips, op. cit.
19. MacCormick, Austin H., ed. Handbook of American Prisons and Reformatories, Pacific Coast States, op. cit., pp. 115-116.
20. Baker, J. E., op. cit., p. 209.
21. SchWeber, Claudine, Ph.D., "Pioneers in Prison," Federal Probation Quarterly, Vol. 44, No. 3, September 1980, p. 34.
22. Baker, J. E., op. cit., p. 215.
23. Letter from Z. S. Grzegorek, Regional Director, Northeast Regional Office, Philadelphia, Pennsylvania, November 15, 1982.
24. "Constitution," Warden's Council, Federal Correctional Institution, Alderson, West Virginia, October 2, 1981 (supercedes Constitution dated April 6, 1979).
25. Baker, J. E., op. cit., p. 219.
26. Letter from D. W. Hasty, op. cit.
27. "Program Advisory Committee," Memorandum, J. B. Bogan, Associate Warden, Federal Correctional Institution, Butner, North Carolina, May 6, 1977.
28. Baker, J. E., op. cit., p. 221.
29. Letter from Z. S. Grzegorek, op. cit.
30. Baker, J. E., op. cit., p. 218.
31. Letter from G. E. Killinger, Regional Correctional Program Administrator, South Central Regional Office, Dallas, Texas, October 28, 1982.
32. Baker, J. E., op. cit., p. 221.
33. Letter from Art Espinosa, Executive Assistant, Federal Correctional Institution, Englewood, Colorado, November 9, 1982.
34. Keating, Gilligan, McArthur, Lewis, and Singer, op. cit., p. 32 (based on site visit in November 1973).
35. Ibid., pp. 35-36.
36. Baker, J. E., op. cit., p. 226.
37. Letter from G. E. Killinger, op. cit.
38. Baker, J. E., op. cit., p. 222.
39. Letter from R. L. Phillips, op. cit.
40. Baker, J. E., op. cit., pp. 219-221.
41. Letter from Z. S. Grzegorek, op. cit.
42. Baker, J. E., op. cit., pp. 218-219.
43. Letter from Z. S. Grzegorek, op. cit.
44. "Inmate Ad Hoc, Advisory Groups and Committees," Unit Management Manual, Section 5045 (PLE 5321.2), Federal Correctional Institution, Pleasanton, California, March 30, 1982 (supersedes policy of March 17, 1981); letter from Ron Burkhart, Acting Warden, Federal Correctional Institution, Pleasanton, California, November 18, 1982.

45. Baker, J. E., _op. cit._, p. 222.
46. _Ibid._, p. 222.
47. _Ibid._, pp. 222-223.
48. Letter from R. L. Phillips, _op. cit._
49. Baker, J. E., _op. cit._, pp. 223-224.
50. _Ibid._, p. 224.
51. Letter from G. E. Killinger, _op. cit._
52. Baker, J. E., _op. cit._, pp. 224-225.
53. Letter from G. E. Killinger, _op. cit._
54. MacCormick, Austin H., ed. (1942), _op. cit._, pp. 181-182.
55. Letter from Luis F. Cortez, Associate Warden (Programs), Federal Correctional Institution, Terminal Island, California, December 28, 1982.
56. Baker, J. E., _op. cit._, p. 225.
57. Letter from Superintendent Bill R. Story, Federal Prison Camp, Boron, California, November 9, 1982.
58. Letter from Superintendent C. H. Young, Federal Prison Camp, Safford, Arizona, November 17, 1982.
59. Baker, J. E., _op. cit._, p. 227.
60. Letter from Z. S. Grzegorek, _op. cit._
61. Baker, J. E., _op. cit._, pp. 215-218.
62. _Ibid._, p. 219.

CHAPTER V

OTHER JURISDICTIONS

Although there are numerous facilities administered at other than the state or federal level, only those in the District of Columbia, the Department of Defense, the cities of New York and Philadelphia, and the counties of Cook, Illinois, and Westchester, New York, were included in the survey.

CIVIL

COUNTY OF COOK, ILLINOIS

The Department of Corrections, Chicago, of the County of Cook, administers six divisions (facilities) for adult and youthful felony and misdemeanor offenders.

An ombudsman program was established in 1975 which provided for written responses to grievants.[1] No further information has been obtained.

An Inmate Grievance Procedure has been drafted, with May or June 1983 targeted as the time for full implementation.[2]

Under the proposed procedure, an inmate submits a written grievance to a caseworker from the Human Services Program who has five working days in which to respond. An appeal may be made to an independent reviewer who, within five working days, will make a recommendation to the Executive Director. The Director will issue a written decision within ten days. This is the final level of review.

Grievances may include, but are not limited to, complaints regarding policies, practices, procedures, conditions, acts or omissions, under the jurisdiction of the department. An exception to this process is the disciplinary procedure.

Reprisals against either inmates or staff for use of or participation in the grievance procedure "are strictly prohibited and ... shall be punished by Department disciplinary action."

Decision and implementation of a grievance defined as being of an emergency nature must be made no later than 24 hours following its receipt.

An interesting feature of the procedure is an Inmate and Staff Grievance Committee for the purpose of reviewing the effectiveness of the program and to make recommendations to the Executive Director for procedural modifications. The director is required to make a written reply by the next meeting of the committee. There are 12 members of the committee and a representative of the director. Of six inmate members, two are appointed by the director, the remaining four chosen by random selection. The appointment and selection process must provide for one inmate from each facility. The staff members are two correctional officers, two correctional supervisors, and two non-uniformed personnel. Term of office for members is three months. Individual grievances are not reviewed by this committee.[3]

The Department has never had an inmate council and there are no plans for one in the forseeable future.[4]

Notes

1. Dillingham, David D., and Singer, Linda R., op. cit., p. 59.
2. Letter from Phillip T. Hardiman, Executive Director, Dept. of Corrections, County of Cook, Chicago, April 4, 1983.
3. "Inmate Grievance Procedure," General Orders, Dept. of Corrections, County of Cook, Chicago (proposed).
4. Op. cit.

DISTRICT OF COLUMBIA

Department of Corrections

The Department of Corrections is comprised of three services: Detention, Correctional, and Youth.

An Administrative Remedy Procedure was established on April 21, 1978, to provide a quad-level process in which institution residents may seek formal redress of complaints related to their confinement, except claims made pursuant to the Federal Torts Claims Act or 18 U.S.C., 4126, Claims for Inmate Injury Compensation. The procedure is now tri-level.[1]

If feasible, a resident must file a written complaint, via a prescribed form within 15 days from the date of an incident, with the institution administrator, who will make a written response in not more than 15 working days. If not satisfied, the grievant has ten working days to file an appeal to the Assistant Director (for Detention Services if in the Central Detention Facility; for Correctional

Services if in any of the other six institutions), who has 20 days in which to investigate the grievance, determine a course of action, and make a written reply.

As a final step in the procedure, a grievant may then within 15 working days appeal to the Director, Department of Corrections. The Chief of Judicial Affairs reviews all appeals to the Director and prepares the response.

Complaints of an emergency nature which threaten the resident's health or welfare must be responded to at the administrator level within 48 hours.

Sensitive nature complaints or those the grievant has reason to believe would adversely affect him or her if it became known at the institution that the complaint was being made may be filed with the Director, but must specify why normal channels do not suffice.

The time limits for response at any level of the procedure may be extended for a like period if needed to render a decision. The grievant must be advised in writing in all such instances.

The past and the present regarding inmate advisory councils is presented under each of the three services of the Department of Corrections.

Detention Services: In 1976 a new Central Detention Facility was opened to replace the District of Columbia Jail which had been in operation since 1876. In 1972, it was reported that the organization and operation of an inmate council was not feasible due to the rapid turnover of population.

In 1910, the Reformatory for Women was established at Occoquan, Virginia. In November, 1966, the administration reported a favorable reaction to the results of the inmate advisory council. Under the by-laws, one representative from each housing unit was elected to a six-month term of office. Nominees must have been at the facility for at least 90 days and have six months or more yet to serve. A councilwoman was expected to know all rules and regulations, interpret them to others, and encourage by counsel and example a high standard of conduct. She was also expected to discourage and report any escape plans or attempts and to lend her services to the staff in the event of an escape. Provision was made for removal from office of any councilwoman who became disinterested in her duties, did not attend meetings regularly, continually discussed disapproved council recommendations, engaged in subversive activities, or became involved in disciplinary incidents.

The Reformatory for Women was moved to North Capital Street, N.W., in about 1966, and redesignated as the Women's Detention Center. The Inmate Advisory Council was reported as still active in 1973.

In 1978, the Women's Detention Center was closed and those inmates serving misdemeanant sentences and those who were pretrial detainees were moved to a section of the Central Detention Facility. Female felony offenders serve their sentences in Federal Prison System institutions for women. Currently there is no inmate advisory council.[3]

Correctional Services: The Lorton Correctional Complex, Lorton, Virginia, consists of three institutions for adult male felony and misdemeanor offenders: The Central Facility (formerly designated as the Reformatory), the Maximum Security Facility, and the Minimum Security Facility. The latter is located at Occoquan, Virginia.

An Inmate Advisory Council at the Central Facility was organized in November, 1962, under a constitution and by-laws. Operating with the assistance of a staff committee, the council was the matrix for some successful inmate-staff efforts. Initially there was concern with inmate gripes and somewhat superficial matters, but eventually the group became engaged in activities regarded by the staff as more constructive. The constitution preamble emphasized the blending of inmate-staff endeavors in promoting the re-socialization goals of the institution. A representative and an alternate were elected by secret ballot to represent each housing unit for a six-month period. Those housing units having more than 100 residents elected an additional representative and alternate. Nomination qualifications included six months' residency at the institution, a minimum of six months' time left to serve, no period in segregation or forfeiture of goodtime credits during the six months preceding election, and the absence of any other penalty for the immediate past 60 days. A specific disqualification was having been engaged in a collective action inimical to the best interests of the institution. At least 30 days prior to an election, all office seekers were required to file written intention with the superintendent. Those qualified were given a certificate of eligibility. The Council elected three officers, a chairman, vice-chairman, and secretary. The chairman was empowered to appoint ten standing committees whose chairmen, together with the three Council officers, formed an Executive Committee which had general supervision over the conduct of elections under the direction of the Assistant Superintendent for Training and Treatment. The foregoing information was obtained in December, 1966.[4]

In January, 1973, it was reported that all inmate advisory councils at the Lorton Correctional Complex had become inactive because of inmate dissatisfaction and lack of participation which had developed early in 1972. The administration stated that revival of the councils rested with the inmates.[5] Reportedly, an Office of Resident Concerns was established at the Central Facility. No details have been obtained about this inmate council except that it was activated in 1974 or 1975 and met frequently with the administrator.

A new institution for male misdemeanants, the Occoquan

Facility, became operational in March, 1982, in a section of the former Workhouse at Occoquan, Virginia. To date, no inmate advisory council has been established.[6]

In 1966, the administration of the Workhouse, now the Minimum Security Facility, was experimenting with the use of an inmate advisory council involving only a small segment of the population, the intention being that, should the activity prove satisfactory, all inmates would be given an opportunity to participate.[7]

None of the institutions of the Lorton Correctional Complex has an inmate advisory council at the present time.[8]

Youth Services: Included in the Youth Services are two Youth Centers at Lorton, Virginia, the first opening in 1960, the second in 1972. In January, 1973, an Inmate Advisory Council was reported as being active, meeting once a week, at Youth Center I. As described in 1967, the Council was composed of a representative from each of the 11 dormitories, elected by ballot to hold office for six months. The principal function of the group was to relay inmate wishes and ideas to the administration. At the weekly meetings with staff representatives, the Council considered proposals to be later discussed at an administrative staff meeting. Decisions on these proposals were usually made promptly. A maximum freedom in idea exchange was encouraged. The belief was expressed that this method of contact with inmates was a means of becoming advised of matters which have problem potential if not resolved.[9]

Both Youth Center I and Youth Center II continue to have active councils, now designated as Resident Advisory Councils.[10] Each Council is composed of representatives from the dormitories and from the service areas in which residents are significantly involved. Elections are by secret ballot. Term of office is one year, with reelection permitted. A candidate for office must have been at the Center not less than 45 days and have more than six months remaining to be served on his sentence. Removal from office occurs if a member incurs three disciplinary reports within a six-months' period, acts irresponsibly, or accrues three unexcused absences from meetings. The group has three functions: dissemination of information to the population; contributing to the input of ideas for decison making and evaluation of treatment programs; and relaying to the administration information regarding problem areas and grievances affecting the institution.[11]

Youth Services Administration

The Youth Services Administration, Commission of Social Services, Department of Human Services administers the two facilities for juvenile delinquents. There is no student grievance procedure as such at either facility. However, students may write letters to the Commissioner of Social Services about problems or complaints. An investigator will prepare a report on the issue, a copy of which is sent to the facility superintendent. The deputy superintendent interviews the grievant and attempts to resolve the matter. All allegations of abuse made against staff are fully investigated.[12]

Information was received in 1966 that a Student Council at the Cedar Knoll School, Laurel, a co-educational facility, was sponsored by the administrator and the recreation supervisor. The Council advised on and made recommendations for recreational and leisure time activities such as dances, cottage parties, and special holiday programs. Council members acted as hosts or hostesses at these affairs and assumed responsibility for the conduct of other students. There was also a Clothing Committee made up of representatives from the cottages. Working from catalogues and samples furnished by wholesalers, the group assisted the administration in selecting student clothing. Each chaplain was assisted by student representatives in planning the religious programs.[13] The Council was still active in 1973, together with a staff-student Recreational Council.[14]

Also, in 1966, it was reported that at the Maple Glen School, Laurel, students served as aides to the recreation supervisor, coaching and supervising the younger and newer boys. These junior coaches were regarded as having been very successful. This facility also had a Clothing Committee, and students assisted the chaplains in planning religious programs.[15] The school was closed in about 1976, and is now a Jobs Corps Center.[16]

Notes

1. Department Order No. 4030.1, "Administrative Remedy Procedure," Department of Corrections, District of Columbia, Washington, April 21, 1978. (Originally the second-level appeal was to the superintendent of either the correctional or detention services. Those positions were eliminated circa 1981.)
2. Baker, J. E., op. cit., pp. 231-232.
3. Letter from Mary H. Oakey, Program Analyst, Dept. of Corrections, Washington, received August 8, 1983.
4. Baker, J. E., op. cit., pp. 232-233.
5. Ibid., p. 232.
6. Letter from Mary H. Oakey, op. cit.
7. Baker, J. E., op. cit., p. 233.
8. Letter from Mary H. Oakey, op. cit.
9. Baker, J. E., op. cit., p. 233.
10. Letter from Mary H. Oakey, op. cit.
11. "Resident Advisory Council Constitution," Youth Center I, Lorton, Virginia. (The constitution for the Council at Youth Center II is almost identical.)
12. Telephone conversation with Edward A. Mahlin, Deputy Supt. Oak Hill Youth Center, Laurel, Maryland, June 21, 1983.
13. Baker, J. E., op. cit., p. 233.

14. Letter from William W. Barr, Associate Administrator, Social Rehabilitation Administration, Dept. of Human Resources, October 31, 1973.
15. Baker, J. E., op. cit., pp. 233-234.
16. Telephone conversation with Edward A. Mahlin, June 21, 1983.

THE CITY OF NEW YORK

Department of Correction

The Department of Correction administers all detention and sentence institutions for adult and youthful felony and misdemeanor offenders.

Under a multi-level Inmate Grievance Program established in November, 1982, an inmate may file a grievance about the substance or application of any written or unwritten policy, regulation, or rule of the department, or institution, or the lack of same, or any behavior or action directed toward the grievant.[1] Exceptions are those programs having an internal appeal process, e.g., disciplinary actions, and class action complaints. All complaints, written on a prescribed form, must be filed with a Grievance Officer or Housing Unit Aide within three days of an alleged occurrence. A hearing is then held by the Inmate Grievance Resolution Committee following which a written decision must be made in not more than five working days.

The remaining levels of review whose specified time limits (in working days) for a written response are as follows:

Commanding Officer	- 7
Central Office Review Committee	- 15
Board of Correction/	- 30
and Commissioner's Decision	- 10

A staff grievance coordinator is responsible for the operation of the program in each institution. Grievance Officers and Housing Unit Aides are, with the concurrence of the Commanding Officer, appointed by the coordinator to serve at the latter's discretion. Aides are paid as skilled workers under the inmate incentive wage plan.

The Inmate Grievance Resolution Committee must be a five-member body consisting of two voting inmates elected by their peers, two voting staff members, and a non-voting chairperson who may be a staff member or a volunteer associated with the institution or a civilian grievance coordinator. Members serve a once-renewable three-month term of office. The inmate members, and alternates, are also paid as skilled workers. The chair, a voluntary assignment, has a tenure of six months.

The Board of Correction may delegate its appellate function to any independent arbitrator, whose recommendation must be made to the Commissioner, Department of Correction, in 30 days. No more than ten working days later, the Commissioner will issue a decision, which is final.

Time limits at any level of review may be extended only with the grievant's consent. Copies of grievances may not be placed in either an inmate or personnel file without the signed consent of the affected or referenced persons. Reprisals or adverse actions of any kind against an inmate or employee for using or participating in the grievance procedure are prohibited. Emergency situations are referred directly to the Commanding Officer.

In 1957, there was a fairly sustained attempt by the Department of Correction to test the feasibility of inmate advisory councils at the Correctional Institution on Rikers Island in both the Adolescent and Adult Divisions. Council members were elected on a fairly regular basis in each cell block. Meeting regularly with the warden and occasionally with the commissioner of correction, the councilmen presented suggestions by their constituents for improvements believed by them to be supportive of a good rehabilitation program. Although the administration considered the council program to be a potent factor in promoting the type of self-discipline most useful for success in both learning and community situations, the decision to abandon it had to be made principally because of the transient nature of the inmate population, overcrowded conditions, and lack of funds for required rehabilitation personnel.[2]

Guidelines were issued in late 1972 to assist all institutions in implementing a directive by the commissioner of correction regarding the formation, organization, and implementation of inmate liaison councils. The principal points of the guidelines were:

1. The primary purpose of a Council is to develop new lines of staff-inmate communication as an attempt to promote the solution of problems arising as a result of institutional operations, by serving in an advisory, non-policy making capacity.
2. Techniques for nomination, such as petitions requiring ten to 25 signatures, to be followed by announcements in the institutional newspaper, are suggested.
3. Provision is to be made for closed ballot election in each housing area, to be followed by a run-off election involving the two to four major vote-getters, to serve as delegate or alternate, for a non-renewable term not to exceed three months.
4. Frequency of meetings to insure the opportunity to resolve issues prior to their becoming crises.
5. Staff members chosen to meet with the Council should be those recognized by inmates and staff as possessing both the interest and ability to communicate with inmates.

Additional purposes of the inmate liaison committee system: to provide the staff an opportunity to respond to legitimate grievances, in writing if practical, and to prove the good faith and commitment of the Department of Correction to remedy or to clarify the problems surrounding legitimate grievances; to provide information to the administration for policy-making decisions; to transmit to the institution population the attitudes, values, and commitments of the administration, and be an instrument to assist inmates in obtaining responses to grievances outside the jurisdiction of the Department of Correction. Medical services and courts are cited as examples of the latter.[3]

Currently, inmate councils in New York City correctional facilities are composed of one representative, and up to three alternates, of each housing unit, except at the New York City House of Detention, East Elmhurst, where the numbers are two and five, respectively. Term of office is 60 days. Each council has an executive unit consisting of a chairperson, vice-chairperson, secretary, and three to six additional representatives. This unit meets weekly with the other representatives, and monthly with the institution head.[4]

Notes

1. "Inmate Grievance Program," Directive No. 3375, Dept. of Correction, City of New York, effective November 23, 1982.
2. Baker, J. E., op. cit., p. 234.
3. Ibid., pp. 234-235.
4. Letter from Robert Goldman, Deputy Commissioner, Dept. of Correction, City of New York, April 25, 1983.

THE CITY OF PHILADELPHIA

The Department of Public Welfare has jurisdiction over the prison facilities of the City of Philadelphia which are administered by the Superintendent of Prisons. This city/county system, presently housing some 3700 residents, 80 per cent of whom are in unsentenced status, is comprised of three major facilities, each housing in excess of 1000 persons, and a number of smaller satellite units, including a women's institution.[1]

An independent ombudsman reported directly to a private agency, the Pennsylvania Prison Society, which was established by the Superintendent of Prisons in late 1971, attributed in part to the Holmesburg Prison riot in 1970. However, the project was suspended after a few weeks. Inadequate preparation of prison staff members and dissatisfaction with the personal style of the ombudsman (an ex-offender) are said to have contributed to the failure of the project.[2]

In December, 1980, an Inmate Grievance Procedure was established to conform with the terms of an agreement in a class action suit. (Jackson vs. Hendrick, Court of Common Pleas, Trial Division, February term, 1971, No. 2437.) The deputy warden first seeks to have the parties involved come to an informal resolution of the issue which, if accomplished, is recorded on a grievance form and signed by the inmate. If agreement is not reached, the written grievance is forwarded to the Grievance Committee composed of one inmate member chosen by the Betterment Committee (which is later described), one correctional officer, and a member of the prisons' training staff.[3]

An inmate may file a complaint via a prescribed form about the circumstances or application of written or unwritten policy, regulation, rule, or program; the lack of such policy, regulation or rule; any behavior or action directed toward him or her, and any provisions of the stipulations and agreement regarding the class action suit. Disciplinary actions and issues clearly under litigation are excluded.

The Grievance Committee must process all grievances within three working days. If the issue is a question of policy, the grievance form is returned to the grievant for filing with the superintendent or the Grievance Appeals Committee, which is later described. If the issue is without substance or not within the jurisdiction of the grievance procedure, it is returned, with notation, to the grievant. Otherwise, the Grievance Committee conducts a hearing at which witnesses, as well as the grievant and the respondent, may testify.

Recommendations of the Grievance Committee must be made not later than three days after the hearing, and are subject to the warden's approval if any action by the administration is involved. The latter action must be taken in five working days.

The grievant may appeal an unfavorable decision of the Grievance Committee or warden to the Grievance Appeals Committee. The convenor of the committee is a person not employed by the Philadelphia Prisons and is appointed by the court. Two other voting members are a correctional officer selected by the warden and the convenor from a list of five nominees submitted by the Director of Inmate Services, and an inmate from a pool of three nominees, one from each institution, selected by the institution Betterment Committee membership. A written finding of facts and recommendations are made to the warden. The warden must accept the fact findings unless they are clearly erroneous. Rejection of the recommendations may be made on one or more of the following grounds: implementation would be contrary to law, or institution rules, regulations, or policies; is not fiscally possible; would create a new right of the inmates; would endanger public and/or institution security. Additionally, a recommendation may be denied if it goes beyond the scope of the issues, or is not an appropriate remedy in the specific circumstances of the case. Reasons must be specified as to why the recommendation is not appropriate.

The history of inmate participation in Philadelphia Prisons dates back to mid-1970 when an Inmate Advisory Council was established at the House of Correction on the recommendation of several staff members. Residents of each cell block selected a representative to meet, under the supervision of correctional officers selected from volunteers believed qualified by temperament and attitude, to discuss general prison conditions. Four of the Council members were selected to meet monthly with the administration and initial meetings were regarded as having been very fruitful.[4] As recollected, seven of eight specific recommendations made by the Council at the first meeting were immediately implemented.[5]

By March, 1973, each institution had a council, referred to as the Betterment Committee, and other groups, some being represented by attorneys assigned by the Community Legal Services. These groups may request a meeting with the superintendent and his staff as the need arises. Two instances are cited as evidence of the value of recognizing and working with inmate organizations as opposed to attempts to suppress them. A four-day food strike at the Holmesburg Prison in August, 1972 was resolved as a result of negotiations with various inmate groups. Also in 1972, two similar problems of shorter duration at the House of Correction were resolved through the inmate groups.[6]

By 1973 the role of the Betterment Committee was expanded to include the annual administration of funds granted to the inmates as a result of a class action lawsuit heretofore mentioned. Funding decisions are made in conjunction with the prison administration and relate to the expenditure of monies for musical instruments, movies, entertainment groups, etc. A formal budget cycle and review process has been established and an annual audit of the Inmate Welfare Fund must be performed.[7]

More recent policies have established bi-annual elections of Block Representatives and alternates (together forming the Betterment Committee of each institution) and the selection of officers by internal vote of that group. In addition to meeting with institutional workers and the superintendent on a regular basis to air issues of concern to the inmate population, a member of the Betterment Committee also sits with a correctional officer and a member of the prisons' training staff on the Grievance Committee established at each institution and on the Grievance Appeals Committee, as already described.[8]

Notes

1. Letter from David S. Owens, Jr., Superintendent of Prisons, City of Philadelphia, May 17, 1983.
2. May, Edgar. "Prison Ombudsmen in America." Corrections Magazine, Vol. 1, No. 3, January/February 1975, pp. 45-55, 58-60.
3. J v H Stipulation and Agreement III, Paragraphs 25-45, "Grievance System."

4. Letter from David S. Owens, Jr., Superintendent of Prisons, City of Philadelphia, May 17, 1983; Letter from Louis S. Aytch, then Superintendent of Prisons, City of Philadelphia, March 14, 1973.
5. Letter from Louis S. Aytch, op. cit.
6. Ibid.
7. Letter from David S. Owens, Jr., op. cit.
8. Ibid.; "Guidelines for Inmate Organizational Meetings," City of Philadelphia, March 31, 1983; "Proposed Organization of Block Representatives," March 29, 1982; Procedural Directive, E.O. 79-02, "Inmate Welfare Fund," Philadelphia Prisons, January 15, 1979 (revised April 5, 1979), (designed to conform with terms of Interim Decree II, of the Jackson vs. Hendrick case signed October 31, 1978).

WESTCHESTER COUNTY PENITENTIARY

Department of Correction

All of the correctional operations of the county were merged under the Department of Correction, Westchester County, Valhalla, New York, in 1969.[1]

An Inmate Complaints and Grievances Procedures was established in October, 1981, to supersede all such previous procedures,[2] which probably were of an informal nature.

An inmate must, except as later noted, present a complaint to the housing unit correctional officer, who will make reasonable efforts toward resolution. Should this not be possible, the inmate completes a complaint form for delivery to the unit complaint coordinator, who must be of sergeant rank. The grievant will be interviewed by the coordinator and a reasonable attempt made to resolve the issue. A written response to the grievant must be made within three working days.

If for any reason the inmate feels the complaint could not or should not be called to the attention of the housing unit officer, a complaint form may be given directly to the complaint coordinator.

In the event the coordinator is unable to resolve the complaint successfully, an appeal to the department warden may be made. The warden will convene a Grievance Committee composed of the division head of the grievant's housing unit, a shift supervisor, and a member each from the correction and program staffs. With the warden as chairman, the committee, within five working days, will review previous investigations and findings, hear any additional information from the grievant or other involved or affected persons, and prepare a response indicating the decision made and its rationale.

The grievant may appeal to the Department Commissioner via

sealed letter, and if not satisfied with the response may, within seven days, appeal to the Local Facilities Complaint Unit of the New York State Commission for Correction, Albany, a three-member group responsible for inspecting and monitoring the level of care provided prisoners in all correctional facilities of New York, including those confined in municipal lockups, county jails, and state prisons.

Any complaint of an urgent or emergency nature is investigated immediately by the shift supervisor and a written report made within 24 hours. Such complaints will be escalated, as appropriate, to other levels of the procedure.

An account of the past and present concerning the inmate council known as the Effort League is given in Chapter I, Notable Early Experiences.

Notes

1. Letter from Commissioner John J. Maffucci, Dept. of Correction, Westchester County, Valhalla, March 17, 1983.
2. "Inmate Complaints and Grievances," Policy No. 80-1, Dept. of Correction, County of Westchester, Valhalla, New York, October 8, 1981 (supersedes all previous inmate complaints and grievance procedures).

FEDERAL

DEPARTMENT OF HEALTH AND WELFARE

The United States Public Health Service opened two hospitals in the 1930s for the care and treatment of both term and voluntary narcotic addict patients. Both were transferred to the Federal Prison System in the 1970s. The following accounts are included for historical reasons and as examples of inmate council structure variations.

Clinical Research Center, Lexington

The Clinical Research Center, Lexington, Kentucky, was opened on May 25, 1935, as the United States Public Health Service Hospital, for the treatment of persons addicted to the use of habit-forming drugs. The population included male and female prisoners, voluntary addicts, and a limited number of non-addict neuropsychiatric patients. The first council of patients was organized in July, 1956. It consisted of 20 addict patients elected to represent the various units of the hospital. It functioned until 1964, disbanding because of inability of the members to present and relay projects or programs, due largely to an excessive attention to individual petty gripes.

A constitution drawn in July, 1959 designated the group as the Male Patients' Council and provided for ballot election of two representatives from each housing unit to a six-month term of office. No qualifications for office were stipulated, but provision was made for expulsion "for cause" by a two-thirds vote of the membership subject to concurrence of the medical officer in charge. The editor of the patient newspaper was accorded all the privileges of an elected member except the holding of Council office. A chairman, vice-chairman, recording secretary and sergeant-at-arms were elected by the Council. Meetings with the medical officer in charge were scheduled bi-monthly. Closed meetings of the Council were held weekly. The president was authorized to appoint standing and ad hoc committees on the advice and recommendations of the Council.

In 1958, a Puerto Rican group was organized by the chief of general services to represent approximately 140 Spanish-speaking patients. Members acted as interpreters of their language, culture, and customs for the staff and other patients. Eight delegates from this group met bi-weekly with the chief of general services. They provided an orientation group for new admissions to promote racial-cultural understanding, formed a Spanish music group, took part in helping to lessen incidents of adverse behavior, and organized an Alcoholics Anonymous chapter.

The clinical director organized a Patients' Activities Group in 1959. Its purpose was to encourage patients to participate in the hospital programs, hold competitive meetings, and support special groups, such as drama, art, writers, music and other talents, athletics and pastimes. All of these were interwoven with mental health meetings and closer relationships between and among patients and personnel. This group existed until 1965.

Following passage in 1966 of the Narcotic Addict Rehabilitation Act, the facility limited its patient load to narcotics addicts civilly committed to a six-months' in-patient period and a 36-months' aftercare program. Autonomous living areas were provided, each comprising a small, therapeutic community in which input from both residents and staff provided the basis for all major decisions. Each living area was encouraged to sponsor projects, including research. A Social Affairs Committee was formed principally to plan extra- and intramural social events and to select movies. A staff member and one resident from each living area were the members. This facility was transferred to the jurisdiction of the Federal Prison System in 1974 and is now designated as the Federal Correctional Institution, Lexington, Kentucky.[1]

Clinical Research Center, Fort Worth

From November, 1938 until 1972 (when jurisdiction was transferred to the Federal Bureau of Prisons and the designation changed to Federal Correctional Institution), the facility at Fort Worth, Texas functioned as a United States Public Health Service Hospital. Until

1942, the patient population was composed of term and voluntary narcotics addicts. From 1942 to 1949, the population consisted largely of neuropsychiatric patients on active duty with the Navy, Marine Corps, and Coast Guard. From 1949 until 1972, the hospital cared for a wide variety of psychiatric patients, about one-third of whom were addicted to narcotics.

An Inmate Advisory Council was organized in 1951. Members, elected by popular vote, met with the clinical director and others of the professional staff. An excerpt from the 1951 annual report of the hospital indicated a positive impact on both program and patients:

> Council presented to the staff's attention many needed reforms and changes which were adopted to the betterment of the patients in the hospital. The council served to disseminate information and staff attitudes to the population through Ward Representatives. It played a therapeutic role in the lives of the individual council members in that it gave them a greater sense of responsibility and self-determination within the hospital setting and helped them to resolve some of their conflicts with authority.

In the same year the Honor Ward concept was established, featuring single rooms and minimum security. The selection of patients and the operation of the ward were functions of the Classification Committee whose primary intent was to develop a high degree of democratic self-government.

In November, 1964, staff-led Self-Help Groups were formed, in which patient-leaders encouraged the general patient group to a total involvement in the therapeutic program. A patient-leader was allowed evening use of a group therapy room, which stimulated much enthusiasm among patients for the self-help concept. It is known that between March, 1965 and March, 1967 an entire ward was devoted to the Self-Help Program. It functioned as a minimum security unit in which its 30 patients met twice weekly in 90-minute afternoon sessions with a psychiatrist-psychologist-social worker team. Each of the seven wards also had an eight-member Council, which sent one representative to a weekly Council meeting with the chief of addiction service, a security officer, and a nursing staff member. Minutes of these meetings were distributed to all wards. On its own initiative the Council assumed responsibility for influencing ward milieu favorably.[2]

Notes

1. Baker, J. E., op. cit., pp. 236-237.
2. Ibid., p. 238.

DEPARTMENT OF DEFENSE

The Departments of the Army, Navy, and Air Force, and the United States Marine Corps each operate correctional facilities for their members convicted and sentenced to confinement under court-martial proceedings.

Service members confined in Army correctional facilities retain the right of access to members of the chain of command for the redress of grievances.[1]

No current information about inmate councils was received. However, in December, 1972, it was reported that there had never been councils at the Army facility known as the United States Disciplinary Barracks, Fort Leavenworth, Kansas, or the United States Army Retraining Brigade, Fort Riley, Kansas.[2]

Department of the Navy facilities, called brigs (from 1969 to 1980 they were named correctional centers), provide confinement for detained, adjudged, and sentenced confinees of the Navy, Marine Corps, and Coast Guard. "Detained" means pre-trial; "adjudged" includes those already tried but whose cases have yet to be reviewed, and "sentenced" means that all appellate processes have been completed. There are no grievance procedures in Navy facilities, but each confinee has a "right to redress" for wrongs committed by the commanding officer under the provisions of Article 138, Uniform Code of Military Justice. Unless the individual is satisfied, such complaints must be forwarded to the Secretary of the Navy.[3]

Some Navy brigs have or have had inmate councils that made recommendations on topics of general interest, such as the athletic and recreational programs. Establishment of a council is discretionary with brig officers-in-charge within clearly defined limits.

The Department of the Air Force has one institution, the 3320th Retraining Correction and Rehabilitation Squadron, opened in 1952 at the Amarillo Air Force Base, Texas, and relocated in 1967 to its present location, Lowry Air Force Base, Colorado. (The original name of the facility was the 3320th Retraining Group.)

The entire population of the facility meets with the Corrections Officer once a week to express any grievance. Answers to issues raised are given immediately unless higher authorization or coordination is necessary.[4]

In December, 1972, a Retrainee Council was reported as having been established several years earlier on an informal basis. Two members each from five 40-man treatment groups, elected by retrainees or appointed by counselors and team staff, plus two additional members--selected at the discretion of the division chief from a Corrections Division program for men who have failed to be selected for Retraining Program participation or eliminated from it and returned to confinement to serve out their sentence--made up the 12 members.

Council meetings were held twice monthly at a specified time with the group commander and the security police superintendent present. Discussion topics ranged from petty complaints to the reorganization and revamping of Air Force penal and rehabilitation programs. The only topic not open for discussion was that of staff personalities. While members were cautioned not to expect action or immediate results on all topics considered, the frequency of changes occurring from their discussions was sufficient to cause them to realize they were taken seriously by the administration. Staff input had resulted in a more effective dissemination of information than by traditional written directives.[5]

Since 1976, a rehabilitee council, currently named the Grassroots Council, has been in operation. Council members are elected at-large. Nominees for election are reviewed for appropriateness by the staff. Weekly meetings are held with the Squadron Commander to discuss topics ranging from petty complaints to policy and programmatic issues. The only topic not open for discussion is that of staff personalities. As with the council previously described, members are cautioned not to expect immediate results on all topics considered; the frequency of changes occurring from these discussions is sufficient to cause them to realize their inputs are taken seriously by the administration. Each issue raised is fully coordinated with staff before any answer is given to the council.[6]

No information has been received regarding the Correctional Facilities under the jurisdiction of the Law Enforcement Section Division, United States Marine Corps.

Notes

1. Letter from Thomas A. McDonnell, Colonel, GS, Chief, Office of Army Law Enforcement, Dept. of the Army, Washington, D.C., September 28, 1982.
2. Baker, J. E., op. cit., p. 239.
3. Letter from A. A. Davis, Commander, U.S. Navy, Director, Law Enforcement and Corrections Division, Dept. of the Navy, Washington, D.C., September 30, 1982.
4. Letter from Shelby N. Cordon, Lt. Col., USAF, Commander, 3320th Correction and Rehabilitation Squadron, Lowry Air Force Base, Colorado, September 28, 1982.
5. Baker, J. E., op. cit., pp. 239-240.
6. Letter from Shelby N. Cordon, op. cit.

CHAPTER VI

THE ATTAINMENT OF POWER

From information obtained in surveys made in 1960, 1966-67, 1972-73, and 1982-83, we have drawn a cross-sectional view of the participation of inmates in prison administration. This view is augmented by the work of others to whom credit has been given throughout this volume.

In 1960, most corrections programs were based on the treatment, or medical, model. The report of the President's Commission on Law Enforcement and Administration of Justice, published in 1967, and the subsequent Task Force Reports, made many recommendations for coping with the problem of crime in the nation. Of the recommendations made for corrections, 96 per cent concerned improving treatment and rehabilitation efforts.

As a consequence of the reports by the President's Commission, the Law Enforcement Assistance Administration (LEAA) was created under the provisions of the Omnibus Crime Control and Safe Streets Act. The proportion of the millions of dollars allocated to the LEAA being used for corrections rose dramatically and continued until the demise of that agency in 1982. While controversy about the effectiveness of such massive expenditures still lingers, there can be no question that had the effort not been commenced, the situation in corrections would be doubly as desperate as it is today. The effort did stimulate innovation which generated new experiences, and, vitally important, created an atmosphere for the reception of new thought, a willingness to try new approaches, and an emerging realization that corrections must move with the times and be willing to alter many of its traditions, including--importantly for our study--those regarding the relationship of the keeper and the kept.

By the late 1960s doubts about the efficacy, effectiveness, and even the wisdom of the treatment model were beginning to appear, and finally came out of the closet after the publication of an article entitled "What Works ..."[1] by R. Martinson and colleagues, and a 1975 book, Effectiveness of Correctional Treatment--A Survey of Treatment Evaluation Studies,[2] which was a compilation and analysis of local, national and foreign research studies conducted between January, 1945 and December 31, 1967, to evaluate the treatment of criminal and juvenile offenders. The latter study and, among others, David Fogel's We Are The Living Proof ...,[3] became the rationale for abandoning the treatment model and embracing the justice model. One of the principal components of the justice model is determinate sentencing. Those jurisdictions which adopted the model have watched in fascinated horror as their prison populations escalated to undreamed-of levels.

Despite the justice model and the euphemistic name changes--e.g., prison to correctional institution; isolation to seclusion; segregation to protective custody--the prison in the United States of America faces a crisis, as it has again and again during the 200 years of its existence. It has been an existence in which it has functioned apart from the social mainstream, largely ignored, and relegated to a hand-me-down status as was Cinderella, fulfilling neither the purpose for which it was originally established nor the aspirations and dreams of the handful of dedicated men and women who dared step off the treadmill of tradition.

As each day, each week, each month and each year goes by, the laser beam of publicity is penetrating the concrete and psychological walls, exposing to the view of all what transpires therein. It is a sight that gives little encouragement, Rather, it is a sight of shame--the shame of a long neglect which has caused the piecemeal fashioning of programs, the modus operandi of reacting to situations rather than planning for them, and a host of other ills and shortcomings. The deficiencies, both quantitatively and qualitatively, of men, money and material are not unique to the current scene. Any historical perspective finds that triad of burdens. Additionally, the lack of guidelines, the absence of any means by which to evaluate the efficacy and efficiency of correctional efforts, has resulted in the sorry saga and spectacle of legislators continuing to pass laws, officials making policy, and huge sums of tax dollars being expended on ineffective methods and, in some instances, on programs akin to rediscovering fire or the wheel.

The role of the prison must be defined. There must be a policy which will say what the prison is, what it is not, and, most importantly, a policy by which a determination can be made of what the prison can be. Fortunately, within the past three years, the American Correctional Association has been at work on a plan to identify significant issues affecting corrections so that a national correctional policy can be developed and operationalized. Another source of hope is the establishment of standards by the Commission on Accredition in Corrections.

As has been previously stated, an objective of the prison--disputed by some and championed by many--is to assist the individual prisoner, who so wishes, to acquire modes of coping in his/her life style which do not result in conflict with authority. Direct participation by the individual in the process is essential, possibly mandatory, to insure the attainment of that objective. However, there has been, and continues to be, much debate on the definition of participation.

Some persons concerned with corrections believe that progress in prisons will occur only when inmates are enlisted into the decision-making process and democratically share power with staff. Others view that idea as ridiculous and reject it out of hand.

Sykes' study of a New Jersey prison suggested that under democratic governance, there is a greater chance that goods, rights and privileges will be distributed equitably among large numbers of inmates.[4]

Others view democratic participation as a useful means of negotiating prison conflict providing there exists an effective means of enforcing inmate interests, e.g., an inmate advocacy group or an inmate union. This assumes that inmates have the moral and logical ability to seriously weigh policy claims and to administer justice to other inmates.[5]

Scharf and Hickey also point out, quite realistically, "... that prison democracy, given the contemporary realities of the prison, reflects an almost hopeless enterprise. Unless there is a massive reordering of both the prison as well as the idea of imprisonment, the democratization of the prison is, at best, an unlikely avenue of reform."[6]

Almost any effort at prison democracy must be recognized as a limited democracy, existing within the limits defined by the inmates' captivity.[7]

Inmates have no legal right to democratic participation in prison management. They cannot vote themselves out of prison, nor can they vote to imprison their captors.[8] It has been pointed out, and rightly so, that at this point in history, the mass media and popular sentiment would most certainly overwhelmingly oppose any extension of democratic rights to prison inmates; prison staff and inmates would feel threatened and endangered, the latter probably preferring the certain rule of the prison warden to a justice administered by their peers. Additionally, jurists would, no doubt, object to the notion of inmates judging and legislating for other inmates.[9]

As previously mentioned, inmates have always occupied roles having an impact on prison operations, procedures, and sometimes on policy. Those roles were, in some instances, formal and officially sanctioned. The first attempts to enlist the inmate formally in the administration of the prison were manifested by self-government programs which evolved into an arrangement known as the advisory council.

The concept of inmate self-government grew out of the harshness of the old prison regime, to provide a framework within which the inmate could express some freedom of expression and choice. Certainly, such a concept was unique to the prevalent social patterns of the periods in which we find it first emerging, most often only briefly.

Some persons and groups are critical of inmate councils, dismissing them as artificial or fraudulent fronts by which inmates are conned into being further controlled. A popular disparaging view is that such advisory relationships (council to administration) offer influence but not power. It must be remembered, however, that people with influence are people with power. That is a fact of life in both the public and the private sectors of our society. Inmate councils have the power that influence creates. Councils have the ear of the prison administration, and do bring about changes by responsible presentation of population problems, needs, and wishes.

In the 1982-83 survey, and those made earlier by the author as well as studies by others, administrators have consistently stated that the inmate council provides a vehicle for inmates and staff to discuss their mutual concerns, problems, and in some instances, grievances. In addition, both are able to have input into issues, policies, and procedures affecting their lives, work, and institutional conditions. From the administration viewpoint, the council increases its ability to gain access to inmate attitudes, assess needs, better communicate with the entire population, and manage the prison in a pro-active rather than re-active style. Staff also take the opportunity in council meetings to raise and discuss their own concerns and to become actively involved in decision-making. Many institutions report resulting improvement in staff-inmate relations. Concurrently, the inmate representatives may assist staff by explaining to their peers the staff point of view.

Participants themselves may experience some personal change as a result of being elected to and serving on a council. They improve their leadership skills; they learn to take responsibility for their decisions, to develop long-range plans and to apply this knowledge to their own planning for the future. Just as leadership roles on appointed or elected boards and councils in the community may enhance prestige and self-esteem, so may these roles, despite the aspect of incarceration.[10]

Inmates cannot, of course, be permitted power to administer a prison. Despite the evidence of mismanagement of prisons in some jurisdictions throughout the history of the nation, it would be illogical, aside from being illegal, to abandon management by staff. However, there are other methods by which inmates can participate meaningfully in the administration of the prison. Those methods are based on participatory management or leadership.

Participative leadership is a leadership style which seeks, as far as practical and possible, to embrace the greatest feasible number of organization members in the maximum number of decision-making episodes. Its democratic flavor rests on the view that people support what they help create. It makes managers, or perhaps "mini-managers," of almost the entire organization. Its advantages are many:[11]

1. It tends to increase collaboration and reduce competition between interdependent units.

2. It encourages a very healthy situation where decisions are made on the basis of information sources rather than organizational roles, thus favoring a norm of "the authority of knowledge" rather than one of "the authority of position."
3. It can use the talents and resources of group members, permitting them to invest in the goals and problem-solving mechanisms of the organization so that there is greater compliance and teamwork in achieving objectives.

However, it must be kept in mind that participation in and of itself is no panacea. What is sought after is a particular kind of participation: "participation which is no more than pooling of ignorance will not yield 'best' solutions. Reaching commitment to decisions based on opinions rather than fact may merely be motivation to produce erroneous action."[12]

Whether prison administrators recognized it or not, there has always been a high degree of participatory management in their institutions. Some call this phenomenon a heightened communication or shared decision-making. By whatever name, it translates to inmate participation.

As the accounts in previous chapters reveal, inmates have attained power also via complaint procedures and the courts. Wholesale changes in both policy and procedure have been mandated by the courts on the basis of inmate initiatives.

There is a growing sophistication among inmates in the use of their influence on those who have the power to change conditions. In addition to complaint procedures and the courts, inmates exert influence via the numerous prison reform groups to whom legislators often listen. Another source of influence is the activist attorney who has a monetary, as well, perhaps, as a philosophical stake in assuring that inmate rights are protected through litigation.

Correctional administrators must be aware that today we see an altering of the relationship between the individual and whichever insititution of society, for whatever reason, has assumed some degree of control over his destiny. This alteration is taking place through several social movements whose collective thrust is that those who are to be affected have a legitimate interest in the actions taken by that social institution, and perforce the right to voice an opinion which will be given serious consideration in the formulation of philosophy as well as policy.

Movements by and in behalf of students, the mentally ill, welfare recipients, and consumers are examples of this striving for a new kind of relationship between the dispenser of largesse and the receiver. Again and again, in the swiftly swirling events of the last two decades, there are repeated demonstrations of the fact that policies and procedures produced in the isolation of Washington, the State Capitol, or the County or City Courthouse are not always the best. In order for any agency of government to do even an adequate job of meeting the needs of those it is to serve, and to promote the general good of all the nation, there needs to be established and preserved a relationship of serious communication. The correctional process is the manifestation of society's assumption of control over the destiny of the offender.

Reason reveals to us that almost without exception, all offenders are engaged, either positively or negatively, in the correctional process. Wagner pointed out many years ago that, while the status of inmate participation in correctional institutions is controversial, and therefore uncertain, one thing is definite--all institutions do have some form of inmate participation, whether planned or unplanned, and if properly channeled it can be an important constructive force in the rehabilitation of offenders. He defined inmate participation primarily as free and easy avenues of communication between inmates and administration, with inmate participation in both the planning and the operation of the institution program as an almost natural corollary.[13]

Perhaps many of those who have seriously believed that the administration controlled the direction and the destiny of the institution have never fully comprehended the extent and the impact of offender influence on planning and operations. As the characteristics of those in confinement change, to that extent the institution changes. From that strata of society euphemistically designated as the disadvantaged, the places of confinement have traditionally received their clientele. What the institution provided, or failed to provide, was of little consequence to persons whose social consciousness was undeveloped or thoroughly inhibited. But the person in confinement today is no longer the acquiescent "good inmate" of yesterday. The mainstream of the confined population today contains in disproportionate numbers the products of the urban scene, well aware of the life of abundancy and affluence which surrounds them: they have seen it on the tube and the screen, want what they want now, and are convinced that the continuing discontinuities of our social order block their escape from the status they believe to be the reason for their present situation. They have had it with authority which seems to be blind or insensitive to the individual without power or influence.

As the characteristics by which the confined population can be generally described have changed, so it is with the place of confinement. In some, the change has been evolutionary. As the needs of the offender changed in response to expectancies aroused by multitudinous social stimuli, the institutional program shifted in accommodation. Perhaps a school was added, or a new series of studies introduced--black culture, for instance, a work release program, or a furlough plan.

In other places of confinement--alas, too many--offenders have brought about changes in program and practice by revolution, as witness the disturbances of varying degrees of severity that send shockwaves throughout a state, and, in some instances, across the nation.

In either case, evolution or revolution, correctional residential facilities have responded. They have responded in a variety of ways, but they have responded, just as there have been responses to the communication efforts of the human beings involved in the social movements already mentioned.

In the correctional residential facility, the voice of the inmate, prisoner, resident, ward, student, client--or whatever designation has been adopted--is being raised, and reason tells us that this will continue. Psychology tells us that the provision of channels of communication, so that the individual can be assured of being heard, will provide the kind of satisfactory emotional outlet that will make collective shouting unnecessary.

It has often been said that prisoners are people. This so obvious fact is too often overlooked. People want and need to be heard, and need the satisfaction of knowing that what they say will be given serious consideration. This is important in dealing with others, either individually or collectively. It assumes added importance in the confinement situation, which purports to resocialize the offender to the end that he will become a law-abiding, productive member of society upon release. This goal cannot be accomplished if his voice is stilled, his thoughts stifled, and his opinion unsought or ignored.

Corrections administrators also need to be aware of the extent to which each new idea, policy, procedure or program may add to the power of others, perhaps at the expense of an administration's ability effectively to guide and control the consequences of actions which may be taken by the shareholder-of-power on the basis of either explicit or implied power.

Each successful effort by inmates via court orders, consent decrees, or otherwise to be granted a privilege or to restrict an action by corrections administration is a diminution of the power of the warden in the institution and the top person in the central office. That power does not atomize or disappear. Power is like matter; it is indestructible. It always exists in some form and in some area. In the case of the prison, any power that is lost by the administration generally passes to the inmate.

There are many ways in which power is eroded, and ceaseless attempts are being made in that regard. For example, several inmates at the Pontiac Correctional Center, Pontiac, Illinois, had filed various lawsuits involving disciplinary hearing officers. Included in the list of grievances was the complaint that some of the officers sitting on the committee that heard charges against those inmates were persons against whom the inmates had previously filed lawsuits. The inmates contended that, as a result, those members were prejudiced against them. A lower court agreed that those members should not have been allowed to rule on disciplinary matters, even though the two problems were unrelated. Had this ruling stood it would have been possible, within a relatively brief period, for those inmates and others to file lawsuits against all staff members, and thus block them from sitting as members of a disciplinary committee. Fortunately, a federal court of appeals disagreed and reversed that decision. Disqualification is not necessary in every case, the court said, and pointed out that if each staff member who had been named in such lawsuits had to refrain from sitting on the disciplinary committee, a severe burden on the institution would result. The court also noted that, since an inmate is able to name many staff members as defendants, he could gain control of the committee make-up. The case is Redding v. Fiarman, 717 F.2nd 1105(7th Cir., 1983) and was reported in Corrections Compendium, Vol. 8, No. 7, published by Contact, Inc., Lincoln, Nebraska. The lower court was asked to determine if disqualifications were needed based on all the circumstances surrounding each case.

Nothing in the foregoing three paragraphs should be construed as being in opposition to the adoption of complaint procedures and/or inmate councils. There are positives and negatives to any program, and both must be weighed in any decision to establish, modify, or terminate. The detailed accounts given in this book will be helpful in connection with any such decision-making.

The necessity for informed decision-making gives emphasis to the necessity that the correctional administrator be a competent professional, truly a correctional administrator. There is much argument about the qualifications of a correctional administrator. Many management purists teach as holy writ the philosophy that a top-level manager can manage any kind of endeavor, be it the manufacture of left-handed widgets, the operation of a coal mining enterprise, a prison, a group of prisons, or a correctional system encompassing both confinement facilities and community service programs. The core of that view is that a manager manages people and an organization is, after all, simply a collection of people performing whatever tasks have been assigned to them in a particular division of labor scheme.

But such a philosophy does not wash in corrections. Despite the occasional example of an outsider successfully presiding as such, a correctional administrator should be either an experienced corrections worker or an experienced administrator in a people-oriented service organization. A comparison of the qualifications of those who administer correctional facilities today with the qualification of administrators of several decades ago will reveal a marked increase in the ranks of those who are truly competent correctional administrators. The author has no survey results to support that view, only his own observations over a 43-year span of time.

Ten years ago, in a prior book, the author made an observation about changes then in progress which is still valid:

> "... throughout the nation, at all levels of government, there is a growing realization that simply because of his confined status, the offender should not suffer the loss of

> all rights. With increasing frequency the Courts are mandating changes in prison procedures...."[14]

Additionally, a suggestion was made for adoption by the corrections profession:

> It is high time for corrections to acknowledge an additional right, and to guarantee that right, not under the compulsion of a Court decree, but on the basis of professional wisdom. Every person in a correctional confinement facility should be assured of: The right to participate in matters relating to his personal welfare by contributing his point of view.[15]

The accounts in this book of the establishment throughout the many corrections jurisdictions of ombudsman programs, grievance commissions, multi-level grievance procedures, and the increasing number of inmate councils indicates that the corrections profession is assuring that such a right for all confined persons is being assured by a variety of means.

Notes

1. Martinson, Robert. "What Works? Questions and Answers About Prison Reform," The Public Interest, Spring 1974.
2. Lipton, D., Martinson, R., and Wilks, J. The Effectiveness of Correctional Treatment. New York: Praeger Publishers, c/o Holt, Rinehart, Winston, 1975.
3. Fogel, David. We Are the Living Proof: The Justice Model for Corrections. Cincinnati: W. H. Anderson Company, 1975.
4. Sykes, G. The Society of Captives. Princeton, N.J.: Princeton University Press, 1958.
5. Scharf, Peter, and Hickey, Joseph. "Thomas Mott Osborne and the Limits of Democratic Prison Reform," The Prison Journal, Pennsylvania Prison Society, Philadelphia, Vol. LVII, No. 2, Autumn-Winter 1977, pp. 5-6.
6. Ibid.
7. Scharf, Peter. "Democracy and Prison Reform: A Theory of Democratic Participation in Prison," The Prison Journal, Vol. LV, No. 2, Autumn-Winter 1975, p. 21.
8. Ibid.
9. Scharf, Peter, and Hickey, Joseph, op. cit., p. 3.
10. Neto, Virginia V., and Bainer, LaNelle Marie. "Offender Participation in Corrections: Methods for Involving Offenders and Ex-Offenders in the Correctional Process." Social Action Research Center, San Rafael, California, 1981, pp. 80-81.
11. McConkie, Mark L. The Role of Interpersonal Trust in Correctional Administration. Southeastern Regional Management Training Council, The University of Georgia, Athens, September 1975, p. 40.

12. Blake, R., and Mouton, J. Building a Dynamic Corporation Through Grid Organization Development. Reading, Massachusetts: Addison-Wesley, 1969.
13. Wagner, Albert C. "Inmate Participation in Correctional Institutions," The Prison World, Vol. 13, No. 5, (Sept.-Oct. 1951), p. 9-11.
14. Baker, J. E. The Right to Participate: Inmate Involvement in Prison Administration. Metuchen, N.J.: The Scarecrow Press, Inc., 1974. p. 251.
15. Ibid.

APPENDIX A

CIVIL RIGHTS OF INSTITUTIONALIZED PERSONS ACT

Public Law 96-247 (94 Stat. 349 (42-U.S.C. 1997)
Effective Date: May 23, 1980

An Act to authorize actions for redress in cases involving deprivations of rights of institutionalized persons secured or protected by the Constitution or Laws of the United States.

This bill was initially introduced as S.1393 on April 26, 1977 and considered by the Senate during 1977 and 1978. Its intent was to give the U.S. Attorney General authority to initiate and intervene in civil rights suits on behalf of those confined in state institutions: mental patients, the handicapped, residents of home for juveniles and the elderly and state and county prisoners. The courts had ruled that, absent such specific legislation, the U.S. Department of Justice lacked legal standing to bring such suits (U.S. v. Solomon, 419 F. Supp., 358 [D. Md. 1976] and U.S. v. Mattson, CA. No. 74-138 [D. Mont. 1976]).[1]

The bill was vigorously opposed by the National Association of State Attorney Generals whose position was that substantial opportunity for federal intervention in such cases already existed. They pointed to the growing number of inmate suits brought under Section 1983 of the Federal Civil Rights Act of 1871, and demanded relief. A substitute bill was offered requiring state prisoners bringing such lawsuits to first exhaust administrative grievance mechanisms where they existed. It died aborning.

During the next session of Congress, the 96th, in 1979, the bill was reintroduced as S.10 and H.R.10. Both provided that state prisons and local jails be encouraged, but not required, to develop inmate grievance procedures along minimum guidelines based on the model grievance procedure of the California Youth Authority. If this suggestion was adopted, and then approved by the Justice Department, a state or county could move successfully in court to require exhaustion of the administrative remedy in all inmate civil cases. A 90-day deadline for completing the exhaustion was set.

Prisoners' rights advocates objected strenuously. Generally

they believed the exhaustion provision was "designed to treat prisoners differently from all other citizens in the United States, institutionalized or not.... Granting the Attorney General the authority to vindicate the rights of institutionalized persons, and in the same statute imposing an exhaustion requirement on private civil rights suits by prisoners, is an unnecessary and unacceptable tradeoff."

The bill, with the limited (90-day) exhaustion provision, passed both houses of Congress and became law on May 23, 1980. Standards were first published in the Federal Register on January 16, 1981, to take effect 30 legislative days later. However, four days later a new president took office. One of his first actions was to order an immediate freeze on all such regulations, pending further review.

New proposed standards were published in the Federal Register on July 16, 1981, and adopted by the Attorney General on September 25, 1981, differing significantly from previous proposals published in the Federal Register on November 28, 1980 and January 16, 1981. Those differences are:

1. Remedies: The original proposals stated: "The grievance procedure shall afford a successful grievant a meaningful remedy. Acceptable forms of relief may include, but are not limited to, monetary remedies, restitution of property, reclassification, correction of records, personnel actions, agreement by institution officials to remedy an objectionable condition within a reasonable, specified time, and a change in an institution policy or practice. Although available remedies may vary among institutions, a reasonable range of meaningful remedies in each institution is necessary."

The final standards contain only the first and last sentences of the foregoing.

2. Inmate and employee participation: The original proposals provided that some employees and inmates shall be permitted to participate directly in an advisory capacity in the disposition of grievances challenging general policy and practices and to review the effectiveness and credibility of the grievance procedure.

A sentence was inserted in this section that states: "In any instance in which inmates and employees are afforded an advisory role in the disposition of an individual grievance, the opportunity for such participation shall occur before the initial adjudication of the grievance." This scuttled the idea of California Youth Authority-style mediation panels.

3. Review: The original proposals calling for outside review by a person or other entity, not under the supervision or control of the institution or correctional agency, was modified to read: "... not under the institution's supervision or control...."

The standards apply only to persons confined in an institution for adults who have been convicted of a crime.

As of December 1983, certification had been approved for Wyoming and Virginia. Final action was pending on requests by Arizona, California, Iowa, and New York.[2]

Notes

1. Corey, Bruce. "Politics and the Institutionalized Persons Act," Corrections Magazine, Vol. VIII, No. 5, (October 1982), p. 25.
2. Telephone conversation with James A. Finney, Administrator, Rules and Remedies, Office of the General Counsel, Federal Prison System, Washington, D.C., May 17, 1982; telephone conversation with James Ralph, FPS.

DEPARTMENT OF JUSTICE

Attorney General

28 CFR Part 40 [Order No. 957-81]

STANDARDS FOR INMATE GRIEVANCE PROCEDURES*

AGENCY: Department of Justice.

ACTION: Final Rule

SUMMARY: The "Civil Rights of Institutionalized Persons Act," Pub. L. 96-247, requires that the Attorney General promulgate minimum standards for inmate grievance procedures and establish a method of certifying such procedures. The following document fulfills these requirements. Specifically, this document amends Part 40 of Title 28, Code of Federal Regulations by revising Subpart A ("Minimum Standards for Inmate Grievance Procedures") and by adding a new Subpart B ("Procedures for Obtaining Certification of a Grievance Procedure"). This document is intended to provide the public with notice of the rule in this area, not just changes from prior policy.

EFFECTIVE DATE: November 1, 1981.

SUPPLEMENTARY INFORMATION: The Civil Rights of Institutionalized Persons Act, Pub. L. 96-247, 94 Stat. 349 (the "Act"), grants the Attorney General of the United States authority to initiate and to intervene in civil actions against states and their political subdivisions to protect the federal rights of institutionalized persons. It also promotes the protection of constitutional rights of adults in correctional facilities by encouraging the development and implementation of administrative mechanisms for the resolution of prisoner grievances within institutions.

---

*From the Federal Register, vol. 46, no. 190, Oct. 1, 1981.

The Act requires that the Attorney General develop standards for prisoner grievance mechanisms in adult correctional and detention facilities and procedures to certify grievance mechanisms which meet those standards. States and their political subdivisions voluntarily may submit plans for grievance mechanisms to the Attorney General for such certification. A court may continue for a period of up to 90 days, a case filed pursuant to 42 U.S.C. 1983 by an adult confined in a correctional or detention facility in order to require that adult to exhaust administrative remedies that the Attorney General or the court determines are in substantial compliance with the standards promulgated by the Attorney General. Such continuances should only occur if the issues raised in the action pursuant to 42 U.S.C. 1983 reasonably can be expected to be resolved by the grievance mechanism.

Section 7 of the Act, to be codified at 42 U.S.C. 1997e, requires that the standards for grievance mechanisms provide for an advisory role for employees and inmates in the formulation, implementation, and operation of the mechanism; specific time limits for written replies to grievances including explanations of decisions; priority processing of emergency grievances; safeguards to prevent reprisals against grievants; and independent review of grievance decisions "by a person or other entity not under the direct supervision or direct control of the institution."

Proposed standards on this rule were initially published November 28, 1980 (45 FR 79095 et seq.). Following receipt of comments, a final rule was published January 16, 1981 (46 FR 3843 et seq.). Pursuant to the provisions of the Act, the standards set forth in the final rule became effective March 9, 1981, thirty legislative days after final publication. By Order dated March 6, 1981 (46 FR 16100), however, the effective date of those parts of the rule that established methods of certification of inmate grievance procedures and an Office of Inmate Grievance Procedure Certification were deferred until March 30, 1981. In the same Order, the Attorney General gave notice of his intent to review and, if necessary, to revise the part of the rule that became effective March 9, 1981. Subsequently, by Order dated March 30, 1981 (46 FR 19935), the Attorney General again deferred, until June 30, 1981, the effective date of both Subpart B, which established methods of certification, and 0.18 which established an Office of Inmate Grievance Procedure Certification.

Following further review, the Attorney General, as stated in his March 6, 1981 Order, determined that the rule on Standards for Inmate Grievance Procedures should be republished as a proposed rule. Accordingly, by Order dated July 10, 1981 (46 FR 36843), the Attorney General removed 28 CFR Part 40, Subpart B and § 0.18 to Part 0 of Title 28, Code of Federal Regulations. This action was taken to prevent the confusion which would result from permitting the Department's regulations on methods of certification to go into effect while new procedures were simultaneously being proposed.

The Department of Justice republished its proposed Standards for Inmate Grievance Procedures July 16, 1981 (46 FR 36865 et seq.). That document contained a revision of Subpart A (Minimum Standards for Inmate Grievance Procedures) and a new Subpart B (Procedures for Obtaining Certification of a Grievance Procedure). Interested persons were invited to submit comments on the proposed rule and public comments were received from various sources. On the basis of comments received, some changes have been made in the final rule. Members of the public may submit further comments concerning this rule by writing the previously cited address. These comments will be considered but will receive no further response in the Federal Register.

After review of the law and regulations, the Attorney General certifies that this final rule, for the purpose of the Regulatory Flexibility Act (5 U.S.C. 601 et seq.), will not have a significant impact on a substantial number of small entities. Further, the Attorney General has determined that the proposed standards do not constitute a "major rule" within the meaning of Executive Order 12291.

Summary of Changes/Comments

1. § 40.1--Proposed § 40.17 is renumbered § 40.1. Comments requested clarification on whether the rule applies to pretrial inmates, as the definition of "inmate" in § 40.1(e) states "who has been convicted of a crime," while the definition of "institution" includes "pretrial detention facility." A comment favored including pretrial inmates within the scope of this rule; however, section 7 of the Act, specifies "an adult convicted of a crime confined in any jail, prison, or other correctional facility." To clarify this, the definition of "institution" is revised to specify that the Standards apply to institutions which house adult inmates. "Inmate" is defined in § 40.1(e) as "an individual confined in an institution for adults, who has been convicted of a crime." Any state, at its option, may elect to apply the standards to persons in pretrial status whether they are detained in a separate institution or in the same institution as adult inmates.

2. § 40.2--Comments on this section objected to the provision that inmates be afforded an advisory role in the formulation and implementation of a grievance procedure. One comment stated that prisoners in county jails are in custody for short periods of time and are poor advisors because they are "inexperienced and unaware of the problems of the jail." Another commenter suggests the use of ex-offenders as advisors. Another commenter believed that the system itself provides an advisory role in both the implementation and reviewing phases of the procedure, as the inmate can call attention to procedural shortcomings through use of the system itself. Another commenter suggested that the rule lends a greater level of specificity to inmate advisory roles than is desirable or practicable. The commenter favors inmate/employee advisory roles through regular monthly "forum" meetings, which focus on numerous

subjects, including the grievance procedure. Section 7(b)(2)(A) of the Act requires that employees and inmates have an advisory role in the formulation, implementation, and operation of the system. Correctional authorities have latitude in selecting a method to ensure that the advisory role is provided. This method may include periodic "forum" meetings, written notices with solicitation of comments, advisory committees, etc. While jail prisoners may be inexperienced and unaware of the problems of the jail, the Act requires an "advisory role" only, and gives correctional authorities latitude to determine the method of participation and the feasibility of suggestions.

3. § 40.3--Comments objected to the provision that the written grievance procedure be distributed to all employees and inmates in the institution. One commenter stated that implementation of this provision would require "large expenditures of precious few dollars and staff time to make available to each and every new employe and inmate a copy of the entire and, presumbly, lengthy procedure." Another commenter stated that some institutional employees have no direct contact with or responsibility for inmates and therefore would have no substantive need for an individual copy of the procedure.

Although it is essential that all inmates and staff know that the procedure exists, the value of individual copies for every person is not clear. The cost factor and the administrative burden are not inconsequential, especially in facilities where large numbers of inmates are detained for relatively short periods of time. Accordingly, the final rule is revised to require the written grievance procedure to be "available" to all employees and inmates of the institution. This provision may be met by posting copies of the written procedure on inmate and staff bulletin boards, in inmate law libraries, etc. The rule also requires that each new inmate and employee receive both a written notification (possibly as part of an institution handbook) and an oral explanation (possibly as part of the institution orientation program) of the procedure.

We do not agree with a comment that this section needs to recognize that participating employees and inmates equally need training. Section 40.11(b) of the certification procedure clearly states that staff and inmates are to be afforded instructional materials.

4. § 40.5--A commenter suggests that it would be unwise to allow a staff/inmate committee to review all complaints against staff and inmates since some complaints require absolute confidentiality, while other complaints result in the head of the institution having his actions or decisions reviewed by a group of subordinates. This section does not establish one required method for review of grievances, but only requires that the grievance procedure apply to a broad range of complaints and state specifically the type of complaints covered and excluded. There is no requirement that grievances be reviewed by a committee, as suggested by the commenter. An applicant may exclude from review by inmates participating in an advisory role, a grievance which is not against general policy and which poses a threat

to institutional security (for example, a serious allegation against an employee which may affect the security of the institution). As to the comment that the head of the institution may have his actions or decisions reviewed by subordinates, we point out that inmate/staff participation is advisory only, but this review can be useful in assessing how policy is perceived.

5. § 40.7--A commenter suggests that § 40.7(a) encourages attempts at informal resolution of a grievance before formal filing to ensure that an inmate makes an initial effort to solve the problem with the appropriate person(s). Prior to the commenter's initiation of an informal resolution procedure, inmates "were ignoring the usual way of doing business which resulted in an extraordinarily high volume of appeals entering the system." An informal resolution process is highly desirable, and § 40.7(a) is revised accordingly.

The majority of all comments received related to § 40.7(b) and concerned the provision for inmate and employee participation in the operation of the system. The words "and use" were removed from the first sentence because inmate and employee participation is intended to promote the credibility of the system, but not to promote the use of the procedure. In response to concern that the third sentence of proposed § 40.7(b) was vague and difficult to understand, that sentence was redrafted to more clearly state its intent. Most comments opposed the concept of inmate participation. Commenters stated that such a provision creates a specific hardship on management, that the matter should be left to the discretion of prison officials (dependent on the situation at a given institution), that it may potentially impact on institution security, that it may subject inmate participants to exertion of pressure, criticisms and perhaps retaliatory actions from others, and that inmates may be perceived by other inmates to exercise a leadership role (thereby constituting a security risk). Several commenters pointed out specific problems which would be encountered with a jail population. One commenter said that inmates in their jail have an average stay of 62 days, and that the longer term inmates are "hard core, repeat offenders," with "no real interest in the efficient lawful operation of the jail." Another commenter pointed out that the short stay would make selection and evaluation of inmates for an advisory position "difficult and meaningless."

Several commenters favored inmate participation but believe that the proposed rule fails to accurately meet the Act's requirement for employees and inmates to be afforded an advisory role in the formulation, implementation, and operation of the system. One commenter suggests that the proposed rule "permits prisoner participation far short of that required under any reasonable interpretation of the statutory language." Another commenter objects to the limitation of inmate participation to general policy matters, as distinguished from specific actions or incidents relating to individual inmates.

The Act and its legislative history require an advisory role for employees and inmates in the formulation, implementation, and operation of the system. The Act also recognizes the need to solicit and incorporate the suggestions of correctional experts, as it requires that the Attorney General shall "after consultation with persons, State and local agencies, and organizations with background and expertise in the area of corrections, promulgate minimum standards * * *." The rule as written accommodates the legitimate security concerns of correctional persons and complies with the minimum requirements of the Act. One commenter believed the language is insufficient, that the rule should provide guidance more specific than the statute. The rule is considerably more detailed than the statute. The rule language sets the framework and the tone for what is expected, and the applicant has discretion to determine how best to fulfill the requirement. Different approaches may be considered. If the method chosen is not sufficient, the Attorney General will not award certification.

In respect to comments that there is no support in the Act or its legislative history for limiting inmate participation to grievances on general policy matters, the Act does not require that inmates and staff advise on all grievances, and it calls for the establishment of minimum standards after consultation with corrections authorities. Because some commenters believe the inmates' advisory role in resolution should be restricted to no more than general policy matters, and because most commenters believe it is unwise and even dangerous to place one inmate in an apparent or quasi decision-making role in the specific grievance of another, we believe it is unwise to require as a minimum standard a more extensive advisory role for inmates than required in the present rule. These rules set minimum standards which applicants may then expand if they wish. For example, inmate participation may be solicited in a grievance concerning an institution's administrative detention policy. For reasons addressed by most correctional authorities, however, inmate participation in a grievance concerning another inmate's placement in detention is considered inappropriate, as it may permit one inmate to unreasonably intrude on the privacy of another, it may affect institution security, it may subject inmate participants to undue pressure and retaliation, and it may invite corruption. While two commenters believe that limiting inmate participation to grievances of general policy would diminish the inmates' perception of the system's credibility, the majority of comments on that issue are best described by one comment that inmate trust and inmate belief in the credibility of the system are not a function of inmate participation, since that participation in any event is advisory, but depend on how well correctional officials, who are and must be the final decision-makers, operate the system.

We disagree with a comment that this section conflicts with Standard 1.11 (which requires "an advisory role for inmates and staff in the formulation, implementation and general policy operation of the system") of the Department of Justice Federal Standards for Prisons and Jails. Section 40.7(b) clearly reflects the same principle, that the advisory role on operation need only relate to general policy questions.

Several commenters addressed the method of inmate participation and many were under the impression that grievance hearings or some form of inmate-employee grievance resolution committee are required. To resolve this misconception, a new sentence has been added to make it clear that these methods of resolving grievances are permitted but not required. The method of participation is intentionally left unspecified so that correctional authorities may consider the applicable constraints and factors which exist at their institutions. The need for this latitude is demonstrated by one state correctional official who reported that while several institutions in his state have been able to operate inmate councils in "an effective and non-disruptive manner," at least two institutions "have recently experienced disruptions caused by misguided and pressured inmate council members." In addition to inmate councils, other examples of inmate participation include the solicitation of written comments on the posted abstract of policy grievances, advisory committee discussions, and inmate/staff town meetings.

We disagree with a comment that inmate review of the effectiveness and credibility of the grievance procedure be at the discretion of the institution if inmates and employees are allowed to actively participate in disposition of grievances challenging policy and practices. Inmate assessment of the procedure, regardless of their participation in the system, is beneficial in both learning how the system is perceived, and in making the effort to strengthen the effectiveness and credibility of the mechanics of the system. Inmate participation "before the adjudication of the grievance" in § 40.7(b) means before the first formal level of adjudication, and is amended accordingly.

No change is contemplated in response to a comment that § 40.7(c) should specifically state that the institution establish a procedure for investigating the allegations and establishing the facts of each grievance. The title of § 40.7(c), "Investigation and consideration," clearly indicates an investigation is to occur, and such a rule would simply belabor the obvious. Nor do we believe it necessary to revise this section to specify that no direct party to the grievance should be involved. The existing language is intended to exclude persons who, although not directly involved, may have been indirectly involved in the subject of the grievance (for example, a witness to an act which is the subject of the grievance). It is not intended, as suggested by a commenter, to preclude the Warden from responding to a grievance about an institutional policy promulgated by the Warden.

We disagree with a comment to § 40.7(d) that the rule should require that the grievant file a reasoned, written statement as to why he wishes to appeal further. The commenter objected to a common practice whereby a grievant appeals, stating only "appeal further." While some states may wish to require further specificity, as to the exact substance of an appeal, this is a matter better left to the applicant's discretion than to this rule. Another comment to this section states that the rule does not identify decision levels. This is intentional to give each applicant latitude to establish its own levels of decision and review in compliance with § 40.7(f). With respect to a comment that suggests deletion of the phrase "if available," we note that administrative appeal is not available after the final stage.

Comments on § 40.7(e) objected to the requirement that grievances must be processed from initiation to final disposition in less than 90 days, unless the grievant agrees in writing to an extension. While some grievances may require in excess of 90 days, for resolution (for example, on a policy issue), the Act in § 7(a)(1), permits continuance for exhaustion for no more than 90 days. To clarify, § 40.7(e) substitutes the phrase "within 90 days" for "in less than 90 days."

Two commenters to § 40.7(f) favored the provision that the required review be conducted by a person or other entity not under the supervision or control of the correctional agency. Such a requirement, however, would clearly go beyond the provision of the Act which requires "independent review * * * by a person or other entity not under the direct supervision or direct control of the institution." Further, there are strong arguments for not having review outside of the agency. The existing rule language does not prohibit review by an authority outside the correctional agency but leaves this determination to individual applicants.

We do not agree with another comment to § 40.7(f) that inmates will always exercise this review provision or that the correctional system itself cannot effectively serve as an objective third party. Experience with, and knowledge of existing grievance procedures clearly indicate that inmates don't automatically exercise their right to appeal nor do appeal responses within the correctional system routinely show a lack of objectivity.

A commenter to both § 40.7(f) and § 40.8 asked who had responsibility to select or appoint a person or persons outside of the institution to serve as the reviewing official. Such a selection is presumed to be made by the applicant.

6. § 40.8--Several commenters to § 40.8 objected to the need for an emergency procedure. One commenter believed that the use "of multi-level grievance procedure requiring inmate, employee and outside participation is inefficient for this purpose." The commenter favored the development of an alternative approach, for example, directing the grievance to the appropriate administrator. Another commenter believes that an emergency provision "unnecessarily complicates the entire process," stating that failure to act promptly will undermine the validity of the system and be detrimental to the correctional institution. The language of the Act requires the development of a procedure for "priority processing of grievances which are of an emergency nature." While an individual is encouraged to go to the "appropriate administrator" prior to filing a grievance, the rule does provide an inmate an alternative course of action in the event that the emergency situation is not expeditiously

handled. Another comment assumes the need to initially refer the emergency complaint to a grievance committee, but there is nothing in the Act which requires that a committee exist for any reason in the grievance procedure. The rule allows for an emergency appeal directly to the decision level of the grievance process. In the event that the grievance does not warrant an emergency review, it may be returned to the inmate for routine submission.

There is merit to comments that the grievance procedure needs to provide guidance in determining emergency matters to be reviewed. The proposed language requiring specificity, however, is unnecessary and may result in applicants inadvertently omitting subjects which may constitute an emergency. The basis for emergency review is described in the existing rule language as a matter which could "subject the inmate to a substantial risk of personal injury, or cause other serious and irreparable harm to the inmate." Accordingly, the final rule deletes language requiring that the grievance procedure state specifically the matters to be reviewed.

7. § 40.9--In response to comments, § 40.9 is revised. The final rule is expanded to prohibit reprisals against anyone for their good faith use of or good faith participation in the grievance procedure. This revision satisfies public comments that employees be included within the provisions of this section. The "good faith" condition is added as a result of comments, and changes the rule so that appropriate disciplinary action is not precluded in cases of deliberate, malicious filings. We consider it impractical and unnecessary to adopt a suggestion that the rule require an applicant to specify steps that will be taken to prevent and redress reprisals, and the penalties for engaging in reprisals, though individual applicants are free to do so. Reprisals are a form of employee misconduct which is governed, as to procedures and sanctions, by provisions other than the grievance procedure.

8. § 40.10--We do not agree with a comment to § 40.10(a) that the minimal reporting and recording system for grievance matters is meaningless. The requested information can be provided in a single-line log, card, or data entry per case, which easily provides a general overview of the system's operation.

Commenters to § 40.10(b) opposed the provisions on confidentiality. One commenter stated that staff may need to review grievances for many non-clerical reasons, including certain transfer decisions (a grievance could have been filed against placement in a particular institution), to determine whether an inmate has exhausted administrative remedies, etc. Another commenter stated that § 40.9, by prohibiting reprisals, clearly prohibits misuse of the grievance information. Recognizing these concerns, the final rule incorporates the substance of a comment that the records regarding the participation of an inmate in the grievance procedures shall be considered confidential and shall be handled under the same procedures used to protect other confidential case records.

9. § 40.11 (Proposed)--Several commenters objected to the annual comprehensive evaluation required by § 40.11. Commenters believed that it places an unjustified burden upon small entities and that the necessary resources (staff and hardware) will not be available. Another commenter believes that it is impossible to report accurately the costs generated or saved by compliance with 42 U.S.C. 1997e "due to the myriad of other factors affecting the cost associated with the correctional system."

In assessing these comments and after a review of the Act, it has been determined that inclusion of § 40.11 is neither necessary nor cost-effective, and that it would be of questionable value. Accordingly, proposed § 40.11 is deleted from the final rule. Section 40.10(a) requires maintenance of records and establishes the minimum information that is to be retained. Additional information and/or evaluation may be maintained at the discretion of the applicant.

One commenter to this section indicates that there is a need to continually monitor the program, preferably by a person or entity within the agency that is outside the chain of command of the institution. While an applicant may wish to establish a separate monitoring procedure, we believe that the appeal process can be adequately monitored by that entity designated to be the final level of appeal. We do not believe it necessary for the rule to require a separate provision for monitoring.

Based on the deletion of proposed § 40.11, proposed §§ 40.12-23 become final §§ 40.11-22.

10. § 40.11--We do not believe, as suggested by a commenter, that the absence of a separate office for grievance certification will adversely affect the certification process. While a separate office might have some useful aspects, administrative costs do not warrant its establishment now. If the need exists at some future date, consideration can then be given to the establishment of a separate office for certification.

There is no requirement in the proposed rule that each inmate or employee receive training in the operation of the grievance system. As specified in § 40.3, each inmate and employee is to be afforded written notification of and is to be orally advised of the existence of the procedure. The training required in the latter part of final § 40.11(b) is only for those persons who are directly involved in the operation of the system. "If any" was added to recognize that special training for inmates may not be necessary for some methods of advisory inmate participation.

11. § 40.12--A commenter objected to proposed § 40.13 (now final § 40.12), stating that the published notice requirement is a waste of tax dollars and that it is vague in respect to what is required. In response to this comment, the publication requirement has been replaced by a requirement that an applicant can post notice of its intent to apply for certification in prominent places in each

affected institution and provide a similar notice to the U.S. District Court(s) with jurisdiction over the institution(s). Proposed § 40.12(h) has been deleted because its requirements are not applicable under the terms of the final rule.

12. § 40.13--A commenter believes that proposed § 40.14 (now final § 40.13) is vague and, in conjunction with the notice provision, that it creates a situation whereby the applicant is placed in the "middle of a political controversy with those 'groups and persons' which have developed and attempted to promulgate philosophies of corrections for and against the rights of incarcerated persons." The commenter believes that the net effect of these requirements is to discourage rather than encourage state applicants. A final objection is based on the view that since the Federal District Court with jurisdiction over 42 U.S.C. 1983 actions can determine if a 90-day continuation is in order, the requirements of final § 40.13 are subjecting the state applicant to political pressures.

It is not the intent of the proposed rule to create the situation identified by this commenter. The posting of the notice and inviting of comments provide interested persons with the knowledge that an application for certification is to be filed. The Attorney General's review of the comments received is limited to the certification process, and is not intended, nor expected, to create a "political controversy."

A commenter requests clarification on what constitutes a reasonable amount of time for a response by the Attorney General. The rule requires that a response be prepared as promptly as the circumstances permit. It is not now possible to set a specific time frame, since the number and complexity of the applications and the volume of information to be reviewed are unknown.

13. § 40.20--The word "whether" is changed to "if" in the last sentence of § 40.20 to make it clear that the Attorney General need notify an applicant only if a proposed change would result in suspension of certification.

14. § 40.22--It is not appropriate to add the phrase, as suggested by a commenter, that "these standards create no legally enforceable rights or expectations of any kind." In suggesting this language the commenter refers to the revised Preamble (see 46 FR 39515-16) to the Federal Standards for Prisons and Jails. The Federal Standards for Prisons and Jails were not statutorily created as is the case with this present publication. As for this grievance procedure, certification of the procedure will give a U.S. Court the authority to continue an inmate's claim under 42 U.S.C. 1983 for 90 days in order to exhaust these administrative remedies.

15. Additional comments--Several commenters objected to the grievance procedures in their entirety. One commenter believed that the proposed procedure "is a series of mistakes," that it is "far too burdensome on a jail administration." Other comments

suggested that the Commission on Accreditation for Corrections Standards serve as the definitive set of standards for jails, with one commenter stating that imposing additional standards only serves to impose an additional level of regulations that is unnecessary. We believe these Standards, as revised, are adaptable to jail situations (with frequent turnover of population) if an applicant chooses to apply them to jails. We concur with the statements supporting definitive standards for corrections: we do not believe that these standards for grievance procedures conflict with those published by the Commission on Accreditation for Corrections. Rather, the rule deals with a certification process for the grievance procedure, and describes what the system should include in order for the Attorney General to award certification.

Another comment suggested that the grievance standards need to retain flexibility to accommodate the "healthy diversity" that exists among various states. We agree, and believe that this is accomplished in the existing standards, which set guidelines, but leave specific procedures to each applicant. These revised standards recognize, as suggested in a comment, the "assumption that state correction officials by and large seek to discharge their duties with the utmost good faith * * *."

A suggestion that the Commentary published in the January 1981 final rule be retained is not adopted, as this information is believed extraneous to the substance of the rule. Another commenter suggested that the implementation of this grievance procedure would be better served if federal assistance were granted. Federal assistance is a separate issue, not required to be addressed by the Act in these standards. These rules have been adopted on the basic assumption that each state should develop its own grievance procedure. Federal assistance in the form of consultation, as opposed to monetary support, is available upon request. In response to a final comment, the rule does not require periodic review by the Attorney General. It is expected that reviews will be conducted as the need arises, based on specific requests or information.

For the reasons set forth in the preamble and under the authority of Pub. L. 96-247, 94 Stat. 349 (42 U.S.C. 1997) the Attorney General amends Part 40 of Title 28, Code of Federal Regulations by revising Subpart A and by adding a new Subpart B.

40 CFR is amended by revising Subpart A and by adding a new Subpart B to read as follows:

PART 40--STANDARDS FOR INMATE GRIEVANCE PROCEDURES

Subpart A--Minimum Standards for Inmate Grievance Procedures

Sec.
40.1 Definitions.

Subpart B--Procedures for Obtaining Certification of a Grievance Procedure

Authority: Pub. L. 96-247. 94 Stat. 349 (42 U.S.C. 1997).

Subpart A--Minimum Standards for Inmate Grievance Procedures

§ 40.1 Definitions.

For the purposes of this part--

(a) "Act" means the Civil Rights of Institutionalized Persons Act, Pub. L. 96-247, 94 Stat. 349 (42 U.S.C. 1997).

(b) "Applicant" means a state or political subdivision of a state that submits to the Attorney General a request for certification of a grievance procedure.

(c) "Attorney General" means the Attorney General of the United States or the Attorney General's designees.

(d) "Grievance" means a written complaint by an inmate on the inmate's own behalf regarding a policy applicable within an institution, a condition in an institution, an action involving an inmate of an institution, or an incident occurring within an institution. The term "grievance" does not include a complaint relating to a parole decision.

(e) "Inmate" means an individual confined in an institution for adults, who has been convicted of a crime.

(f) "Institution" means a jail, prison, or other correctional facility, or pretrial detention facility that houses adult inmates and is owned, operated, or managed by or provides services on behalf of a State or political subdivision of a State.

(g) "State" means a State of the United States, the District of Columbia, the commonwealth of Puerto Rico, or any of the territories and possessions of the United States.

(h) "Substantial compliance" means that there is no omission of any essential part from compliance, that any omission consists only of an unimportant defect or omission, and that there has been a firm effort to comply fully with the standards.

§ 40.2 Adoption of procedures.

Each applicant seeking certification of its grievance procedure for purposes of the Act shall adopt a written grievance procedure. Inmates and employees shall be afforded an advisory role in the formulation and implementation of a grievance procedure adopted after the effective date of these regulations, and shall be afforded an advisory role in reviewing the compliance with the standards set forth herein of a grievance procedure adopted prior to the effective date of these regulations.

§ 40.3 Communication of procedures.

The written grievance procedure shall be readily available to all employees and inmates of the institution. Additionally, each inmate and employee shall upon arrival at the institution, receive written notification and an oral explanation of the procedure, including the opportunity to have questions regarding the procedure answered orally. The written procedure shall be available in any language spoken by a significant portion of the institution's population and appropriate provisions shall be made for those not speaking those languages, as well as for the impaired and the handicapped.

§ 40.4 Accessibility.

Each inmate shall be entitled to invoke the grievance procedure regardless of any disciplinary, classification, or other administrative or legislative decision to which the inmate may be subject. The institution shall ensure that the procedure is accessible to impaired and handicapped inmates.

§ 40.5 Applicability.

The grievance procedure shall be applicable to a broad range of complaints and shall state specifically the types of complaints covered and excluded. At a minimum, the grievance procedure shall permit complaints by inmates regarding policies and conditions within the jurisdiction of the institution or the correctional agency that affect them personally, as well as actions by employees and inmates, and incidents occurring within the institution that affect them personally. The grievance procedure shall not be used as a disciplinary procedure.

§ 40.6 Remedies.

The grievance procedure shall afford a successful grievant a meaningful remedy. Although available remedies may vary among institutions, a reasonable range of meaningful remedies in each institution is necessary.

§ 40.7 Operation and decision.

(a) Initiation. The institution may require an inmate to attempt informal resolution before the inmate files a grievance under this procedure. The procedure for initiating a grievance shall be simple and include the use of a standard form. Necessary materials shall be freely available to all inmates and assistance shall be readily available for inmates who cannot complete the forms themselves. Forms shall not demand unnecessary technical compliance with formal structure or detail, but shall encourage a simple and straightforward statement of the inmate's grievance.

(b) Inmate and employee participation. The institution shall provide a role for employees and inmates in the operation of the system in such a manner as to promote the credibility of the grievance procedure. At a minimum, some employees and inmates shall be permitted to participate in an advisory capacity in the disposition of grievances challenging general policy and practices and to review the effectiveness and credibility of the grievance procedure. In any instance in which inmates and employees are afforded an advisory role in the disposition of an individual grievance, the opportunity for such participation shall occur before the initial adjudication of the grievance. Such participation may be limited to advisory comment on policy questions which are raised or implicated in a grievance, without identification of individual names or specific facts. No inmate shall participate in the resolution of any other inmate's grievance over the objection of the grievant. In-person hearings and formally established inmate-employee committees are permitted, but are not required as part of the grievance procedure.

(c) Investigation and consideration. No inmate or employee who appears to be involved in the matter shall participate in any capacity in the resolution of the grievance.

(d) Reasoned, written responses. Each grievance shall be answered in writing at each level of decision and review. The response shall state the reasons for the decision reached and shall include a statement that the inmate is entitled to further review, if such is available, and shall contain simple directions for obtaining such review.

(e) Fixed time limits. Responses shall be made within fixed

time limits at each level of decision. Time limits may vary between institutions, but expeditious processing of grievances at each level of decision is essential to prevent grievances from becoming moot. In all instances grievances must be processed from initiation to final disposition within 90 days unless the grievant agrees in writing to an extension for a fixed period. Expiration of a time limit at any stage of the process shall entitle the grievant to move to the next stage of the process, unless the grievant has agreed in writing to an extension of the time for a response.

(f) Review. The grievant shall be entitled to review by a person or other entity, not under the institution's supervision or control, of the disposition of all grievances, including alleged reprisals by an employee against an inmate. A request for review shall be allowed automatically without interference by administrators or employees of the institution and such review shall be conducted without influence or interference by administrators or employees of the institution.

§ 40.8 Emergency procedure.

The grievance procedure shall contain special provision for responding to grievances of an emergency nature. Emergency grievances shall be defined, at a minimum, as matters regarding which disposition according to the regular time limits would subject the inmate to a substantial risk of personal injury or cause other serious and irreparable harm to the inmate. Emergency grievances shall be forwarded immediately, without substantive review, to the level at which corrective action can be taken. The procedure for resolving emergency grievances shall provide for expedited responses at every level of decision. The emergency procedure shall also include review by a person or entity not under the supervision or control of the institution.

§ 40.9 Reprisals.

The grievance procedure shall prohibit reprisals. "Reprisal" means any action or threat of action against anyone for the good faith use of or good faith participation in the grievance procedure. The written procedure shall include assurance that good faith use of or good faith participation in the grievance mechanism will not result in formal or informal reprisal. An inmate shall be entitled to pursue through the grievance procedure a complaint that a reprisal occurred.

§ 40.10 Records--nature; confidentiality.

(a) Nature. Records regarding the filing and disposition of grievances shall be collected and maintained systematically by the institution. Such records shall be preserved for at least three years following final disposition of the grievance. At a minimum, such records shall include aggregate information regarding the numbers, types and dispositions of grievances, as well as individual records of the date of and the reasons for each disposition at each stage of the procedure.

(b) Confidentiality. Records regarding the participation of an individual in the grievance proceedings shall be considered confidential and shall be handled under the same procedures used to protect other confidential case records. Consistent with ensuring confidentiality, staff who are participating in the disposition of a grievance shall have access to records essential to the resolution of the grievance.

Subpart B--Procedures for Obtaining Certification of a Grievance Procedure

§ 40.11 Submissions by applicant.

An application for certification shall be submitted to the Office of the Associate Attorney General, Department of Justice, Main Justice Building, Washington, D.C. 20530, and shall contain the following:

(a) Written statement. A written statement describing the grievance procedure, including a brief description of the institution or institutions covered by the procedure, with accompanying plans for or evidence of implementation in each institution.

(b) Instructional materials. A copy of the instructional materials for inmates and employees regarding use of the grievance procedure together with a description of the manner in which such materials are distributed, a description of the oral explanation of the grievance procedure, including the circumstances under which it is delivered, and a description of the training, if any, provided to employees and inmates in the skills necessary to operate the grievance procedure.

(c) Form. A copy of the form used by inmates to initiate a grievance and to obtain review of the disposition of a grievance.

(d) Information regarding past performance. For a procedure that has operated for more than one year at the time of the application, the applicant shall submit information regarding the number and types of grievances filed over the preceding year, the disposition of the grievances with sample responses from each level of decision, the remedies granted, evidence of compliance with time limits at each level of decision, and a description of the role of inmates and employees in the formulation, implementation, and operation of the grievance procedure.

(e) Plan for collecting information. For a procedure that has operated for less than one year at the time of the application, the applicant shall submit a plan for collecting the information described in paragraph (d) of this section.

(f) Assurance of confidentiality. A description of the steps taken to ensure the confidentiality of records of individual use of or participation in the grievance procedure.

(g) Evaluation. A description of the plans for periodic evaluation of the grievance procedure, including identification of the group, individuals or individual who will conduct the evaluation and identification of the person or entity not under the control or supervision of the institution who will review the evaluation, together with two copies of the most recent evaluation, if one has been performed.

§ 40.12 Notice of Intent to apply for certification.

The applicant shall post notice of its intent to request certification in prominent places in each institution to be covered by the procedure and shall provide similar written notice to the U.S. District Court(s) having jurisdiction over each institution to be covered by the procedure. The notices shall invite comments regarding the grievance procedure and direct them to the Attorney General.

§ 40.13 Review by the Attorney General.

The Attorney General shall review and respond to each application as promptly as the circumstances, including the need for independent investigation and consideration of the comments of agencies, and interested groups and persons, permit.

§ 40.14 Conditional certification.

If, in the judgment of the Attorney General, a grievance procedure that has been in existence less than one year is at the time of application in substantial compliance with the standards promulgated herein, the Attorney General shall grant conditional certification for one year or until the applicant satisfies the requirements of § 40.15, whichever period is shorter.

§ 40.15 Full certification.

If, in the judgment of the Attorney General, a grievance procedure that has been in existence longer than one year at the time of application is in substantial compliance with the standards promulgated herein, full certification shall be granted. Such certification shall remain in effect unless and until the Attorney General finds reasonable cause to believe that the grievance procedure is no longer in substantial compliance with the minimum standards and so notifies the applicant in writing.

§ 40.16 Denial of certification.

If the Attorney General finds that the grievance procedure is not in substantial compliance with the standards promulgated herein, the Attorney General shall deny certification and inform the applicant in writing of the area or areas in which the grievance procedure or the application is deemed inadequate.

§ 40.17 Reapplication after denial of certification.

An applicant denied certification may resubmit an application for certification at any time after the inadequacy in the application or the grievance procedure is corrected.

§ 40.18 Suspension of certification.

(a) Reasonable belief of non-compliance. If the Attorney General has reasonable grounds to believe that a previously certified grievance procedure may no longer be in substantial compliance with the minimum standards, the Attorney General shall suspend certification. The suspension shall continue until such time as the deficiency is corrected, in which case certification shall be reinstated, or until the Attorney General determines that substantial compliance no longer exists, in which case, except as provided in paragraph (b) of this section, the Attorney General shall withdraw certification pursuant to § 40.19 of this part.

(b) Defect may be readily remedied; good faith effort. If the Attorney General determines that a grievance procedure is no longer in substantial compliance with the minimum standards, but has reason to believe that the defect may be readily corrected and that good faith efforts are underway to correct it, the Attorney General may suspend certification until the grievance procedure returns to compliance with the minimum standards.

(c) Recertification after suspension pursuant to paragraph (c). The Attorney General shall reinstate the certification of an applicant whose certification was suspended pursuant to paragraph (a) of this section upon a demonstration in writing by the applicant that the specific deficiency on which the suspension was based has been corrected or that the information that caused the Attorney General to suspend certification was erroneous.

(d) Recertification after suspension pursuant to paragraph (b). The Attorney General shall reinstate the certification of an applicant whose certification has been suspended pursuant to paragraph (b) upon a demonstration in writing that the deficiency on which the suspension was based has been corrected.

(e) Notification in writing of suspension or reinstatement. The Attorney General shall notify an applicant in writing that certification has been suspended or reinstated and state the reasons for the action.

§ 40.19 Withdrawal of certification.

(a) Finding of non-compliance. If the Attorney General finds that a grievance procedure is no longer in substantial compliance with the minimum standards, the Attorney General shall withdraw certification, unless the Attorney General concludes that suspension of certification under § 40.18(b) of this part is appropriate.

(b) Notification in writing of withdrawal of certification. The Attorney General shall notify an applicant in writing that certification has been withdrawn and state the reasons for the action.

(c) Recertification after withdrawal. An applicant whose certification has been withdrawn and who wishes to receive recertification shall submit a new application for certification.

§ 40.20 Contemplated change in certified procedure.

A proposed change in a certified procedure must be submitted to the Attorney General thirty days in advance of its proposed effective date. The Attorney General shall review such proposed change and notify the applicant in writing before the effective date of the proposed change if such change will result in suspension or withdrawal of the certification of the grievance procedure.

§ 40.21 Notification of court.

The Attorney General shall notify in writing the Chief Judges of the United States Court of Appeals and of the United States District Court(s) within whose jurisdiction the applicant is located of the certification, suspension of certification, withdrawal of certification and recertification of the applicant's grievance procedure. The Attorney General shall also notify the court of the certification status of any grievance procedure at the request of the court or any part in an action by an adult inmate pursuant to 42 U.S.C. 1983.

§ 40.22 Significance of certification.

Certification of a grievance procedure by the Attorney General shall signify only that on the basis of the information submitted, the Attorney General believes the grievance procedure is in substantial compliance with the minimum standards. Certification shall not indicate approval of the use or application of the grievance procedure in a particular case.

Dated: September 25, 1981.
William French Smith,
Attorney General

APPENDIX B

PRINCIPLES FOR WARD GRIEVANCE PROCEDURE CALIFORNIA YOUTH AUTHORITY

April 4, 1973

1. Every resident assigned to any program unit shall have available to him a means to file a grievance and use any grievance procedure developed within that program unit.

2. There shall be available to any resident with an emergency grievance or problem a course of action which can provide him redress to his problem within a relatively immediate time frame.

3. There shall be participation by elected residents and staff in the developing of procedures and in the operation of said grievance procedure.

4. The levels of review for a grievance shall be kept to a minimum. Ideally, these levels should coincide with the major decision making levels of the program unit's organization.

5. Residents shall be entitled to representation at all levels, including informal resolution within the procedure.

6. There shall be time limits established for the receipt of all responses for any action which must be taken to put said response into effect.

7. A course of action shall be available to all parties of a grievance, staff or residents, for appealing a decision.

8. A resident filing a written grievance will be guaranteed a written response with reasons for action taken, or shall have recourse in the absence of a written response.

9. There shall be monitoring and evaluation of all procedures, their operation, and their decisions.

10. The procedure shall include, as a final review, some sort of independent review by a party or parties outside of the Youth Authority.

11. There shall not be any reprisals taken against anyone using the grievance procedure.

12. The grievance procedure shall provide an impartial method for determining whether a complaint falls within the procedure.

APPENDIX C

New York Division for Youth
New York State Executive Department

YOUNG PEOPLE'S BILL OF RIGHTS

We The People of New York State Believe In The Right of Every Child To:

1. Affection, Love, Guidance and Understanding from parents and teachers.
2. Adequate Nutrition and Medical care to aid mental, physical and social growth.
3. Free education to develop individual abilities and to become a useful member of society.
4. Special care, if handicapped.
5. Opportunity for recreation in a wholesome, well-rounded environment.
6. An environment that reflects peace and mutual concern.
7. The opportunity for sound moral development.
8. Constructive discipline to help develop responsibility and character.
9. Good adult examples to follow.
10. A future commensurate with abilities and aspirations.
11. Enjoyment of all these rights, regardless of race, color, sex, religion, national or social origin.

INDEX

Baker, J. E., 1917-

Prisoner participation in prison power

$29.50

DATE			
MAR 16 1987			
MAY 13 '91			
APR 13 '92			
APR 19 '93			
MAR 21 '94			
APR 24 '95			